# MIGRATION, REGIONAL INTEGRATION
AND HUMAN SECURITY

# Research in Migration and Ethnic Relations Series

*Series Editor:*
Maykel Verkuyten, ERCOMER Utrecht University

The Research in Migration and Ethnic Relations series has been at the forefront of research in the field for ten years. The series has built an international reputation for cutting edge theoretical work, for comparative research especially on Europe and for nationally-based studies with broader relevance to international issues. Published in association with the European Research Centre on Migration and Ethnic Relations (ERCOMER), Utrecht University, it draws contributions from the best international scholars in the field, offering an interdisciplinary perspective on some of the key issues of the contemporary world.

*Other titles in the series*

East to West Migration: Russian Migrants in Western Europe
*Helen Kopnina*
0 7546 4170 8

Moving Lives: Narratives of Nation and Migration
among Europeans in Post-War Britain
*Kathy Burrell*
0 7546 4574 6

Globalizing Migration Regimes: New Challenges
to Transnational Cooperation
*Kristof Tamas and Joakim Palme*
0 7546 4692 0

# Migration, Regional Integration and Human Security
The Formation and Maintenance of Transnational Spaces

*Edited by*
Harald Kleinschmidt
*University of Tsukuba, Japan*

**ASHGATE**

© Harald Kleinschmidt 2006

All rights reserved. No part of this publication may be reproduced, stored in a retrieval system, or transmitted in any form or by any means, electronic, mechanical, photocopying, recording or otherwise without the prior permission of the publisher.

Harald Kleinschmidt has asserted his right under the Copyright, Designs and Patents Act, 1988, to be identified as the editor of this work.

Published by
Ashgate Publishing Limited
Gower House
Croft Road
Aldershot
Hampshire GU11 3HR
England

Ashgate Publishing Company
Suite 420
101 Cherry Street
Burlington, VT 05401-4405
USA

Ashgate website: http://www.ashgate.com

**British Library Cataloguing in Publication Data**
Migration, regional integration and human security : the
  formation and maintenance of transnational spaces. -
  (Research in migration and ethnic relations series)
  1.Emigration and immigration 2.Emigration and immigration -
  Government policy 3.International economic integration -
  Social aspects
  I.Kleinschmidt, Harald, 1949-
  304.8'2

**Library of Congress Cataloging-in-Publication Data**
Migration, regional integration and human security : the formation and maintenance of Transnational spaces / edited by Harald Kleinschmidt.
       p. cm. -- (Research in migration and ethnic relations series)
    Includes bibliographical references and index.
    ISBN 0-7546-4646-7
  1. Emigration an immigration--Government policy. 2. Regionalism. I. Kleinschmidt, Harald, 1949- II. Series

   JV6271.M54 2006
   325--dc22
                                                                                   2006000110

ISBN-10: 0 7546 4646 7

Library
University of Texas
at San Antonio

Printed in Great Britain by
Antony Rowe Ltd, Chippenham, Wiltshire.

# Contents

| | |
|---|---:|
| List of Figures | vii |
| List of Contributors | ix |
| Introduction<br>*Harald Kleinschmidt* | 1 |

**Part 1: Approaches to Migration**     19

1. International Migration: A Development Practitioner's Perspective     21
*Eimi Watanabe*

2. Migration, Minorities and the Transfer of Technology in Early Modern Europe     45
*Salvatore Ciriacono*

3. Migration, Regional Integration and Human Security: An Overview of Research Developments     61
*Harald Kleinschmidt*

4. Migrants, Human Security and Military Security     103
*Reinhard Drifte*

**Part 2: The Restructuration of Transnational Spaces**     121

5. Migration and Geographical Distance     123
*Leslie E. Bauzon*

6. Community Beyond the Border: An Ethnological Study of Chuukese Migration in Micronesia     139
*Keiji Maegawa*

7. International Migration and Regional Integration: The Case of Central America     153
*Wolfgang Hein*

8. The Kurdish Movement: Ethnic Mobilization and Europeanization     181
*Andreas Blätte*

**Part 3: Regional Approaches to Migrants' Security Concerns**      203

9    Labour Migration and Human Security
in East and Southeast Asia      205
*Motoko Shuto*

10    European Immigration and Asylum Policy:
Scope and Limits of Intergovernmental Europeanization      225
*Dietmar Herz*

11    Migration and Cross-border Cooperation
in Central and East European Countries      245
*Kazu Takahashi*

12    People on the Move:
The Theoretical Challenge of Migratory Movement      259
*Henning Eichberg*

Epilogue      271
*Harald Kleinschmidt*

*Bibliography*      *275*
*Index*      *283*

# List of Figures

| | | |
|---|---|---|
| Table 7.1 | Migration within Central America and between Central and North America | 161 |
| Table 7.2 | Key Indicators of Development for Central American Countries | 166 |
| Table 7.3 | Foreign-born Professionals and Technicians in Costa Rica, according to Occupational Groups and Area of Work | 170 |
| Table 8.1 | Attendance at Kurdish Protests in Germany 1980-2002 | 186 |
| Table 8.2 | Kurdish European-level Protest Activity 1999-2003 | 192 |
| Table 10.1 | Voting Requirements in Selected Fields of European Migration Policy | 243 |

# List of Contributors

**Leslie E. Bauzon**: Professor of History at the University of the Philippines and currently Visiting Professor of Areas Studies (Southeast Asia) at the University of Tsukuba, Japan.

**Andreas Blätte**: Political Scientist, Doctoral Candidate at the University of Erfurt, Germany.

**Salvatore Ciriacono**: Professor of History at the University of Padua, Italy.

**Reinhard Drifte**: Professor of Political Science at the University of Newcastle, UK.

**Henning Eichberg**: Professor of Sociology at the University of Southern Denmark, Denmark.

**Wolfgang Hein**: Professor of Political Science at the University of Hamburg and fellow of the German Overseas Research Institute at Hamburg, Germany.

**Dietmar Herz**: Professor of Political Science and Vice-President of Erfurt University, Germany.

**Harald Kleinschmidt**: Professor of History at the Universities of Tsukuba and of Tokyo, Japan.

**Keiji Maegawa**: Professor of Anthropology at the University of Tsukuba, Japan.

**Motoko Shuto**: Professor of Political Science at the University of Tsukuba, Japan.

**Kazu Takahashi**: Professor of Political Science at Yamagata University, Japan.

**Eimi Watanabe**: culminated her long career with the UN's Children's Fund (UNICEF) as Assistant Secretary General and Director, Development Policy Bureau in the UNDP, and now lives in Denmark and writes and lectures occasionally on development issues.

# Introduction

## Harald Kleinschmidt

Migrants connect. They make borders threadbare. They operate in or even establish spaces in geographical, social, political, economic and cultural respects. If migrants cross international borders, they create transnational spaces and their activities trigger responses from and impact on the policies of institutions of governance of sovereign states, supranational and international institutions and as well as civil society groups. Yet the formulation and implementation of migration policies has most commonly been vested in the decision-making institutions of sovereign states for two-hundred or so years. This has been so although transnational migration, by its very nature, is a border-crossing process and cannot, therefore, be dealt with unilaterally within the confines of only one state. In fact, some of the transnational spaces within which migrants have operated or which they established have existed for a long time, joining together several states or other types of polities. But regional institutions or transnational regimes have rarely been involved in the formulation and implementation of migration policies. Currently, most regional integration and cooperation schemes are only gradually including migration into their agendas or, in the case of the European Union (EU), develop their migration policies along the traditional, regressive lines of national states. There are only three international organizations and institutions dealing with migration, namely the United Nations High Commissioner on Refugees (UNHCR), the International Labour Organization (ILO) and the International Organization for Migration (IOM). There appears to be a clash of perceptions between migrants on the one side and, on the other, law-makers, political decision-makers and administrators in charge of and theorists reflecting on migration. Whereas the latter have looked at migration from the point of view of government, many transnational migrants have been agents of regionalism, if not of globalization, not necessarily by intention but through manifest action.

The conflict between transnational migrants' actions and state government policies poses a number of difficult questions. What can the migration policy of an institution of governance consist in? What are the goals that any migration policy can be designed to accomplish? What are the factors that can stimulate the making of a migration policy? What are the consequences of success or failure of a migration policy? What are the intellectual tools necessary for the making and the execution of a migration policy and how do these tools relate to the execution and evaluation of the success or failure of a migration policy?

## Actors in Migration Policy

The first question touches upon factual, possible and desirable institutional actors in charge of transnational migration. It is relevant because, from the turn of the nineteenth century, the making of migration policy has been ranked among the foremost properties of the sovereign state. The second question emerges from the first. The basic reason why governments of sovereign states have traditionally been credited with the capability of deciding authoritatively on transnational migration issues is that each sovereign state is considered to have to have a population that remains identifiable as a uniform politically active group only as long as it remains stable. One important factor of regulating the stability of the population of a state is control of transnational migration. Over the last two hundred or so years, immigrants have been categorized as a threat and consequently, the foremost instrument of regulating migration has been control of immigration. Hence, whenever governments of sovereign states have developed migration policies during this period, they have put into operation administrative and policing tools. They have done so claiming to act to the ends of preventing uncontrolled trespass into the territory under their control and of providing security to the state population.

As the goals of any migration policy can be subject to critical inquiry, so too can its motives be scrutinized. Hence the third question is only the flip side of the second question. Institutions of governance in sovereign states can want to devise migration policies to the end of adding to their security-providing capabilities. Yet, in areas where regionalization processes are ongoing and supported or accompanied by transnational migration, institutions of regional integration can want to absorb decision-making capabilities from the governments of their member states. Thus, in order to acquire more paraphernalia of sovereignty, regional institutions can try to accumulate competence over migration policy to the end of increasing their own competence vis-à-vis the governments of their member states. Ever since the enactment of the Treaty of Amsterdam in 1997, the European Commission and the European Parliament have tried to increase their influence on migration policy-making. However, as long as the range of migration policy remains confined to the issues on which this policy field has been focused over the last two hundred or so years (namely, the prevention of uncontrolled immigration), regional institutions can only have the desire to generate their own competence over migration policy if, at the same time, they have the administrative and policing tools to manifestly control transnational immigration. In the case of the EU, however, only the governments of the sovereign member states have the technical means and the legitimacy to control transnational immigration. Interests of sovereign states will then clash with regional integration schemes.

The dilemma is this: Under the given focus of migration policy on the prevention of uncontrolled immigration, it makes little sense for a regional institution to devise its own migration policy for lack of means to implement it. Yet, if it leaves this policy field to the exclusive custody of the governments of its member states, it does not contribute to the deepening of regional integration. Nevertheless, the dilemma points to a potential for political action that regional institutions may devote themselves to. They may devise their own migration policy along lines that depart from the conventional habit of formulation and executing migration policies to the end of preventing uncontrolled immigration. The decision to do so is made easier through the empirical observation that conventional migration policy has rarely accomplished its goal. Instead, much of the history of state immigration control is the history of its failure. Prima facie, this has been so because of the difficulty of consistently enforcing complete border control. But the deeper problem is why boundaries are so difficult to control and so attractive to trespass. One answer to this problem is that people will cross boundaries whether or not they are allowed to do so by law if these boundaries divide traditional areas of cohabitation. In these cases the resulting frequency of transnational migration can be an indicator for implicit popular support of or demand for regional integration. The transnational spaces that migrants created at some time in the past can therefore be older than the international borders of currently existing sovereign states. Under this condition, the institutions of governance of sovereign states might act with legitimacy if they allocate the decision-making capability over migration policy to a regional institution in which they are members. However, at present, there is no empirical case where this allocation has happened, even though there is an emergent practice of migration policy coordination among states joining the Central American Common Market. Therefore, in the context of current regional integration schemes, we need to ask what the consequences of success or failure of a migration policy can be.

The question has rarely been asked. This has been so because asking it means reflecting on the notion of migration and the intellectual tools that are necessary to the end of implementing a migration policy. Readiness to do so has not greatly advanced. In fact, most of the intellectual tools informing current migration policies go back to residentialist assumptions inherited from nineteenth-century social and political theories. These theories postulated a long-term metaphysical process of social organization in the course of which groups appeared to have gradually given up their seemingly original 'nomadic' pattern of life became settled and integrated themselves into ever larger group structures. In consequence of these theories, migration was scaled down to an exceptional if not deviant behaviour that individuals appeared to choose who, for some psychic abnormality, seemed to be determined to practice atavistic habits. However, over the past thirty or so years, many of the assumptions on which these theories had been rested have been called into question or been given up right away. If this is so, the conceptualization and implementation of migration policies become difficult that continue to take assumptions for granted that were at best based on ideologies. Hence, once more the question, what the intellectual tools are that are necessary for the conceptualization and implementation of current migration policies.

## Migration and Regional Integration

There has long been much talk about 'walls' in Europe. Down to the end of the eighteenth or the beginning of the nineteenth century, many cities had walls. These walls visualized separation and the lack of possibility of uncontrolled accessibility. Walls marked difference in social, political, economic and cultural terms and divided urban communities from the 'open' countryside. In the nineteenth and twentieth centuries, most of the medieval urban enceintes were torn down or neglected while walls were erected around states. Some of these walls were of stone and concrete, others consisted of administrative regimes. Their task in either case was once again the prevention of trespass. Nineteenth-century geographers, political decision-makers and military organizers likened the international boundaries of states to the skin of the political body. They concluded that penetration into the skin of the political body was a dangerous violation of its integrity and should be prevented by all means. Two kinds of penetrating agents were ranked as highly dangerous: armed forces and migrants. Armed forces were relatively easy to deal with. Late in the nineteenth century, the French military, for one, put up huge fortifications behind the French-German border to the end of keeping the German military out. The German army did care but drew the conclusion that it should circumvent the wall rather than attacking it directly if it were to invade France. Following this plan, German armed forces were marched into France through Belgium when Germany launched World War I. Yet such walls were useless against unarmed migrants as the wall separating the two German states from 1961 to 1989 eventually made clear. The latter wall did have some effect in reducing migration between the two states but its maintenance, surveillance and administration charged prohibitively high costs under which eventually the state collapsed whose government had authorized the building of the wall. In spite of the factual failure of the French and the German walls, political decision-makers and administrators attempting to regulate migration and social scientists advising them in these efforts, have not banned walls from their minds. The walls no longer serve military purposes and are not built of stone and concrete. But debate continues about the question whether or not states should and can impose restrictions against immigration.

The debate ignores the fact that regional integration enforces changes of the public policy of defining who a migrant is and who a resident is, and thereby makes it more difficult to determine what the population of a state is. Properly understood, regional integration renders obsolete the more significant of the postulates on which the migration policies of sovereign states used to rest, namely that transnational migration can and should solely be defined in administrative terms and controlled through state surveillance of international borders. Even international organizations like IOM and international advisory commissions, such as the Commission on Human Security, have continued to follow this state-centric definition of migration to the present day. Neither institutions of governance of sovereign states nor international organizations and regional institutions seem to be willing to accept the given fact that regional integration politicizes migration in the sense that it enhances controversy over the norms and values informing attitudes towards collective identity and security in connection with migration.

Two indicators seem to suggest nevertheless that regional institutions hold sway over migration policy in an indirect way. The first indicator is that any process at regional integration and regional cooperation at any level eases cross-border traffic if several sovereign states are involved in it. Increased frequency of traffic permits an increase of migration potential. If regional integration processes are institutional, the activities of the regional institutions above the sovereign states have a bearing on migration even if the formulation and execution of migration policies do not fall into their competence. The second indicator is the attraction of regionally integrated areas for migrants from other parts of the world. Not only the EU, also the Association of Southeast Asian Nations (ASEAN) and the North American Free Trade Association (NAFTA) provide examples that migrants looking for opportunities focus their attention on areas in which regional integration takes place in one way or another.

Both indicators taken together support the assumption that there is some political connection between migration and regional integration, even where regional institutions are not engaged in implementing migration policies. In other words, the interdependence of migration with regional integration is subject neither to the political will nor to the control of regional institutions. Nor at that of institutions of governance of sovereign states as soon as or as long as their governments engage in policies to the end of enhancing economic, political and cultural ties within a region and smoothing the crossing of international borders. Reduction of government capability to formulate and execute migration policies is part and parcel of regional integration in this broad sense. Regions are demarcated along fuzzy boundaries and because, as a rule, regional identities are multiple, in competition among themselves and do not always relate to identical boundaries. Carl von Clausewitz already observed early in the nineteenth century that the Chinese Great Wall, a piece of 'ultimate defence' as he called it, was useless in military contexts because, once built, it could not be moved when the enemies changed their positions. *Mutatis mutandis,* the same applies to talk about closed regions. Apart from the physical and financial difficulty of walling in regions, against whom should these walls be built and defended and who could guarantee that potential migrants only use tracks blocked by these walls? Walls of administrative constraints have even poorer chances to accomplish any goal. They do not prevent trespass by people determined to cross them. The concept of 'closed regionalism' is a contradiction in itself.

## The Making of Collective Identities

Deciding what constitutes the population of a state politically has been part of nationality legislation for about two hundred years. The overall goal under which population policy and nationality legislation have stood in Europe for about one hundred and thirty years has been the maintenance of population stability. Migration destabilizes populations and regional integration eases migration. Therefore, migration and regional integration can both be construed, perceived or even experienced as an obstacle against the accomplishment of population stability. These constructions, perceptions and experiences have dominated in a world that was considered as a world of states and in which the nation-state ranked as the prototype of the state at large. They have received support from a theory of legitimacy that derives justification for the existence of states and governments from the consent of population groups residing in given areas. Population groups as groups of settlers have been credited with a degree social cohesion sufficient to enter into an agreement to act to the end of establishing a government. From the learned Abbot Engelbert of Admont early in the fourteenth century, to Justus Lipsius at the turn of the seventeenth century, to Thomas Hobbes and John Locke in the seventeenth century, contractualism generated an interventionist migration policy the goal of which was to contribute to population stability through the enhancement of immigration. The reasons for immigration-generating policies were, first, that most cities in the larger territorial polities had a death rate higher than the birth rate; second, that some of the larger territorial polities such as Russia were composed of vast thinly settled lands that rulers tried to populate; third, that in some cases, such as the boundary between the Habsburg territories and the Ottoman Turkish Empire, new settlements were considered necessary for defence purposes. In any case, migration policies were so designed as to create positive, attractive images of and conditions for life at the destinations of migrants. To the extent that such policies were successful, propagandists disseminated the conclusion that the migrants had, in a way, voted by their feet to conclude a contract with the rulers of the areas of their destination. In the seventeenth and eighteenth centuries, several rulers devised such policies simultaneously thereby creating a migration market where they competed over attracting the largest number of immigrants.

In the nineteenth and twentieth centuries, contractualism continued but merged with nationalism. The contract on the establishment of a government was understood to be a contract among nationals, and nationals were considered to be members of a geno group as a group of people whose relationships were described metaphorically in kin terms. The fair degree of openness that had been characteristic of border control regimes up to the early nineteenth century gave way to rigorous measures of border control and migration restriction. Immigration of non-nationals was regarded as a jeopardy to the social cohesion of the geno group. Emigration was taken to be a dangerous reduction of the national war-making capacity. If, under these circumstances, populations were found to decline, such as after major military conflicts, the increase of the birth rate emerged as the main feature of population policy. Under the premise of nationalism, fulfilling the contract between rulers and ruled was identical with closing off one nation against others. Nationals were expected to be settled in a given area and remain settled there. The postulate of residentialism, enshrined in most nineteenth- and twentieth-century theories of society, helped downgrade migration to a deviant form of behaviour for which explanations were sought and found mainly in economic conditions of life. Thus the image of migrants as poor and lonely people pushed and pulled away and around, dominated nationalist migration policy in the nineteenth and twentieth centuries. The categorization of migrant behaviour as deviant entailed a search for reasons that might make people move. Against empirical evidence suggesting that a large number of people moved for private reasons or because of some political dissatisfaction, the authorities usually assumed economic motives. The push- and-pull-model cast these fuzzy perceptions into terms. It suggested that migration occurs where pull factors as factors of 'attraction' meet with push factors as factors of 'repulsion', as the London *Times* put it in 1851. The physicalist model stigmatized migrants as passive targets of anonymous 'factors', a maneuverable mass that, like rivers, flows into a certain direction and precipitates destruction when out of control. Nineteenth-century scientism induced statisticians such as Ernest George Ravenstein to condense recurrent observations about migration into statements that proclaimed to be laws.

Persons migrating nevertheless had to overcome high hurdles to find acceptance at their destinations. Lawmakers, political decision-makers and administrators delved in a plethora of laws and other legal rules apt to define immigrants as non-nationals. In some states, for example the USA, nationality and citizenship were separated. US immigration policy proceeded from the assumption that migrants carried with them and could retain the nationality that they acquired through birth. By contrast, US citizenship was a status that migrants appeared to be able to acquire through state controlled admission and registration procedures. Elsewhere, for example in Germany, citizenship and nationality were defined in ways that established largely overlapping though not completely identical terms. In German, there is still today no word for the US term 'citizenship'. Instead, immigrants were given the status of resident aliens, temporary or permanent. A permanent alien resident is entitled to stay but not to participation in the political activities of the nationals.

Much as these distinctions may have appeared to be mandatory from an administrative point of view, they were nevertheless informed by the nineteenth-century concept of the nation as a geno group. This concept positioned the nation at the highest level of a hierarchy of social groups all of which were modelled upon the kin group occupying the lowest level. Proclaiming this hierarchy of social groups, social theorists insisted that membership in nations should, as a rule, be acquired in the same way as individuals acquired kin membership, namely by birth. Naturalization as an administrative procedure for the integration of immigrants was regarded as a rare exception, usually conditioned by marriage relations. The likening of national identity to kin identity boosted the image that national identity could hardly be changed, even after long-distance international migration. This image has been characteristic of migration and migrants since the nineteenth century and has entailed important consequences for the making and the enforcement of migration policy. While during the *Ancien Régime* when 'national characters' were derived from climate (Montesquieu) or from contractual agreements on human made political order (Hume), change of national identity through migration or political reform and revolution was considered to be perfectly normal. Yet the subsequent conceptualization of the nation as a geno group has promoted political strategies and administrative tactics designed to widen the difference between nations and to make the change of national identity difficult.

Theorists of regional integration and political decision-makers wishing to promote schemes of regional integration in early post-World-War-II Europe sensed the obstacles that the image of nations as isolated geno groups posed against regional integration. In the 1950s, neo-functionalists developed an elaborate theoretical framework to steer regional integration processes against what they perceived as the basic popular option of Europeans in favour of nation-states. This framework soon proved inapt, insufficient and obsolescent. It did so primarily because the perception of the attitude of Europeans allegedly favouring the nation-state was in fact a perception of the political elite with little or no roots in popular attitudes. For the concept of the nation as a geno group was, form the very beginning, the concoction of elites seeking to manipulate consent to their rule. The carnage of World War II disclosed the vanity of this concept and opened the pathway to European integration. However, the emerging European institutions of the 1950s and 1960s and the governments of the sovereign states making up these institutions were too slow to recognize and utilize the potential for regional integration. Stuck in the legacy of the interwar period, the old men at the helm of most European states in the 1950s and 1960s vainly sought to restore the international system of the 1920s.

Lawmakers, political decision-makers, and administrators unanimously and almost everywhere in Europe rated the chances of successful reintegration low and thereby promoted the image of migrants as 'uprooted' people. Hence their primary concern was the prevention of the return of penniless remigrants whom they expected to become a burden for the national social welfare systems. The image of uprootedness was unfounded already in the nineteenth century, as the hundreds of millions of letters show that were sent back and forth only between North America and Europe at the time. Nevertheless, the image became the foundation of much social science research methodology establishing criteria for the determination as well as taxonomies of causes for migration and promoting instruments for the measurement of social integration and disintegration.

### 'New Migration', 'New Regionalism and 'New Security Thinking'

Over the past 20 or so years, most of these core postulates and assumptions have been called into question, even though new images of migration do not seem to have penetrated the minds of political decision-makers, lawmakers and administrators. Empirical data show that migration is frequently not a finite process but a recurrent or even continuing activity. This activity may engage individuals over a long period of their lifetime, or it may connect the life experiences of individuals with those of their kin members, neighbours and friends, even across generations. These experiences may range from continuing migration without specific concern for destinations, return to place or area of origin, the purposeful movement to a specific destination, usually at the advice of friends or relatives. Frequently, migrants establish networks among themselves as well as with people at places of their origin and communicate their experiences. In areas where migration has been frequent over long periods of time, such as across the Atlantic, across the Pacific, in between two or more states, special relationships come into existence creating systems within which migration takes place without specific identifiable push and pull factors. In short, the image of the poor, passive, lonely and 'uprooted' migrant has given way to the picture of well informed, active, well-to-do persons who consciously rank their diffuse desire to move above their concurrent desire to stay. This new picture of the migrant suggests that it is of the same importance to ask the question why people move as it is to ask the opposite question why people stay. Generally speaking, migration takes place when the motives to move win over the motives to stay and a latent potential for migration becomes activated. The critical situation in which individuals or groups opt against residentialism needs to be analyzed at the level of individual behaviour and cannot be reconstructed or hypothesized on the basis of aggregate statistical data.

'New migration' has important consequences for the formulation and execution of migration policy. If migration is recognized as a normal, not a deviant behaviour, migration policies that impose constraints and hardships upon migrants in service to the sovereign state are violations of human rights. Far from conveying security, migration policies provoke insecurity for migrants as well as residents. Migrants' insecurity becomes more severe with the increasing rigidity of border control; residents' insecurity grows because institutions of governance of sovereign state fail to effectively implement border control at feasible costs. Under these conditions, human rights and other transnational civil society organizations will be called in as additional security providers standing against or competing with institutions of governance of sovereign states. Paradoxically, many states have constitutions that guarantee the right to emigrate. But no state exists in which institutions of governance recognize the right to immigrate. International organizations have addressed this paradox as a problem but have so far failed to demand the recognition of the right to immigrate.

'New migration' has therefore sparked the elevation of new security issues onto the international agenda. 'New security' does not merely entail a widening concept of security but also necessitates the inclusion of the subjective consciousnesses of migrants into the formulation and implementation of migration policies. Both consequences are important. A variety of factors, among them the twentieth-century experience that warfare has become more lethal for non-combatants than for combatants, have warranted the inclusion of the human dimension into the concept of security and have sparked extensive cross-border movements, mainly of refugees and asylum-seekers. As a consequence, the conventional, narrow definition of security in terms of protection to be provided by armed forces, has become insufficient, as armed forces, with or without control by institutions of governance of sovereign states, have been found to threaten most elementary aspects of the security of non-combatant civilians. From 1994, human security has featured with increasing prominence on the agenda of international organizations, such as the United Nations Development Program (UNDP). It has been investigated by the international Commission on Human Security that filed its report in 2003. The focus of the work of these institutions, which have received support from governments of several states including Japan and Sweden, has been cast on the reduction of the suffering of individuals in consequence of war and environmental disasters. It has been understood that withholding basic human rights and deprivation of essential conditions of life are likely to result in the increase of the number of migrants, specifically refugees and asylum-seekers. Because many of the involved policy issues concerning the most feasible mode of providing human security have been contested, the concept of security has become subject to intense debate among theorists, policy-makers and administrators. Moreover, the new, extended concept of security expands the meaning of security to concerns about the human individual as the primary recipient of security and, therefore, amplifies the range of potential security providers beyond the army and the police as institutions of the sovereign state. The wider concept of security necessitates the inclusion of local as well as transnational security providers, first and foremost civil society organizations.

The politicization of the debate about human security has boosted the significance of migration as an issue of international relations and deepened the understanding that migration policies can no longer be left to be decided by institutions of governance of sovereign states. By contrast, the second consequence of the widening concept of security, namely the increase of the significance of the subjective consciousness of migrants in connection with human security concerns, has received much less attention. This has been due to the way in which institutions of governance of sovereign states, international organizations as well as transnational civil society groups have so far been concerned with migration. Many of these institutions, organizations and groups have been mostly concerned with refugees and asylum-seekers and their security interests. They have often overlooked that, despite their often heart-breaking experiences, refugees and asylum-seekers represent only a small minority of the total of currently some 175 million migrants worldwide. Even though refugees and asylum-seekers and their human security concerns have to receive appropriate attention on humanitarian and legal grounds, it would be misleading to conceive human security as being mainly relevant for refugees and asylum-seekers. In fact, migrants other than refugees and asylum-seekers have their own human security concerns that are often sharply different from, if not directly opposed to those that institutions of governance of sovereign states, international organizations and transnational civil society groups are willing to acknowledge and place on their agendas. Whereas refugees and asylum-seekers are most frequently in need of quickly provided help concerning essential conditions of life, such as the provision of food, shelter and medical care, most important among the human security concerns of other groups of migrants is the demand for transparent, equitable and fair immigration rules and procedures that are based on widely applied, stated and lasting principles that can be expected to be in operation for an explicitly guaranteed period of time.

This demand has militated against the determination of institutions of governance of sovereign states whose representatives have insisted on their sovereign privilege to the 'freedom of action' concerning immigration regulations and procedures. However, insistence upon this privilege has produced situations in which, according to the Commission on Human Security, governments of 44 per cent of so-called 'developed' countries and 39 per cent of so-called 'developing' countries pursue restrictive immigration policies. Yet increased migration restriction adds to the potential of clandestine or undocumented migration that, in turn, amplifies the hazards for migrants and jeopardizes the security of residents. Moreover, increased migration restriction must be enforced consistently over a long period in order to be effective. But the enforcement costs may ruin the very legitimacy base and public budget of the state that restricted immigration policies seek to protect. Obviously, human security concerns can be best met with at the level of regional institutions above the sovereign states. Empowering regional institutions to administer and police transnational spaces is therefore not merely a means to provide human security more effectively. It is also in the well-understood and legitimate self-interest of institutions of governance of sovereign states to waive their migration-policy-making monopoly and involve regional institutions of governance together with civil society groups, unless they want to risk their own demise.

Yet not merely lawmakers, political decision-makers and administrators in charge of migration are at a loss to reorient their perceptions to deal with migration and regional integration. So too are academics, specifically social scientists. Many social scientists still today rely on statistical data compiled from state-centred sources. This may be a necessary practice that can hardly be changed as long as sovereign states continue to exist. But social scientists are not always aware of the impact that their choice of data can have on their work and its results. As a legacy of the nineteenth century, official statistics are statistics compiled by institutions of governance or subordinate agencies of states. Hence these statistics end at the international borders of the state. Yet regional integration flexibilizes institutions of the sovereign state as migration makes border threadbare and changes the size and composition of the state population. Hence, migration and regional integration obfuscate the statistics of the state. Structural changes in state populations together with changing borders render official demographic data inadequate where they exist at all. Thus essential data for any social science enquiry need careful scrutiny and are of limited value as a starting platform for theorizing. Moreover, official population statistics have been available for no more than approximately 200 years.

Consequently, long-term statistical surveys are impossible and so too are qualified statements on trends of numerical increase or decrease of migration. The frequent claim that migration should have exponentially increased worldwide during the nineteenth and twentieth centuries is unascertainable.

The lack of reliability of data adds to the inadequacy of migration-related perceptions. One of them is the political theory that states are 'black boxes' or uniform 'actors'. The theory is drawn on the assumption that the population of a state is united to the degree that it can act as if speaking with one voice. Thus the population of a state is seen, first and foremost, as a group of settlers. But the residentialist postulate that the population is essentially stable and will eventually integrate immigrants is unwarranted in many cases because of the frequent coexistence of and competition among diverse identities within one state. In these cases, the diversity of collective identities includes or is informed by a variety of memories of and perceptions on past migrations. The sets of identities may be horizontally stratified in a hierarchy manifest in an order of more or less comprehensive institutions of governance at the local, micro-regional, national or macro-regional levels. In regions such as in the EU, the macro-regional level should be the preferred level of social-science analysis.

Awareness of these restrictions and problems pitched against a straightforward application of state-centric social science methods has increased over the past twenty or so years with paradigm shifts from conventional to 'new migration' studies, from neo-functionalist regional integration theory to 'new regionalism', and from etatism to the human security discourse. The common features of all simultaneous paradigm shifts are, first and foremost, that they call into question state-centric perspectives and approaches. Even more importantly, they facilitate the recognition of subjective consciousnesses and perceptions of migrants and the competitive interaction of various coexisting identities in regions. They also promote a degree of relativism and demand a comparative perspective in the process of obtaining definitions and the making of standards. In this respect, 'new migration' studies have added to our knowledge about the various possibilities of experiencing and conceptualizing migration from the points of view of migrants as well as those of lawmakers, political decision-makers and administrators. Likewise, 'new regionalism' has promoted the comparative study of regional integration processes, and one important result of these studies is that the EU has been dismissed as a model and scaled down to one particular and to a large extent, odd case. Hence students of migration have learnt to live with fuzzy definitions in a scope that is limited in terms of space and time. Careful description and analysis have taken priority over grand theory. Finally, 'new security' studies have shed light on the diversity of security demands and widened the spectre of actors that can be considered as security providers.

## Chapter Survey

Changing patterns of twentieth-century migration and changing theoretical positions towards migration have rendered obsolete the assumptions of nineteenth-century European social thought according to which societies were defined as territorialized groups of residents under the control of norm-setting institutions. This tradition of social thought is thus not only incapable of dealing with mobile societies but it also supports attitudes that subject migrants to discrimination and other acts of injustice. In the light recent of the recent revisions on migration, regional integration and security thinking, how do the economic, social, political and cultural frameworks have to be adjusted so that they can respond more adequately to migration as a normal activity, regional integration as a regular instrument for the accomplishment of political, economic and cultural change and security as a good provided to individuals? This book does not ask why people move but what can be done to regularize migration processes at regional leves, reduce the hazards for migrants and to accommodate the needs of giving and receiving societies with migrants' demands. The four chapters included in Part I approach these issues in general terms. Parts II and III feature three chapters each on the western Pacific Rim and the EU. Both regions are juxtaposed because they represent to types of processes of regionalization, one through intergovernmental contractualization, the other through institutionalization. The comparison between both types of regionalization allows insights into the various conditions that can shape the interdependence of migration, regional integration and security together with their joint effects on the sovereign state. In addition, one chapter in Part II focuses on Central America as a region in which institutional integration is weak while intergovernmental cooperation includes issues of migration policy.

Part I examines migration in general terms. It opens with Eimi Watanabe's survey 'International Migration: A Development Practitioner's Perspective'. She calls for a transdisciplinary approach to the study of transnational migration. Yet in her view, current debates on international migration, particularly post-September 11 with the global preoccupation on internal security, are increasingly focused on achieving tighter controls to keep out 'unwanted migrants' and ensuring better and faster integration of 'new citizens'. She criticizes that too little distinction is being made between asylum-seekers and refugees on the one side and migrants on the other. Given that the incentives for emigration are unlikely to abate in the years to come, and as industrialized countries will be increasingly under pressure to look to migration as a solution to their problems of labour shortages due to aging population, Watanabe demands a more balanced perspective that would constitute the basis of rational and longer term immigration policies. Such a perspective might view international migration as a livelihood strategy and a development issue, in a human development framework, thus analyzing the impact of emigration and immigration on growth and human development at the global and regional levels as well as in connection with communities and families.

Salvatore Ciriacono extends Watanabe's empirical investigation to the past and focuses on the role of migrants as technological innovators. Looking at migration in early modern Europe, he emphasizes the openness of early modern European urban and territorial polities and the comparative ease with which migrants were integrated into their host communities. He points towards the existence of early modern migration networks that effectively connected urban and territorial polities even at times of war and other kinds of dispute. Contrary to much nineteenth-century nationalistic myth-making, early modern Europe emerges as an intensely interconnected and socially integrated continent, despite the plethora of mostly tiny polities into which the continent was divided politically. It is important to note the fact that state-centric migration policies have been in operation only for little more than two hundred years and are thus likely to be transient.

In the following research review, I focus on the consciousnesses of migrants as an emerging research interest and discuss, in theoretical terms, the interrelationship of migration with regional integration and security together with their joint effect on institutions of governance of sovereign states. I emphasize the paradigm change in migration research from the prevalence of state-centric approaches that held sway up until the early 1990s to the widening horizon of perceptions and attitudes that can only be considered from the vantage point of the migrants themselves.

In his empirical study of the interconnectedness of migration and security, specifically in East Asia, Reinhard Drifte reviews the literature about the relationship between security in general and human security in particular. Following Mutiah Alagappa's lead, Drifte defines security as 'the protection and enhancement of values that the authoritative decision makers deem vital for the survival and well-being of a community'. Based on this definition, Drifte shows that for a long time, migration failed to attract the attention of policymakers and security theorists because its linkage with security was not immediately evident. He identifies the eastern rim of the Eurasian continental block as an area where non-traditional security concerns, such as human rights, economic deprivation, health problems and environmental degradation have been linked to migration processes. He thus concludes that the most promising approach to reduce the threat of migration on national security is the advancement of sustainable development, the improvement of governance, that is, the widening of the attention paid to human security concerns.

Part II explores the making of transnational spaces through migration and regional integration and reviews changes of government attitudes toward migrants against the backdrop of changing consciousnesses of the migrants themselves. Government attitudes toward migrants are laid down in nationality legislation and immigration policies. To the extent that they are drawn on nineteenth-century theories of social organization, nationality legislation and immigration policies have put into force rules that have classed migrants according to such external administrative categories as citizenship, professional status, income and migration motivation. These categories have been authoritatively imposed upon migrants through administrative acts, largely without giving due respect to the subjective consciousnesses of the people on the move. For example, migrants have been classed as refugees because departure from their native country was judged to have been involuntary. This judgment has usually entailed the expectation that their stay in the host country was intended to be limited. Likewise, migrants have been categorized as aliens if their citizenship differed from that of their host country, again without due respect being paid to the subjective assessment of collective identity by the migrants themselves. Moreover, immigration rules have been applied differently, pending whether or not immigration officers judged incoming migrants to have a certain 'desired' professional status and income level. Migrants could then be rejected on the grounds that they would not meet entrance requirements, even if they did not accept these verdicts. However, new thinking on migration has increased the demand that the consciousnesses of migrants should be given deeper attention by authorities as well as social science students of migration. Specifically, migration research has confirmed the impression, already gained towards the end of the nineteenth century, that most migration takes place across short distances but that migrants' perception of distances will undergo changes in accordance with changing transport facilities and perceptions of space. If modern transport technology allows migrants to choose their destinations with an higher degree autonomy than in the past two or so centuries, perceptions of distance may change accordingly, and what appeared to be a remote destination may now turn into a nearby place. Therefore, the mental maps of migrants matter as much as the political conditions that shape border control regimes. Part II critically reviews these changes with an eye on the possibilities to do more justice to individual migrants and to assess the reallocation of competences for the making of migration policy from the governments of sovereign states to overarching institutions, such as those envisaged for the EU in the Amsterdam Treaty.

Leslie Bauzon looks at the Philippines as a major sending state whose citizens and their descendants can be found virtually everywhere in the world. He examines perceptions of geographical distance in the minds of migrants on the basis of a survey he conducted in the Philippines in the summer of 2002. He observes that populations in Africa, Asia and Latin America may be leaving their homes for basic necessities of food, shelter and education. He shows that a large majority of the migrants interviewed were well educated. Bauzon finds that migrants are strongly motivated and concludes that geographical distance is only one among a variety of factors that can trigger or prevent migration. Not necessarily do migrants move to the closest possible destination; instead, if they organize themselves in groups or retain kin and neighbourhood relations while on the move, a more distant destination may appear as the more feasible one preferred under expectations of economic prosperity. Through their networking capability migrants appear as a major factor in the making of transnational spaces.

Keiji Maegawa takes a closer look at perceptions of the effects of migration on sending and host communities. Small island polities in the South Pacific are ideal cases for detailed studies in this field of inquiry because the numbers of migrants are relatively small and allow in-depth scrutiny. Maegawa challenges the conventional anthropological view of local societies as traditional closed units of residents. Instead, he positions them as open systems and traces the making and maintenance of transnational spaces across communities. He reviews two fundamental effects of migration on communities, the outflow of population and the inflow currency remittances. He insists that migrants contribute importantly to their home communities even though the impacts on their host community may be insignificant. He observes a decline of traditional culture in Chuuk Island although Chuukese immigrants in Guam and Saipan find it difficult to integrate into their host communities because of their willingness to preserve their traditional culture. Chuukese in Guam and Saipan have established a network community that maintains strong ties with their communities of origin. These ties facilitate further emigration from Chuuk Island even though prospects for future economic affluence and social integration in the host communities are grim.

Wolfgang Hein directs the attention to Central America where he reviews migration in the context of the making of transnational spaces. Drawing on nearly two decades of fieldwork in Costa Rica, Hein denies that migration has led to any processes of socio-economic integration in Central America but shows that migration has contributed to the formation and stabilization of regional centres in Central America, Costa Rica being one of them. Costa Rica has been able to build on a middle class of immigrant social scientists and entrepreneurs whose continuing relations with their countries of origin contribute to the widening of market access. He takes the activities of these migrants as a contribution towards regional integration and demands that processes of the 'horizontal migration' of people with a fairly high income and a relatively high social status should be recognized as an important contribution to regional integration.

Andreas Blätte examines the impact of migration on changing collective identities, using the case of Kurdish immigration to Germany. Largely labour migrants or their relatives and descendants, Kurds in Germany have mostly been ranked as members of the country's large Turkish immigrant community, based on the categories of Turkish and German nationality legislation. As most Kurds arrived in Germany from Turkey, carrying Turkish passports, German authorities identified them as Turks irrespective of their possibly different 'ethnic' consciousness. Blätte views the emergence of organized protest among Turkish immigrants to Germany as a form of immigrant political participation and reviews what he calls the 'political opportunity structure' as the key variable for explaining how immigrants organize themselves and how they get involved in the politics of their host country. He identifies local, national and European Union levels of participation and traces the various channels used by immigrant lobbyists to articulate their interests and advocate their demands. A key demand is that Kurdish collective identity should be recognized against or jointly with Turkish nationality and that the request for the promotion of Kurdish language and culture should be accepted as a legitimate political goal. Describing the various strategies to implement these demands, Blätte predicts that the European level of participation is likely to rise in political significance with the Turkish bid for accession to the EU.

Part III ventures more deeply into the interconnectedness of migration with regional integration and human security. First, Motoko Shuto discusses labour migration dynamics during the 1990s in Southeast and East Asia. She specifies the migration flows in this part of the world as 'temporary migration', largely excluding female migration. She observes that the intention of migration policy-makers in the host countries not primarily directed towards the promotion of integration of immigrants but to fulfill the needs of domestic labour markets, and she notes a strengthening government determination to combat 'undocumented' immigration. Against these government strategies, migrants appear in vulnerable social positions where their own security needs are often neglected or where civil society groups act as security providers in lieu of government institutions. Remarkably, she categorizes some Southeast Asian economies, among them Thailand and Malaysia, as labour-sending and as labour-receiving countries. Other economies, like those of Singapore and Hong Kong, have depended heavily on immigrant labour. While some labour-sending countries have launched schemes of cooperation on migration policy, the migration policies of most states in East and Southeast Asia have continued to be defined at the national level and in ways that have merely responded to current needs without tackling long-term issues. Thus, while the migrants themselves have strengthened the ties among states in East and Southeast Asia through their own movements, governments have long been reluctant to respond in ways that might have helped alleviate social hardships and legal burdens of migrants.

Moving from the Pacific Rim to Europe, Dietmar Herz divides his review of the migration policy of the EU into three parts. In the first part, he sketches the development of European migration policy. In the second part, he relates theories of regional integration, such as neo-functionalism and intergovernmentalism, to migration policy and examines to what extent these theories can explain migration policy. In the third part, he argues the position that European migration policy can be understood as part of a project to form a European citizenship or something equivalent to conventional nationality. Thus EU migration policy appears to be extrapolated from the migration policies of the sovereign member states, even though the European Commission took a more liberal stance towards immigration in some of its directives than governments of member states. Through a discussion of the mechanisms of inclusion and exclusion that are connected with the definition of citizenship, he warns that European identity should not and can not be accomplished through administrative processes excluding those who are found to be in need of assistance.

Kazu Takahashi examines border-policing regimes in the context of the eastern expansion of the EU. She directs attention to a particular set of two so-called Euregions on the eastern fringes of the EU before 1 May 2004. She looks at Euregions that were established on the borders between Germany and the Czech Republic as well as between Germany, the Czech Republic and Poland in 1990. Euregions are cross-border communities of towns and villages with established commercial and cultural ties. For centuries, these ties have crisscrossed the borders of polities and states, even when they were severed by the Iron Curtain after World War II. In the two cases under review, job-related cross-border movements are frequent in either direction and cooperation among local authorities receives support from EU funds. However, the development potential of the cooperation has been reduced through the effects of EU and member state immigration policies aimed at restricting immigration to its states. There is thus a conflict of political goals between the EU and its member states on the one side and the job-creating efforts of the local communities cooperating in the Euregions. Whereas the cooperation within the micro-regions had the potential of stimulating the local economies, of promoting mutual understanding among residents on either side of international borders and of mitigating frictions, the immigration policies of the EU and its member states enforced border control and migration restriction.

Lastly, Henning Eichberg pulls together the various contributions and pleads for the recognition of the bottom-up perspective in formulating policies and conducting academic discussions on the interconnectedness of migration, regional integration and security issues. He concludes with the demand that genuinely democratic migration policies must recognize felt needs and desires of the people rather than fulfill the concerns of lawmakers, policy-makers and administrators.

The contributions to this volume were first read at an international conference organized by the University of Tokyo from 27 to 29 September 2002 with the generous support of its German and European Study Centre (DESK). The conference panels scrutinized changing perspectives on, new approaches to and a widening horizon of international migration in an effort to develop new research paradigms in migration studies. It is hoped that the volume can contribute to the same purpose.

# PART 1
Approaches to Migration

Chapter One

# International Migration: A Development Practitioner's Perspective

Eimi Watanabe[1]

**Introduction**

Some 175 million people live outside the country of their birth (2000 estimate)[2], including some 12 million refugees and 1 million asylum seekers (UNHCR 2000 figures). Each year, more than 5 million people migrate, through formal and informal channels. This paper will refer mainly to migration from developing countries into OECD countries, though significantly, the great majority of international migration takes place among developing countries. The term international migration is used loosely to refer to movement of people across borders, whether as job seekers, refugees or asylum seekers, for shorter or longer periods of time.

While migration has existed throughout the history of humankind, present day international migration is characterized by the greater diversity and often, the lack of predictability of flows. The distinction between economic migrants, refugees and asylum seekers has become blurred. This reflects both the tightening restrictions on immigration, as well as the complexity of factors that result in people leaving their countries. With such tightening, the numbers of undocumented or illegal migrants have increased (UN estimates for 1998 of 4 million people trafficked, producing a profit of 7 billion US$).

With the development of communication and transportation, most migrant communities now maintain close economic, social, political, cultural and religious links with their extended families, communities and institutions in their countries of origin, exercising significant impact on the latter. Repeat, return and onward

---

[1] The writer, while trained as a sociologist, has spent her career as a development professional in the United Nations, in both field and headquarters locations, performing operational and policy level work.
[2] United Nations Department of Economic and Social Affairs, *World Economic and Social Survey 2004: International Migration* (New York: United Nations, 2004).

migrants are not uncommon, thus intensifying the multiple identities of migrants straddling multiple societies and cultures.

Public apprehension over the perception of haphazard and uncontrolled immigration has intensified in recent years in OECD receiving countries, though not necessarily proportionate to actual numbers. The so-called 'immigration crisis' has become a hotly debated political issue. In addition to the grievance that immigrants are taking away jobs and abusing generous social services benefits, September 11 has added fuel to the terror of being swamped by great waves of unwanted foreigners who are causing a threat to internal security through terrorism, crime, drugs, disease, and so forth.[3] In the months following September 11, immigration featured as a key election issue in several EU countries, resulting in part in centre/right coalition governments in Denmark and Netherlands, or, at least tightly fought elections as in the cases of Sweden and Germany. Niessen and Schibel summarize the current situation as follows:

> It is probably fair to say that in the nineties, Europe saw itself confronted with unsolicited and undesired immigration. This is reflected in the terms used in the debates. Asylum-seekers and refugees were indeed admitted in great numbers, but seen as a burden that had to be shared among countries. Policies became based on suspicion: asylum was granted when not proven manifestly unfounded. Spouses were reunited after the primary purpose of their marriage was established. Bogus asylum seekers, economic refugees – terms frequently used in official parlance – and clandestine migrants were out to enter Europe's backdoor in order to benefit from the welfare state. Migration management and prevention came to mean migration restriction, border control and combating clandestine migration, trafficking in and smuggling of human beings. Migration became associated with organized crime and terrorism (especially after the 11th of September). Immigrants were associated with criminals and terrorists. Security issues began to dominate the policy agendas at national and European level, just as re-admission began to dominate the relationship with countries of origin.[4]

Terrorism was being associated with lack of democratic values, and thus, post September 11, the 'uncontrolled outflow' from poor countries is perceived as being

---

[3] See, for instance, the testimony for the Senate Judiciary Committee Subcommittee on, Technology, Terrorism and Government Information, USA, by the Director of Research, Centre for Immigration Studies, on 12 October 2001: '[T]errorists of September 11 were all foreign citizens and entered the US legally. While it is absolutely essential that we do not scapegoat immigrants, especially Muslim immigrants, we also must not overlook the most obvious fact: the current terrorist threat to the USA comes almost exclusively from individuals who arrive from abroad. Thus, our immigration policy, including temporary and permanent visas issuance, border control, and efforts to deal with illegal immigration are all critical to reducing the chance of an attack in the future.'

[4] Jan Niessen and Yongmi Schibel, *EU and US Approaches to the Management of Immigration. Comparative Perspectives* (Brussels: Migration Policy Group, May 2003), p. 5. (http://www.migpolgroup.com/uploadstore/electronic%20version.pdf).

linked not just with development failure, but also with failure of governance. Is the 'migration crisis' a misguided fallacy or can it be substantiated? Zolberg and Benda conclude as their most significant finding in *Global Migrants, Global Refugees*, that 'recent developments in the sphere of international migration, including both voluntary and forced movements, do not provide evidence of a "crisis" and that this holds as well for realistic projections into the near future'.[5] Crises or not, the perception is real, and there is mounting pressure for rationalizing policies and practices surrounding international migration.

Rationalizing, from a receiving, OECD country perspective, focuses on strengthening the control of international population flows, or put bluntly, keeping out unwanted immigrants, rejecting and returning bogus asylum seekers.

From an emigrating developing country perspective, however, international migration, whether permanent or temporary, is one among a mix of strategies, which households, communities and countries activate to improve their well being, and is thus part and parcel of the development process. Thus, rationalization would imply policy mixes that optimize the gains from migration while minimizing the losses, namely more of the right kind of migration under the right conditions.

This fundamental disparity manifests itself in two other ways. One is in the commonly accepted notion of 'globalization', which covers the free flow of money, goods and services, but not of people, especially when it comes to unskilled workers. For example, a World Bank document describes globalization as

> the growing interdependence of countries resulting from the increasing integration of trade, finance, people, and ideas in one global marketplace. International trade and cross-border investment flows are the main elements of this integration.[6]

While the movement of certain categories of professionals and managers is encompassed under the World Trade Organization's General Agreement on Trade in Services ('movement of natural persons'), that of skilled and unskilled workers is not. Given that for a significant number of developing countries, skilled and unskilled workforce are their biggest resource, restrictions on their flow prevent them from maximizing the benefits of globalization. Thus, Dollar and Kraay state: 'Migration from poor locations is the missing factor in the current wave of globalization that could make a large contribution to reducing poverty'.[7] According to an applied equilibrium model study, if people were money, and enjoyed the same freedom of mobility enjoyed by finance today, the world could expect an

---

[5] Aristide R. Zolberg and Peter M. Benda (eds), *Global Migrants Global Refugees* (New York and Oxford: Berghahn Books, 2001), p. 1.

[6] World Bank, *Beyond Economic Growth: Meeting the Challenges of Global Development* (Washington: The World Bank, 2000), p. 66.

[7] David Dollar and Aart Kraay, 'Spreading the Wealth', in *Foreign Affairs*, 81/1 (January/February 2002): 132.

efficiency gain as high as 3.4 trillion US$.[8] Some economists, including Rodrik, have argued for total liberalization in the flow of labour, for 'it is time to redress this balance'.[9]

A developmental perspective to international migration calls for recognizing these disparities and exploring pragmatic measures that reconcile competing policy objectives which can meet the needs of emigrating countries and immigrating countries alike, a highly aspirational goal but nonetheless one that needs to be placed on the global agenda.

**International Migration: A Sustainable Livelihood Strategy**

The impact of international migration on economic development is, in the main, encapsulated in the 'migration hump' theory. That is, it is not the poorest countries, nor the poorest sections of developing countries, where international migration is most prevalent. Rather, it is countries that have 'taken off', when people's incomes as well as aspirations rise, that they are more likely to emigrate. The incentive to emigrate declines, however, when the country reaches a higher level of development, with per capita incomes above 4,000 US$, and the disparity with the industrialized countries become marginal. This then creates the migration hump. According to Peter Stalker, the migration hump is evident first for short distance unskilled migrants and later for the more skilled workers.[10]

The logical extension of the migration hump theory is that, once a country or society has reached a 'higher level' of economic development, migration would more or less cease. Consider, however, that according to the 2001 UK Census, three million people emigrated from the UK over the previous decade, a much higher figure than estimated, and this, notwithstanding the number of immigrants into UK. Many migrated to Australia, where they constituted 9.8 per cent of immigrants between July 2001 and June 2002, second only to New Zealand as

---

[8] W. Moses and B. Letnes, *If People Were Money: Estimating the Potential Gains from Increased International Migration* (Helsinki: World Institute for Development Economics Research / UNU-WIDER, 2003).

[9] Dani Rodrik writes: 'The asymmetry of expectations imposed on the North and South is simply staggering ... developed countries cannot have it both ways. Either they put their money where their mouth is, and include labor flows in the agenda of liberalization; or they recognize the need for national autonomy and space, in which case they must extend to the developing countries the same privileges in the areas of trade and capital flows. ... I am struck by how tolerant we are of the political realities that support an excessively restrictive regime of international labor mobility, while we continually decry the "protectionist" forces that block further liberalization of an already very open trading system. It is time to redress the balance.' Dani Rodrik, Comments on the Conference on 'Immigration Policy and the Welfare State', Triest, 23 June 2001, p. 3.

[10] Peter Stalker, *International Migration* (London: New Internationalist Publications, 2001), p. 129.

country of origin. Among the immigrants into UK in turn, there were 3,500 Danes in 2003, a small number in proportion to the total of immigrants but significant as a proportion of the population of Denmark (6 million). These Danes were largely motivated by the UK tax laws which are among the most attractive in EU, according to the daily newspaper, *Politiken*, which adds that it is the Danes who earn more than 400,000 Danish crowns that consider moving out.[11] The many British migrating to Australia and the Danes to UK are surely not migrating because of 'poverty', and UK and Denmark are usually not branded as 'development failures'. Reasons for such migration are varied – better opportunities for jobs and education, better living environment for self and family (including better climate which is especially important for retirees), lower taxes. In a word, better lives and livelihoods.

Is it not then more appropriate to regard migration as normal human behaviour, that some people will choose migration as their strategy for achieving the goal of better lives and livelihood for themselves and their families whatever the level of societal development?

Many migrants maintain a constant flow of communication, money, visits with their countries of origin, often over generations. This flow over time creates strong linkages between specific regions in emigration and immigration countries, as new migrants follow the channels that have been opened up by earlier migrants.

Families go to considerable lengths to enable migration, often selling meager family assets including land; such investments are made in expectation of returns. Many families dispatch family members to different locations, depending on the opportunities, comparative advantages of these locations and family composition, with young children and the elderly often remaining in the rural area. With time and shifting family composition, the mobility roles of family members change.

Salazaar Parrenas' description of Filipino migrant families vividly illustrates their mobility and resourcefulness:

> Ruth Mercado works in Rome, while her oldest sister is a barmaid in Switzerland, her brother a tricycle driver in Manila, and her other sister a provider of elderly care in Saudi Arabia. Her retired parents stay in the Philippines, where they depend on the remittances sent by their daughters from three different nations. A domestic worker in Los Angeles, Dorothy Espiritu had previously worked in Saudi Arabia, during which time her husband passed away in the Philippines, her oldest daughter began working in Japan, and another daughter was working in Saudi Arabia. Finally, there is the family of Libertad Sobredo, a domestic worker in Los Angeles. Her nine children are either working outside of the Philippines, in Saudi Arabia and Greece, or pursuing their college degrees in Manila. Accentuating the experience of a multinational family, Libertad often deals with family

---

[11] *Politiken, PS* (19 September 2004): 6.

crises occurring across the Pacific in the Philippines by making transatlantic phone calls to her oldest son in Greece.[12]

Thus, international migration can be expressed as continua with two dimensions, one spatial, the other temporal. That is, the spatial continuum involves the destination of the move, covering the spectrum from district towns, capital city, neigbouring country or an OECD destination. The temporal continuum refers to the length of stay, from workers seeking seasonal employment, to permanent migration. With the lowering of international boundaries through globalization and/or regional integration, that movement increasingly takes the form of international migration.

The concept of 'sustainable livelihoods' is frequently applied as a framework for analyzing development policy and practice. Robert Chambers and Gordon Conway define livelihoods as 'the capabilities, assets (including both material and social resources) and activities required for a means of living. A livelihood is sustainable when it can cope with and recover from stresses and shocks and maintain or enhance its capabilities and assets both now and in the future, while not undermining the natural resource base'.[13]

The multi-disciplinary, people-centred sustainable livelihoods perspective is helpful in that it focuses on (1) households and families as an economic unit; (2) not just monetary income but a diverse range of resources and assets including non-material assets such as networks; (3) the dynamic nature of livelihood responses, whose mix evolves with changing socio-economic circumstances, family structure, and opportunities. These characteristics are key to understanding and explaining migration responses. Thus, de Haan and others have applied the sustainable development approach to the analysis of international migration.[14]

De Haan discusses international migration as being among the 'household portfolio' of livelihood strategies,[15] the purpose of which is to spread the financial risks over different economic sectors and types of employment. The examples of Filipino families quoted above portray the extent to which migration is a key livelihood strategy in their household portfolio. Of greatest benefit to the family/household is for those member(s) with the greatest earning potential to go abroad temporarily or for a longer period of time and remit funds. When that

---

[12] Rachel Salazar Parrenas, 'Transgressing the Nation-State: The Partial Citizenship and "Imagined (Global) Community" of Migrant Filipina Domestic Workers', in *Signs: Journal of Women in Culture & Society*, 26/4 (Summer 2001). (http://www.iupui.edu/~anthkb/a104/ philippines/migrationfilipinas.htm).

[13] Robert Chambers and Gordon Conway, *Sustainable Rural Livelihoods: Practical Concepts for the 21st Century*, IDS Discussion Paper 296 (Brighton: Institute of Development Studies, 1992).

[14] Arjan de Haan et al., *Migration and Livelihoods: Case Studies in Bangladesh, Ethiopia and Mali*, IDS Research Report 46 (Brighton: Institute of Development Studies, 2000).

[15] Ibid., p. 33.

family member is beyond her or his maximum earning capacity, he or she can return home to retire where the cost of living is less, to be replaced by another family member with greater earning capacity abroad.

From the sustainable livelihoods perspective, it is clear that maintaining transnational families with migration circulation, which enables the most appropriate household member to go abroad to earn at the appropriate time, rather than permanent moves of family members, is the most rational livelihood strategy. The theme of circulation will be pursued in the next sections.

## New Migrants Occupying Transnational Social Spaces: From 'Brain Strain' to 'Brain Circulation'

Faster, cheaper and more widely available means of communication and transportation today allow the great majority of international migrants to remain connected not just with their own families, but to communities, institutions, businesses, etc. in their countries of origin, individually and as members of immigrant social institutions and networks. The intensity of their connectivity results in migrants identifying themselves as occupying multiple social spaces rather than as belonging to the country of immigration or of origin, as transnationals rather than nationals of one country, regardless of official nationality or citizenship status.[16]

Schiller and Fouron describe US based Haitian immigrants, many of whom not only support families and communities back home but also influence national politics and. the economy at the macro level regardless of citizenship status or whether they intend to return to Haiti or otherwise. The two researchers define these migrants as 'long-distance nationalists', people willing to take specific action to make 'patriotic contributions to the well-being of their homeland', who envision a transnational nation-state, that is a state whose outreach is not confined within

---

[16] Thomas Faist, *The Volume and Dynamics of International Migration and Transnational Social Spaces* (Oxford: Clarendon Press, 2000). The use of the term 'diaspora' to refer to migrant communities in general has become widespread among scholars as well as migrant communities themselves. A quick search on the worldwide web turned up a plethora of self-claimed 'diaspora' sites, for Greeks, Africans, Indians, Ukrainians, Irish, South Asian, Overseas Chinese, Azerbaijan, Timorese, Rumanians, Angolans, Serbians, Filipinos, Telegu-speakers, Russians, Nigerians, as well as Armenians and Jews. Such indiscriminate use of the term 'diaspora' obfuscates rather than clarifies the relationship of migrant communities to their homeland. The term is better confined to a subset of communities that have been dispersed through a history of oppression, racism, war, etc. and whose 'homeland' can sometimes be more notional than real. Here, the term transnational migrants will be used to refer to those occupying multiple social spaces.

their borders.[17] The 'specific actions' taken by the long-distance nationalists are so significant economically, politically and socially that overseas Haitians are referred to as Haiti's 'Tenth Department', Haiti being composed of nine local government departments (the term was first used by President Aristide in early 1990s, and has since been accepted broadly). Concurrently, they are assimilated into US society and culture as 'Haitian Americans', one among many new US ethnic groups in a multicultural society, recognized as a separate and powerful US entity by American organizations and political leaders.

Gardner's work with Bangladeshi migrants to UK[18] vividly illustrates that terms of distinction such as 'sojourners' and 'settlers' are no longer so clear-cut. Bangladeshis from Sylheti villages are often settled in both Bangladesh and the UK, with households transcending geographical boundaries, with members in both countries and movement in both directions, on temporary or on longer-term basis, inter- or intra-generational circulation in families. Migrants' perceptions of where they belong are becoming increasingly complex.

Ammassari's work based in Africa describes how migrants tap social capital in both the countries of origin and destination to sustain themselves. Social capital encompasses information on jobs, social services and housing in receiving countries as well as contacts, knowledge about business and investment opportunities, or loans to finance private enterprises in their countries of origin. The more networking competencies migrants have, and the more they invest in maintaining social capital back home and establishing social capital in the immigration countries, the more they have the freedom of choice to return, to stay away, or to shuttle back and forth. They are more likely to be successful at both ends. Further, the return of this type of migrants has greater likelihood to effect positive changes in the sending country.[19]

These transnational migrants are described by Nikos Papastergiadis in *The Turbulence of Migration* as people of hybrid identity, people for whom departures and returns are rarely final, with identities that are not tied exclusively with one country, with close ties including family ties extending beyond national borders.[20]

One of the most spectacular recent examples of migrants maximizing the benefits of their occupation of transnational social spaces are the Indians and Chinese migrants from Taiwan in Silicon Valley, USA, many of whom originally

---

[17] Nina Glick Schiller and Georges Eugene Fouron, *Georges Woke Up Laughing: Long-Distance Nationalism and the Search for Home* (Durham and London: Duke University Press, 2001), pp. 22-3.

[18] Katy Gardner, *Global Migrants, Local Lives. Travel and Transformation in Rural Bangladesh* (Oxford: Clarendon Press, 1995), p. 5.

[19] Savina Ammassari and Richard Black, *Harnessing the Potential of Migration and Return to Promote Development: Applying Concepts to West Africa* (Brighton: Sussex Centre for Migration Research, 2001), p. 20.

[20] Nikos Papastergiadis, *The Turbulence of Migration. Globalization, Deterritorialization and Hybridity* (Cambridge: Polity Press, 2000).

came to the US as engineering students, as described by Anna Lee Saxenian. Chinese and Indians run 29 per cent of the region's high-technology companies started between 1995 and 1998. Most significantly, many have returned home, temporarily or for longer periods of time, and launched new enterprises, thus driving the growth of high tech industries in their countries of origin as well. Capitalizing on their networks in both countries, they could identify new market opportunities, raise capital, establish partnerships, build management teams and so forth.

Transnational entrepreneurs – US-educated immigrant engineers whose activities span national borders – are creating new economic opportunities for formerly peripheral economies around the world. Talented immigrants who have studied and worked in the US are increasingly reversing the 'brain drain' by returning to their home countries to take advantage of promising opportunities there. In so doing they are building technical communities that link their home countries to one of the world's leading centers of information and communications technologies, Silicon Valley. As the 'brain drain' increasingly gives way to a process of 'brain circulation', networks of scientists and engineers are transferring technology, skill, and know-how between distant regional economies faster and more flexibly than most corporations.[21]

These 'footloose engineers whose long-distance professional networks allow technology entrepreneurship to flourish far from world centers of wealth and skill',[22] are the cutting-edge example of highly skilled communities optimizing the benefits of globalization for themselves, the countries of origin as well as of immigration, through their occupation of transnational social spaces. It exemplifies the developmental potential of such transnational migrants, a potential that is dependent on maintaining their social capital and operational capacity in both countries. Rather than being 'footloose', then, they have firm footholds in two places. I shall revert to the ways in which governments and the private sector in the country of origin have recognized this potential, facilitating their entrepreneurship and investments, in the final section.

Similar, if not so spectacular, examples abound. Not just among the highly skilled, but among those with entrepreneurial initiative that have benefited from their transnational linkages and ethnic networks. Such migrants transmit not only physical capital, but also human and social capital, contributing significantly to the

---

[21] Anna Lee Saxenian., *Transnational Communities and the Evolution of Global Production Networks: The Case of Taiwan, China and India* (Honolulu: University of Hawaii, East-West Center, December 2001).
(http://www.eastwestcenter.org/stored/pdfs/ECONwp037.pdf#search='brain%20circuktaion%30brain%20drain').

[22] Anna Lee Saxenian, 'Back to India: Indian Software Engineers are Returning with Enthusiasm and Entrepreneurial Know-how', in *Wall Street Journal: Technology Journal Asia* (24 January 2000)
(http://www.dcrp.ced.berkeley.edu/Faculty/Anno/Writings/WSJ20%20Back%20to%20India.htm).

development of communities and enterprises in the various social spaces they occupy. Based on decades of comparative study of Pakistani communities with large UK based emigrants, Ballard concludes:

Although each network was slightly differently structured, they had in each case provided their users with a means of circumventing a huge range of exclusionary obstacles, from immigration controls onwards, and having done so to exploit all sorts of novel opportunities in the global labour market. Hence a central focus of my most recent work has been on the organization, dynamics and ever-growing reach of these self-constructed transnational networks. In my view it is precisely the effectiveness and efficiency of such networks which is the key to the success of all those involved in processes of transnational migration 'from below', no matter where in the developing world they may have their original roots.[23]

Thus transnationalism, bolstered by circular migration, can benefit not only the migrants themselves but development in receiving and sending countries.[24]

As an afterthought on transnationalism, migration scholars will hopefully monitor the impact of Business Process Outsourcing (BPO) on migration and transnationalism. One recent poll indicates that already 76 per cent of large companies throughout North America and Europe are outsourcing technical and clerical work,[25] in financial analysis, computer programming, customer service, back office finance and human resources. India has been the biggest beneficiary of BPO, with an income in 2004 from exports of software and services, and from outsourced services such as call-centres, reaching nearly 17 billion US$ (4 per cent of GDP). In addition to the impact on the economy, the BPO work environment has resulted in extensive life style changes among the young Indian workers involved, to the extent of being described as constituting a 'virtual migration'. On the other hand, the 'BPO backlash' in the USA has resulted in a reduction in the

---

[23] Roger Ballard, *Growth and Poverty Reduction: Reflections on the Basis of South Asian Experience. A Report for DFID* (Manchester: Centre for Applied South Asian Studies, University of Manchester, 2003.
(http://www.art.man.ac.uk/CASAS/ pdfpapers/remittances.pdf).

[24] There can also be excess of transnationalism, or a sojourner mentality carried to its extreme, as described by Pieke about Fujianese migrants: 'Fujianese show as yet little evidence of grafting themselves more permanently onto local Chinese communities and the wider societies of destination. Fuzhou/Fujian migration therefore raises the important question whether such extreme transnationalism is to the long-term benefit of the people involved. If it proves to be more than a temporary phenomenon characteristic of the first stages of a new migratory flow, extreme transnationalism may very well lock the Fujianese into a permanently exploited position. Contrary to the benefits that are commonly expected to derive from transnational ties, Fujianese transnationalism possibly renders the dream of self-employment elusive but for the very few who manage to sever at least some the ties with Fuzhou/Fujian and the Fuzhou/Fujian diaspora.' Frank N. Pieke, *Recent Trends in Chinese Migration to Europe: Fujianese Migration in Perspective* (Geneva: International Organization for Migration, 2002).

[25] *Financial Times*, (26 January 2005).

number of H1B visas issued to IT service workers, from 195,000 to 65,000 starting 2004.[26] One might speculate whether greater BPO will result in decreased migration as jobs move to potential migrants rather than vice versa, or, perhaps the experience of 'virtual migration' might stimulate more actual migration. With clerical and technical jobs moving to lower income countries on top of manufacturing processes that have already moved, migrant workers may be even more restricted to the service and the care industries in the decades to come.

*Measures in Support of Transnationalism*

In the sections above, I have postulated that transnationalism reinforced through circular migration can benefit the development of both immigration and emigration countries, as well as migrant families themselves. In this section, supportive policy measures at the national and international or global levels are explored.

*Measures in Receiving OECD Countries*

While traditional countries of immigration, namely the USA, Canada and Australia, have clearly defined immigration policies that seek to attract specified categories of migrants, the explicit focus in most other OECD countries at present is on restricting the entry of unwanted immigrants, refugees and asylum seekers, and integrating those already in the country on a permanent basis. Thus these policies are aimed at controlling rather than managing migration. Yet the population projections for most OECD countries call for a much more proactive policy on labour migration to counteract their aging population structure.[27]

The increasing need for labour has resulted in growing numbers of illegal immigrants, and keeping open some form of backdoor channels. Such is the case of

---

[26] *Frontline*, (6-19 December 2003).
[27] The population in EU countries and Japan is expected to fall by 10 and 14 per cent between 2000 and 2050 and, with the ageing process, the dependency ratio will increase in the same period from 27.9 to 55.7 per cent in the EU, and in Japan from 20.3 to 43.1 per cent. Improved productivity and use of surplus labour cannot meet the growing labour shortage and thus, international migration will play a key role (UN Population Division, 2001). According to Eberstadt, to prevent an eventual decline in the size of the 15 to 64 grouping (the 'working-age' population), Europe's net migration will have to nearly quadruple to a long-term average of about 3.6 million a year. Migration of this magnitude would change the face of Europe: By 2050, under these two scenarios, the descendants of present-day non-Europeans will account for approximately 20 to 25 percent of Europe's inhabitants. To maintain total population size, Japan would have to accept a long-term average of almost 350,000 newcomers a year for the next 50 years, and it would need nearly twice that number to keep its working-age population from shrinking. Under the first contingency, over a sixth of Japan's 2050 population would be descendants of present-day *gaijin* (foreigners); under the second contingency, that group would account for nearly a third of Japan's total population. Nicholas Eberstadt, 'The Population Implosion', in *Foreign Policy*, 123 (March-April 2001): 42-53.

Japan, where unskilled workers have been arriving under the guise of 'technical internship schemes' and students. Thus first and foremost, EU countries and Japan need to recognize the reality and establish immigration management policies that might include some of the following points.

Secondly, governments need to regularize undocumented and/or illegal migrants. Nick Pearce and Dhananjayan Sriskandarajah compare Spain, which has recently declared an amnesty on low-skilled illegal immigrants by offering them a one-year residence permit, with UK. They argue that while such regularization may be counterintuitive, it is not only more realistic and humane, but also, in the long term, a more economically effective approach.

Regularization reduces the exploitation of migrant workers in the shadow economy by giving them formal rights. It also recognizes that migrants often end up working in unskilled jobs – in Spain, migrants are twice as likely to be in these jobs as locals. In the absence of legal opportunities to work, illegal channels become more attractive and larger. Regularization and the implementation of formal channels for low-skilled migration is a more realistic approach than denying the need for low-skilled migrants or being overconfident about the ability to control them. With rapidly ageing populations, it also makes sense to maximize the fiscal contributions of the population. The more people are working legally, the larger their contribution.[28]

It is also worth noting that when the US government regularized undocumented Mexican workers under a 1986 legislation, rather than increasing the flow of immigrants, it led to a significant return flow to Mexico, as the legalized immigrants now felt that they could circulate freely between the two countries.

Thus regularizing undocumented and illegal immigrants is a key component of active migration management.

Thirdly, regulations on residency, citizenship and so forth, need to be reviewed against the reality of transnationalism. Current regulations tend to assume that migrants want to stay permanently once they have arrived, which is not necessarily the case. For example, residence permits, in the main, do not allow migrants who have been granted residency in a country to reside elsewhere, including in her or his country of origin, for significant lengths of time. That is, migrants must either stay, or give up their residency. Thus while some migrants may want to return to their countries of origin for some time or move to another, they dare not for risk of forsaking their options. If they retain the right of entry and residence, it may well be that for instance, post-retirement migrants would spend their old age in countries of their origin.

Going beyond permanent residency, currently, not many countries allow their citizens to hold dual nationality or citizenship, Canada and Australia being among the few that do. If transnationals are law-abiding productive citizens of both countries, what is the logic against dual citizenship and nationality? If the concern

---

[28] Nick Pearce and Dhananjayan Sriskandarajah, 'Out of the Shadows' in *The Guardian*, (9 February 2005) (http://www.ippr.org.uk/articles/index.asp?id=1257).

is about loyalty and patriotism, then acquiring nationality or citizenship by no means automatically ensures greater loyalty. Governments can and do negotiate agreements on issues such as tax payments, pension benefits, etc. for transnational citizens. Dual citizenship or nationality would be the ultimate manifestation of transnationalism.

Regulated, but a more open migration regime conducive to transnationals would require countries to try new approaches. From the perspective of sustainable livelihoods, why not, for instance, a residence quota for migrant families rather than for individual migrants? That is, migrant families obtain a 'right' to, say, five family members residing in the country of immigration at any given time, with the choice of members being left to them. In terms of a sustainable livelihood strategy, it would make sense for the family member(s) with the greatest earning potential to migrate and remit, returning home to retire, and to be replaced by a younger family member. Such a family will continue to have stakes in two countries. Instead of the current policy of family reunification, which tends to increase the financial burden on receiving countries as the majority of the new entrants are likely to be dependents, the presence of greater numbers of working age migrants would be more beneficial to the receiving country as well.

Fourthly, migration needs to feature in a much broader framework of both bilateral and multilateral relations. Migration should be discussed, negotiated and agreed upon between nations in the context of a broader framework of transactions between them, including trade, financial flows, development cooperation etc.

OECD governments in recent years have emphasized the need for greater coherence and consistency in donor country policies, recognizing that the impact that they have on developing countries derives from the totality of their policies and action. Thus, benefits that are brought about through development cooperation programmes targeted towards poverty reduction can be wiped out, several times over, by the negative effects of adverse trade, investment, agricultural and energy policies and so forth. The latter policies therefore need to be coherent and consistent with the development cooperation objectives. While there is growing recognition that immigration should also be part of the 'coherence' agenda, this has yet to be fully reflected in national policies. After September 11, there have been moves to use development cooperation to achieve immigration control objectives as part of the security and stability agenda that was the key preoccupation. For example, during the Seville EU Summit of June 2002, Spain, backed by 12 out of the 15 EU countries, proposed to suspend financial assistance to developing countries which fail to crack down on people-smugglers and take back their own nationals; while these proposals were not adopted, due to opposition from Sweden, France and Luxembourg, there was a significant majority that saw development as a tool for migration control.

Sweden recognized the need for a more comprehensive approach, attempting to combine the asylum and migration policies with aspects of foreign and economic policies in one common approach, migration management being considered as an integrated part of these policies:[29]

> When we work to promote democracy, respect for human rights, good governance and the rule of law in order to facilitate poverty reduction, we also prevent involuntary emigration. In humanitarian assistance in measures to prevent violent conflicts, the links are obvious. The same is true when aid funds are used for reconstruction after a conflict allowing refugees and internally displaced persons to return.[30]

Thus, while the link between migration and development is being made, the focus is on preventing unwanted migration rather than on optimizing the development impact of migration.

In more recent years, the UK and the Nordic countries are among those applying a more developmental emphasis on their perspectives on migration. Denmark, for instance, commissioned a paper on the Development and Migration Nexus, followed by an international conference on the subject in April 2002.[31] The UK House of Commons International Development Committee issued a report Migration and Development: How to make migration work for poverty reduction.[32]

At the multilateral level, while an earlier call for a United Nations conference on international migration and development in 2001 did not win sufficient support, the International Organization for Migration, the International Labour Organization and the Population Division of the Department of Economic and Social Affairs have consistently worked to keep the issue of the migration-development nexus on the international agenda.[33] These multilateral efforts have led to the scheduling of a

---

[29] The Ministry of Foreign Affairs, Sweden, for instance, organized an international conference on the subject in 1999: *International Migration, Development and Integration: Towards a Comprehensive Approach* (Stockholm: Ministry of Foreign Affairs, 1999).

[30] Gun-Britt Andersson, Speech by State Secretary. Bern, International Symposium on Migration, 14-15 June 2001.

[31] Ninna Nyberg Soerensen, Nicholas Van Heer and Poul Engberg-Pedersen, *The Migration-Development Nexus: Evidence and Policy Options: Policy Study* (Copenhagen: Centre for Development Research, April 2002).

[32] United Kingdom House of Commons International Development Committee, *Migration and Development: How to make migration work for poverty reduction*, Sixth Report of Session 2003-2004
(http://www.parliament.thestationeryoffice.co.uk/pa/cm200304/cmselect/cmintdev/79/79.pdf#search='policy%20coherence%20development%20and%20international%20migration').

[33] For example, IOM hosted a workshop in February 2005 entitled 'Pursuing policy coherence in migration and development policy agendas' to 'share approaches and practices, which incorporate migration into national, regional and international development policy agendas of developing as well as developed countries and identify gaps where this can be taken further'. It is, however, noted that there were very few representatives from the 'development community' participating in this workshop. Greater engagement of the latter, including multilateral development agencies, is needed if coherent policies are to be developed and abided by.

High Level Dialogue on International Migration and Development during the General Assembly in 2006, 'to discuss the multidimensional aspects of international migration and development in order to identify appropriate ways and means to maximize its development benefits and minimize its negative impacts' with 'a strong focus on policy issues'. It is hoped that such international processes have an impact at the national levels in terms of concrete shifts in favour of migration policies that benefit development.

Fifthly, bilateral discussions between receiving, OECD and sending, developing countries might also feature how financial systems and instruments for remittances, which now constitute a far greater amount of transfers than ODA for many developing countries, can be made more beneficial for migrants and for development. Much of the migrants' cash is currently transferred via informal systems such as *hawalas* rather than through formal channels.

Finally, more informed national debates on immigration, including what constitutes integration are needed. Public debates should be guided by facts and figures and fed by findings from the large volume of migration studies, and misperceptions, misrepresentation and irrational fears challenged. An example of such a finding that can dispel popular misperception is a UK study which shows that the migrant workforce contributes disproportionately more in income tax than non-migrants.[34] Sriskandarajah and Morrell argue that highlighting the scale of the contribution of migrants to the UK health services – almost one in three doctors, one in six dentists and one in ten nurses in the UK are overseas trained – 'will be an important step in gaining much-needed public support for managed migration'.[35]

There is an underlying fear that as long as migrants remain attached to the countries and cultures of their origin, they cannot become fully-fledged, functional citizens in the new, so that transnationalism hinders integration. The recent ban of wearing of headscarves in French schools and the ensuing heated debates on the same issue in other European countries illustrate this fear. A major Transnational Communities Programme established and funded by UK's Economic and Social Research Council in 1997 reviewed how transnational communities develop their long-distance activities and what impact these had for politics, economics and society. The study concludes that '[m]ultiple attachments do not hamper integration in the country of settlement',[36] the reason being that 'two or more sets of attachment do not necessarily compete with each other. Further, when we accept

---

[34] Here the migrant workforce makes up 8.7 per cent of the population but contributes 10.2 per cent of all income tax collected, according to an article in *The Guardian* (27 April 2005).

[35] Dhananjayan Sriskandarajah and Gareth Morrell, 'Immigrants - What Migrants do for the NHS', in *Health Service Journal*, (14 March 2005).
(http://www.ippr.org.uk/articles/ index.asp?id=1254).

[36] *Transnational Communities Programme: Synopsis* (Oxford: Institute of Social and Cultural Anthropology, University of Oxford, for the Economic and Social Research Council, 2003), p.4 (italics mine).

the fact that people are attached to their countries of origin, it gives migrants the self-confidence to interact much more dynamically and creatively with the cultural lives of the country of settlement. It also makes them feel that they are being valued for who they are. It is wrong to believe that if migrant communities would stop being communities and break up, it would be easier to integrate them into the mainstream society'.[37] They also conclude 'although transnational communities show transnational attachments and loyalties, this does not mean that they do not value national citizenship. Indeed, national citizenship remains something that diasporic communities desperately want and cherish as the emblem of their acceptance and as a means to their flourishing in a new environment'.[38]

The conclusions from this Programme in the UK thus indicate that transnationalism might help, rather than hinder, integration, a vital finding, not just for policy makers, but for the public at large that live in a multi ethnic society, if immigration policy is to embrace transnationalism.

As charged a field it is for governments to take a lead on, reality and future population structures impel them to generate and maintain public support for rational immigration policies, as advocated by the authors of the Transnational Communities Programme:

> ... so then let's take the debate out to the public, let's be transparent about the real choices to be made, the challenges and the opportunities. Of course there will be fears that doing this will provide a platform for unacceptable views. It would also be an opportunity to put the facts on the table, to debunk some myths and for migrant communities themselves to be heard. I think it is time that we had that debate.[39]

*Measures in Sending, Developing countries*

Emigration countries can optimize the migration development link and minimize the losses through changes in existing policies and practices. As has been long recognized, the brain drain is a major negative impact of emigration particularly for smaller African countries. According to Sriskanandaraj, for instance,[40] there are apparently more Malawian doctors working in the city of Manchester, UK, alone, than in Malawi itself. It is, however, important to note that the brain drain can also have a positive effect on development, as has been shown by Beine et al. in a study of migration data by education levels in a cross section of some 50 countries. They conclude that:

The magnitude of the losses and gains, expressed in terms of annual growth rate of the GDP per capita, remains relatively limited for most countries. Notable exceptions are Jamaica and Guyana, which have extremely high migration rates.

---

[37] Ibid.
[38] Ibid., pp. 4-5.
[39] Ibid., p. 7.
[40] *Financial Times* (12 April 2005).

Except for these two countries, the net variation of the annual GDP per capita growth rate is always lower than 0.20 per cent.

Most countries combining low levels of human capital and low emigration rates of their highly-educated are positively affected by the brain drain.

By contrast, the brain drain appears to have negative growth effects in countries where the migration rate of the highly educated is higher than 20 per cent and/or where the proportion of highly educated in the total population is above 5 per cent.[41]

Accordingly, these researchers conclude that there are both winners and losers from the brain drain in sending countries, pointing 'to the necessity of a better understanding of the circumstances and factors favoring the occurrence of a detrimental brain drain'.[42] It is thus critical to develop differentiated strategies for countries that are affected differently by the brain drain, some to further build on current benefits, some to minimize the losses:

We need interventions that acknowledge that mobility is, in itself, not necessarily the problem. Rather, we should pay attention to the impact of that mobility. Improving the development prospects of the Guyanese and the Malawis of the world will require targeted strategies such as limiting active recruitment from the most vulnerable sectors and creating incentives for return. But the most enduring interventions may lie outside the remit of immigration policies. Financing additional training facilities in vulnerable sectors may help meet local demand. Delivering aid to bolster local wages may promote the retention of key workers. Additional funding for professionals in the developed world to spend time in poorer countries could also be effective, certainly in the short term.[43]

There are already many small-scale initiatives that facilitate beneficial brain circulation rather than detrimental brain drain. For example, some projects enable professionals and skilled workers settled overseas to contribute to development work in their home countries for a limited period of time. Afghanistan is attracting many such initiatives; for instance, 4,000 Afghans from 27 countries that have applied to the International Organization for Migration (IOM) (The Return of Qualified Afghans Programme) for slots in a new programme that places college-educated professionals in private sector and government jobs in Afghanistan for up to a year.

'Virtual' brain circulation can take the form of networking. TIE (The IndUS Entrepreneur), a not-for-profit global network of entrepreneurs and professionals founded in 1992 in Silicon Valley, has rapidly grown to more than forty chapters in nine countries, providing networking, mentoring and education support. Another

---

[41] Michel Beine, Frédéric Docquier and Hillel Rapoport, *Brain Drain and LDCs' Growth: Winners and Losers*, IZA DP, No 819 (Bonn: IZA [Institute for the Study of Labour], 2003), pp. 34-5.

[42] Ibid.

[43] Dhananjayan Sriskandarajah, 'Migration can aid development', in *Financial Times* (12 April 2005).

example is the South African Network of Skills Abroad (SANSA), a knowledge network that provides a vital link between skilled emigrants and local experts and projects. Information of the qualification and location of South Africans residing abroad and willing to participate in local development is stored into a database and can be easily retrieved. Nationals residing abroad participate in joint research with their South African counterparts, initiate commercial projects, provide support in transferring technology to South African institutions and transmitting research unavailable locally, receive South African students in training programs and facilitate business contacts. Clearly, governments need to do much more to tap on 'brains' overseas and encourage circulation.[44]

Governments in labour exporting countries such as Philippines and Bangladesh take the position that their overseas workers constitute their biggest comparative advantage. Thus, Bangladesh, for instance, has a Ministry of Expatriate Welfare and Overseas Employment, specifically devoted to ensuring the well being of their workers overseas, and facilitating further employment opportunities abroad, as well as in facilitating their remittances. The Philippines Department of Labor and Employment (DOLE) 'maintains jurisdiction over overseas contract workers through the Philippine Overseas Employment Agency (POEA), which monitors the exit of workers, and the Overseas Workers Welfare Agency (OWWA), which provides services to migrants in receiving nations [such as] free legal assistance and counseling, assistance with repatriation, insurance coverage, and loan programs for housing and small business enterprises'.[45] However, Salazaar Parrenas demonstrates that the Department is often made ineffective as they have no jurisdiction on overseas soil as illustrated by the case of a Philippine government-sponsored welfare center in Saudi Arabia that had to close down 'because the Saudi government thought that providing shelter to runaway maids constituted foreign intervention in their internal affairs'. Bilateral negotiations may have limited impact in resolving issues of migrant protection. Thus, all the more, it is important that both migrant sending and receiving countries abide by multilateral norms and resolve issues within such a framework. A key instrument is ILO's UN Convention on the Protection of the Rights of All Migrant Workers and Members of Their Families of 1990 which entered into force finally in 2003. As of May 2005, however, none of the major migrant receiving countries have ratified or signed it.

Fundamentally, labour exporting countries will benefit from more flexible policies that will enable greater labour migration, a free flow of labour. Some have argued for a multilateral framework for migration, the equivalent of the World

---

[44] Incidentally, it is not only developing countries but also OECD governments that are attempting to tap into transnational ties. For example, in 2005, Japan hosted a symposium entitled 'The Role of Japanese Descendants in the Economic Development of Latin American and Caribbean Countries: Review and Prospects', 'to search for further business opportunities and cooperation through utilizing the Japanese descendants' community network linking Japan and the Latin American and Caribbean countries' (Ministry of Foreign Affairs, Japan, 7 March 2005).

[45] Salazar Parrenas, 'Transgressing the Nation-State'.

Trade Organization, with binding powers. An ILO Report in 2004 concluded that '[a] major gap in the current institutional structure for the global economy is the absence of a multilateral framework for governing the cross-border movement of people'.[46] A UN Report notes that there is an 'increasing convergence of ideas on the need for a multilateral framework ... to maximize the potential benefits of cross-border movement of people for migrants and their families, and for their countries of origin and destination, while minimizing the drawbacks',[47] the hope being that the 2006 High Level Dialogue would move the process forward towards such a multilateral framework. Given the 'fundamental moral contradiction' discussed earlier between the universal right of emigration and the sovereign right of governments to determine whom to admit and to whom citizenship may be granted,[48] a multilateral framework with powers of binding arbitration similar to WTO, may not be very realistic. However, some form of a multilateral forum, that seeks to harmonize policies and develop guidelines that take into account developing country requirements can be envisaged. It could then form the basis for bilateral or regional negotiations towards binding agreements.

In addition to formal support services for migrants offered by governments, informal networks of migrants providing mutual support thrive wherever large numbers of migrants are concentrated. In many cities in Europe and Asia, it has become commonplace to see large gatherings of Filipino domestic workers on Sundays in specific city parks, plazas and around Catholic churches – informal networking at work. Virtual networking takes place on the World Wide Web, as well as through publications such as Tinig Filipino, a glossy monthly magazine specifically for migrant Filipinos published in Hong Kong and Italy and distributed in more than a dozen countries.[49] Receiving and sending governments can both support such networking, critical for transnationals to sustain their linkages, by making available suitable meeting places, for example.

Recent works indicate that remittances have far greater positive impact on communities in developing countries than previously acknowledged,[50] at the macro-, meso- and micro-levels. Ballard estimates remittance flows from North to South to be around US$ 150 billion, far exceeding the level of Official Development Assistance of US$ 69 billion in 2003. Most significantly, the

---

[46] International Labour Organization, *A Fair Globalization: Creating Opportunities for All, Report of the World Commission on the Social Dimension of Globalization* (Geneva: ILO, 2004) (http://www.ilo.org/public/english/wcsdg/docs/report.pdf).

[47] United Nations Department of Economic and Social Affairs, *World Economic and Social Survey 2004: International Migration* (New York: United Nations, 2004).

[48] Myron Weiner, *The Global Migration Crisis. Challenge to States and to Human Rights*, (New York: HarperCollins, 1995).

[49] Salazar Parrenas, 'Transgressing the Nation-State'.

[50] Susan F. Martin, *Remittances as a Development Tool. A Regional Conference Organized by the Multilateral Investment Fund* (Washington: Inter-American Development Bank, 2001), p. 3.

majority of the remittances go to poor households, as grants, with no policy conditionality. Even when the remittances are used for consumption rather than in investment, they can stimulate development, particularly when spent locally. Research has shown that the developmental impact on communities can differ greatly, stimulating local entrepreneurial activity in some, while precipitating economic decline and dependency on others. In a study for the UK's Department of International Development, Ballard identifies the blockages which currently inhibit the development potential of remittances, recommending DFID to focus its development cooperation on these areas:

- Lack of obvious niches into which their savings can profitably be invested;
- Lack of infrastructural resources such as roads, bridges, irrigation facilities, electricity and telephone connections etc.;
- The obstructive capacity of the local state.[51]

These shortcomings apply widely, not just in hindering the effective investment of remittances but investment in general, and should, most importantly, be addressed to developing country governments who have the greatest interest in better utilization of remittances. Countries need to learn from successful examples in the use of remittances for development and introduce policy incentives and eliminate disincentives.

As mentioned previously, migrants from some countries transmit their earnings through *hawalas* and other informal channels. A key reason for the popularity of such systems is their capacity to deliver money safely even to rural areas, which are often underserved by formal banks. In addition, the latter, when they do exist, are not user-friendly, especially for the poor. Thus, for greater development potential, the involvement of micro finance institutions (MFI) with proven track records and extensive rural networks, for instance CrediAmigo in Brazil or Grameen Bank in Bangladesh, in the delivery of remittances might be explored, possibly to designate them as the correspondent bank of choice. An ILO Workshop in 2000 identified several cases where MFIs were already becoming involved, or are currently observing the developments with a view to future involvement. The general agreement of the workshop was that 'MFIs were well placed to handle transfer payments, due to their proximity to remittance-receiving families and their potential to reach out to poor communities. Besides, MFIs had the potential to produce positive returns on investments.' The Workshop also identified three reasons why MFIs were particularly suited for this purpose: (i) they deal with small-scale transactions where personal relations were important, (ii) they extensively involve groups and associations of intermediaries and (iii) they

---

[51] Roger Ballard, *Remittances and Economic Development* (submitted for consideration by the House of Commons Select Committee on International Development in the course of the inquiry into Migration and Development, 2003-4), p. 3.
(http://www.art.man.ac.uk/CASAS/ pdfpapers/selectctte.pdf).

integrate the formal and the informal sector practices.[52] Multilateral organizations including ILO, IMO and possibly the World Bank through its Development Gateway, are well placed to facilitate the sharing of positive experiences in effective ways of managing remittances.

Private sector entities have seized on the potential of remittances, and have initiated schemes that facilitate the migrants' capacity to maintain their stakes in their home countries. India, for instance, has long recognized the potential of Non-Resident Indians (NRIs), and banks and other financial institutions, insurance agencies, real estate developers, providing service such as investment, real estate management, taxation advice, and so forth. Governments may support these measures through further policy incentives for investment, or at least, by reducing disincentives such as excessive red tape.

Meso-level linkages are significant. A negative consequence of emigration and remittances often pointed out by researchers is the growth in inequality between households that receive remittances and those that do not, between villages and regions that do and those that do not.[53] Remittances channelled to community projects, especially for infrastructure such as water supply, schools, health centers and road improvement, could go in some way to address these community level inequalities. There are strong incentives for immigrants to contribute to such community initiatives as they are visible means of maintaining their ties to their home communities and bring them prestige as generous benefactors. Ballard discovered among Pakistani immigrants that '[m]embers of the second and third generation are much more willing to give generously to such charitable projects than to support their elders' passion for buying more land'.[54] There are many examples whereby migrant communities abroad support community development initiatives collectively, such as hometown associations of migrants which provide financial support to villages, helping them to improve roads, water and sanitation systems, health clinics, schools and other community infrastructure.

One such scheme is the 3-for-1 Programme in Zacadecas, Mexico, where each dollar remitted by migrants or hometown clubs in the USA is matched by three additional dollars, one each from the federal, state and local governments, to be spent on local development schemes. With approximately 600,000 to 1 million

---

[52] International Labour Organization, *Making the Best of Globalisation: Migrant Worker Remittances and Micro-Finance: Workshop Report* (Geneva: ILO, 20-21 November 2000), pp. 14-15.

[53] Gardner's study, for example has identified that overseas migration has contributed to economic and social polarization, with remittances enabling households with migrant remittances to buy up local resources pushing up local prices far beyond the reach of those without access to foreign wages; when new economic opportunities are introduced to hierarchical societies, such polarization results. (Gardner, *Global Migrants*, p. 271). However, Gardner also suggests 'whilst the rich have grown richer, and economic differentiation is now drawn up along the lines of migration, the poor have not in fact become poorer in real terms' (ibid., p. 279).

[54] Ballard, *Remittances*, pp. 37-8.

Zacatecans living in USA, it is a significant resource. Such schemes not only bring physical benefits to communities, but also reinforce the continued linkage and identity of migrants with their home communities. Positive examples can be disseminated and emulated widely.

While transnational families enjoy the economic benefits of remittances, there can be potentially negative consequences from separation, particularly for children. The concern is greatest where women constitute the majority of emigrants, leaving younger children in care of husbands or extended family members. Such is the case in the Philippines, where fully two-thirds of migrant workers are women filling domestic jobs. According to Salazaar Parrenas who has conducted in-depth interviews with children of such transnational families, while they had to endure emotional hardships, their hardships were diminished when 'they received support from extended families and communities, when they enjoyed open communication with their migrant parents, and when they clearly understood the limited financial options that led their parents to migrate in the first place'.[55] Likewise, John Bryant has studied the impact of migration on children in Southeast Asia for the UNICEF Innocenti Research Centre and concludes that children of migrants 'do not, on average, suffer greater social and economic problems than their peers', because migration is alleviating household poverty and extended families are filling the gaps left by absent parents.[56] This corroborates the view of international migration as a sustainable livelihood strategy for households (see above, Section 2). However, as Bryant suggests, migrant networks can further minimize the potentially negative impact through sharing of experiences, mutual support and advice on long-distance parenting.

## Concluding Remarks

A development perspective on international migration calls for migration policies that embrace transnationalism, more flexible migration regimes that enable circulation. Such policies require the support of a public, fostered through open debates about the challenges as well as advantages brought about by migration, based on solid facts, figures and findings rather than demagogy. Most importantly, receiving countries need to recognize migration as normal human activity, and a valid strategy for development. As development cooperation partners, they need to reflect their stated commitment to development goals throughout their migration

---

[55] Rachel Salazaar Parrenas, 'The Care Crisis in the Philippines: Children and Transnational Families in the New Global Economy', in Barbara Ehrenreich and Arlie Russell Hochschild (eds), *Global Woman – Nannies, Maids and Sex Workers in the New Economy* (London: Granta Books, 2003), p. 41.

[56] John Bryant, *Children of International Migrants in Indonesia, Thailand, and the Philippines: A Review of Evidence and Policies*, Innocenti Working Paper 2005-05 (New York: UNICEF, Innocenti Research Centre, 2005), p. 23.

policies and instruments. Emigration countries, in turn, need to identify more effective means of benefiting from emigration while minimizing the negatives. A multilateral framework, with a greater development perspective, may be useful within which bilateral or region-to-region negotiations can take place. Immigration policies, if properly managed, monitored, and constantly adjusted, can work to the benefit of both sending and receiving countries, as well as migrants themselves.

Chapter Two

# Migration, Minorities and the Transfer of Technology in Early Modern Europe

Salvatore Ciriacono

**Introduction**

The history of workforce migration – be it skilled or unskilled labour – has a long and complex history, with different features characterizing the phenomenon in different historical periods. Sometimes it has been viewed with suspicion by certain political authorities and by those social classes and categories which have felt threatened by the newcomers; and very often it has been the selfsame political élites – together with a certain hostility of the majority towards particular minorities in their midst – which have triggered the process of migration in the first place. However, there is no denying the importance that such migratory movement has had on the spread of knowledge and know-how between various areas of the world, and within Europe in particular: according to Heinz Schilling, for example, 'in Early Europe unlike present times, the propagation of innovations and their interregional penetration did not come about primarily through books or technical and professional journals. It took place rather through the migration of skilled craftsmen, financiers and entrepreneurs, setting out voluntarily or in consequence of expulsion from foreign countries'.[1] Though one may not be able to agree with these observations in their entirety, they do serve to show how, in itself, migration is a phenomenon that inevitably runs into conflict with all those policies that aim at establishing and maintaining some sort of social equilibrium within a specific territory. As Harald Kleinschmidt makes clear, a rigidly functional interpretation – 'which defines societies as territorialized groups of settlers under the control of norm-setting institutions'[2] – can only lead to some

---

[1] Heinz Schilling, 'Innovation through Migration: the Settlements of Calvinistic Netherlanders in Sixteenth- and Seventeenth-Century Central and Western Europe', in *Histoire sociale – Social History*, 16/31 (May 1983): 7-33.

[2] Harald Kleinschmidt, 'Migration, Regional Integration and Human Security. An Overview of Research Developments', Chapter Three in this volume. See also Kleinschmidt, *Menschen in Bewegung. Inhalte und Ziele historischer Migrationsforschung* (Göttingen: Vandenhoeck & Ruprecht, 2002). Jacques Bottin and Donatella Calabi (eds), *Les étrangers dans la ville* (Paris: Maison des Sciences de l'Homme, 1999). Umberto Curi and Bruna Giacomini (eds), *Xenos. Filosofia dello straniero* (Padua: Il Polifilo, 2002).

sort of latent conflict between a social organisation which has developed in a certain place at a given time and the very phenomenon of migration, which inevitably marks a rupture in that territorialized group. However, in following Schilling's conclusions one would have to accept the image of a simple overflow of knowledge, spilling from one region or continent to another; as if the host region (the place in which the technological innovation is received and developed) played no essential role as the vessel within which such knowledge was deposited. I would like to look at the historical facts from a different point of view, underlining the importance of the attraction centres of trade and economic activity exercised over potential 'emigrants'. In other terms, the two aspects (on the one hand, migration as a vehicle of information and knowledge, and, on the other, the role played by 'world-economies') must both be taken into consideration, together with a number of variables, which make the picture even more complex. These variables might be summarized as: the role played by religion and the persecution of religious minorities; the relative or absolute decline in the standing of certain economic areas; high demographic growth in such areas, which rendered emigration inevitable; the imposed emigration of artisans who were part of a servant, non-independent work force; emigration as a structural and functional factor within a given community; the comparative advantages to be gained in moving from one region to another; and immigration as a phenomenon compensating for the demographic decline that was a characteristic feature of *Ancien-Régime* Europe, in which structural factors such as war, plague and famine prevented constant population growth. And, of course, one should not forget that all of these factors were operative within the context of a general phenomenon that profoundly influenced the migratory process – that is to say, the emergence of the modern state.

## Migration in Early Modern Europe

In effect, migration in the early modern period was different from that of the Middle Ages and from that of the present-day world at that. Here we must distinguish between a structural and an institutional aspect. With regard to the former, one must underline how the country-to-city migration during these centuries made it possible to correct the demographic shortfall caused by the above-mentioned structural factors (disease, famine, war). This migration brought to the possible areas of in-take (cities and regions) not only specialized craftsmen but also common labourers and workers (both of these cases have to be taken into consideration in the medieval-modern and the contemporary setting, even if with a different focus. I will return to this point). The reception offered to this influx by states and cities was also not uninfluenced by fiscal considerations (the desire to increase tax revenues).

As for the institutional aspect, the reactions and actions of a medieval city were very different from what one would see in modern states. First of all, they were concerned with a more limited spatial area; and secondly, they acted in unison with the craft guilds. These latter only opened up their ranks when, first, they wanted to make good a shortage of numbers and, second, after the potential new members had passed through a specific apprenticeship that demonstrated the development of a specific craft skill, thus permitting the move from assistant labourer to master craftsman. Here one might cite many examples and specific legislation from cities not only in Italy but also in Flanders and Germany. Nevertheless, one must underline how the notion of a 'nation' was bound up with ethnic considerations, with the notion of a social group speaking the same language or boasting the same geographical origin. In the German world, ethnic origins played a key role, whilst in France a 'foreigner' was anyone born outside the country, even if to French parents.[3]

Cities – especially those of greater economic importance – showed themselves open to the influx of groups of merchants and craftsmen who contributed to the wealth of the city. In Venice, special areas or buildings were reserved for the use of Turkish, German and Jewish merchants, where they might live temporarily or settle in a more stable fashion. The latter was the case, for example, with the Jews, Greeks and Albanians, who occupied specially delimited areas of the city (in the case of the Jews, thus giving birth to the very word ghetto). There were also the so-called Fondaco dei Tedeschi and Fondaco dei Turchi, where German and Turkish merchants in the city found warehouses and living accommodation.

Obviously, national states were concerned with a much vaster spatial area than medieval cities; above all, they pursued the creation of institutions which contained the population within precise social and territorial frameworks, thus guaranteeing that they could exercise control and discipline. At the same time, the first political economies were emerging, with an attempt being made to outline and define the economic activity of a nation's inhabitants (for example, in the most advanced countries, primarily France and England). The most significant policies were those intended to control manufacturing activities within national states, encouraging the import of raw materials and the export of finished goods. These were essentially mercantile policies, paying particular attention to specialised crafts and to the technical and technological know-how necessary to the development of those products, which were considered of essential importance to the national interest. The migration of skilled labour was, therefore, encouraged by the states that had moved in this direction most intelligently. However, the process was far from straightforward: whilst there might be forms of openness and

---

[3] Claudine Billot, 'Les italiens naturalisés français sous le règne de François I$^{er}$ (1514-1547)', in Rinaldo Comba, Gabriella Piccinni and Giuliano Pinto (eds), *Strutture familiari, epidemie, migrazioni nell'Italia medievale* (Naples: Edizioni Scientifiche Italiane, 1984), p. 477. For an analysis of the concept of *émigrant* and *immigrant* in the French meaning see Norman Laybourn, *L'émigration des alsaciens et des lorrains du XVIIIe au XXe siècle* (2 vols, Strasbourg: Association des publications près des Universités de Strasbourg, 1986), vol. 1: Les noms des lieux, pp. 10-13.

tolerance, it was also true that in certain countries and in certain economic situations, mercantilist polices led to forms of protectionism rather than the free movement of goods and people. In Europe, and probably elsewhere, the modern state developed in this contradictory fashion. At the same time as it aimed to establish an institutional and political framework that could control the movement of populations and further economic activity, which was in the national interest, it could not prevent the arrival of new immigrants (though it might encourage the arrival solely of those who could serve the national interest). The same fluctuations and contradictions can also be seen in contemporary emigration and immigration.

Moreover, one would be wrong in thinking that the population policies of the modern state –or restrictive measures concerning migration – truly managed to exercise full control over the stable resident population (just as one would be wrong in taking such a group as the sole constituent of the 'population' of a given country). In fact, the states of modern Europe were characterized by the seasonal migration of peddlers and chapmen. As Laurence Fontaine has shown, mobility should not necessarily be considered as a transitory phase between departure and arrival; it might well constitute a *modus vivendi*, a way of appropriating territory that is just as legitimate as settlement. Migrants are not marginal figures when compared to the settled majority; they set up a network of personal relations between groups bound together by economic links – for example, access to credit made possible by the bonds of solidarity within a particular network – and by social or familial ties (of an extended and not necessarily nuclear type).[4]

Emigration did not necessarily mean an economic and cultural rupture with the country of origin, given that many links with it might still remain active. Charles Tilly has here distinguished between 'circular' and 'chain' migration. The former 'takes a social unit to a destination through a set of arrangements which returns it to the origin after a well-defined interval'.[5] This category might include seasonal labourers in agriculture (for example, mowers, reapers or rice-weeders), herdsmen with transhumant herds and flocks, domestic workers who leave their jobs when they marry, soldiers, the wide range of mountain folk who leave the valleys of the Alps for the plains and then return to the mountains when they have sufficiently supplemented their income and building labourers who leave their fields during the spring and summer months to then return in the winter. 'Chain migration', on the other hand, 'moves sets of related individuals or households from one place to another via a set of social arrangements in which people at the destination provide aid, information and encouragement to new migrants.' There is a wide range of such cases in medieval and modern Europe. Cities themselves used to allow or

---

[4] Laurence Fontaine, *Histoire du colportage en Europe, 15e-19e siècle* (Paris: A. Michel, 1993).

[5] Charles Tilly, 'Migration in Modern European History', in William Hardy McNeill and Ruth S. Adams (eds), *Human Migration* (Bloomington, IN and London: Indiana University Press, 1978), p. 52.

encourage 'these clusters of people to organize as "nations" sharing well-defined privileges and bearing collective responsibility for the policing and welfare of their members'.[6] Such communities would specialize in a specific activity. For example, in Venice there were 'German cobblers' or even 'German lute-makers' (from cities in which it had been difficult for them to practice their craft).[7] And in Renaissance Rome a large number of the courtiers were of Spanish origin. A third aspect has also been identified, namely 'career migration' which enabled migrants to better their social and professional prospects through a whole series of work opportunities provided by 'organized trades, firms, governments, mercantile networks, armies and the like'. Here encouragement and assistance did not come from relatives and acquaintances but from colleagues; and the persons involved in such migration were 'scientists, technicians, military officers, priests and bureaucrats'.[8] Thus, in some areas, for example, Kent as studied by Peter Clark, migration during the sixteenth century has been identified as dual-faceted, with unskilled labourers willing to move to fairly distant cities and accept humble jobs, and, as a result of the expansion during the course of the century, a wave of migration involving 'peddlers, chapmen and other itinerant retailers with their own trade routes across counties'.[9]

Very often these people did not aim to achieve social integration. In an Italian city of the Middle Ages (and later), immigrants or members of a 'nation' wanted to retain their status, preserving their own language and links with their ethnic groups of origin.[10] The Fondaco dei Tedeschi in Venice had a fixed population of some 100-120 merchants, together with porters, cooks and packers, most of whom were of German origin – in all, some 200 people involved in commerce and trade.[11]

Thus migration was a sort of underground river, a social variable that made its presence felt in national or urban policies, a factor that undoubtedly enriched the social contexts in which it occurred. With varying degrees of success, cities and states strove to control or integrate the new arrivals and minorities within more homogeneous social groups; but historical evidence shows that this process was generally contradictory, even if sometimes it might be described as successful and

---

[6] Ibid., p. 53.

[7] Salvatore Ciriacono, 'Les manufactures de luxe à Venise: contraintes géographiques, goût méditerranéen et compétition internationale (XIVe-XVIe siècles)', in *Les villes et la transmission des valeurs culturelles au bas Moyen Age et aux temps modernes* (Brussells: Crédit Communal, 1996), pp. 235-51.

[8] Tilly, 'Migration', p. 54.

[9] Peter Clark, 'The Migrant in Kentish Towns, 1580-1640', in Peter Clark and Peter Slack (eds), *Crisis and Order in English Towns, 1500-1700: Essays in Urban History* (Toronto: University of Toronto Press, 1972), pp. 117-63, especially at p. 146.

[10] Rinaldo Comba, 'Emigrare nel Medioevo. Aspetti economico-sociali della mobilità geografica nei secoli XI-XVII', in *Strutture familiari*, p. 63.

[11] Philippe Braunstein, 'Appunti per la storia di una minoranza: la popolazione tedesca di Venezia nel Medioevo', in *Strutture familiari*, pp. 515-16.

coherent. There is no doubt, however, that the influx of people and know-how was beneficial to the recipient countries (the vast majority of the literature agrees on this point). However, though this end-result is clear when viewed from a historical perspective, one has to acknowledge that migrants often faced policies predicated on little more than simple toleration, if indeed they did not become victims of active exclusion, persecution and expulsion.

## Migration of Religious Minorities

Religious minorities provide a perfect illustration of how the attitudes of states can vary; and very often enforced emigration – dictated by a desire to preserve or enforce some supposed religious or racial homogeneity – has turned out to be counterproductive, having results very different to those envisaged by the makers of such policies. Religious minorities thus represented in an emblematic way the different types of reception offered by the states. Forced emigration caused by intolerant politics whose aim was the implementation of a theoretical religious and racial homogeneity, eventually produced results that contradicted the hopes informing these policies. Perhaps Jews provide the best example of this contradiction. Sometimes, medieval states or cities might be cautiously welcoming them, exhibiting a certain tolerance, but in most cases such an attitude eventually resulted in segregation and strict confinement of their economic activities within a specific area.[12] The institution of the ghetto in Venice is the first example of this desire to impose institutionalised control over the relatively rich Jewish community, even if the main inspiration for such a policy was not necessarily racial (the word ghetto has, as it's well known, an Italian and more exactly, a Venetian origin).

However, the overall picture is certainly much more complicated than this; and whilst the term 'essential outsiders' has been applied to both the Jewish and Chinese communities,[13] how can one omit mention here of Armenians, Greeks, Spanish Moriscos, the various Protestant communities (Huguenots, Quakers, Amish and Waldensians), or even all those European populations that from the sixteenth century onwards set out to colonize the world? Indeed, such minorities have been studied either with a focus on religious ideology and *mentalité*, or with the emphasis being placed on economic considerations and the prevailing international situation. Quite rightly, emphasis is placed on an international

---

[12] Maurice Aymard, 'La Sicile, terre d'immigration', in *Les migrations dans les pays méditerranéens au XVIIIe siècle et au début du XIXe siècle* (Actes des journées d'études, Bendor, 6 et 7 avril 1973), Cahiers de la Méditerranée, Série Spéciale, vol. 2 (Nice: Université de Nice, Centre de la Méditerranée moderne et contemporaine, 1973), pp. 4-24.

[13] Daniel Chirot and Anthony Reid (eds), *Essential Outsiders: Chinese and Jews in the Modern Transformation of Southeast Asia and Central Europe* (Seattle: University of Washington Press, 1997).

context for these issues, which is sometimes overlooked; religion and *mentalité* inevitably tended to fall into the background when there was a key change in the economic or international situation. It has been pointed out that the influence and success of the Jewish communities at different levels of society varied according to economic circumstances and to the international role played by the country in which they found themselves.

Probably, the point being made here is best illustrated by reference to Werner Sombart's contribution to the debate on the relationship between Jews and capitalism.[14] He argued that the Jewish community showed itself to be the most open to economic rationalism, and that the Jews were therefore the ones most inclined to develop business and commerce. Unaffected by certain strains of asceticism found in Catholicism, Judaism itself encouraged the nurture of such aptitudes; there was no contradiction between economic success and the contract stipulated between God and the Faithful. More importantly, the fact that, as a racial group, the Jewish community had lived on the margins of other communities for millennia further encouraged the development of an entrepreneurial spirit, dictated by the need to adapt to the most difficult and varied circumstances.[15] However, these conclusions are far from being universally accepted. Had not Catholic merchants shown the same ability in commerce and business practice? Others argued that, over the long term, the racial and mental particularities of the Jewish *mentalité* were far from being proven. The economic success of the Jews was the result of the historical *milieux* and the circumstances with which they had been faced. Moreover, it was totally wrong to overlook the elements of mysticism that do exist in Judaic theology: the Talmud did concede that Jews could engage in money-lending and the buying and selling of goods but, whilst respecting certain moral and religious requirements; it certainly did not open the way to the invention of modern capitalism.[16] Marx, in fact, claimed that the role of the Jews in modern society could not be analysed along religious and racial lines, but must be seen in terms of history, with the Jews' financial and commercial activities being the one way they could achieve social recognition and status. The true emancipation of the Jews would come about within an entirely renewed society, within which the constrictions of money and capital had been overthrown – and Judaism itself would no longer exist.[17]

---

[14] Werner Sombart, *Die Juden und das Wirtschaftsleben* (Leipzig: Duncker and Humblot, 1922).

[15] On this point see Natalie Zemon Davis, 'Religion and Capitalism Once Again? Jewish Merchant Culture in the Seventeenth Century', in *Representation*, 59 (Summer 1997): 57-8. See also C.B. Stuczynski, The Marrano Economic Network: Religion and Capitalism, unpublished paper for the Thirteenth Economic History Congress, Session 10 (Diaspora entrepreneurial networks, c. 1000 to 2000), Buenos Aires, 22-26 July 2002.

[16] Raphael-Georges Lévy and Moses Hoffmann, quoted by Davis, 'Religion and Capitalism', pp. 80-81.

[17] Dennis K. Fischman, quoted by Zemon Davis, 'Religionand Capitalism', p. 80.

For his part, Max Weber saw the Jews as perennial 'outsiders', the agents of a 'pariah capitalism' that was limited to lending money to the ruling classes or providing pawn facilities for the middle and lower classes. The Jews never became part of that 'bourgeois capitalism' which truly opened the way to modern capitalism.[18] But Weber's main contribution was to shift attention from the Jewish to the Protestant and Puritan communities which, as we know, saw economic success as a confirmation of the divine grace freely bestowed on the Elect; the Calvinist communities were thus the ground for the emergence of a new concept of society and economic activity.[19]

However, given that within the Early Modern State they might themselves be seen as an obstacle to the implementation policies inspired by the very notion of a 'nation', Protestant communities might not always be able to exercise their capacity for economic renewal and growth. Once again, emigration and technology transfer seem to be the most obvious result of this clash with the structure of the state. It was, in fact, the Calvinists who probably played the greatest role in technology transfer, not only from the Mediterranean area to the north but also across the whole of the continent (even if one should not underestimate the contribution made by such sects as the Anabaptists, Waldensians and Mennonites). Nevertheless even Protestant communities encountered a broken ground showing their capabilities to implement more rational economics forms, often being considered as an obstacle to the national interests that the modern state aimed to realise. Migration and technology transfer have again been the more evident consequences of this confrontation with national order. Dismissing a previous estimate of some half a million, Heinz Schilling claims that at least one hundred thousand Huguenots came from the Low Countries during the course of the sixteenth and seventeenth centuries. They escaped from the policies of intolerance and persecution first introduced by Charles V (1530) and then applied in the Low Countries by the Spanish authorities – emigrants who went to France, England, Germany, Poland and the Scandinavian peninsula, in particular, Sweden. Many would return to the Seven Provinces once these had established themselves as a Republic; but the fall of Antwerp to Alessandro Farnese in 1585 meant that the southern regions of the Low Countries remained under Spanish influence, and thus the centre of technological innovation shifted northwards.[20]

The other Huguenot migration – that from France after the revocation of the Edict of Nantes in 1685 (the number of around 200,000 refugees has been

---

[18] Ibid., p. 58.

[19] Max Weber, *The Protestant Ethic and the Spirit of Capitalism*, with a foreword of Richard H. Tawney (London: Allen & Unwin, 1930); reprint (New York: Scribner, 1958). For the debate on this work see Hartmut Lehmann and G. Roth (eds), *Weber's "Protestant Ethic": Origins, Evidence, Contests* (Cambridge: Cambridge University Press, 1993).

[20] Schilling, 'Innovation through Migration', pp. 9-11.

suggested)[21] – will be even larger than this first flow from the Low Countries.[22] Both phenomena are examples of 'confessional migration' which was characteristic of these centuries, whereas many of the migratory movements in the Late Middle Ages have been described as 'betterment or subsistence migration'. Further the transitional character of sixteenth-century Europe permitted the introduction of innovations without state control, whereas in the late seventeenth century the absolutist bureaucracy controlled the settlement of Huguenots much more intensively and determined the scope and direction of their economic activities.[23] Indeed these innovations had a direct influence on manufacturing activities and can be characterized as examples of the technological diffusion which was essentially imitative in nature, occurred between areas that were relatively close together – or which could be reached via contacts for the exchange of goods and information – and ultimately led to 'the gradual replacement of old methods by the new'.[24] It is no accident that in the German cities which received influxes of Walloons, Antwerpenaar and Dutch refugees during the second half of the sixteenth century, bitter conflicts erupted between local corporations and guilds (particularly in Frankfurt but also in Cologne, Aix-la-Chapelle, Augsburg, Nuremberg, Hamburg and Wesel) and the Protestant entrepreneurs who set up small and medium size manufacturing activities that undercut the tradition of domestic craft production. New water-powered machines could perform the work of a dozen old looms, inevitably provoking a bitter reaction from craftsmen. These clashes also had a strong religious component, with the Calvinists opposed not only by the Catholics but also by the Lutherans (thus opening up a division within the Protestant communities themselves). All of this led to the Calvinist communities in German cities becoming rather closed social entities, laying the groundwork for that formation of entrepreneurial elites that would still be active in the nineteenth century; and thus one might see in them the first historical confirmation of Max Weber's theories concerning 'capitalism and Calvinism', with the constitution of an 'early modern business bourgeoisie'.[25]

In effect, in the sixteenth century the regions that received these refugees revealed themselves to be backward precisely in those areas of activity in which the newcomers excelled. The wool industry in England lagged behind that in the Low Countries, and the migrants introduced 'looms with multiple shuttles' and

---

[21] Another Huguenot migration occurred from Salzburg around the same time.

[22] Warren Candler Scoville, *The Persecution of Huguenots* (Berkeley: University of California Press, 1960), pp. 120-121. See also Jean Hémardinquer, 'Les conséquences de la revocation de l'Édit de Nantes: une révision', in *Annales E.S.C.*, 16 (1961): 1212-7. Scoville strengthens the significance of solidarity among the different actors of the society versus the thesis of Max Weber and Arnold Toynbee who stressed the marginalisation of the minorities.

[23] Schilling, 'Innovation through Migration', p. 9.

[24] Warren Candler Scoville, 'Spread of Techniques: Minority Migrations and the Diffusion of Technology', in *The Journal of Economic History*, 11 (1951): 347.

[25] Schilling, 'Innovation through Migration', p. 30.

'new drapery' (combed wool cloth that was lighter and less expensive than the old carded wool) which would develop on the basis of a 'putting-out system' (one particular type of thread in Maidstone was actually known as 'Dutchwork'). The expansion of dye works meant that England no longer had to send its cloth abroad to be finished. And in other areas we know that Elizabethan England had some 150 jewellers, diamond-cutters and workers of fine metals who came from Flanders or Holland. Another group of Protestants, this time from Italy, would introduce silk-weaving and the cultivation of mulberry trees to Switzerland, which also received numerous French Huguenots, especially in the city of Geneva (though the Swiss watch industry does not appear to owe anything to the arrival of French Protestants).

Thus the impact of this first wave of Protestant migration on the technological know-how and manufacturing industries of the host countries seems to have been profound. However, we cannot completely underestimate the influence of the other wave of Huguenot migration that started after 1685. Indeed it is true that the early migrants introduced previously unknown methods of manufacture ex novo, but we cannot conclude for this reason that the arrival of the French Huguenots resulted in a lack of 'more capitalistic forms of production', as Warren Scoville claims.[26] In fact, one might reverse this argument and emphasize that the second wave of migration reinforced the various trades that were developing in the different countries, interacting in a situation where private consumption was expanding and a system of fashions made for a 'consumer society' that was very different from that at the end of the sixteenth century.

For instance, the famous Edict of Potsdam issued by the Elector of Brandenburg, who accepted many of the Huguenots in his state in 1685, meant that a whole series of manufacturing activities became established in the area, from glass (with the 'plate-glass factory' at Neustadt) to wool, light steel and the working of leather and printed cottons. Scoville himself points out:

> In Prussia, in particular, they made rugs and tapestries and introduced the manufacture of gold and silk galloons ... [Whilst] silk workers from Tours, Lyons and Nîmes settled in London and Canterbury and made damasks, lustrous black taffetas, brocades, moires, satins and velvets, which in richness of colour and fineness of quality at least rivalled those exported from France.[27]

Protestant minorities had a significant effect on both the financial and the agricultural sectors. In France, historians have spoken of the creation of what amounted to a *banque protestante* that could influence the political and economic policies of the kingdom; and both in the latter years of the sixteenth and throughout the seventeenth centuries.[28] The City of London itself and the financial

---

[26] Scoville, 'Spread of Techniques', pp. 353-5, esp. at p. 355.
[27] Ibid., p. 357.
[28] Herbert Lüthy, *La banque protestante en France: de la révocation de l'Édit de Nantes*

market of Amsterdam even benefited from the arrival of refugees at the end of the sixteenth and the beginning of the seventeenth centuries. It is probably true that the techniques of finance within Europe did not change significantly during the course of the sixteenth century (with Italy providing the dominant models for commercial and financial practice), yet the drop in interest rates that occurred in Amsterdam towards the end of the seventeenth century can be seen in connection with the arrival of the French Huguenots and the capital they brought with them.[29] More importantly, if the fall of Antwerp and other Flemish cities a century earlier led to a massive shift of adventure capital and technological know-how towards the northern Low Countries, as is well-known, a similar movement occurred towards France, where this capital funded a number of land reclamation and improvement projects.[30]

The protestant minorities exerted an equally important influence in the agricultural sector. In Germany itself the introduction of such 'crops as tobacco, artichokes, asparagus, cauliflower, fine fruit trees and wood' is seen as a consequence of the arrival of a group of entrepreneurs. And in late-seventeenth-century Ireland, the introduction of the linen industry accompanied a policy of re-population intended to make good the demographic losses during Oliver Cromwell's campaigns on the island (there were at least twelve settlement colonies in 1695 and the number of Protestant refugees in 1711 totalled at least 10,000). Schools were set up to introduce women and craftsmen to the new fibre and the new looms; and at the same time, dye works were established so that the whole production cycle could be completed on the island, without the need to send the fabric abroad for finishing (as had been the case in England).[31]

Schemes for land reclamation and improvement obviously required much more sizeable funds than more individual forms of technological implantation, and the results were not always as noteworthy successes as in the financial and manufacturing sectors. Nevertheless, the input from the minority came up against the degree of openness and backwardness in the host country. Holland, England and – to a lesser extent – Switzerland undoubtedly benefited from the influx of refugees; whilst in France and the German *Länder*, political and institutional structures (sometimes still feudal in character) left very little space for the more advanced projects and undertakings that could have brought about a break with the past. As a result, a certain type of international finance capitalism linked with the Protestantism of Northern Europe was for a long time at loggerheads with the political and national strategies of the French monarchy (though a member of the Herbart family did become Contrôleur Général des Finances). Many financiers

---

à la Revolution (Paris: SEVPEN, 1959).

[29] Scoville, 'Spread of Techniques', p. 357.

[30] Salvatore Ciriacono, 'Land Reclamation in Early Modern Europe. Dutch Windmills, Private Enterprises and State Intervention', in *Review. Fernand Braudel Center*, 18 (1995): 281-304.

[31] Scoville, 'Spread of Techniques', pp. 355-6.

and entrepreneurs were forced to leave the country after the revocation of the Edict of Nantes, though their difficulties with the monarchy dated from some time before. However, the influence of la *banque protestante* was far from over (as can be judged, for example, from the role played by Geneva).[32]

Whilst there can be no doubt that both Judaism and Protestantism had a profound effect upon economic life in modern Europe, one should not ignore the results of another migratory movement – that of the Spanish Moriscos, who (especially after the 1492 Reconquista) played an important role in the spread of technological know-how through the Mediterranean basin. In effect, the Spanish Jews and Muslims (the Marranos and Moriscos) can be seen as posing a single challenge to domestic know-how in numerous areas of the continent, offering input with which all the various technological cultures of Europe had to interact. However, whilst there is no doubt that such minorities were bearers of know-how of general importance, it is also true that the influence of the Marranos and Moriscos in areas such as Italy and Holland was much less significant than it was in the regions of the Ottoman Turkish Empire (even if the former did benefit from the know-how they had to offer, especially during the Middle Ages).

Moreover, as Thomas Glick rightly points out,[33] the assessment of the actual extent of technology transfer is a problem not only of precise knowledge of facts but also of objective interpretation (the latter often being coloured by nationalist prejudices and self-celebration). In effect, though certain Spanish historians of the sixteenth century tried to diminish the influence of the Moriscos, their continuation of the Arab-Andalusian traditions did continue to make their effects felt (above all, in the agricultural sector). However, Morisco influence was much greater in North Africa, where the sixteenth century saw the arrival (via Spain) of such New World crops as tomatoes, types of beans and American peppers, whilst irrigation – a great boast of the Arab-Muslim tradition – made it possible to cultivate such crops as olives. Spanish-Arab technology would also have an effect on the very crafts and skills of the Ottoman world, which continued to oppose 'the weapons and devices [of the infidel]' in the name of a policy that posited (who can know with how much success?) the promotion of a technology that followed the dictates of Islamic Law.

In the area of civilian industries, for example, it has been shown beyond question that the Moriscos had a clear influence on wool production; they had a near monopoly on the production of the typical Tunisian cap known as the *sah-shiya*, and also introduced such terms as *ma-ki-na* (which replaced the Arabic, *alat*).

The migration of the Spanish (Sephardite) Jews would have a clear influence in both the Low Countries and throughout the Mediterranean, above all in the Ottoman Empire, where they are considered to have played an important role in

---

[32] Ciriacono, 'Land Reclamation in Early Modern Europe'.

[33] Thomas Glick, 'Moriscos and Marranos as Agents of Technological Diffusion', in *History of Technology*, 17 (1995): 114-22, esp. at p. 116.

the wool industry, printing, armaments, astronomy, glass-making, medicine and mechanical engineering (fulling mills and water-wheels). Saloniki, in Ottoman Greece, was in fact considered practically a Spanish city due to the number of its Sephardite immigrants, who introduced not only the wool industry but also the making of particular fabrics (*velarde*) that had previously be worked primarily in Islamic areas of Spain. And there is a solid historical tradition that the Venetians themselves were very careful about not expelling their Jews once they saw the contribution they had made to the armaments of the Ottoman Empire. Of course, it may well be true that a power of the size of the Ottoman Empire would in any case have learnt to benefit from the technological know-how that was circulating within the Mediterranean area: the predominant influence and greater dynamism of technological sectors in the West is, after the studies of Eliyahu Ashtor,[34] something that cannot be denied (even if concepts as 'path dependency' and 'exposure effect', according to Joel Mokyr,[35] do not always seem to apply to the Ottoman Empire which, as Thomas Glick argues, may have been resisting innovation for religious reasons). However, there does seem to be no doubt that numerous artisans, technicians and scholars of Jewish origin brought with them know-how and abilities from which the Ottoman Empire benefited greatly.

And this gives us pause for thought before making any conclusive statement with regard to the 'exceptional' role played in such migration by specific minorities, of whatever religion or creed. This does not mean that beliefs, *mentalité* and philosophy of life have not been important factors in the social and economic success of such communities at certain fundamental moments in history, but simply that one has to look very carefully at their long-term role in an international context that has undergone radical economic change. Hence, one cannot help but see all the inevitable limitations of the age-old debates regarding the relation between 'Protestantism and Capitalism', 'Judaism and Capitalism' or the supposed 'superiority' of the Western over the Islamic social model.

## Conclusion

Nor should one forget that knowledge might also be diffused by less traumatic routes than the forced migration of religious minorities. Scholars have spoken of an expanding emission of technological know-how generated by international demand, better opportunities and the attraction exerted by economic areas in which development was most intense. In other words, when a social and political context was no longer capable of satisfying the expectations of the more dynamic sectors of society, these economic factors could be just as effective as religious

---

[34] Eliyahu Ashtor, *Technology, Industry, and Trade: the Levant versus Europe, 1250-1500* (Aldershot: Ashgate, 1992).

[35] Joel Mokyr, *The Lever of Riches: Technological Creativity and Economic Progress* (New York and London: Oxford University Press, 1990).

persecution in stimulating temporary or definitive emigration. And sometimes this migration occurred even though the state – for example, seventeenth-century Venice and Japan – threatened emigrants with arrest, punishment or even death in the unlikely event of their return.[36] Through such clandestine migration the Venetian glassmakers carried the know-how behind the manufacture of Venetian crystal (a very pure type of glass of very low lead content, obtained by the skilful mix of various chemical components) to numerous countries throughout Europe, which then produced their own *façon de Venise* glassware. The transfer of entire groups of lace-makers from Venice to France had a similar impact on French luxury industries at the time of Colbert, who also stimulated the French glass industry by bringing in numerous glassmakers from the historic island of Murano to set up the Saint-Gobain factory.[37]

In effect, the case of Italy would seem to be a paradigm of the complex problem posed by emigration, in which one can identify a religious component (even if this was not of predominant importance here; neither in human nor technological terms can the emigration of the Waldensians and the Veneto or Neapolitan Protestants be compared with that of the Moriscos, the Jews, the Armenians, the Chinese or other communities), a financial component (the great financier-merchants who were famous in the major cities of Europe), a craft component (with craftsmen leaving either for good or temporarily) and a component of need (with emigration brought about by underdevelopment).[38] All of these variables interacted in the social and economic history of the relations between Italy and the rest of the European and world economy. Whilst the world of Italian finance – Aldo de Maddalena has described it as 'the international aristocracy of money'[39] – was active and dynamic in Europe from the twelfth to the fifteenth century, introducing advanced and sophisticated financial techniques to numerous European countries (double-entry book-keeping, endorsed bills, bills of exchange), from the sixteenth century onwards it was the country's artisans who probably

---

[36] Francesca Trivellato, *La fondamenta dei vetrai* (Rome: Donzelli, 2000); Paolo Preto, *I servizi segreti di Venezia* (Milano: Il Saggiatore, 1994). William D. Wray, The 17th Century Japanese Diaspora: questions of boundary and policy, unpublished paper for the Thirteenth Economic History Congress, Session 10 (Diaspora entrepreneurial networks, c. 1000 to 2000), Buenos Aires, 22-26 July 2002.

[37] Salvatore Ciriacono, 'Per una storia dell'industria di lusso in Francia. La concorrenza italiana nei secoli XVI e XVII', in *Ricerche di storia religiosa e sociale*, 14 (1978): 181-202. Ciriacono, 'Silk Manufacturing in France and Italy in the XVIIth Century: Two Models Compared', in *The Journal of European Economic History*, 10 (1981): 167-99.

[38] Giovanni Pizzorusso, 'I movimenti migratory in Italia in antico regime', in Piero Bevilacqua, Andreina de Clementi and Emilio Franzina (eds), *Storia dell'emigrazione italiana* (Rome and Bari: Laterza, 2001), pp. 3-16. Donna R. Gabaccia and Fraser M. Ottanelli (eds), *Italian Workers of the World: Labor Migration and the Formation of Multiethnic States* (Urbana and Chicago: University of Illinois Press, 2001).

[39] Aldo de Maddalena and Hermann Kellenbenz (eds), *La Repubblica internazionale del denaro tra XV e XVII secolo* (Bologna: Il Mulino, 1986).

made up the most noticeable group of emigrants, at a time that saw a shift in the 'world-economy' from Northern Italy towards Northern Europe.[40] And as the fortunes of the country declined during the nineteenth century, another type of migration took over, with thousands of emigrants moving as far apart as the Americas and Australia. Technological know-how seemed to play a lesser role here – unless one includes within that term the ability of people to adapt to and make the most of what circumstances had to offer. The case of North America – a country that was capable of absorbing and rewarding such abilities – is perhaps the most significant example for the exploration of this human phenomenon.

---

[40] On the concept of 'world-economy' see Fernand Braudel, *Civilisation matérielle, Economie et Capitalisme, XVe-XVIIIe siècle* (3 vols, Paris: Colin, 1979), vol. 3: Le Temps du Monde, pp. 12-70. For another approach see Imanuel Wallerstein, *The Modern World-System. Capitalist Agriculture and the Origins of the European World-Economy in the Sixteenth Century*, (3 vols, New York: Academic Press, 1974-2004), vol. 1.

Chapter Three

# Migration, Regional Integration and Human Security: An Overview of Research Developments

Harald Kleinschmidt

**Introduction**

For most of the postwar period, migration has been studied in its effects on the populations and institutions of the sovereign state. During the same period, migration policies of governments of sovereign states have mainly consisted in attempts to enforce immigration reduction. Migration has been categorized as a factor of the destabilization of state populations as putative groups of residents. By contrast, institutions of governance other than governments of sovereign states and national as well as transnational civil society institutions have hardly been allowed to play an active role in the formation and implementation of migrations policies. Similarly, at least, if not only, in Europe, regional integration has been approached with the goal of moulding institutions of the state. Thus, within and with regard to Europe, theorists as well as practical decision-makers have looked at regional integration in attempts to predict the likelihood or lack of likelihood that regional institutions might absorb institutions of governance pertaining to the sovereign state, thereby reducing the significance of international borders. Even though processes of regionalism elsewhere in the world have had less impact on the transformation of institutions, regional integration theorists have continued to be about potential consequences of regionalism for the destabilization of state institutions. Lastly, security has been the subject of inquiry mainly under the presumption that the state can and should be the unit which can provide security and for which security has to be provided in military terms. However, issues beyond military matters, such as environmental degradation, resource scarcity and political inequality, have been securitized over a period of some twenty years and the human individual has been recognized as a unit for whom security in a broader sense should be provided. Nevertheless, recognition of the widening range of issues covered in security discourses has been slow. Thus as late as in 2003, the UN-sponsored international Commission on Human Security could take the view that what they termed 'human security' was a new issue in international politics.

By contrast, it is far from obvious that the interrelationship between migration, regional integration and security should be approached from the point of view of the sovereign state, even though theorists of the realist schools[1] and high-ranking decision-makers in military matters and foreign policy continued to give priority to the security of the state as a sovereign political entity over regional integration down to the early 1990s, as they are continuing to rank the perceived interests of states above the manifest interests of migrants. Among the many instances that provide evidence for this contention are the failure of the Latin American Free Trade Association (LAFTA) in 1980 as only one of the several regional integration schemes in Latin America that gave way to persisting perceived state interests under pressure from military governments in the area,[2] the dissolution in 1984 of the first East African Community (EAC) which had been paralyzed from 1971 by the lack of willingness of the rulers of the involved states to build common security regimes, the negative impact of interstate and domestic warfare in Southeast Asia on regional integration schemes such as Maphilindo and the early Association of Southeast Asian Nations (ASEAN),[3] the lack of involvement of the European institutions in the process of the merging of the two German states in 1989 and

---

[1] For a recent case of state-centric security theory see Robert Gilpin, 'No One Loves a Political Realist', in Benjamin Frankel (ed.), *Realism. Restatements and Renewal* (London and Portland, OR: Cass, 1996), pp. 3-26.

[2] See Gary Clyde Hofbauer, Jeffrey J. Schott and Diana Clark, *Western Hemispheric Economic Integration* (Washington: Institute of International Economics, 1994). Anneke Jessen and Ennio Rodriguez, *The Caribbean Community* (Kingston: Institute for the Integration of Latin America and the Caribbean, 1999). Ritter N. Diaz, The Political Economy of Regional Integration in the Common Market of the South (Mercosur). Unpublished M.A. Thesis. University of Tsukuba, Graduate School of International Political Economy, 2000. It is a euphemism to say that LAFTA was replaced by the Latin American Integration Association (LAIA), as John McCormick [*Understanding the European Union* (Basingstoke: Palgrave, 1999), pp. 23-4] has suggested. This is so because the ending of LAFTA came after the admission that a multilateral design for free trade agreements was not considered desirable by the then involved governments.

[3] For a recent survey of African regional integration see Aderemi Ajibewa, *From Regional Security to Regional Integration in West Africa. Lessons from the ASEAN Experience* (London: Cass, 2002). Daniel C. Bach (ed.), *Regionalisation in Africa. Integration and Disintegration* (Oxford and Bloomington, IN: Indiana University Press, 2000). Stefan Collignon, *Regionale Integration und Entwicklung in Ostafrika* (Hamburg: Institut für Afrikakunde, 1990). Sheila Page, *Regionalism among Developing Countries* (Basingstoke: Macmillan; and New York: St Martin's Press, 2000). Victor Hermann Umbricht, *Multilateral Mediation. Practical Experiences and Lessons* (Dordrecht and Boston: Nijhoff, 1989). On ASEAN see: Amitav Acharya, *The Quest for Identity. International Relations of Southeast Asia* (Singapore: Institute of Southeast Asian Studies, 2000). Acharya, *Constructing a Security Community in Southeast Asia. ASEAN and the Problem of Regional Order* (London and New York: Routledge, 2001). Suthiphand Chirathivat, Franz Knipping, Poul Henrik Lassen and Chia Siow Yue (eds), *Asia-Europe on the Eve of the 21$^{st}$ Century* (Singapore: Institute of Southeast Asian Studies, 2001). Simon S. C. Tay, Jesus P. Estanislao and Hadi Soesastro (eds), *Reinventing ASEAN* (Singapore: Institute of Southeast Asian Studies, 2001).

1990,[4] the lack of willingness of the governments of many states to allow or promote schemes of dual citizenship and the use of security arguments against demands to that extent,[5] as well as such incidents as the establishment of checkpoints on the Czech-Slovak border in consequence of the German demand to control immigration from Eastern European states.[6]

However, from the late 1980s, voices have become more frequent which have articulated different perceptions. In this chapter, I address these new perceptions and try to systematize the interconnectedness of new approaches to migration, regional integration and security in their joint effects on the sovereign state. I assume that these joint effects are more significant as factors transforming the structure and capabilities of state institutions than the political impacts of globalization. The latter impacts, analyzed in the work by Susan Strange and Ken'ichi Ohmae, refer largely to processes of world market integration that began its acceleration under the auspices of European colonialism and imperialism at the turn of the twentieth century. These processes have left core tasks of governance under the control of institutions of sovereign states, such as the definition of

---

[4] On the interconnectedness of German unification and European integration see Jeffrey Anderson, *German Unification and the Union of Europe* (Cambridge: Cambridge University Press, 1999). Wesley D. Chapin, *Germany for the Germans? The Political Effects of International Migration* (Westport, CT and London: Greenwood, 1997). Mark Fisher, *After the Wall. Germany, the Germans and the Burdens of History* (New York: Simon and Schuster, 1995). Andrew Geddes, *Immigration and European Integration. Towards Fortress Europe?* (Manchester, and New York: Manchester University Press, 2000). Manfred Görtemaker, *Unifying Germany. 1989 – 90* (New York: St. Martin's Press; and Basingstoke: Macmillan, 1994). Gisela Hendriks, *Germany and European Integration* (New York: St. Martin's Press; and Basingstoke: Macmillan, 1991). Andrei Markovits and Philipp Gorski, *The German Predicament. Memory and Power in the New Europe* (Ithaca and London: Cornell University Press, 1997). Barbara Marshall, *The New Germany and Migration in Europe* (Manchester and New York: Manchester University Press, 2000). Paul Stares (ed.), *The New Germany and the New Europe* (Washington: Brookings Institution, 1992).

[5] On the controversies over dual citizenship see John Breuilly, 'Sovereignty, Citizenship and Nationality. Reflections on the Case of Germany', in Malcolm Anderson and Eberhart Bort (eds), *The Frontiers of Europe* (London: Pinter, 1998), pp. 36-67. Irene Goetz (ed.), *Zündstoff doppelte Staatsbürgerschaft* (Munster and Hamburg: LIT, 2000). Dieter Gosewinkel, 'Staatsbürgerschaft und Staatsangehörigkeit', *Geschichte und Gesellschaft*, 21 (1995): 533-56. Gosewinkel, *Einbürgern und Ausschließen. Die Nationalisierung der Staatsangehörigkeit vom Deutschen Bund bis zur Bundesrepublik Deutschland* (Göttingen: Vandenhoeck & Ruprecht, 2001), pp. 422-9. Rolf Grawert, *Staat und Staatsangehörigkeit* (Berlin: Duncker & Humblot, 1973). Grawert, 'Staatsangehörigkeit und Staatsbürgerschaft', *Der Staat*, 23 (1984): 198-204. Henry Ashby Turner, Jr, 'Deutsches Staatsbürgerrecht und der Mythos der ethnischen Nation', in Manfred Hettling and Paul Nolte (eds), *Nation und Gesellschaft in Deutschland. Historische Essays* (Munich: Piper, 1996), pp. 142-50.

[6] See Kazu Takahashi, 'Cross-border Cooperation among Local Governments between Western and Eastern Europe, in *Roshia nishigawa shûhen ni okeru kannaigai chiiki kyôryoku no kenkyû* (Sapporo: Hokkaidô Daigaku Surabu Kenkyû Sentâ, 1998), pp. 53-82.

collective identities through migration legislation, the regulation of border control, and the provision of security. Likewise, manifold counter-processes of localization and glocalization have mitigated globalization. Some of these processes appear to have even entailed a re-territorialization of institutions of governance.[7] I intend to show that the new forms of migration, regional integration and security thinking are flexibilizing state populations, reducing or even abolishing the border-controlling capability of governments of sovereign states, and increasing the number and capability of institutions that can act as security providers through the inclusion of private Multinational Corporations (MNCs), national as well as international Non-Government Organizations (NGOs) and transnational civil society groups. Migration, regional integration and the widening notion of security appear to contribute to the formation of transnational spaces that place institutions of sovereign states into competition with international public, multinational private and transnational civil society actors.

The making of transnational spaces has fuelled demands that notions of citizenship should be extended to make possible participation in local politics by resident aliens on the one side[8] and, on the other, to link citizenship to universalistic principles from which rights and obligations can be derived

---

[7] For the debate about globalization, localization, glocalization and re-territorialization see Hartmut Behr, 'Transnationale Politik und die Frage der Territorialität', in Karl Schmitt (ed.), *Politik und Raum* (Baden-Baden: Nomos, 2003, pp. 59-78. Behr, *Entterritoriale Politik. Von den internationalen Beziehungen zur Netzwerkanalyse* (Wiesbaden: Verlag für Sozialwissenschaften, 2004). Lothar Brock and Mathias Albert, 'Entgrenzung der Staatenwelt', *Zeitschrift für internationale Beziehungen*, 2 (1995): 259-85. Ludger Pries, 'Transnationale soziale Räume', *Zeitschrift für Soziologie*, 25 (1996): 456-72. Ken'ichi Ohmae, *The Borderless World. Power and Strategy in the Interlinked Economy* (New York: HarperBusiness, 1990). Ulrich Beck, *Was ist Globalisierung?* (Frankfurt: Suhrkamp, 1998). Roland Robertson, *Globalization* (London: Sage, 1992). Susan Strange, *States and Markets* (London: Pinter, 1988).

[8] On the debate on local citizenship see Geoffrey Alderman, J. Leslie and V. Pollman *Governments, Ethnic Groups and Political Representation* (Aldershot: European Science Foundation, 1992). Veit Bader, 'Citizenship and Exclusion', *Political Theory*, 23 (1995): 222-35. Philip Cole, *Philosophies of Exclusion* (Edinburgh: Edinburgh University Press, 2000). Thomas Faist, 'How to Define a Foreigner? The Symbolic Politics of Immigration in German Partisan Discourse. 1978 – 1992', in Martin Baldwin-Edwards and Martin A. Schain (eds), *The Politics of Immigration in Western Europe* (London: Cass, 1994), pp. 50-71. Faist, 'Transnationalization in International Migration. Implications for the Study of Citizenship and Culture', *Ethnic and Racial Studies*, 23 (2000): 189-222. Herman R. van Gunsteren, 'Admission to Citizenship', *Ethics*, 98 (1998): 731-42. José Itzigsohn, 'Immigration and the Boundaries of Citizenship', *International Migration Review*, 34 (2000): 1126-54. Christian Joppke, 'How Immigration is Changing Citizenship', *Ethnic and Racial Studies*, 22 (1999): 629-52. Maxim Silverman, *Deconstructing the Nation. Immigration, Racism and Citizenship in Modern France* (London and New York: Routledge, 1992).

irrespectively of loyalty to a particular institution of statehood.[9] Observers of what has come to be termed 'new immigration' have pointed out that the administrative capability of the governments of sovereign states to control migration has declined as non-state actors such as NGOs and MNCs, civil society groups as well as regional institutions and international organizations have acquired more influence on migration processes.[10] For example, international organizations, such as the International Organization for Migration (IOM) and the International Labour Organization (ILO), have advanced proposals for international regulations apt to reduce the decision-making capability of institutions of sovereign states with regard to immigration rules.

These proposals formed the basis for the international Convention on the Protection of the Rights of All Migrant Workers and Members of Their Families that was approved by the United Nations General Assembly in 1991 and went into force in December 2002. It has been the purpose of this convention to secure the provision of essential human rights to immigrants who are found to have violated

---

[9] See Yasemin Nuhoğlu Soysal, *Limits of Citizenship. Migrants and Postnational Membership of Europe* (Chicago and London: University of Chicago Press, 1994). Soysal, 'Citizenship and Identity. Living in Diasporas in Post-War Europe', *Ethnic and Racial Studies*, 23 (1999): 1-15.

[10] For the debate on New Migration see Pieter Boeles, *Fair Immigration Proceedings in Europe* (The Hague, Boston and London: Nijhoff, 1997). Caroline B. Bretell and James F. Hollifield (eds), *Migration Theory. Talking across Disciplines* (London and New York: Routledge, 2000). Robin Cohen, *Global Diasporas* (London: UCL Press, 1997). Cohen (ed.), *Theories of Migration* (Cheltenham and Brookfields, VT: Elgar, 1997). Wayne A. Cornelius, Philip L. Martin and James F. Hollifield (eds), *Controlling Immigration. A Global Perspective* (Stanford: Stanford University Press, 1994). Nancy Foner, Ruben G. Rumbaut and Steven J. Gold (eds), *Immigration Research for a New Century* (New York: Russell Sage Foundation, 2000). W. T. S. Gould and A. M. Finlay (eds), *Population Migration and the Changing World Order* (Chichester and New York: Wiley, 1994). Kay Hailbronner, David Martin and Hiroshi Motomura, *Immigration Control. The Search for Workable Policies in Germany and the United States* (Providence, RI, and Oxford: Berghahn, 1998). P. Jadoul and E. Mignon (eds), *Le droit des étrangers. Statut, évolution européenne, droits économiques et sociaux* (Brussels: Facultés universitaires Saint-Louis, 1993). Russell King (ed.), *Mass Migrations in Europe. The Legacy and the Future* (London: Belhaven Press, 1993). James Mittelman, 'Production and Migration', in Y. Sakamoto (ed.), *Global Transformation. Challenges to the State System* (Tokyo: United Nations University, 1994), pp. 34-62. Peter H. Schuck and Rainer Münz (eds), *Paths to Inclusion. The Integration of Migrants in the United States and Germany* (New York and Oxford: Berghahn, 1998). Muhammed Abu B. Siddique and Reginald Appleyard, 'International Migration into the 21st Century', in Siddique (ed.), *International Migration into the 21st Century. Essays in Honour of Reginald Appleyard* (Cheltenham and Northampton, MA: Elgar, 2001), pp. 1-13. Myron Weiner, *The Global Migration Crisis. Challenge to States and to Human Rights* (New York: HarperCollins, 1995). Aristide R. Zolberg, 'The Next Waves. Migration Theory for a Changing World', *International Migration Review*, 23 (1989): 403-30.

immigration rules.¹¹ Likewise, regional institutions such as the European Union (EU) have granted the freedom of movement to all nationals of the EU member states while they have simultaneously forced governments of member states to take measures for the rigorous control of immigration from non-EU states.¹² Private NGO's such as Amnesty International have requested the freedom of emigration as a human right, and intellectuals have demanded that the right to emigrate should be supplemented by an internationally guaranteed right to immigrate.¹³ Apparently, a multitude of private organizations exist as part of the so-called 'migration industry' that is capable of bringing almost anyone anywhere for pay, usually outside the bounds of legality.¹⁴ Serious arguments in favour of these activities except for the

---

¹¹ See *The Role of Regional Consultative Processes in Managing International Migration* (Geneva: International Organization for Migration, 2001) The text of the UN convention on undocumented immigration has been edited in *International Migration Review*, 25/4 (1991): 873-919. The same issue of the journal is devoted to discussions about the convention. For related case studies, especially on the problem of undocumented immigration of Mexicans to the USA, see Arthur F. Corwin (ed.), *Immigrants – and Immigrants. Perspectives on Mexican Labor Migration to the United States* (Westport, CT: Greenwood, 1978). Catherine Dauvergne, *Challenges to Sovereignty. Migration Laws for the 21$^{st}$ Century* (New York: UNHCR, 2003). Paul R. Ehrlich, Loy Bilderback and Anne H. Ehrlich, *The Golden Door. International Migration, Mexico and the United States* (New York: Ballantine, 1979). Richard C. Jones (ed.), *Patterns of Undocumented Migration. Mexico and the United States* (Totowa: Rowland & Littleton, 1984). Yann Moulier Boutang, Jean-Pierre Garson and Roxane Silberman, *Economie politique des migrations clandestines de main-d'oeuvre* (Paris: Pulisud, 1986). Gerald C. Neumann, *Strangers to the Constitution. Immigrants, Borders, and Fundamental Law* (Princeton: Princeton University Press, 1996). Suzan Pozo, ed., *Essays on Legal and Illegal Immigration* (Kalamazoo: W. E. Upjohn Institute for Employment Research, 1986). J. Edward Taylor, 'Undocumented Mexico-US Migration and the Return to Households in Rural Mexico', *American Journal of Agricultural Economics*, 69 (1987): 616-38. Previous relevant conventions were the 1961 Convention on the Reduction of Statelessness, the 1965 Convention on the Elimination of all Forms of Racial Discrimination, the 1966 Convention on Civil and Political Rights, the 1979 Convention on the Elimination of all Forms of Discrimination against Women and the 1990 Convention on the Rights of the Children.

¹² Treaty on European Union, Maastricht 7 February 1992, Art. 8a.

¹³ See Anthony Fielding, 'Migration and Culture', in Tony Champion Fielding (ed.), *Migration Processes and Patterns* (2 vols, London: Belhaven Press, 1992), vol. 1, pp. 201-14. Fielding, 'Migrations, Institutions and Politics. The Evolution of European Migration Policies', in Russell King (ed.), *Mass Migrations in Europe. The Legacy and the Future* (London: Belhaven Press, 1993), pp. 40-62. Aristide R. Zolberg, 'International Migration in Political Perspective', in Mary M. Kritz, Charles B. Keely and Silvano M. Tomasi (eds), *Global Trends in Migration* (Staten Island: Center for Migration Research of New York, 1981), pp. 3-27.

¹⁴ For a recent study avoiding to address this difficult issues see Ralph Rotte, 'Immigration Control in United Germany', *International Migration Review*, 34 (2000): 357-89. See also the report by the international Commission on Human Security, *Human Security Now* (New York: Commission on Human Security, 2003), pp. 40-55.

latter are that the notion of citizenship is state-centric, may do little to convey an identity on a person and that, consequently, personhood and the complex of subjective wishes, perceptions and opinions should be taken into consideration rather than purportedly objective standards deemed to inform the administration of citizenship and laid down in passports as official documents.[15]

Migration has thus emerged as a process and an issue that has begun to impact on affairs of the state as well as civil society. Neither are state institutions continuing to be solely legitimized to deal with migration nor has civil society so far acquired sufficient legitimacy to compete with institutions of the state. Because migrants can establish or transform transnational space, state institutions and civil society can be in a position where they compete with regard to migration regulation and frequently take opposing attitudes to migration. The dividing line, which frequently separates institutions of statehood from groups acting as parts of civil society, is state security.[16] Demands have been raised that the subjective

---

[15] See William Rogers Brubaker (ed.), *Immigration and the Politics of Citizenship in Europe and America* (Lanham, MD: University Press of America, 1989). Brubaker, 'Einwanderung und Nationalstaat in Frankreich und Deutschland', *Der Staat*, 28 (1989): 1-30. Brubaker, *Citizenship and Nationhood in France and Germany* (Cambridge, MA, and London: Harvard University Press, 1992) [German version: *Staats-Bürger. Deutschland und Frankreich im historischen Vergleich* (Hamburg: Junius, 1994)]. For a critical review of Brubaker's arguments see Andreas Fahrmeir, *Citizens and Aliens. Foreigners and the Law in Britain and the German States. 1789 – 1870* (Oxford and New York: Berghahn, 2000).

[16] For social science migration definitions see Marianne Amar and Pierre Milza, *L'immigration en France au XXe siècle* (Paris: Colin, 1990). Bernhard Blanke (ed.), *Zuwanderung und Asyl in der Konkurrenzgesellschaft* (Opladen: Leske und Budrich, 1993). Jochen Blaschke, 'Internationale Migration. Ein Problemaufriss', in Manfred Knapp (ed.), *Migration im neuen Europa* (Stuttgart: Steiner, 1994), pp. 23-50. Andreas Bös, 'Weltweite Migration und Schließungstendenzen westlicher Industriegesellschaften', in Lars Clausen (ed.), *Gesellschaften im Umbruch. Verhandlungen des 27. Kongresses der Deutschen Gesellschaft für Soziologie in Halle an der Saale 1995* (Frankfurt and New York: Campus, 1996), pp. 395-412. Joseph H. Carens, 'Migration and Morality. A Liberal Egalitarian Perspective', in Brian Barry and Robert E. Goodni (eds), *Free Movement. Ethical Issues in the Transnational Migration of People and of Money* (New York: Harvester, 1992), pp. 25-47. Stephen Castles and Mark J. Miller, *The Age of Migration* (Basingstoke: Macmillan, 1993) [second edn (Basingstoke, Macmillan, 1998)]. Adrian Favell, *Philosophies of Integration. Immigration and the Idea of Citizenship in France and Britain* (Basingstoke: Macmillan; and New York: St. Martin's Press, 1998). Guy S. Goodwin-Gill, 'Immigration, Nationality and the Standards of International Law', in Ann Dummett (ed.), *Towards a Just Immigration Policy* (London: Cobden Trust, 1986), pp. 3-32. Peter Marschalck, 'Aktuelle Probleme der Migrationsforschung', in Michael Matheus and Walter G. Rödel (eds), *Landesgeschichte und Historische Demographie* (Stuttgart: Steiner, 2000), pp. 177-89. Michael C. May, *Anatomy of a Public Policy. The Reform of Contemporary American Immigration Law* (Westport, CT, and London: Praeger, 1994). Mark J. Miller, 'Towards Understanding State Capacity to Prevent Unwanted Migration. Employer Sanctions Enforcement in France. 1975 – 1990', in Martin Baldwin-Edwards and Martin A. Schain

consciousnesses and intentions of migrants should be given priority over ultimately arbitrary administrative standards.[17]

Finally, the conventional, ultimately nineteenth-century perception that migrations result from certain pull and push factors, which were taken to be measurable, has been called into question. Instead of viewing migrations as linear finite processes connecting a sending and a receiving state, migration systems have been constructed within which migration takes place over longer periods and in various directions. These migration systems can deterritorialize culture, lead to hybrid or multiple identities and define areas within which migration has occurred frequently and has followed established patterns.[18] Within these migration systems, the capability of the involved governments of sovereign states to control migration is declining. This effect of migration systems has been amplified by the fact that migrants have become accustomed to operate within networks that convey a degree of autonomy in migration decision-making.[19] These migration networks provide sources of information about immigration procedures and help accommodating migrants in their target areas. Hence, it is no longer possible to differentiate unequivocally between sending and receiving states and to apply to migrants the ultimately nineteenth-century images of uprootedness (Oscar Handlin). Migration systems and migration networks are interactionistic devices through which migrations can continue indefinitely and without any particular direction, allow migrants a fair degree of autonomy of action and thereby become less subject to government surveillance.

---

(eds), *The Politics of Immigration in Western Europe* (London: Cass, 1994), pp. 140-67. Franz Nuscheler, *Internationale Migration, Flucht und Asyl* (Opladen: Westdeutscher Verlag, 1995). Saskia Sassen, *Migranten, Siedler, Flüchtlinge. Von der Massenauswanderung zur Festung Europa* (Frankfurt: Fischer, 1996) [English version: *Guests and Aliens* (New York: Free Press, 1999)]. Aaron Segal, *An Atlas of International Migration* (London, Melbourne and Munich: Zell, 1993). Raphael-Emmanuel Verhaeren, *Partir? Une théorie économique des migrations internationales* (Grenoble: Presses Universitaires, 1990). Myron Weiner, 'On International Migration and International Relations', *Population and Development*, 11 (1985): 441-55. Hania Zlotnik, 'The Concept of International Migration as Reflected in Data Collection Systems', *International Migration Review*, 21 (1987): 925-45.

[17] Saskia Sassen, *Losing Control? Sovereignty in the Age of Globalization* (New York: Columbia University Press, 1996), pp. 59-99. Weiner, *Global Migration Crisis*. Aristide R. Zolberg, 'The Next Wave. Migration Theory for a Changing World', *International Migration Review*, 23 (1989): 403-30.

[18] Mary M. Kritz, Lean Lim Lin and Hania Zlotnik (eds), *International Migration Systems. A Global Approach* (Oxford: Oxford University Press, 1992). Nikos Papastergiadis, *The Turbulence of Migration. Globalization, Deterritorialization and Hybridity* (Cambridge: Polity Press, 2000).

[19] On migration networks see James F. Fawcett, 'Networks, Linkages and Migration Systems', *International Migration Review*, 23 (1989): 671-80. Mary M. Kritz, Charles B. Keely and Silvano M. Tomasi (eds), *Global Trends in Migration* (Staten Island, NY: Center for Migration Research, 1981).

Simultaneously with 'new migration', the notion of 'new regionalism' has emerged. The notion suggests a shift in theories about regional integration and demands recognition that regional integration may proceed in a variety of ways that differ from the assumptions that had been shared by neo-functionalist theorists of the 1950s and 1960s.[20] 'New regionalism' came into existence in response to manifest regional integration processes which were ongoing or in the making from the 1980s and 1990s when theorists had neither explanations for them nor even analytical tools to study them.[21] 'New regionalism' emerged from the challenge that these new or newly intensified integration processes provided for the making of international theory. Specifically, it turned out to be of importance to take seriously the variety of impacts that regional integration processes might have on the existence and continuity of sovereign states. Whereas old style regional integration theory had focused monistically on the prediction that regional integration processes were to absorb existent sovereign states into larger polities, if they were to be successful, advocates of 'new regionalism' suggested that integration processes might leave existing states untouched, take a variety of directions and that the intended or accomplished results might not be uniform or drawn on one single model only.

Moreover, the late 1980s and early 1990s witnessed the restructuring of security thinking. The 'new security' discourse demanded a substantive widening of the then conventional concept of security to cover not only military and foreign policy issues but also environmental matters, economic, social and cultural factors. Theorists began to suggest that the concept of security should not be limited exclusively to affairs of the state but should include a human dimension and a selection of issues related to personhood or the affairs of the individual.[22] Notably, migration and regional integration have begun to feature within the security discourse.

---

[20] See Ernest B. Haas. *The Uniting of Europe* (Stanford: Stanford University Press, 1958) [second edn (ibid., 1968)]. Karl Wolfgang Deutsch, *Political Community and the North Atlantic Area* (Princeton: Princeton University Press, 1957). Amitai Etzioni, *Political Unification* (New York: Holt, Rinehart and Winston, 1965) [revised version (Huntington, NY: Krieger, 1974)]. Etzioni, *Political Unification Revisited* (Lanham, MD: Lexington Books, 2001). For reviews of these theories see Charles Pentland, *International Theory and European Integration* (London: Faber, 1973). Walter Mattli, *The Logic of Regional Integration* (Cambridge: Cambridge University Press, 1999). James Patrick Sewell, *Functionalism and World Politics* (Princeton: Princeton University Press, 1966). See also below, note 36.

[21] Specifically in Africa and the Asia Pacific where, until then, such processes had not attracted the attention of scholars in the Western world.

[22] For work on human security see below, note 50.

## Craving for Novelty: 'New Migration', 'New Regionalism', 'New Security Thinking'

The common denominator of 'new migration', 'new regionalism' and 'human security' is the focus on the needs and demands of the individual as a person who is on the move, claims participation rights in an area of settlement and is the recipient of security. But the question that needs to be raised at this point is how new these features of 'new migration', 'new regionalism' and 'human security' actually are in the light of a long-term perspective on the history of international theory.[23] Is the migrants' capability to sidetrack government migration restrictions a new phenomenon? Is regional integration in theory and practice peculiar to the twentieth century? Is human security an invention of the 1990s?

With regard to migration, it may well be that persons desperately willing to immigrate into or emigrate from a certain state have at their disposal today a wider range of technological means and organizational strategies than in previous periods. Nevertheless, the principal observation holds true that the general history of government migration control has been the history of its failure. At the very best, governments of sovereign states have, during the nineteenth and twentieth centuries, been able to limit temporarily the numbers of persons crossing international boundaries in the one or the other direction. In a few cases, governments of sovereign states were able to develop regimes of surveillance apt to maintain a degree of border control that was close to perfect. But these states, most notoriously the German Democratic Republic, paid the highest thinkable price for this accomplishment, namely their own destruction. For the surveillance required funds and manpower to an extent that rendered impossible economically sound fiscal policies. When, finally late in 1989, the East German government gave in and allowed border crossing without much control, the irony became recognizable that the number of the persons who sought to emigrate from East Germany immediately was marginal, namely below 5 per cent of the total population. The maintenance of extensive bureaucracies for the management of border control undermined the legitimacy of the government and enhanced the collapse of the state. Without the risk of self-destruction, no government has so far empirically been able to completely suppress undocumented migration. The reason appears to be plain and obvious. Unlike refugees and expellees, migrants move voluntarily across boundaries of recognized significance and must therefore count as determined and highly motivated persons many of whom will have the intellectual capability, economic resources and technical means to carry out their plans in one way or another and sooner or later. Consequently, what is new about 'new immigration' is neither a larger number nor some increased capability of migrants to get where they want to go but the admission by government institutions of the fact that migration control cannot be complete.

---

[23] For a summary see Harald Kleinschmidt, *The Nemesis of Power* (London: Reaktion Books, 2000).

But is this admission the result of a declining capability of government institutions to control migration? If we take a long-term historical perspective, we notice that up until the end of the eighteenth century, governments displayed little interest in curbing migration. Instead, governments were willing to cope with and tolerate situations in which about 10 per cent of the resident population would be constantly on the move,[24] conducted active immigration policies[25] and did little to control emigration beyond often vain attempts to prevent the desertion of trained soldiers.[26] It seems that the demand that governments should control migration was informed by the nineteenth-century European conceptualization of statehood that awarded to governments the task of moulding or maintaining the coherence or integrity of the nation.[27] From the same time, migrants came to be regarded as poor people and were criminalized. Likewise, controlling immigration came to be considered a part of a more comprehensive set of measures designated for the provision of security to the resident population as the group of nationals living within the borders of a state. Correspondingly, these borders were understood as the skin of the body politic[28], whence migration control obtained the status of an instrument for the preservation of the security of the nation through government activities. Nineteenth-century nationalism shaped a political legacy which continued to be characteristic mainly of European states or states shaped on the European tradition. Outside Europe, China, the USA and the former British Dominions, few states developed policies of migration control before the 1990s.

By contrast, is the increasing concern for migrants' motives and goals new? Put differently, have governments only recently become willing to acknowledge the

---

[24] Carsten Küther, *Menschen auf der Straße. Vagierende Unterschichten in Bayern, Franken und Schwaben in der zweiten Hälfte des 18. Jahrhunderts* (Göttingen: Vandenhoeck & Ruprecht, 1983).

[25] Johann Heinrich Gottlob von Justi, *Grundsätze der Policeywissenschaft*, third edn (Göttingen: Dieterich, 1782), pp. 77-84 [reprint (Frankfurt: Keip, 1969)]. For a discussion of this text see Harald Kleinschmidt, *Menschen in Bewegung* (Göttingen: Vandenhoeck & Ruprecht, 2002), pp. 123-31.

[26] See Michael Sikora, *Disziplin und Desertion* (Berlin: Dumblot & Humblot, 1996). For sixteenth- and eighteenth-century attempts by city councils to restrict the emigration of skilled craftsmen see Francesca Trivellato, *La fondamenta dei vetrai* (Rome: Donzelli, 2000). Klaus Jürgen Bade, 'Altes Handwerk, Wanderzwang und Gute Policey. Gesellenwanderung zwischen Zunftökonomie und Gewerbereform', in Bade, *Sozialhistorische Migrationsforschung* (Göttingen: Vandenhoeck & Ruprecht, 2004), pp. 64-5 [first published in *Vierteljahrschrift für Sozial- und Wirtschaftsgeschichte* 69 (1982), pp. 1-37]. Albrecht Bruns, Die Arbeitsverhältnisse der Lehrlinge und Gesellen im städtischen Handwerk in Westdeutschland bis 1800, Ph.D. Thesis (University of Cologne, 1938), p. 119.

[27] Johann Gottlieb Fichte, *Der geschloßne Handelsstaat* (Tübingen: Cotta, 1800), pp. 58-9 [ed. by Reinhard Lauth and Hans Gliwitzky, Fichte, *Werke. 1800 – 1801* (Stuttgart: Frommann-Holzboog, 1988), p. 69 (Fichte. Gesamtausgabe. I/7.)]

[28] Friedrich Ratzel, *Politische Geographie,* third edn, ed. by Eugen Oberhummer (Munich and Berlin: Oldenbourg, 1923), p. 434 [first published (ibid., 1897)].

possibility that there can be a gap between migrants' strategies and government-enforced policies? Much evidence supports the assumption that this is so. First, there is, in the academic world, the widening recognition that generalizing external categories are insufficient means for an understanding of migration. That is to say that the previous positivist conviction has weakened that migration should be defined objectively and authoritatively without recourse to the subjective perceptions of the migrants. More recently, scholars have adopted more circumspect approaches suggesting that precise theory-based definitions cannot be superimposed upon the diversity of migration processes.[29] Post-positivist admission of a lack of certainty in academic research has fully impacted on migration studies calling into question the justice of a procedure by which analysts could claim to be able to deal with migration only from an external, as it were, bird's eye perspective.[30] Increasingly, attention has shifted to the subjective cultures of migrants, and methods pertaining to anthropology as well as history have obtained significance in migration research equal to those of sociology and economics.[31]

This shift includes a focus on migrants' perceptions of borders. If the premise has to be accepted that migrants' perceptions of borders can differ from what governments may take for granted and if migrants' perceptions can be culturally specific and change over time,[32] the consequence is that governments of sovereign states as well as the international community of sovereign states loose part of their legitimacy to request unconditional respect for existing international borders. This is so because migrants may not see any requirement to recognize borders drawn by former colonial powers or through international agreements at the end of wars. The borders would then conflict with conventional habits or daily needs and desires of local population groups in areas where these borders were established. Therefore, international migration renders threadbare international borders as one important definitional element of the state, if the perceptions and attitudes of migrants are taken into consideration. The coming into existence of new states over the past twelve or so years and the plethora of secessionist movements in many parts of the world point towards the salience of taking seriously migrants' perceptions of

---

[29] Among others see Daniel Kubat and Hans-Joachim Hoffmann-Nowotny, 'Migrations. Vers un nouveau paradigme', *Revue internationale des sciences sociales*, 33 (1981): 335-59. Weiner, *Global Migration Crisis*. Virginia Yans-MacLaughlin (ed.), *Immigration Reconsidered. History, Sociology, and Politics* (Oxford: Oxford University Press, 1990).

[30] Michael J. Piore, *Birds of Passage* (Cambridge: Cambridge University Press, 1979).

[31] See Kleinschmidt, *Menschen*, Chapter I. Keiji Maegawa, 'An Anthropological Approach on Social Change in the Modern World-System', *Rekishi Jinrui (History and Anthropology)*, 22 (1994): 49-88. Maegawa, 'From Articulation to Translative Adaptation. Methodological Inquiries into the Localization Process of Western Culture', *Journal of Asian Pacific Communication*, 9 (1999): 131-43.

[32] Among others see Han van Dijk, Dick Foeken and Kiky van Til, 'Population Mobility in Africa', in Mirjam de Bruijn, Rijk van Dijk and Dick Foeken (eds), *Mobile Africa* (Leiden, Boston and Cologne: Brill, 2001), pp. 23-4.

international boundaries rather than continuing to insist that border-making should be recognized as the privilege of governments of sovereign states.

Consequently, the international convention on the rights of migrants signed in 1991[33] obliges governments to grant unalienable human rights to persons who have managed to emigrate from and immigrate into a state without proper documentation. The convention thus forces governments of sovereign states to give proper treatment to persons who have been found to have violated state laws, and therefore reduces the rights of these governments regarding border control. It takes into the fact that empirically, most undocumented migrants eventually accomplish the legalization of their status, of they manage to stay on long enough. These are grim prospects from the point of view of conventional realist international theory but they are not necessarily so from the point of view of constructivism (or for that matter, deconstructivism) as the latter demands recognition of perceptions, motives and intentions of individuals.[34]

Likewise, the question is legitimate what is new about 'new regionalism'. As in the case of 'new migration', the notion of 'new regionalism' represents a theoretical refinement of the transformations that can be sparked by regional integration processes. Which are these transformations? Conventional regional integration theory of the 1950s and 1960s had been state-centric in the sense that it had proceeded from the assumption that regional integration must be launched from the platform of existing sovereign states. Hence, the prospects of regional integration vis-à-vis the believed perseverance of institutions of the sovereign state were a central issue of this brand of regional integration theory.[35] Proponents of this theory assessed the prospects of regional integration most cautiously.[36] In the

---

[33] See above, note 11.

[34] Nicholas Greenwood Onuf, *World of Our Making* (Columbia, SC: University of South Carolina Press, 1989), pp. 33-65.

[35] Especially Ernest B. Haas and Philippe C. Schmitter, 'Economics and Differential Patterns of Political Integration', *International Organization*, 18 (1964): 705-37. Haas, 'The Uniting of Europe and the Uniting of Latin America', *Journal of Common Market Studies*, 5 (1966/67): 315-43.

[36] Leon N. Lindberg and Stuart A. Scheingold (eds), *Regional Integration* (Cambridge, MA: Harvard University Press, 1971). Joseph Samuel Nye, Jr, 'Patterns and Catalysts in Regional Integration', *International Organization*, 19 (1965): 870-9. Nye, *Pan-Africanism and East African Integration* (Cambridge, MA: Harvard University Press, 1965). Philippe C. Schmitter, 'Central American Integration', *Journal of Common Market Studies*, 9 (1970/71): 49-66. Miguel S. Wionczek, 'The Rise and Decline of Latin American Economic Integration', *Journal of Common Market Studies*, 9 (1970/71): 135-74. The same focus on institutions is still to be found in a comparative paper by Joseph M. Grieco, 'Systemic Sources of Variation in Regional Institutionalization in Western Europe, East Asia, and the Americas', in Edward D. Mansfield and Helen V. Milner (eds), *The Political Economy of Regionalism* (New York: Columbia University Press, 1997), pp. 164-87. Grieco ignores non-institutional integration processes and, consequently, arrives at moderately optimistic statements on regional integration in the Americas but very skeptical assessments of regional

world picture shared by these theorists, national identity had a paramount status that would admit only loyalties to the institutions of the national state. Hence the moulding of national identities into regional identities was considered to be a difficult task.

By contrast, recent theorists have taken into account actors other than institutions of the sovereign state, among them local governments,[37] NGOs[38] and MNCs,[39] and have included the broad spectre of institutions and associations thought to represent civil society[40] as private or privately organized agents of regional integration. Moreover, whereas conventional regional integration theory had confined regional integration to processes of institutionalization, recent theory has ranked intergovernmental contractualization equal to institutionalization as means to promote regional integration.[41] The admission that there is a choice of instruments for the promotion of regional integration has had implications for the specification of the goals that were considered to be achievable through regional integration. For contractualization makes it possible to construct regional integration as a process the end of which is not the absorption but the continuation of existing state institutions and the promotion of the ultimately free movement of persons, goods and services across the borders of regionally integrated states. Thus, 'new regionalism' has been constituted as a body of theory that takes into account migration as one factor of regional integration and thereby shifts the focus from

---

integration schemes in Asia and the Pacific.

[37] Harald Kleinschmidt, *Württemberg und Japan* (Stuttgart: Fay, 1991). Kazu Takahashi, 'Political Reorganization and Regional Cooperations in "East Europe"', in Mikiko Iwasaki (ed.), *Varieties of Regional Integration* (Munster and Hamburg: LIT, 1995), pp. 117-35.

[38] See Andrew Hurrell and Benedict Kingsbury (eds), *The International Politics of the Environment* (Oxford: Clarendon, 1992). Vandana Shiva, 'Ecological Balance in an Era of Globalization', in Paul Wapner and Lester Edwin J. Ruis (eds), *Principled World Politics* (Lanham, MD, Boulder, New York and Oxford: Rowman & Littlefield, 2000), pp. 130-49. Oran R. Young, *International Cooperation. Building Regimes for Natural Resources and the Environment* (Ithaca and London: Cornell University Press, 1989).

[39] See Robin Broad and John Cavanagh, 'Global Backlash. Initiatives to Counter Corporate-Led Globalization', in Paul Wapner and Lester Edwin J. Ruis (eds), *Principled World Politics* (Lanham, MD, Boulder, New York and Oxford; Rowman & Littlefield, 2000), pp. 191-207.

[40] For a review see Louise Fawcett and Andrew Hurrell (eds), *Regionalism in World Politics* (Oxford and New York: Oxford University Press, 1995).

[41] Morton Boas, 'Regions and Regionalisation. A Theoretical View', in *Regionalism and Regional Integration in Africa* (Uppsala: Almqvist & Wiksell for Nordiska Afrikainstitutet, 2001), pp. 27-39. Björn Hettne, András Inotai and Osvaldo Sunkel (eds), *Globalism and the New Regionalism* (Basingstoke: Macmillan; and New York: St Martin's Press, 1998). Harald Kleinschmidt, 'A Preparatory for a New Regional Integration Theory', in Mikiko Iwasaki (ed.), *Varieties of Regional Integration* (Munster and Hamburg: LIT, 1995), pp. 47-71. Michael Niemann, *A Spatial Approach to Regionalism in the Global Economy* (Basingstoke: Macmillan; and New York: St Martin's Press, 2000). Raimo Värynen, 'Regionalism Old and New', *International Studies Review*, 5 (2003): 25-51.

concerns of the state to the wishes and desires of the people.⁴²

Whereas the nineteenth-century conceptualization of international borders as the skins of the sovereign states made it possible to juxtapose regional and national identities of population groups, states had hardly been conceived as autonomous entities with no more than necessary interconnections with the rest of the world up until the end of the eighteenth century. Europe then consisted of more than three hundred polities most of which had at least some attributes of sovereignty or could claim to be under the control of sovereign rulers. The populations over which these rulers were invested to rule were made up of multifarious groups whose members shared multiple identities and cultivated multiple loyalties to a variety of institutions and persons.⁴³ Changes of loyalties were frequent, specifically for military personnel so that the degree of control by rulers over the ruled was limited.⁴⁴ Therefore, what is new about 'new regionalism' is not the seemingly sudden appearance of the possibility of multiple identities and loyalties but their recognition by theorists and decision-makers in government.

Finally, what is new about human security thinking? It can be said that much security theory from the 1950s to the 1980s dealt with military and foreign policy in the context of the East-West controversy. This was done so on defendable grounds. For one, the UN charter allocated matters of defence to the competence of the sovereign states.⁴⁵ Moreover, various notions of comprehensive security were deliberated, most prominently in Asia,⁴⁶ and the notion of collective security

---

⁴² Sarah Collinson, *Beyond Borders. West European Policy Towards the 21st Century* (London: Royal Institute of International Affairs, 1993), pp. 100-104. Collinson, *Europe and International Migration,* second edn (London: Royal Institute of International Affairs, 1994), pp. 43-63 [first published (ibid., 1993)]. Geddes, *Immigration,* p. 120. The conventional view was upheld by Mark Gibney ['The Citizenship and Freedom of Movement and the Welfare State', in Gibney (ed.), *Open Borders? Closed Societies? The Ethical and Political Issues* (New York, Westport, CT and London: Greenwood, 1988), p. 34] and Michael Bommes ['Introduction. Immigration and the Welfare State', in Bommes and Andrew Geddes (eds), *Immigration and Welfare. Challenging the Borders of the Welfare State* (London and New York: Routledge, 2000), p. 1] who defended the necessity of immigration control on the grounds of maintaining the stability of states and population groups as nations and democratic legitimacy.

⁴³ For a description see Harald Kleinschmidt, *Geschichte der internationalen Beziehungen* (Stuttgart: Reclam, 1998).

⁴⁴ See Gerhard Oestreich, *Strukturprobleme der frühen Neuzeit,* ed. by Brigitta Oestreich (Berlin: Duncker & Humblot, 1980). Oestreich, *Neostoicism and the Early Modern State,* ed. by Helmut Georg Koenigsberger and Brigitta Oestreich (Cambridge: Cambridge University Press, 1982).

⁴⁵ Charter of the United Nations, Art. 2 (1). For a wide-ranging study see: Sabine Jaberg, *Systeme kollektiver Sicherheit in und für Europa in Theorie, Praxis und Entwurf* (Baden-Baden: Nomos 1998). I owe this reference to the kindness of August Pradetto, Hamburg.

⁴⁶ For the notion of comprehensive security in early postwar Japan see D. A. Baldwin, 'The Concept of Security', *Review of International Studies,* 23 (1997): 5-26. Andrew

formed one basis for the conclusion of the Helsinki Final Act of 1975.[47] Nevertheless, the UN as a whole were not generally regarded nor even accepted as an institution that could alone safeguard the security of its member states.[48]

Against this background, human security thinking has cast into terms the demand that security should be sought and provided for not mainly by institutions of the state through national armies but through international regimes, institutions and organizations which appear to be capable of maintaining the political, social, economic and physical environment in a sustainable equilibrium.[49] While some theorists concerned with new security thinking take the view that this demand can be fulfilled only through the cooperation of state and regional institutions within international organizations,[50] others, including the Commission on Human

---

Bennett and Joseph Lepgold, 'Reinventing Collective Security After the Cold War and Gulf Conflict', *Political Science Quarterly* 108 (1993): 213-37. J.W.M. Chapman, Reinhard Drifte and I.T.M. Gow, *Japan's Quest for Comprehensive Security* (London: Pinter, 1983). Reinhard Drifte, *Sicherheit als Faktor der japanischen Außenpolitik* (Bochum: Brockmeyer, 1981) [English version (Ripe: Saltire, 1983)]. Paul M. Evans, 'Human Security and East Asia", *Journal of East Asian Studies* 4 (2004): 263-84. Liang Pan, Japanese Multipurpose Cooperation with United Nations Organization. 1946-92. Ph.D. Diss. University of Tsukuba, 2000 [to be published by Harvard University Press in 2005]. Kurt W. Radtke and Raymond Feddema (eds), *Comprehensive Security in Asia. Views from Asia and the West on a Changing Security Environment* (Leiden: Brill, 2001). For the different notion of collective security in the 1970s see Helmut Schmidt, *A Grand Strategy for the West* (New Haven: Yale University Press, 1985).

[47] Krisztina Vigh, Helsinki and After. The Invention of the Concept of Human Security. Unpublished M. A. Thesis (University of Tsukuba, Graduate School of International Political Economy, 2000), pp. 49-60.

[48] For the exceptional position that the Japanese government took in its formulation of a UN-centric security policy in the late 1940s and early 1950s, see Pan, Cooperation.

[49] See Richard Falk, *On Humane Governance* (Cambridge: Polity Press, 1995).

[50] Emanuel Adler and Michael Barnett (eds), *Security Communities* (Cambridge: Cambridge University Press, 1998). Muthiah Alagappa, *Asian Security Order* (Stanford: Stanford University Press, 2003). Baldwin, 'Security': 5-26. Morton Bøås, 'Security Communities: Whose Security?', *Cooperation and Conflict*, 35 (2000): 298-309. Ken Booth, 'Security and Emancipation', *Review of International Studies*, 17 (1991): 313-26. Booth, 'Security in Anarchy', *International Affairs*, 63 (1991): 527-45. Booth (ed.), *Statecraft and Security* (Cambridge: Cambridge University Press, 1998). Barry Buzan, 'Societal Security', in Ole Waever, Barry Buzan, M. Kelstrup and P. Lemaitre (eds), *Identity, Migration and the New Security Agenda in Europe* (London: Pinter, 1993). Buzan, 'Rethinking Security After the Cold War', *Cooperation and Conflict*, 32 (1997): 5-28. Buzan, 'The Logic of Regional Security in the Post-Cold War World', in Björn Hettne, András Inotai and Osvaldo Sunkel (eds), *The New Regionalism and the Future of Security and Development* (New York: St. Martin's Press, 2000), pp. 1-25. Buzan and Ole Wæver, *Regions and Powers. The Structure of International Security* (Cambridge: Cambridge University Press, 2003). Björn Hettne, 'Regionalism, Security and Development', in Hettne, András Inotai and Osvaldo Sunkel (eds), *Competing Regionalisms* (Basingstoke: Palgrave, 2001), pp. 7-54. Sören Jesse-Petersen, 'International Migration and Security. A Pragmatic Response', in Kimberly

Security, are convinced that human security emerges primarily from concerns over environmental, economic, political, social and cultural matters over which control cannot be accomplished merely by governments of sovereign states even if they cooperate.[51] The latter theorists thus insist that regional integration, together with the strengthening of international organizations, is a necessary requirement for the provision of human security. The major reason why these theorists take this view is that environmental catastrophes, economic disasters, political problems such as structural injustice, social problems resulting from inequalities and cultural deprivation can trigger migration processes as they may leave to individuals few options other than emigrating from their places of settlement. In including migration into the core factors of insecurity or threats to the stability of particular states and to the sustainability of various aspects of the environment in general, proponents of human security have turned migration from an issue of sociology into one of international relations. The securitization of migration has thus considerably widened the notion of security, likening the concept of human security to the notion of comprehensive security, at least in Asian security discourses. But the question remains whether the late twentieth-century debate about human security can be linked to older notions of security that were in existence elsewhere in the world and more comprehensive than the notion of military security characteristic of the nineteenth and much of the twentieth centuries.

I shall now turn to the problem of how migration and regional integration have emerged as core issues in the security debate and what the gains are that we have when we continue this debate.

---

A. Hamilton (ed.), *Migration and the New Europe* (Washington, DC: Center for Strategic and International Studies, 1994), pp. 1-11. Peter Katzenstein (ed.), *The Culture of National Security* (New York: Columbia University Press, 1996). Keith Krause and Michael C. Williams, 'From Strategy to Security. Foundations of Critical Security Studies', in Krause and Williams (eds), *Critical Security Studies. Concepts and Cases* (London and New York: UCL Press, 1997), pp. 33-61. David A. Lake and Patrick M. Morgan, 'The New Regionalism and Security Affairs', in Lake and Morgan (eds), *Regional Orders* (University Park, PA: Pennsylvania State University Press, 1997), pp. 3-19. Mark J. Miller, 'International Migration and Global Security', in Nana K. Poku and David T. Graham (eds), *Redefining Security. Population Movements and National Security* (Westport, CT: Greenwood Press, 1998), pp. 15-49. Myron Weiner (ed.), *International Migration and Security* (Boulder: Westview Press, 1993).

[51] Commission, *Human Security Now*, pp. 6-7. Mahbub ul-Haq, 'Global Governance for Human Security', in Majid Tehranian (ed.), *Worlds Apart. Human Security and Global Governance* (London and New York: Tauris, 1999), pp. 79-94. Nana K. Poku, Neil Renwick and John Glenn, 'Human Security in a Globalising World', in David T. Graham and Nana K. Poku (eds), *Migration, Globalisation and Human Security* (London and New York: Routledge, 2000), pp. 9-22.

## The Emergence of Migration as a Security Issue

Categorizing migration as a factor of insecurity and a threat to the stability of the world and the states therein is not self-evident. On the one side, it is arguable that governments of states have the task and ought to be given the means to control migration.[52] However, because the history of government attempts to control migration is the history of its failure, there seems to be a lack of aptitude of government institutions to accomplish this task. On the other side, most voluntary migrants move in perfect legality and often with encouragement from government institutions. Moreover, most undocumented immigrants, that is, persons who are found to have violated immigration laws, eventually accomplish government recognition of their status as immigrants. Obviously, governments, specifically those subscribing or bound to subscribe to principles of liberalism, are under constraints not to fully exploit their legal rights to control migration.[53] The implication seems to be that the formulation and execution of anti-migration policies, justified on the grounds that migration is a factor of insecurity, follow from the specific mindsets of those who devise these policies and are informed by peculiar attitudes towards and perceptions of migration. These government attitudes and perceptions are frequently in conflict with the attitudes and perceptions of the migrants themselves.[54]

The twentieth century witnessed and the present is witnessing circumstances under which solitary migrants or small groups appear most frequent as actors in migration processes, and there is no obvious reason why these migrants should be less risk-prone today than in previous periods. Hence, the expectation is sound that there will be many migrants who will do their very best to accomplish the goals that they have set for themselves by whatever means and sooner or later even if they have to evade or ignore existing restrictions. This tendency seems to apply to migrants of various statuses and degrees of financial affluence. Specifically, it can be shown to have applied to people who were categorized by the authorities as

---

[52] Particularly from the point of view of contractualist theories of legitimacy. See, for an example, the British Alien Act of 1905 [5 Edward VII, c. 13], printed in: Myer Jack Landa, *The Alien Problem and Its Remedy* (London: P.S. King, 1911), pp. 299-308.

[53] For a review of immigration restriction policies see Gary P. Freeman, 'Can Liberal States Control Unwanted Migration?', in Mark J. Miller (ed.), *Strategies for Immigration Control* (Thousand Oaks, London and New Delhi: Sage, 1994), pp. 17-30. James F. Hollifield, *Immigrants, Markets and States* (Cambridge, MA: Harvard University Press, 1992), pp. 214-32. Mark J. Miller, 'Towards Understanding State Capacity to Prevent Unwanted Migration. Employer Sanctions Enforcement in France, 1975 – 1990', in Martin Baldwin-Edwards and Martin A. Schain (eds), *The Politics of Immigration in Western Europe* (London: Cass, 1994), pp. 140-67. Rotte, 'Immigration Control'. Christian Joppke, 'Why Liberal States Accept Unwanted Immigration', *World Politics*, 50 (1998): 266-93. Myron Weiner, 'Ethics, National Sovereignty and the Control of Immigration', *International Migration Review*, 30 (1996): 171-97.

[54] Kleinschmidt, *Menschen*.

belonging to the poor. There are records of eighteenth-century beggars who were repeatedly expelled from several places and still were able to lead a relatively decent life with some degree of business success.[55] Even threats to punish returning beggars seem to have had little effect of keeping them at bay.[56] Likewise, bureaucratic policies aimed at criminalizing migrants were hardly preventive of migration. Instead, migrants became wary of society, tried their utmost to avoid police and made every effort to stay clean rather than stay at places that they considered unfavourable for themselves. Migration hump theorists may be correct in predicting that the willingness to migrate increases when income rises above levels of extreme poverty.[57] Migrants' willingness and ability to evade administrative prohibitions will thus be far more substantial than the available means of bureaucratic control. There is no reason to justify the claim that bureaucratic migration control has become more effective or efficient since the end of the eighteenth century.

However, government institutions have frequently resorted to simplistic or simplifying perceptions of migrants over the past two hundred or so years. Migration policies have sought to categorize migrants rather than understand or recognize their specific motives and goals. Ever since the nineteenth century, governments in Europe, North America and the European settlements in the South Pacific have applied heterostereotypes which described migrants as lonely, marginal, uneducated, lazy, disobedient, poor people who were expected to commit themselves to unlawful actions. The primary source for these heterostereotypes has been a social theory, widespread in nineteenth-century Europe, according to which residentialism was taken to be the seemingly natural condition of life.[58] Within the bounds of this social theory, migrants were identified as persons who renounced

---

[55] Among others, see Thomas McStay Adams, *Bureaucracy and Beggards. French Social Policy in the Age of the Enlightenment* (New York and Oxford: Oxford University Press, 1990). Olwen H. Hufton, *The Poor in Eighteenth-Century France* (Oxford: Oxford University Press, 1974). Ingeborg Titz-Matuszak, 'Mobilität der Armut', *Plesse-Archiv*, 24 (1988): 9-338. Otto Ulbricht, 'Die Welt eines Bettlers um 1775', *Historische Anthropologie*, 2 (1994): 379-98.

[56] Archiv der Hansestadt Lübeck, Abt. 268, No 650.

[57] Lucy Luck, 'A Little of My Life', *London Mercury*, 13 (1925/26): 354-73. For a study of the behaviour of poor migrants see Edith Saurer, *Straße, Schmuggel, Lottospiel* (Göttingen: Vandenhoeck & Ruprecht, 1989), pp. 137-216. Elisabeth Schepers, 'Regieren durch Grenzsetzungen. Struktur und Grenzen des Bettelrechtes in Bayern im 16. und 17. Jahrhundert', in Wolfgang Schmale and Reinhard Stauber (eds), *Menschen und Grenzen in der Frühen Neuzeit* (Berlin: Spitz, 1998), pp. 244-6. For migration hump theory see: Peter Stalker, *International Migration* (London: New Internationalist Publications, 2001), p. 129. I am grateful to Dr Eimi Watanabe for this reference.

[58] Johann Baptista Fallati, 'Die Genesis der Völkergesellschaft', *Zeitschrift für die gesamte Staatswissenschaft*, 1 (1844): 183-4. Albert Schäffle, *Bau und Leben des socialen Körpers* (6 vols, Tübingen: Mohr, 1881), vol. 4, pt 2, pp. 216-9. Herbert Spencer, *Principles of Sociology* (3 vols, New York and London: Appleton, 1910), vol. 1, pp. 449-53.

residentialism and preferred to live either outside society as permanent migrants or switch membership from one to another society.[59] The former decision was construed as unnatural at best and criminal in the worst case, the latter decision was understood as evidence for lack of loyalty.[60] These government-sponsored heterostereotypes created negative images about migration and migrants and demanded the search of reasons of migration. Already late in the nineteenth century, social scientists began to devise research projects designed to determine migration factors. Rather than investigating why people stay, the sole heuristic question leading these projects was why people move.[61] Moreover, the heterostereotypes were to be applied generically to all migrants, irrespective of what may have been true in a given case. The perception of migration as a threat to the stability of the world and the states therein has thus been informed by the residentialist bias of nineteenth-century social theory but has little connection with the perceptions and attitudes of the migrants themselves. How did the gap between migrants' attitudes and perceptions and government perceptions on migrants come about?

Obviously, answers to this question depend on the specific socio-cultural systems within or in between which migrations have taken place. Within a European setting, it is remarkable that a persistent government migration policy has been on record only since the late seventeenth century. Up until the end of the seventeenth century, territorial rulers and governments of towns and cities usually abstained from efforts to control migration although they might on occasions resort to measures of expulsion or try to prevent emigration. At times of crisis, such as during the period of the Black Death during the middle of the fourteenth century, an estimated 20 per cent of local populations were permanently on the move where they joined professional travellers such as merchants, apprentices, roving bandits, unpaid mercenaries and regular warrior bands. The image of a 'feudal' population confined to the soil belongs to the realm of nineteenth-century academic mythology and has nothing to do with the Middle Ages and the early modern period.[62]

---

[59] Theodor Bödiker 'Die Einwanderung und Auswanderung des Preußischen Staaates', *Preußische Statistik*, 26 (1874): I-IX. Fritz Joseephy, *Die deutsche überseeische Auswanderung seit 1871 unter besonderer Berücksichtigung der Auswanderung nach den Vereinigten Staaten von Amerika* (Berlin: Welt-Verlag, 1912). Wilhelm Mönckmeier, *Die deutsche überseeische Auswanderung* (Jena: Fischer, 1912).

[60] For such attitudes in Germany see C. Herzog, 'Was fließt den Vereinigten Staaten durch die Einwanderung zu, und was verliert Deutschland durch die überseeische Auswanderung?', *(Schmollers) Jahrbuch für Gesetzgebung, Verwaltung und Volkswirtschaft*, 9 (1885): 37. For the USA see Edward Young, *Special Report on Immigration* (Washington: GPO, 1872). Henry Pratt Fairchild, 'The Restriction of Immigration', *American Journal of Sociology*, 17 (1912): 637-46 [newly ed. by John J. Appel, *The New Immigration* (New York: Pitman, 1971), pp. 184-193]. Fairchild, *The Melting Pot Mistake* (Boston: Little, Brown & Co, 1926) [reprint (New York: Arno Press, 1977)].

[61] Eugen von Philippovich (ed.), *Auswanderung und Auswanderungspolitik in Deutschland* (Leipzig: Duncker & Humblot, 1892).

[62] Gerhard Jaritz and Albert Müller (eds), *Migration in der Feudalgesellschaft* (Frankfurt

The revocation by Louis XIV in 1685 of the toleration edict of Nantes of 1589 indicated the beginning of a change of attitudes towards migration. This was so because the plight of the Huguenots triggered positive responses from territorial rulers elsewhere in Europe. Some of these rulers, such as the Elector of Brandenburg, later King in Prussia, and the Landgrave of Hesse-Kassel, invited the expellees to settle in their lands at dedicated places and gave them special privileges. These rulers did so because of a cluster of motives among which political digs at the rule of Louis XIV, anti-Catholic religious partisanship and a deliberate population policy featured most prominently.[63]

Only the third motive deserves closer scrutiny in the present context. The emergence of a systemic population policy has to be seen against the background of contemporary demographic and political theories that formulated hypotheses about population change. Throughout the seventeenth and much of the eighteenth centuries, these theories were drawn on the Bible. According to the Book of Genesis, all humankind had descended from the primordial couple through Noah and his sons. The biblical creation myth thus supported the assumption that all humankind had spread across the world through migration since the Flood. As the mythology contained in the Book of Genesis was taken for granted, human beings all over the world had to descend from Noah. The theorists attempting to solve this problem gleaned from the Book of Genesis the argument that the earliest of Noah's descendants had been gifted with extreme longevity and superfecundity so that they could accomplish unproportionately high population growth rates. The rapid growth appeared to allow the dissemination of the human species through migration. With the spreading of human settlements all across the inhabitable surface of the earth, longevity and superfecundity would decline together with the growth rate and accomplish a stability of populations through a balance of birth and death rates. This was the theoretical postulate that, among others, the Berlin

---

and New York: Campus, 1988).

[63] Among others see Johannes E. Bischoff, 'Hugenotten und Hugenotten-Nachkommen als städtische Minderheiten', in Bernhard Kirchgässner and Fritz Reuter (eds), *Städtische Randgruppen und Minderheiten* (Sigmaringen: Thorbecke, 1986), pp. 115-28. Jon Butler, *The Huguenots in America. A Refugee People in New World Society* (Cambridge, MA: Harvard University Press, 1982). Heinz Duchhardt (ed.), *Der Exodus der Hugenotten. Die Aufhebung des Edikts von Nantes 1685 als europäisches Ereignis* (Cologne and Vienna: Böhlau, 1985). Richard M. Golden (ed.), *The Huguenot Connection. The Edict of Nantes, Its Revocation, and Early French Migration to South Carolina* (Dordrecht and Boston: Kluwer, 1988). Frédéric Hartweg and Stefi Jersch-Wenzel (eds), *Die Hugenotten und das Refuge* (Berlin: de Gruyter, 1990). Michelle Magdeleine and Rudolf von Thadden (eds), *Die Hugenotten* (Munich: Piper, 1985). Ingrid Mittenzwei (ed.), *Hugenotten in Brandenburg-Preußen* (Berlin: Akademie-Verlag, 1987). Margret Zumstroll, 'Die Gründung von "Hugenottenstädten" als wirtschaftspolitische Maßnahme eines merkantilistischen Landesherren. Am Beispiel Kassel und Karlshafen', in Volker Press (ed.), *Städtewesen und Merkantilismus in Mitteleuropa* (Cologne and Vienna: Böhlau, 1983), pp. 156-221.

Protestant church superintendent Johann Peter Süßmilch[64] upheld in the middle of the eighteenth century.[65]

However, this postulate militated against empirical evidence that was recognized already in the late seventeenth as displaying declining populations. Theorists concluded that the postulate of theory remained unfulfilled, not because the information provided by the Bible should have been wrong but because many individuals through carelessness or on purpose ended their lives prematurely or were put to death before their time through natural disasters, war or other acts of human violence. Among other theorists, the Prussian cameralist Johann Heinrich Gottlob Justi derived the practical advice from their observations that rulers should devise active population policies to as to end the population decline and accomplish a stable population in their territories. They demanded that the population decline should be reversed through proper education, the prevention of epidemics, the improvement of health care, the avoidance or at least the limitation of war and, when all these measures proved insufficient, a policy of immigration stimulation.[66] It was the latter of these demands that was taken up eagerly by rulers who used domestic political crises in territories of other rulers to lure qualified migrants into their territories by granting them special privileges of the freedom of religious practice, exempting them from taxation and allocating to them land for settlement at favourable conditions.[67]

---

[64] Johann Peter Süßmilch, *Die göttliche Ordnung in den Veränderungen des menschlichen Geschlechts,* third edn (3 vols, Berlin: Buchhandlung der Realschule, 1765), vol. 1, pp. 13-4, 17, 19-20, 25-6, 35, 39, 416-8, 556-73 [reprint, ed. by Jürgen Cromm (Göttingen: Cromm, 1988)].

[65] On Süßmilch and the history of demography see Herwig Birg (ed.), *Ursprünge der Demographie in Deutschland. Leben und Werk Johann Peter Süssmilchs* (Frankfurt and New York: Campus, 1986). Birg, 'Johann Peter Süßmilch und Thomas Robert Malthus', in Rainer Mackensen, Lydia Thill-Thoner and Ulrich Stark (eds), *Bevölkerungsentwicklung und Bevölkerungstheorie in Geschichte und Gegenwart* (Frankfurt and New York: Campus, 1989), pp. 53-76. Jacqueline Hecht, *'L'ordre divin' aux origines de la démographie,* vol. 1: Biographie, Correspondence, Bibliographie (Paris: Institut national d'études démographiques, 1979). Johann Christian Förster, *Nachricht von dem Leben und den Verdiensten des Oberconsistorialraths Johann Peter Süßmilchs* (Berlin: Buchhandlung der Realschule, 1768) [reprint, ed. by Jürgen Cromm (Göttingen: Cromm, 1988)]. R. A. Horvák, 'L'Ordre divin de Süssmilch', *Population*, 1 (1962): 267-8. Horvák, 'Le bicentenaire de la mort de Johann Peter Süssmilch (1707 – 1767) et la discipline statistique', *Revue de l'Institut Internationale de Statistique*, no 1 (1969): 36-44. Wolfgang Neugebauer, 'Johann Peter Süßmilch. Geistliches Amt und Wissenschaft im friderizianischen Berlin', *Berlin in Geschichte und Gegenwart. Jahrbuch des Landesarchivs Berlin* (1985): 33-68.

[66] Justi, *Grundsätze.*

[67] On Justi and the formulation of population policy in the eighteenth century see Otto Friedrich Bollnow, 'Die philosophischen Grundlagen der Staats- und Wirtschaftslehren bei Johann Heinrich Gottlob Justi', *Finanz-Archiv,* N. F., vol. 8 (1941): 381-402. Horst Dreitzel, 'Justis Beitrag zur Politisierung der deutschen Aufklärung', in Horst E. Bödeker and Ulrich Herrmann (eds), *Aufklärung als Politisierung – Politiserung der Aufklärung* (Hamburg:

Moreover, rulers' toleration of a substantive degree of migration was supported by contractualist theories of the legitimacy of government. These theories were drawn on the assumption that the population of a territory constituted one or several political groups with social bonds and ties that were strong enough to act as the conveyors of legitimacy to their government through some hypothetical contract. Contractualism had been advocated as a theory of legitimacy from the early fourteenth century[68] but it was only in the course of the eighteenth century that migrations came to be understood as acts of voting by the feet to the advantage of the rulers in whose territories the number of immigrants exceeded the number of emigrants.[69] Consequently, rulers could enlist groups of new immigrants simply as an addition to the groups of subjects on territories under their control. The absence of nationalism prevented rulers and political theorists from categorizing immigrants as a threat to the security of their territories and jeopardy of national identity.

Nevertheless, the degree of success of active immigration policies remained behind the expectations of the theorists. For obvious reasons, active immigration policies were not feasible without toleration of emigration. On balance, immigration rates as well as emigration rates remained high in many territories, so that populations were in fact unstable rather than stable and difficult to be subjected to efficient and sustained bureaucratic control. A strong general population increase began to occur only towards the end of the eighteenth century and was due to factors that had not been considered by demographers of the time.[70]

New attitudes developed at the turn of the nineteenth century and were closely intertwined with the rise of nationalism. To be sure, throughout the nineteenth century governments continued to tolerate emigration,[71] at times even using

---

Meiner, 1987), pp. 158-77. Ferdinand Frensdorff, *Über das Leben und die Schriften des Nationalökonomen Johann Heinrich Gottlob Justi* (Göttingen: Akademie der Wissenschaften, 1903) [reprint (Glashütten: Auvermann, 1970)]. Harm Klueting, *Die Lehre von der Macht der Staaten* (Berlin: Duncker & Humblot: 1986). Marcus Overt, *Die naturrechtliche 'politische Metaphysik' bei Johann Heinrich Gottlob von Justi (1717 – 1771)* (Frankfurt and Bern: Lang, 1992). Justus Remer, *Johann Heinrich Gottlob Justi, ein deutscher Volkswirt des 18. Jahrhunderts* (Stuttgart and Berlin: Kohlhammer, 1938).

[68] Engelbert of Admont, 'De ortu, progressu et fine regnorum et praecipue regni seu imperii Romani', cap. 2, ed. by Melchior Goldast of Haiminsfeld, *Politica imperialia* (Frankfurt: Bringer, 1614), p. 755. John Quidort of Paris, *De potestate regali et papali,* cap. I, ed. by Fritz Bleienstein (Stuttgart: Kohlhammer, 1969), pp. 71-5. Marsilius of Padua, *Defensor pacis,* lib. I, cap. 15, lib I, cap. 16, ed. by Richard Scholz (2 vols, Hanover: Hahn, 1932), vol. 1, pp. 84-112 (Monumenta Germaniae Historica, Fontes iuris Germanici antiqui in usum scholarum separatim editi. 7.)

[69] Justi, *Grundsätze*.

[70] Arthur Erwin Imhof, *Von der unsicheren zur sicheren Lebenszeit* (Darmstadt: Wissenschaftliche Buchgesellschaft, 1988).

[71] Mönckmeier, *Auswanderung*, pp. 229-30, gives a list of years in which, in his view, nineteenth-century governments of German states granted the freedom of emigration.

emigration as a strategy of poverty alleviation.[72] But migration policy became increasingly interconnected with social and defence policy. The reason was that, in the course of the century, the task of providing social welfare shifted from parishes and other local communities to the central governments of states. Necessarily, already up until the end of the eighteenth century, local communities had tried to reduce the burden of social welfare provision by forcing beggars out and trying to avoid the settlement of poor immigrants.[73] But rulers had been able to counterbalance such measures by allocating to immigrants newly founded settlements in suburban or even remote areas.[74] At the central or national level, provision of social welfare became a means to strengthen national identity in the course of the nineteenth century.[75] The conversion of social policy from an instrument of poverty alleviation to a means proffering national identity entailed the consequence that a debate arose whether and, if so, to what extent, immigrants should be able to receive social welfare benefits.[76]

---

[72] See Charlotte Erickson, *Leaving England. Essays on British Emigration in the Nineteenth Century* (Ithaca and London: Cornell University Press, 1994).

[73] K. L. Ay, 'Unehrlichkeit, Vagantentum und Bettelwesen in der vorindustriellen Gesellschaft', *Jahrbuch des Instituts für deutsche Geschichte*, 8 (1979): 13-38. A. L. Beier, 'Vagrants and the Social Order in Elizabethan England', *Past and Present*, 64 (1974): 3-29. Beier, *Masterless Men. The Vagrancy Problem in England. 1560 – 1640* (London and New York: Methuen, 1986). Martin Dinges, *Stadtarmut in Bordeaux. 1525 – 1675* (Bonn: Bouvier, 1988). Bronislaw Geremek, 'Criminalité, vagabondage, pauperisme. La marginalité à l'aube des temps modernes', *Revue d'histoire moderne et contemporaine*, 21 (1974): 337-75. František Graus, 'Randgruppen der städtischen Gesellschaft im Spätmittelalter', *Zeitschrift für historische Forschung*, 8 (1981): 385-437. Bernd-Ulrich Hergemöller (ed.), *Randgruppen der spätmittelalterlichen Gesellschaft* (Warendorf: Fahlbusch, 1990). Hergemöller, '"Randgruppen" im späten Mittelalter. Konstruktion – Dekonstruktion – Rekonstruktion', in Hans-Werner Goetz (ed.), *Die Aktualität des Mittelalters* (Bochum: Winkler, 2000), pp. 165-90. Eric John Hobsbawm, *Social Bandits and Primitive Rebels* (Cambridge: Cambridge University Press, 1959). Robert Jütte, *Poverty and Deviance in Early Modern Europe* (Cambridge: Cambridge University Press, 1994) [German version: *Arme, Bettler, Beutelschneider. Eine Sozialgeschichte der Armut* (Weimar: H. Böhlau, 2000)]. John Pound, *Poverty and Vagrancy in Tudor England* (London: Longman, 1971). Martin Rheinheimer, *Arme, Bettler und Vaganten. Überleben in der Not. 1450 – 1850* (Frankfurt: Fischer, 2000). Bernd Roeck. *Außenseiter, Randgruppen, Minderheiten* (Göttingen: Vandenhoeck & Ruprecht, 1993). Ernst Schubert, *Fahrendes Volk im Mittelalter* (Bielefeld: Verlag für Regionalgeschichte, 1995). Alexandre Vexliard, *Introduction à la sociologie du vagabondage* (Paris: Ribière, 1956).

[74] On Huguenot policy see above, note 63.

[75] Gerhald Albert Ritter (ed.), *Vom Wohlfahrtsausschuß zum Wohlfahrsstaat* (Cologne: Markus, 1973). Ritter, *Sozialversicherung in Deutschland und England* (Munich: Beck, 1983) [English version (Oxford: Berg, 1986)]. Ritter, *Der Sozialstaat* (Munich: Oldenbourg, 1989) [second edn (ibid., 1991)].

[76] For example the issue of Polish immigrants in the German Empire. See Bade, *Sozialhistorische Migrationsforschung*, pp. 89-388. Knuth Dohse, *Ausländische Arbeiter*

Moreover, nineteenth-century theorists such as Carl von Clausewitz understood nations as defence communities of settled people and argued that wars could only be fought with success if the nations were united behind their armed forces. The image of the 'nations in arms' as contending parties in warfare supported the categorization of war as a 'struggle for survival of nations'.[77] Within the confines of this theory, emigration meant a loss of defence capability, whereas immigration could be judged as a process of the admission into the state of people whose

---

*und bürgerlicher Staat. Genese und Funktion von staatlicher Ausländerpolitik und Ausländerrecht. Vom Kaiserreich bis zur Bundesrepublik Deutschland* (Königstein: Athenaeum, 1981). William W. Hagen, *Germans, Poles, Jews. The Nationality Conflict in the Prussian East. 1772 – 1914* (Chicago and London: University of Chicago Press, 1980). Ulrich Herbert, *Geschichte der Ausländerbeschäftigung in Deutschland. 1880 – 1980* (Berlin and Bonn: Bouvier, 1986). Christoph Kleßmann,: *Polnische Bergarbeiter im Ruhrgebiet. 1870 – 1945* (Göttingen: Vandenhoeck & Ruprecht, 1978). Kleßmann, 'Polish Miners in the Ruhr District. Their Social Situation and Trade Union Activity', in Dirk Hoerder (ed.), *Labor Migration in the Atlantic Economies* (Westport, CT, and London: Greenwood, 1985), pp. 253-75 [first published in: Hans Mommsen and Ulrich Borsdorf (eds), *Glückauf Kameraden! Die Bergarbeiter und ihre Organisationen in Deutschland* (Cologne: Bund-Verlag, 1979)]. John J. Kulczycki, 'Scapegoating the Foreign Worker. Job Turnover, Accidents, and Diseases among Polish Coal Miners in the German Ruhr. 1871 – 1914', in Camille Guerin Gonzales and Carl Strickwerda (eds), *The Policies of Immigrant Workers* (New York and London: Routledge, 1993), pp. 133-52. Hans Linde, 'Die soziale Problematik der masurischen Agrargesellschaft und die masurische Einwanderung in das Emscherrevier', in Hans-Ulrich Wehler (ed.), *Moderne deutsche Sozialgeschichte* (Cologne: Kiepenheuer & Witsch, 1968), pp. 456-70. Ewa Morawska, 'Labor Migrations of Poles in the Atlantic Economy. 1880 – 1914', *Comparative Studies in Society and History*, 31 (1989): 237-72 [reprint in Dirk Hoerder and Leslie Page Moch (eds), *European Migrants* (Evanston: Northwestern University Press, 1996), pp. 170-208]. Richard Charles Murphy, Polish Immigrants in Bottrop. 1891 – 1933. Ph.D. Diss., typescript (University of Iowa, 1977). Murphy, 'Polnische Berarbeiter im Ruhrgebiet. Das Beispiel Bottrop', in Hans Mommsen and Ulrich Borsdorff (eds), *Glückauf Kameraden! Die Bergarbeiter und ihre Organisationen in Deutschland* (Cologne: Bund-Verlag, 1979), pp. 89-108. Murphy, *Guestworkers in the German Reich. A Polish Community in Wilhelmian Germany* (New York: Knopf, 1983). Krystyna Murzynowska, *Polskie wychodzstwo zarotkow w zagłebin Ruhry. 1880 – 1914* (Wrocław: Ossolineum, 1972) [German edition (Dortmund: Harenberg, 1979)]. Robert E. Rhoades, 'Foreign Labour in German Industrial Capitalism. 1871 – 1978', *American Ethnology*, 5 (1978): 553-73. Stanislaus T. Ruziewicz, *Le problème de l'émigration polonaise en Allemagne* (Paris: Sirey, 1930). Adelheid von Saldern, 'Polnische Arbeitsmigration im Deutschen Kaiserreich – Menschen zweiter und dritter Klasse', in Hans-Heinrich Nolte (ed.), *Deutsche Migrationen* (Munster and Hamburg: LIT, 1996), pp. 102-13. Hans-Ulrich Wehler, 'Die Polen im Ruhrgebiet bis 1918', in Wehler (ed.), *Moderne deutsche Sozialgeschichte* (Cologne: Kiepenheuer & Witsch, 1968), pp. 437-55. Arthur Young, Bismarck's Policy towards the Poles. 1870 – 1890. Ph.D. Diss. typescript (University of Chicago, 1970).

[77] Carl von Clausewitz, *Vom Kriege,* Teil I, Buch I, Kap. III (Berlin: Dümmler, 1832) [newly ed. (Berlin: Ullstein, 1980), pp. 52-72].

trustworthiness in military matters had not been tested. Emigration could be admitted only if the emigrants could be classed as poor 'undesirables',[78] whereas immigration was to be fended off so as to prevent the settlement of allegedly unreliable subjects.[79]

The demand following from both perceptions was that governments should control migration in order to guarantee the domestic stability and the international security of the nation in its state. Toward the end of the nineteenth century, one of the driving forces behind European colonial expansion resulted from the attempt to channel overseas emigration into areas over which the one or the other European government held some degree of – usually illegitimate – control. Governments with colonial aspirations at the turn of the twentieth century competed over their relative success in the accomplishment of this goal because resettling emigrants in colonial dependencies did not have to be counted as a statistical loss of population. As the German government displayed little success in directing 'emigration flows' to dependencies under its control, it appeared to be losing out in its rivalry with the more successful British government. In 1913, a German colonial administrator listed merely 24,389 Europeans in the German dependencies (Qingdao excepted).[80] The larger the state, the more theorists and practical political decision-makers were ready to assume that nations should be unified so as to convey the image of military strength to the outside world. In the view of these theorists, only small states, such as Belgium or Switzerland, could afford to comprise a heterogeneous population, rely solely on production and trade as sources of revenue and dispense of the sizeable armed forces.[81] By contrast, big states were credited with 'security demands' that were judged as accomplishable solely through a united population and policies of rigid migration control. Migration was a security threat against the backdrop of these theories.[82]

The consequence of these government perceptions on migration was that the gap widened between attitudes of governments towards migrants and attitudes of migrants themselves. Governments tended to downgrade the social status and economic achievements of emigrants whereas migrants themselves did not necessary regard extreme poverty as incentives for emigration[83] and made strong efforts to remain within the bounds of legality.[84] Emigrants often responded with

---

[78] *Times* 1870. Quoted from: Charles Manning Hope Clark (ed.), *Select Documents in Australian History. 1851 – 1900* (Sydney: Angus & Robertson, 1955), p. 247.

[79] Wilhelm Rüstow, *Die Grenzen der Staaten* (Zurich: Schulheiss, 1868), pp. 1-5.

[80] Bade, *Sozialhistorische Migrationsforschung*, p. 141. Sönke Neitzel, *Weltmacht oder Untergang* (Paderborn, Munich, Vienna and Zurich: Schöningh, 2000). Ute Mehnert, *Deutschland, Amerika und die 'Gelbe Gefahr'* (Stuttgart: Steiner, 1995).

[81] Rüstow, *Grenzen*.

[82] John Frederick Maurice, *The Balance of Military Power in Europe* (Edinburgh and London: Blackwood, 1888).

[83] See Günter Moltmann (ed.), *Aufbruch nach Amerika* (Tübingen: Wunderlich, 1979) [new edn (Stuttgart: Metzler, 1989), pp. 97, 100, 126-7, 175-87].

[84] Luck, 'Life'.

sensitivity to political pressure and excessive taxation and chose to go when they saw no prospect of improvement. Or migrants simply decided to move without having a particular incentive to do so while governments tried to downscale political incentives.[85] Governments thus took the point of view that migration is a type of action that deviates from the assumed norm that people should stay where they were. This residentialist attitude was informed by nineteenth-century evolutionist social theory but not in conformity with the perceptions and attitudes of migrants.[86] Contrary to historical evidence, social theorists in the academic world as well as political decision-makers in government took for granted a vision of world history according to which mass migration was a phenomenon of relatively recent times.[87] Little has changed in the assessment of long-distance as well as local migration in the context of security policy ever since then.[88] Realist theorists of the state as an integrated actor have relied on nineteenth-century assumptions in so far as they have classed governments of sovereign states as prime actors in international relations and have restricted security theory to a matter of state policy.[89]

Obviously, only a small part of all migration takes place across international boundaries. But international migration epitomizes the predicament of the state as long as it remains defined in accordance with realist theories. This is so because realism takes for granted a degree of unity of states so that they can – for the purposes of theory – speak with one voice and appear as consolidated actors.[90] But international migration jeopardizes this supposition because it displays the populations of states as heterogeneous, diverse and disunited. In other words, with the paradigm change of migration studies the wisdom of nineteenth-century social theory has been challenged[91] and international migration has ceased to be a security issue in confinement to the state. Rather than using force to secure existing boundaries most of which are arbitrary anyway and can, if understood as contingent products of history, hardly be expected to find general acceptance and approval, it is more salient for governments of states to support schemes of regional integration within areas in which migration is found to have occurred most frequently over a longer period of time. Under this premise, human security would be extendable to those who move and those who stay. The question then remains how and to what extent regional integration can advance human security.

---

[85] Moltmann, *Aufbruch*.
[86] Schäffle, *Bau*.
[87] On the German debate of nationality law 1912/13 see Kleinschmidt, *Menschen*.
[88] Colin G. Pooley and Jean Turnbull, *Migration and Mobility in Britain since the Eighteenth Century* (London: UCL Press, 1998).
[89] On the history of realism see Kleinschmidt, *Nemesis*.
[90] Kenneth Neal Waltz, *Theory of International Politics* (Reading, MA: Addison Wesley, 1979), pp. 161-2.
[91] See above, note 29.

## Regional Integration as an Impediment of Security?

I assume that official activities in international relations can take place at five levels. These are: international institutions operating at the global level; regions above sovereign states or other polities; the sovereign states or other polities themselves; regions below the sovereign states or other polities; and local communities. Four of these five levels are less than global, define collective identities and demarcate them in more or less loose terms. In the course of the twentieth century, actors in and theorists of international relations have been concerned with these four levels of regionality or regionalness with varying degrees of intensity.[92] The sovereign states or similar types of polity have attracted most attention, even where they were contested, and the largest number of activities in international relations have been launched from the level of the sovereign states. This is the empirical background against which, from the turn of the twentieth century, realists have devised their theoretical position that states are paramount actors in international relations. However, this position is untenable when applied to previous periods of history and Eurocentric when related to the experiences of population groups outside Europe and North America.

The level of regionality or regionalness that has been neglected most in its impacts on international relations is that of regions above and below the sovereign states or other polities. Between the end of World War I and the end of the 1980s, most international theorists concerned with these levels of regionality or regionalness have assumed that the formation of institutions above or schemes of cooperation among sovereign states as aspects of regional integration emerged in Europe only during the immediate postwar period, were rare in earlier parts of the twentieth century and unknown in Europe as well as to the world at large in previous centuries.[93] But this assumption is far from true. The sole reason that it could have emerged is the lack of historical interest on the part of the theorists who studied regional integration.

Up until the superimposition of European colonial domination in Africa, South and Southeast Asia as well as Oceania in the course of the nineteenth century, the world was a world of regions, and notions of statehood played only a marginal role. Some of these regions came into existence through the use of force, such as the Qing Chinese Empire of the eighteenth and nineteenth centuries,[94] the Russian Empire which was expanded to the Pacific coasts, Central Asia and the Black Sea

---

[92] Kleinschmidt, 'Preparatory'.
[93] Haas, *Europe*.
[94] Jeremy Black, *Why Wars Happen* (London: Reaktion Books, 1998), p. 99. Eva Kraft (ed.), *Zum Dschungarenkrieg im 18. Jahrhundert. Berichte des Generals Funingga* (Leipzig: Harrassowitz, 1953).

in the course of the eighteenth and nineteenth centuries,[95] the Ottoman Turkish Empire which was no longer expanding during the eighteenth century but, in many areas, was successfully defended against external pressure,[96] the Spanish colonial empire in America which was extended to include much of California in the eighteenth century,[97] the Mughal Empire in India[98] or the empires of the Ashanti,[99] Dahomey[100] and the Zulu[101] which emerged during the eighteenth and early nineteenth centuries. Other regions were integrated through more peaceful means, mainly the acceptance of common legal norms and rules, the exchange of goods and the practice of cooperation among rulers. This was not only the case in central, western and southern Europe during the eighteenth century[102] but also in the Interlacustrine Area of East Africa during the eighteenth and nineteenth centuries,[103] among the polities joined into the 'Kula Ring' in the Pacific by the nineteenth century if not before,[104] and institutions established among Native Americans such as the Iroquois League of the eighteenth and nineteenth centuries.[105]

That is to say that regional institutions and schemes for regional cooperation have a much longer tradition than most of the sovereign states that exist today. The same applies to institutions of governance at levels of regionalness or regionality below the sovereign states. Often these institutions are successors to polities with a

---

[95] James Forsyth, *History of the Peoples of Siberia. Russia's North Asian Colony. 1581 – 1990* (Cambridge: Cambridge University Press, 1994).

[96] Halil Inalcik, *The Ottoman Empire* (London: Weidenfeld & Nicolson, 1973) [new edn (London: Phoenix, 1994)].

[97] *The Cambridge History of Latin America* (6 vols, Cambridge: Cambridge University Press, 1984). C. de Parrel, 'Pitt et l'Espagne', *Revue d'histoire diplomatique*, 64 (1950): 58-98.

[98] *The Cambridge History of India,* new edn (6 vols, Dehli: Chand, 1987).

[99] Robert Sutherland Rattray, *Ashanti* (Oxford: Clarendon Press, 1923).

[100] Archibald Dalzel, *The History of Dahomey* (London: s.n., 1793) [reprint, ed. by John D. Fage (London: Cass, 1967). For studies of the Dahomey slave trade see Werner Peukert, *Der atlantische Sklavenhandel von Dahomey. 1740 – 1797* (Wiesbaden: Steiner, 1978) Karl Polanyi, *Dahomey and the Slave Trade* (Seattle: University of Washington Press, 1966).

[101] Leonard Thompson, *A History of South Africa* (New Haven and London: Yale University Press, 1990). Jacob Festus Ade Ajayi, *UNESCO General History of Africa. Africa in the Nineteenth Century* (Berkeley and Los Angeles: University of California Press, 1998).

[102] Among others, see Ludwig Martin Kahle, *La Balance de l'Europe considerée comme la règle de la paix et de la guerre* (Berlin, Göttingen: the author, 1744).

[103] Apolo Kaggwa, *The Kings of Buganda,* ed. by Matia Semakula M. Kiwanuka (Nairobi: East African Publishing House, 1971). John Roscoe, *The Baganda* (London: Macmillan, 1911) [reprint (London: Cass, 1965)].

[104] Jitendra Pal Singh Uberoi, *Politics of the Kula Ring. An Analysis of the Findings of Bronislaw Malinowski* (Manchester: Manchester University Press, 1962).

[105] William N. Fenton, *The Great Law and the Longhouse. A Political History of the Iroquois Confederacy* (Norman, OK: University of Oklahoma Press, 1998).

history longer than that of sovereign states. There were three processes that reduced the significance of these institutions and schemes, first the globalization of the European international system through imperialist colonialism at the turn of the twentieth century, second, the simultaneous creation and strengthening of international institutions and, third, the conceptualization and establishment of national states in the course of the nineteenth and twentieth centuries. Imperialist colonialism was detrimental to regional institutions and schemes for regional integration because it created or enhanced demands for global military, economic, political and cultural competition. This strategy was pursued by military planners, business leaders, diplomats and other decision-makers in government who displayed their readiness to perceive international relations as under the impact of global conflict and strove to analyze global interdependencies among actions of governments, armed forces and the various business communities.[106] The pursuit of peace through global international organization was positioned against regional integration because regional institutions appeared to obstruct global cooperation under the goal of accomplishing peace in the world. Activists of the international peace movement, some journalists and non-partisan intellectuals favoured this strategy for the purpose of counterbalancing the politics of imperialistic expansion, and advocated the promotion of world organization through world organizations.[107]

Nationalism was inimical to institutions and schemes of regional integration because it favoured state making and nation building at the expense of communication among neighbours within a region. Nationalists assumed that international boundaries were significant dividing lines in military, economic, political and cultural respects. They advocated the fortification of these boundaries in service of the perceived security of the states, which they strove to organize as autonomous self-sufficient entities. And they demanded that the boundaries of the states should overlap with the areas each of which were inhabited by only one group that was perceivable as a single, homogeneous, social coherent and politically uniform nation.[108] Nationalists could perceive relations with neighbours in the region merely under the guidance of power politics and were fearful that regional integration could weaken the defence capability, make the governments of sovereign states subject to political and economic pressures at the hands of their neighbours and thereby increase the vulnerability of the sovereign states. Keeping

---

[106] Neitzel, *Weltmacht*.

[107] Alfred Hermann Fried, *Handbuch der Friedensbewegung* (Vienna and Leipzig: Verlag der 'Friedens-Warte', 1905). Jost Dülffer, *Regeln gegen den Krieg? Die Haager Friedenskonferenzen 1899 und 1907 in der internationalen Politik* (Berlin, Frankfurt and Vienna: Ullstein, 1981). Verdiana Grossi, *Le pacifisme européen* (Brussels: Bruylant, 1994).

[108] Richard Boeckh, *Der Deutschen Volkszahl und Sprachgebiet* (Berlin: Guttentag, 1869) [reprint (ibid., 1870)]. For recent studies of nationalism in Germany see Otto Dann, *Nation und Nationalismus in Deutschland* (Munich: Beck, 1998). Heinz Duchhardt and Andreas Kunz (eds), *Reich oder Nation? Mitteleuropa. 1780 – 1815* (Mainz: Zabern, 1998). Wolfgang Hardtwig, *Geschichtskultur und Wissenschaft* (Munich: Beck, 1990). Michael Hughes, *Nationalism and Society. Germany 1800 – 1945* (London: Edward Arnold, 1988).

close watch over the population of the state under its control was regarded as the prime government task as the lack of government capability to provide for domestic stability could jeopardize the external security of the state.[109] Therefore, the regional concerns that were considered to be possible by the nationalists were focused on the exercise of power by one government over its neighbouring states, such as the designs that were enshrined in the German *Mitteleuropa* policies.[110] Hence, while imperialism and colonialism promoted competition and global internationalism sought to absorb states and regions into the future world community, nationalism was divisive and prioritized the self-sufficiency of the sovereign states.

Internationalism and nationalism even shared the common belief that the world as a whole together with the national states represented or should represent integrated and well-'functioning' 'organisms' wherein the whole was larger than the sum of its parts and wherein the operations of all parts were considered to have to be supportive to the whole.[111] Hence the political language of nineteenth- and early twentieth-century internationalists as well as nationalists abounded with biologistic metaphors drawn on the model of the living body. While nationalists likened international boundaries to the skin of the state, sealing off the state against its environment,[112] internationalists equated the entire world with a comprehensive system that should 'organize' relations among specific units and integrate them into an overarching superstructure.[113] Internationalists as well as nationalists could easily agree that institutions and schemes of regional integration were dangerous because they ignored the purported 'national desires and passions' and obstructed the integration of the world into only one single international system. Both parties could then easily denounce institutions and schemes of regional integration as part of the seemingly dusty legacy of *Ancien Régime* mechanicism.[114] If theorists were

---

[109] For German attacks on the notion of the balance of power in the early twentieth century see Karl Jacob, 'Die Chimäre des Gleichgewichts', *Archiv für Urkundenforschung*, 6 (1918): 341-4. A. von Kirchheim, 'Politisches Gleichgewicht', *Deutsche Revue*, 40/4 (1915): 308-15. Heinrich Otto Meisner, 'Vom europäischen Gleichgewicht', *Preußische Jahrbücher*, 176 (1919): 222-45. Ferdinand Jakob Schmidt, 'Das Ethos des politischen Gleichgewichtsdenkens', *Preußiche Jahrbücher*, 158 (1914): 1-15.

[110] For a contemporary view on the *Mitteleuropa* ideology see Friedrich Naumann, *Mitteleuropa* (Berlin: Reimer, 1915).

[111] Schäffle, *Bau*.

[112] Ratzel, *Geographie*.

[113] Harald Kleinschmidt, *Federalism, Functionalism and the Quest for International Order* (Tsukuba: Special Research Project on the New International System, 1995).

[114] Otto Hintze, 'Imperialismus und Weltpolitik [1907]', ed. by Fritz Hartung, Hintze, *Staat und Verfassung* (Leipzig: Koehler & Amelang, 1941), p. 459. Hintze, 'Imperialismus und Weltpolitik', *Die deutsche Freiheit* (1917): 117. Walther Max Adrian Schücking, 'Die Organisation der Welt', in *Staatsrechtliche Abhandlungen. Festgabe für Paul Laband* (Tübingen: Mohr, 1908), pp. 594-5. Hans Wehberg, 'Ideen und Projekte betr[effend] die Vereinigten Staaten von Europa in den letzten 100 Jahren', *Die Friedenswarte*, 51 (1941):

at all willing to conceive regions in biologistic terms, they positioned regions as the fertile grounds on which nations as well as international organization could 'grow'.[115]

Consequently, most twentieth-century international relations theorists have had a distanced relationship with regional integration. Realists ignored it because it appeared to be dangerous for the state.[116] Functionalists as theorists ignored it because it was dangerous for global integration.[117] Functionalists in office made efforts to prevent it.[118] Although neo-functionalists shifted the focus of their theoretical inquiries from global to regional integration, they conceived regional integration solely as a process of the absorption of national states into larger polities[119] and used their remaining intellectual resources mainly to the end of predicting and explaining the failure of regional integration processes.[120] The neo-functionalist approach had immensely negative consequences for the regional integration processes of the 1950s and 1960s because it suggested that the degree of success of regional integration should be measured according to the ascertainable capability of regional institutions to 'incorporate' institutions of existing sovereign national states. As most regional integration processes at the time displayed few ascertainable results of 'spill over' effects of state bureaucratic decision-making onto the advancement of regional integration, theorists passed negative verdicts on the work of regional institutions. Bureaucrats and political decision-makers followed suit and began to bicker over relative gains and losses on the various sides of the parties involved in regional integration processes. In Latin America, these disputes contributed to the collapse of institutions of regional integration in the course of the 1960s,[121] in East Africa, the first East African Community, which had been modelled on the European Economic Community

---

11-82 [separately ed. by Karl Holl and Jost Dülffer (Bremen: Edition Temmen, 1984)].

[115] Goldmann, *Die europäische Pentarchie* (Leipzig: s.n., 1839), p. 1.

[116] Carl Joachim Friedrich, *Foreign Policy in the Making* (New York: Norton, 1938), p. 138. Hans Joachim Morgenthau, *Politics among Nations,* fifth edn (New York: Knopf, 1973), pp. 548-50 [first published (1948)]. Nicholas John Spykman, *America's Strategy in World Politics* (New York: Harcourt Brace, 1942), p. 460.

[117] Lassa Francis Lawrence Oppenheim, *International Law,* fourth edn, ed. by Arnold D. McNaire (3 vols, London: Longman, 1928), vol. 1, p. 99. David Mitrany, *The Progress of International Government* (London: Allen & Unwin, 1933). Alfred Eckhard Zimmern, *Learning and Leadership* (London: Oxford University Press, 1928).

[118] Woodrow Wilson, *The Public Papers,* vol. 40 (Princeton: Princeton University Press, 1982), pp. 535-6, vol. 45 (ibid., 1984), pp. 534-5, vol. 53 (ibid., 1986), pp. 532, 599. See also Kwame Nkrumah [*Africa Must Unite* (Nairobi: Heinemann, 1963)], who equated regional integration with balkanization.

[119] See above, note 20.

[120] Ernest B. Haas, *The Obsolescence of Regional Integration Theory* (Berkeley: Institute of International Studies, University of California, 1975). Haas, 'Why Collaborate?', *World Politics,* 32 (1979/80): 357-405.

[121] See above, note 2.

(EEC), ended in 1984.[122] Moreover, neo-functionalism appealed primarily to political and administrative elites who tended to conceptualize regional integration as a process of inter-government negotiation and accommodation among sovereign states without taking seriously popular attitudes and perceptions.[123] The consequence of this bias was that regional integration could hardly proceed if disagreement arose among the governments involved. For example, the first East African Community ceased to operate due to disagreement over the adjustment of relative gains and losses from the integration process and, paradoxically, required a joint effort from the heads of the involved states to allow its dissolution under World Bank mediation.

Whereas neo-functionalist theory and its practical application remained unconcerned with security issues, realist opposition against regional integration was fed by security concerns. Realists were contractualists who tied the legitimacy of a government to the existence of a sovereign population group within the borders of a state.[124] Hence realists assumed that it was the legitimate task of governments to provide for the security of the population under their control. Therefore, within the confines of realist theory, governments were to be sole providers of security, domestically against crime and other disturbances, and internationally against threats from other states.[125] Insofar as realism was informed by contractualism, it was and had to be state-centric. Realists could accept neither regional or global nor civil society institutions as security providers because these institutions could not be legitimized through contractualist means. Therefore, the lack of possibility to provide security by institutions above, below or beside the sovereign state became the core realist argument against multilateralism or regional integration.[126] In consequence, the perceived security concerns of states obtained priority over the 'human' aspect of security in the course of the nineteenth and twentieth centuries.[127]

---

[122] See above, note 3.

[123] Andrew Moravcsik ['Preferences and Power in the European Community', *Journal of Common Market Studies*, 31 (1993): 473-524. Also: Moravcsik, *The Choice for Europe* (Ithaca and London: Cornell University Press, 1998)] tried to revive this approach in the 1990s with, however, a mixed response.

[124] See Kleinschmidt, *Nemesis*.

[125] Rüstow, *Grenzen*. Maurice, *Balance*. Morton A. Kaplan, *System and Process in International Politics* (New York: Wiley, 1957). Kaplan, *Macropolitics* (Chicago: Aldine, 1969), pp. 209-42.

[126] For a recent restatement of this realist orthodoxy see John J. Mearsheimer, *The Tragedy of Great Power Politics* (New York and London: Norton, 2001), pp. 338-47.

[127] This aspect of the military security concerns was recognized already during World War by Otfrid Nippold, professor of international trade and traffic law at the University of Bern, in his manuscript Die Ursachen des europäischen Krieges [1915], Nippold Papers, Burgerbibliothek Bern. Edited by Harald Kleinschmidt and introduced by Akio Nakai (Munich: Iudicium, 2005).

However, the realist assumptions are far from obvious.[128] The state-centricity of realist international theory has led to the postulate that the population groups inhabiting state territories should be united in one collective identity and should display a single loyalty to the institutions of that state. By contrast, according to this venue of thought, multiple loyalties attached to other institutions, should they persist, ought to be destroyed.[129] From the end of the nineteenth century, realists have accepted the principal postulate that nation-states should be the only institutional framework for sovereign polities[130] within which class distinctions and ethnic or gender discriminations can be overcome and the democratically controlled rule of justice can be guaranteed.[131] But the belief that states are and, of right, should be the only legitimate sovereign polities has been rendered unwarranted by the fact that communitarian ideologies and regional identities have persisted for a period that is much longer in most parts of the world than the temporal dimension within which sovereign states have been on record.[132] These ideologies and identities have enforced the continuity of multiple loyalties and governments of sovereign states have met with serious resistance in their attempts to constitute themselves as the only focal points of loyalty. By contrast, admitting the pluralism of potentially competing loyalties and identities, the description of ongoing political processes may not only gain in adequacy but, more importantly, such processes as state succession can be analyzed more appropriately as the results of long-term shifts in loyalties and identities rather than as abrupt collapses

---

[128] See Barry M. Blechmann, 'International Peace and Security in the Twenty-First Century', in Ken Booth (ed.), *State and Security* (Cambridge: Cambridge University Press, 1998), pp. 289-307. Jose V. Ciprut (ed.), *Of Fears and Foes. Security and Insecurity in an Evolving Global Political Economy* (Westport, CT, and London: Praeger, 2000).

[129] John J. Mearsheimer, 'The False Promise of International Institutions', *International Security*, 19 (1994/95): 5-49.

[130] Aleksandr Nikolaevič de Shtiglits [Stieglitz], *De l'équilibre politique, du légitimisme et du principe des nationalités* (3 vols, Paris: Pedone-Lauriel, 1893), vol. 1. Waltz, *Theory*.

[131] Philipp Zorn, 'Streitfragen des deutschen Staatsrechtes', *Zeitschrift für die gesamte Staatswissenschaft*, 37 (1881): 292-322. Paul W. Schroeder, 'Historical Reality vs. Neo-realist Theory', *International Security*, 19 (1994): 108-48.

[132] Johann Stephan Pütter, *Beyträge zur näheren Erläuterung und richtigen Bestimmung einiger Lehren des teutschen Staats- und Fürstenrechts* (2 vols, Göttingen: Vandenhoeck, 1777), vol. 1, pp. 30-32. John Caldwell Calhoun, 'A Discourse on the Constitution and Government of the United States [c. 1849]', in Calhoun, *A Disquisition of Government and A Discourse on the Constitution and Government of the United States*, ed. by Richard Kenner Crallé (New York: Russell & Russell, 1968), pp. 120-1 [new edn (ibid., 2002)]. Georg Waitz, 'Das Wesen des Bundesstaats', Waitz, *Grundzüge der Politik* (Kiel: Homann, 1862), pp. 153-218 [reprint (New York: AMS Press, 1979); first published *Allgemeine Monatsschrift für Wissenschaft und Literatur* (1853)]. Max von Seydel, 'Der Bundesstaaatsbegriff', *Zeitschrift für die gesamte Staatswissenschaft*, 28 (1872): 185-256 [newly ed. in Seydel, *Staatsrechtliche und politische Abhandlungen* (Freiburg: Mohr, 1893), pp. 1-85]. For a recent study of the emergence of regional identities see Peter Blickle, *Kommunalismus* (2 vols, Munich: Oldenbourg, 2000), vol. 1.

of institutions. Vice versa, regional integration processes may be understood as similar shifts that can but do not have to entail the destruction of existing state institutions.

As one consequence of this revision of regional integration theory, security concerns can be connected with multiple identities and loyalties and can thus be focused on transnational civil society groups as more suitable as security providers. It may be remarked in this context that, up until the end of the eighteenth century, regional institutions as well as non-government organizations such as churches and private companies[133] were accepted as regular providers of the human aspect of security together with governments. Only within the framework of ideologies of the nation-state did governments of sovereign states assume the role of the sole

---

[133] Among them the international trading companies of the seventeenth and eighteenth centuries. See Sinnapali Arasaratnam, *Maritime Trade, Society and European Influence in Southern Asia. 1600 – 1800* (Aldershot: Variorum, 1995). Maurice Aymard (ed.), *Dutch Capitalism and World Capitalism* (Paris: Maison de science de l'homme; and Cambridge: Cambridge University Press, 1982). Charles Ralph Boxer, *The Dutch Seaborne Empire* (London: Hutchinson, 1965). Boxer, *Jan Campagnie in War and Peace* (Hong Kong: Heinemann Asia, 1979). Kirti N. Chaudhuri, *The English East India Company. The Study of an Early Joint-Stock Company. 1600 – 1640* (London: Cass, 1965) [reprint (London and New York: Routledge, 1999)]. Chaudhuri, *The Trading World of Asia and the English East India Company 1660 – 1760* (Cambridge: Cambridge University Press, 1978). Pieter C. Emmer and Magnus Mörner (eds), *European Expansion and Migration* (New York: Berg, 1992). Emmer and Femme S. Gaastra (eds), *The Organization of Interoceanic Trade in European Expansion. 1450 – 1800* (Aldershot: Variorum, 1996). Emmer, *The Dutch in the Atlantic Economy. 1580 – 1880* (Aldershot: Variorum, 1998). Jörg Fisch, *Hollands Ruhm in Asien* (Stuttgart: Steiner, 1986). Holden Furber, *Rival Empires of Trade in the Orient. 1600 – 1800* (Minneapolis: University of Minnesota Press, 1976). Femme S. Gaastra, 'De Verenigde Oost-Indische Compagnie in de zeventiende en achttiende eeuw', *Bijdragen en mededelingen betreffende de geschiedenis der Nederlanden*, 91 (1976): 249-72. Kristof Glamann, *Dutch-Asiatic Trade. 1620 – 1740* (Copenhagen: Danish Science Press, 1958) [second edn (The Hague: Nijhoff, 1981)]. Jonathan I. Israel, *Dutch Primacy in World Trade. 1585 – 1740* (Oxford and New York: Oxford University Press, 1989). Martin Krieger, *Kaufleute, Seeräuber und Diplomaten. Der dänische Handel auf dem Indischen Ozean (1620 – 1868)* (Cologne, Weimar and Vienna: Böhlau, 1998). Douglas M. Peers, *Warfare and Empires. Contact and Conflict between European and Non-European Military and Maritime Forces and Cultures* (Aldershot: Variorum, 1997). Marie Antoinette Petronella Meilink-Roelofsz, *De VOC in Azië* (Bussum: Fibula van Dishoeck, 1976). Om Prakash, *Precious Metals and Commerce. The Dutch East India Company in the Indian Ocean Trade* (Aldershot: Variorum, 1994). Eberhard Schmitt, Thomas Schleich and Thomas Beck (eds), *Kaufleute als Kolonialherren* (Bamberg: Buchner, 1988). Niels Steensgaard, *The Asian Trade Revolution of the Seventeenth Century* (Chicago and London: University of Chicago Press, 1974. Sanjay Subrahmanyan (ed.), *Merchant Networks in the Early Modern World. 1450 – 1800* (Aldershot: Variorum, 1996). James D. Tracy (ed.), *The Rise of Merchant Empires* (Cambridge: Cambridge University Press, 1990). Tracy (ed.), *The Political Economy of Merchant Empires* (Cambridge: Cambridge University Press, 1991).

providers of security at the disadvantage of the security concerns of the individual. Consequently, institutions and schemes of regional integration do not have to be classed as security hazards but, instead, as one condition for the provision of security in the human dimension.

## The Widening Horizon of the Security Discourse

The concept of security has undergone an unexpected change from the 1980s. Objections against the realist security discourse have emerged from the request that the principal unit of security should not be the state or some other form of polity but the individual. Supporters of the request have argued that justice and equality follow from the respect for personhood rather than the recognition of nationality and can only be established and maintained if the needs and desires of individuals are taken seriously as matters of public policy.[134] Moreover, an increasing number of security theorists have displayed their willingness to consider Mahbub ul-Haq's request that security should be defined in terms of the safety of the individual against starvation, loss of property, violations of bodily integrity, torture and other forms of aggression together with the protection of the integrity of states. These demands suggest a paradigm shift from state security to human security as the more comprehensive security concept that combines the security interests of the individual with those of the state.

The most widely accepted perception is that the paradigm shift began in the 1980s and has been fuelled by the several cases of state succession in the 1990s, the tripling of PKOs since 1988 from 13 in the period between 1948 to 1987 to 39 from 1988 to 2000, the increasing vulnerability of civilian non-combatants in military conflicts, and, last but not least, the deepening sense of the urgency of the prevention of further global ecological devastation. However, much as these indicators are straightforward, the perception is not self-evident that concerns for what has been termed human security are actually new. The evidence that the notion of human security, not the word, may have a longer tradition behind it can be grouped into three categories: First, sources earlier than the 1980s show that human security concerns were on the agenda of diplomatic negotiations even though the word 'human security' was not then in use. Second, sources before the turn of the nineteenth century put on record that the protection of the individual was considered to be the prime task of rulers and a powerful means of constraining warfare. Third, sources of medieval origin disclose that the accomplishment of peace as a condition for the temporal security of the individual and the perennial welfare of humankind was a demand enshrined in the ideologies of universalism and, in this respect, the provision of human security was a religious concern.

Sources of the first category can be discussed here in brief. It is well known that human security concerns were made explicit as early as in the Mouraviev

---

[134] Soysal, *Limits*.

Memorandum of 1898 beginning a series of diplomatic negotiations that lead to convocation of the Hague Peace Conference of 1899.[135] There are also traces of the notion of human security in Mitrany's peace proposal of 1943.[136] Debates about the notion of human security at the Helsinki conference were not always controversial and were conducted about issues distinct from human rights. Moreover, they featured strongly in a variety of reports by international commissions whose work followed the 1975 Helsinki Accord.[137] Therefore, the 1994 UNDP report making official Mahbub ul-Haq's definition concluded a process that had already began at the very end of the nineteenth century[138] and had consolidated itself for some twenty years, when the term appeared in official records.

The second category of sources shows that the conceptualization of human security during the twentieth century replaced another process, which might be referred to as the militarization of security from the end of the eighteenth century. This process was innately connected with the surge of nationalism and the militarization of society in consequence of the French Revolution of 1789. Thus early nineteenth-century military theory provided the first general theory of war ever in a European context. Within this theory, the dialectics of the buildup and resolution of friction and tensions appeared to demand the subordination of the interests of the individual to those of the nation as a whole.[139] Early nineteenth-century legal philosophers concurred and were most vocal in insisting that personhood was to be determined through nationality so that the personal identity of the individual should be a derivative of the national identity.[140] It was thus a consistent conclusion to request that individuals should be ready to risk their lives in service to the nation.[141]

---

[135] Nicholas II, Imperial Rescript [May 1898], ed. by Gwyn Prins and Hylke Tromp, *The Future of War* (The Hague, Boston and London: Kluwer, 2000), pp. 59-60.

[136] David Mitrany, *A Working Peace System,* ed. by Hans Joachim Morgenthau (Chicago: Quadrangle Books, 1966), pp. 54-5, 62-71 [first published (London: Royal Institute of International Affairs, 1943)].

[137] Vigh, Helsinki, pp. 49-60.

[138] United Nations Development Programme, *New Dimensions of Human Security* (New York: Oxford University Press, 1994).

[139] Heinrich Gottlieb Tschirner, *Ueber den Krieg* (Leipzig: Barth, 1815). Clausewitz, *Krieg.*

[140] Georg Wilhelm Friedrich Hegel, '[Die Verfassung Deutschlands, c. 1802]', in Hegel, *Frühe Schriften* (Frankfurt: Suhrkamp, 1971), p. 46. Johann Gottlieb Fichte, *Reden an die deutsche Nation* [1807/08], Erste Rede, ed. by Immanuel Hermann Fichte, Fichte, *Sämmtliche Werke* (6 vols, Berlin: Veit, 1846), vol. 1, pp. 264-79 [reprint (Berlin and New York: de Gruyter, 1971)].

[141] Georg Simmel, 'Deutschlands innere Wandlung [Nov. 1914; first published (Strasbourg: Trübner, 1914)]', Simmel, *Der Krieg und die geistigen Entscheidungen* (Berlin and Leipzig: Duncker & Humblot, 1917), pp. 7-29 [new edn., ed. by Otthein Rammstedt, Simmel, *Gesamtausgabe,* vol. 16 (Frankfurt: Suhrkamp, 1999), pp. 7-29]. Max Scheler, *Der*

However, twentieth-century theorists have been wrong in postulating that the demands of nineteenth-century military theorists and legal philosophers had made explicit perennial truths. This was not the case, first and foremost, because the concepts of nation and state underlying the request for sacrifice to the nation emerged in their current meanings only during the second half of the eighteenth century.[142] Moreover, there is positive evidence that, up to the end of the eighteenth century, security was defined in a broader sense than the mere protection against military attacks on states. Instead, theorists of international law and a wide range of seventeenth- and eighteenth-century theoretical tracts, diplomatic memoranda and administrative records on the balance of power provide ample evidence for a notion of security that was integrated into the normative framework of policy-making rules.[143] Rules for the maintenance of the balance of power were expressed in static terms as norms that theorists claimed to have existed throughout history.[144] The most elaborate eighteenth-century system of balance of power rules is contained in the work of Emerich de Vattel, the Swiss born legal theorist who portrayed the balance of power in legal rather than in political terms and insisted that breaches of balance of power rules were reasons for just warfare.[145] Vattel argued in favour of an elaborate casuistry to be employed prior to any decision for war, and this casuistry required much observation on rulers' attitudes, the financial and political capabilities of governments and the general wealth of populations. Hence, even a breach of balance of power rules could automatically serve as a reason for just warfare.[146] Next to Vattel's legalism,

---

*Genius des Krieges und der Deutsche Krieg* (Leipzig: Verlag der Weißen Bücher, 1915), pp. 370-3 [newly ed. by Manfred S. Frings, Scheler, *Politisch-pädagogische Schriften* (Berlin and Munich: Francke, 1982)].

[142] See above, note 108. Emma Rothchild ['What is Security?', *Daedalus*, 124 (1995): 53-98] does not discuss the sources noted here.

[143] Foremost among many Thomas Hobbes, *De Cive. The English Version Entitled in the First Edition Philosophicall Rudiments Concerning Government and Society* [first published (Amsterdam: Elsevier, 1647)] [new edn, ed. by Howard Warrender (Oxford: Clarendon Press, 1983), pp. 170-1 [reprint (ibid., 2004)]. See also Hobbes, *De Corpore politico. Or the Elements of Law, Moral and Politic* (London: Martin and Ridley, 1650). On the balance of power see Heinz Duchhardt, *Balance of Power und Pentarchie. 1700 – 1785* (Paderborn, Munich, Vienna and Zurich: Schöningh, 1997). Christoph Kampmann, *Arbiter Europae* (Paderborn, Munich, Vienna and Zurich: Schöningh, 2001). Arno Strohmeyer, *Theorie der Interaktion. Das europäische Gleichgewicht der Kräfte in der frühen Neuzeit* (Vienna, Cologne and Weimar: Böhlau, 1994).

[144] David Hume, 'Of the Balance of Power [1752]', in Hume, *Essays, Moral, Political and Literary*, ed. by Thomas Hill Green and Thomas Hodge Grose (2 vols, London: Alex Murray, 1882), vol. 1, pp. 348-56 [reprint (Aalen: Scientia, 1964)].

[145] Emerich de Vattel, *Le droit des gens* (London: s.n., 1758), pp. 9-10 [reprint, ed. by Charles G. Fenwick (Washington: Carnegie Institution, 1916; reprint of the reprint (Geneva: Slatkine, 1983]).

[146] Vattel, *Droit*, pp. 139-40.

other theorists were more inclined to follow moral arguments. These theorists proceeded from the rationalist assumption that it was in the legitimate self-interest of every ruler to act in fulfillment of moral obligations and to abide by the general principles of reason, and they requested caution and constraint in decisions to go to war.[147] In either case, the salience of the maintenance of the balance of power was defended on the grounds that it was unjust to jeopardize the life and safety of the population under the control of a ruler and that upsetting the balance of power was ultimately not beneficial to rulers. According to this argument, rulers ignoring the balance of power rules, were to face dissent and opposition from among the ruled, devastation of the land, emigration of subjects, severe economic disadvantages and, last but not least, political isolation.[148]

Hence, concerns for the security of individuals became an issue of great importance also in military matters. Theorists assigned to rulers the task of providing security for the populations subject to their control. Unlike in the sixteenth and earlier seventeenth centuries, when the ratio of the war dead in relation to the total of combatants in battle could amount to about 50 per cent on the side of the loser, eighteenth-century military organization made significant and successful efforts to limit the carnage of battle primarily because it was costly and difficult to replace well-trained soldiers killed or turned invalid through battle action.[149] Instead of using soldiers as cannon fodder, commanders developed their capability to make soldiers execute given commands, to preserve their lives and to prevent them from deserting in masses. This capability was considered the core of the achievement of successful military organizers.[150] All this adds up to the perception that, prior nineteenth century, the provision of security was a comprehensive, not merely military concept and a core condition of the maintenance of stability and peace as well as a crucial task for rulers.

The third category of sources on the history of the concept of human security suggests that this notion did not originate in the particularistic political concerns of rulers of territorial polities but in the theological foundations of late medieval universalism. Late medieval universalism was characterized by a dualism of one divinely willed institution of universal rule ranked and a plethora of particularistic polities resulting from contractual agreements between rulers and ruled.[151] The universalistic creed was eschatological in kind and positioned the Roman Empire

---

[147] Kahle, *Balance*.

[148] Johann Heinrich Gottlob Justi, *Die Chimäre des Gleichgewichts von Europa* (Altona: s.n., 1758).

[149] Harald Kleinschmidt, *Tyrocinium militare* (Stuttgart: Autorenverlag, 1989), pp. 196-270.

[150] Some of them laid down their thoughts in their correspondence or in pragmatic writings, such as drill manuals. See Prince Eugene of Savoy, *Militärische Korrespondenz*, 2 vols, ed. by Friedrich Heller von Hellwald (Vienna: s.n., 1848). The Duke of Marlborough, *New Exercise of Firelocks and Bayonets* (London: s.n., 1708). Leopold Daun, *Richtschnur und unumänderliche gebräuchliche Observations-Puncte* (Luxemburg: s.n., 1733).

[151] Engelbert of Admont, 'Ortu'.

as the guarantor of the stability of the world. It was fundamental in shaping both the theory of empire and the practical conduct of imperial politics in the later Middle Ages because it demanded that emperors should accomplish the task of providing stability and security for the world in the dual sense of safety of individuals against hazards of daily life as well as safeguarding the tranquillity of the world and securing the continuity of life after death. The combination of diffuse eschatological hopes with manifest political and economic interests emerges from the multitude of late medieval political tracts on the origin and the end of the Roman Empire,[152] from the more principled treatises on political philosophy written by Dante and Marsilius of Padua in the first half of the fourteenth century on the condition of a general peace[153] as well as from the widening scope of imperial and territorial peace legislation of the twelfth and the subsequent centuries.[154] The demand that emperors should be the foremost providers of peace, stability and security in temporal as well as eschatological terms was thus imbued with religious values and, consequently, biased in favour of the Christian religion.

Human security, in this understanding, was a universal category only in so far as it applied to Christian believers, whereas non-Christians, especially Muslims, as well as heretics, such as the Hussites, were excluded from the desired peace regimes and became the targets of the use of military violence and brutal persecution. Although the notion of divinely willed natural law was used in the theory of war from the thirteenth century,[155] it remained a theoretical construct with little or no impact on the practical matters of human security beyond the confines of the Christian world. The frequency of the appeals to natural law and the preservation of peace in the later Middle Ages have to be judged against the

---

[152] Engelbert von Admont, 'Ortu', John Quidort of Paris, *Potestate*.

[153] Dante Alighieri, 'De monarchia', lib. I, cap. 2-3, ed. by Bruno Nardi, Dante, *Opere minori*, (2 vols, Milan and Naples: Ricciardi, 1979), vol. 2, pp. 328-30.

[154] For recent work on the peace of God and the *landfrieden* see Arno Buschmann and Elmar Wadle (eds), *Landfrieden. Anspruch und Wirklichkeit* (Paderborn, Munich, Vienna and Zurich: Schöningh, 2001). Johannes Fried (ed.), *Träger und Instrumentarien des Friedens im hohen und späten Mittelalter* (Sigmaringen: Thorbecke, 1996) Thomas Head and Richard Landes (eds), *The Peace of God. Social Violence and Religious Response in France around the Year 1000* (Ithaca and London: Cornell University Press, 1992). Ernst Dieter Hehl, 'Kirche, Krieg und Staatlichkeit im hohen Mittelalter', in Werner Rösener (ed.), *Staat und Krieg* (Göttingen: Vandenhoeck & Ruprecht, 2000), pp. 17-36. Dietrich Kurze, 'Krieg und Frieden im mittelalterlichen Denken', in Heinz Duchhardt (ed.), *Zwischenstaatliche Friedenswahrung in Mittelalter uind Früher Neuzeit* (Cologne and Vienna: Böhlau, 1991), pp. 1-44. Elmar Wadle, 'Zur Delegitimierung der Fehde durch die mittelalterliche Friedensbewegung', in Horst Brunner (ed.), *Der Krieg im Mittelalter und in der Frühen Neuzeit* (Wiesbaden: Reichert, 1999), pp. 73-91.

[155] Thomas Aquinas, 'Summa theologiae', Secundae Secunda, cap. 2, qu 40 ar 1-4, ed. by Roberto Busa, SJ, *Sancti Thomae opera omnia* (4 vols, Stuttgart: Frommann-Holzboog, 1980), vol. 2, pp. 579-80.

background of the intensification of military activity and the rapid increase of the number of war dead and war-related expenses. Theorists could do little more than deplore these developments while emperors appeared too weak to be able to execute their tasks.[156] It was only in the course of the sixteenth century that the secularization of political institutions promoted the de-institutionalization and ethicization of universalism.[157] Following these processes the Roman Empire ceased to be an administrative framework for universal rule and turned into a territorial polity like all others.[158] Theorists responded to these processes by redefining universalism as a set of norms and rules that they took to follow from the general principles of reason and to have validity without specific enforcement through human action.[159] It was only in consequence of the de-institutionalization and ethicization of universalism in the course of the sixteenth century that the pursuit of human security could emerge as a demand of international law and in application to all humankind.

I have traced the history of the concept of human security very roughly backwards from the Helsinki Accord of 1975 to the later Middle Ages, as if, so to speak, to turn the clock back. I have done so in order to show the changeability of the concept in its European context and in what appears to be a time span of about 900 years. The concept of human security reflects the experience of human insecurity together with the expectation that human insecurity can be turned into human security through human efforts. Both, the increased sense of human insecurity and the increased demand for the provision of human security were a consequence of the intensification of warfare during the high and late Middle Ages. Within the *longue durée* of little less than a thousand years, the period of less than two hundred years appears as an aberration during which the concept of security was militarized and focused on institutions of statehood rather than on human individuals. In the Middle Ages, the European concept of human security was tied to a universalistic institution with a strong bias in favour of Christianity. Whether it is still so today might be decided on the basis of a comparison between the legacies of universalism in Europe and the Atlantic World on the one side and, on the other, China and the island worlds of Western Pacific.

---

[156] Honore Bonet [Bouvet], *L'arbre des batailles* (Paris: s.n., 1493), frontispiece.

[157] Kleinschmidt, *Geschichte*.

[158] Harald Kleinschmidt, *Charles V. The World Emperor* (Stroud: Sutton, 2004).

[159] Jean Bodin, *Les six livres de la République*, Lib. I, cap. 8 (Paris: Du Puy, 1576), p. 122. Justus Lipsius, *Six Bookes of Politics*, ed. by W. Jones (London: R. Field, 1594), p. 128 [reprint (Amsterdam and New York: Theatrum orbis, 1970); first published (Antwerp: Plantin, 1589)]. Lipsius, *Two Bookes of Constancie*, ed. by John Stradling (London: R. Johnes, 1595), pp. 77-9, 95-6, 98 [first published (Antwerp: Plantin, 1584)]. For a study of the *lois fondamentales* see: Arlette Juana, 'Die Debatte über die absolute Gewalt im Frankreich der Religionskriege', in Ronald G. Asch and Heinz Duchhardt (eds), *Der Absolutismus – ein Mythos* (Cologne, Weimar and Vienna: Böhlau, 1996), pp. 70-1.

## Conclusion

If the sovereign state represents the triad of unities of population, government and territory, the frequently observed 'decline of the state' has been caused not primarily by economic activities and the patterns informing economic actions. Instead, the sovereign state has come under pressure because two of the three unities constituting it have been disclosed to be programmatic rather than factual. Rather than assuming that states comprise a united population in the tradition of realism, political theorists as well as practical decision-makers in government have been forced to admit that migration flexibilizes the population and that the government capability to counteract the flexibilizing effects of migration are limited. Moreover, rather than perceiving resort to border surveillance and the resulting regional disintegration as proper means to counteract the flexibilizing effects of migration, governments of sovereign states have been induced to contribute to schemes of regional integration or cooperate in institutions of regional integration. They have done so with full awareness that institutions and schemes of regional integration have the effect of further flexibilizing institutions of government.

As a result, it has become more difficult for governments of sovereign states to act as main or even as sole providers for domestic stability and external security. The term 'welfare state', as Nicholas Onuf has recently remarked,[160] has become an oxymoron and, that means in political terms, a nuisance. While the sovereign states have remained the sole legitimate providers of external security, the private sector through MNCs and NGOs has emerged as a powerful competitor to the state for the provision of domestic stability. The private sector easily becomes integrated into regional or even global networks that in turn reduce the range of activities of the governments of sovereign states. Likewise, civil society groups can operate transnationally with the intention of contributing to domestic stability and external security and thereby emerge as further checks against the activities of government of sovereign states. Migration is a factor supporting, if not initializing, these processes. Migrants may create the transnational spaces within which MNCs NGOs and civil society groups can operate. Consequently, regional integration cannot be conceptualized on the basis of the residentialist models of the state but must incorporate the flexibilizing effects of migration. Moreover, the concept of security, narrowly defined in terms of safety against military threats, has been rendered inapt as a means to respond to the flexibilization of state populations and government institutions. Therefore, the comprehensive concept of human security is innately regional. Governments of sovereign states have the choice between redefining domestic stability and external security along the idea and concept of comprehensive human security and living with a widening gap between the demand for security and the declining capability and legitimacy to provide for it.

---

[160] Nicholas Greenwood Onuf, *The Republican Legacy in International Thought* (Cambridge: Cambridge University Press, 1998).

Chapter Four

# Migrants, Human Security and Military Security

Reinhard Drifte

**Introduction**

Migration in its various forms has become part of an enlarged security concept which has grown popular with scholars, politicians and NGO's alike, particularly since the end of the Cold War. The enlarged security concept has also brought with it a clear shift of focus from the security of the state which has been the focus of the traditional security concept to that of the individual. The linkage between migration and an expanded security concept is therefore particularly appealing to the adherents of the latter concept because migration, like famine or draught, refers to the security of the individual. Moreover, migration can be both part of traditional as well as non-traditional security concerns (for example, refugees fleeing war or famine).

In this contribution, I want first to examine the literature on the reasons and problematique of enlarging the security concept. In the second part I examine the links between on the one hand migration and on the other hand conventional and non-conventional security concerns before illustrating these issues with the example of Asia. Finally I briefly review regional approaches in Asia dealing with migration, thus providing yet another example of the limited and inchoate nature of regional cooperation in the region despite the objective need for closer cooperation in view of the nature of the challenges. The example of Asia also shows the practical disadvantages of using the concept of human security as a tool for mobilization because it invokes with most Asian leaders a concern about interference into domestic politics and it leads to difficulties in prioritizing the growing and apparently limitless list of 'non-conventional security challenges'.

**The Widening of the Concept of Security in Security and International Relations Studies**

In security and international relations studies, the concept of security has until now mostly been defined by Realists for whom the referent is the state whereas the contents is narrowly related to military security. As in the general public discourse, particularly since the end of the Cold War, this understanding has been increasingly challenged, and security now includes for many not only the survival of human collectivities and individuals (rather than just the nation state), but also the conditions of existence which are affected by political, economic, societal, and environmental factors, in addition to military factors.[1] It is obvious that there are links between traditional security concerns, namely the maintenance of borders, and non-traditional security concerns like hunger, pollution and privation. Moreover even Realists have to acknowledge that these non-traditional security issues while not directly resulting in a military clash, may create an environment in which such a clash becomes more likely and/or more sustainable. Interstate war, the traditional focus of Realism, has become increasingly rare while intrastate violence has risen. An important development facilitating this enlargement of the concept of security is globalization in many forms which gradually undermines sovereignty as a key concept for the focus on the nation state in the Realist School. Increased mobility as well as migration in all its forms plays an important part in this development.[2] The UNDP report in 1994 on 'Human Security' with its emphasis on the welfare of the individual played a crucial role in popularizing the securitization of certain economic, environmental and political dislocations.[3] This expansion of security has broadened the concept of security but it is neither clear nor agreed upon where this enlargement should stop.[4] For some proponents of this enlargement, security is not an objective condition like it is for the Realists, but a social construct with different meanings in different societies.[5] Keith Krause explains that the basic claims of critical and constructivist approaches leading to the broadening of security are that 'security' is not an objective condition, that threats to it are not simply a matter of correctly perceiving a constellation of material forces, and that the object of security is not stable or unchanging. Instead, questions are becoming central about how the object to be secured (nation, state or other groups) is constituted, and how particular issues (economic well-being, the risk of violence, environmental degradation) are placed under the 'sign of security'.[6]

---

[1] For a critical review and rethinking of security see Muthiah Alagappa (ed.), *Asian Security Practice. Material and Ideational Influences* (Stanford: University Press, 1998), Chapter 1. See also Keith Krause, 'Broadening the Agenda of Security Studies: Politics and Methods', in *Mershon International Studies Review*, 40 (1996): 229-54.

[2] Saskia Sassen, *Losing Control? Sovereignty in an Age of Globalization* (New York: Columbia University Press, 1996).

[3] United Nations Development Programme, *New dimensions of Human Security* (New York: Oxford University Press, 1994). For a discussion of various definitions and problems of 'human security' see Roland Paris, 'Paradigm Shift or Hot Air?', in *International Security*, 26/2 (Fall 2001): 87-102.

[4] Andrew Mack, 'Human Security in the New Millennium', in United Nations University, *Work in Progress*, 16/3 (Summer 2002), p. 6.

[5] Myron Weiner, quoted in Krause, 'Broadening the Agenda', p. 245.

[6] Krause, 'Broadening the Agenda', pp. 242-3.

However, this enlargement of the concept of security is not uncontested.[7] On a practical level, there is the suspicion that the diffuse nature of this enlarged concept is intended as a tool to forge coalitions between various agents and agencies (including NGOs) to address problems which are said to have previously not received sufficient attention, but opponents argue that the costs for this motivation are high in terms of prioritizing.[8] In the case of Japan, a major proponent of human security, the enlargement of the security concept also serves practical objectives which are related to overcoming specific domestic and international problems (see further down). The International Relations School most adverse to this conceptual enlargement is unsurprisingly Realism. In view of the above suspicion, the enlargement of security is dismissed by it as a political act rather than an analytical act.[9] Human security is seen as an attack against the Westphalian system of nation states because it questions the link between national security and national borders and instead transcends the security of the state, expanding it to the whole world or at least to a much wider area. It goes beyond the traditional state conflict because the threat is not necessarily linked to other states. Moreover, responses to these 'new' threats demand international cooperation which reduces the power of the national power elite and infringes on national sovereignty. Realists may agree with some of the non-conventional dimensions of security, but the resolution of most of these threats does not rest only or even primarily on military force.[10] D. Baldwin accuses proponents like Barry Buzan of intermingling conceptual and empirical analysis: 'Understanding the concept of security is a fundamentally different kind of intellectual exercise from specifying the conditions under which security may be attained'.[11] Andrew Mack argues that the 'causal relationships between, say, poverty and political violence can only be explored if these phenomena are treated separately'.[12]

Building on Barry Buzan's seminal work *People, States and Fear*, Ole Wæver is juxtaposing the concept of national security (sovereignty and the survival of the regime) against that of societal security. The latter is related to the identity and survival of the society. Identity means the idea which groups and individuals have of themselves and which allows them to identify themselves as members of a community.[13] In their joint book Morten Kelstrup, Jaap de Wilde and Ole Wæver

---

[7] For a Japanese discussion of this enlargement see *Kokusai Seiji*, No 117: Anzen hosho no riron to seisaku (Tokyo: Nihon Kokusai Seiji Gakkai, March 1998).

[8] Paris, 'Paradigm Shift', p. 88.

[9] For a critical discussion of the Realist opponents to a broadened security concept see Krause, 'Broadening the Agenda'.

[10] Alagappa, *Asian Security Practice*, p. 686.

[11] Quoted in Allan P. Dobson, 'The Dangers of US Interventionism', in *Review of International Studies*, 28/3 (July 2002): 591.

[12] Mack, 'Human Security', p. 6.

[13] On Wæver see Ayse Ceyhan, 'Analyser la securité: Dillon, Wæver, Williams et les autres', in *Cultures & Conflits*, http://www.revues.org (downloaded 9 March 2002). See also Ole Wæver's contributions to Ole Wæver, Barry Buzan, Morton Kelstrup and Pierre

differentiate between societal, state, and systemic security.[14] Agency is no longer only ascribed to the state, but more to non-state actors. The relevance of a threat is determined by five variables: the specificity of the threat, the closeness of the threat in time and space, the high probability of the threat being realized, and the seriousness of consequences the threat will have for the state, the society or the system.[15]

Some of the problems of an enlarged concept of security may be summarized in the following way:

1. precise definition: the problem of clear threat criteria against which relative security environments and situations can be measured;[16]
2. the tension between earmarking the individual as the key unit of analysis and retaining the state as the central referent for countermeasures, even if we accept that the state is not unitary;[17]
3. the long and often complex causality of threats to human security, the difference between 'general' and 'specific' threats;
4. expansion of the concept of security makes prioritization and timing of countermeasures for policymakers more difficult (at what threshold are what measures taken by whom?).

Since I am mostly concerned here with the security of developing countries, in particular Asia, I have found Alagappa's approach to deal with the conceptual problems of enlarging the term security most useful. His generic definition of security, 'the protection and enhancement of values that the authoritative decision makers deem vital for the survival and well-being of a community', is based on three criteria to warrant the security label in order not to dilute the concept of security: the value must be vital to survival, the threat to the value must be urgent, and the value must be determined by the authoritative decision makers.[18] This has also an important operational implication: if the security linkage is not clear, the non-traditional security concern will rank low on the agenda of policymakers.

Alagappa distills two connections between non-conventional concerns and security. The first is the problem of political survival which he puts in Asia as the

---

Lemaitre, Identity, Migration and the New Security Agenda in Europe (London: Pinter Publishers, 1993), pp. 17-40.

[14] Barry Buzan, Ole Wæver and Jaap de Wilde, Security: A New Framework for Analysis (Boulder: Lynne Rienner, 1998).

[15] Summary of Buzan's list by Emil Kirchner and James Sperling, The New Security Threats to Eurasia: Theory and Evidence. Paper for Conference at Renmin University, Beijing 24-26 April 2002, p. 11.

[16] Nicholas Thomas and William T. Town, 'The Utility of Human Security: Sovereignty and Humanitarian Intervention', in Security Dialogue, 33/2 (2002): 181.

[17] Seizaburô Satô, 'Why National Defense Became Security', in Gaikô Forum (English edition) (Summer 2000): 5-19.

[18] Alagappa, Asian Security Practice, pp. 689-91.

main concern of states. Political survival is affected by threats to national identity, political legitimacy, political stability, autonomy, territorial integrity, as well as threats to the state's power, prestige and influence.[19] Economic growth and development are also viewed as critical elements for political survival and any threats to them are therefore also part of the security agenda. Migration may threaten identity and control of state power or may produce domestic and interstate conflict. The second linkage for Alagappa is the impact on the well-being of the community. He suggests to conceptualize security at a higher level of abstraction so that the concept can accommodate diversity and change, beyond an actual referent, a specific value to be protected, or the nature and type of threat to it, and how security is to be achieved.[20]

Alagappa admits that his definition of security may be objected on at least three accounts: its openness to abuse, its subjectivity, and the resulting problems for theory-building.[21] He dismisses the first by rightly pointing out that issues have always been 'securitized' or 'desecuritized' by political leaders to serve their vested interests. The analyst has to detect abuse and take account of it. On subjectivity he simply argues that this is the price to pay for avoiding the creation of a gap between reality and analysis. He defends the third by saying that some shortcomings of this definition cannot be the basis for rejecting alternative conceptions of security, particularly in view of the failures of others based on Neorealist foundations or positivism. He considers that his approach of 'hierarchic conceptualization of security' allows the 'derivation of discrete concepts to specify referents, to delimit the scope, and to identity approaches to security' which facilitates 'comparative analysis and prevents conceptual stretching and obfuscation'.[22]

## Establishing Causal Links between Security and Migration

The issue of migration lends itself very easily to securitization. Refugee movements have been frequently cited in recent times by states and international organizations as a basis for action in both civil and international conflict. As a threat to peace and security, some argue, the imposition of refugees on other states falls under Chapter VII of the UN Charter and thus legitimizes outside intervention.[23] The Japanese Ministry of Foreign Affairs writes in its *Diplomatic Blue Book* of 1999 that refugees 'continue to be not only of humanitarian concern

---

[19] Ibid., p. 685.
[20] Ibid., p. 688.
[21] Ibid., p. 691.
[22] Ibid., p. 696.
[23] Gil Loescher, 'Refugee Movements as Grounds for International Action', in United Nations University, *Work in Progress*, 16/2 (Summer 2002), p. 12.

but also a global issue which could have an effect upon the peace and stability of both the regions concerned and the entire world'.[24]

To start with, even Realists cannot dispute that migration in the form of seeking refuge can occur as the result of interstate conflict although they might stop here because military power as the traditional tool of interstate conflict might not be appropriate for dealing with the problem. Moreover, the broad approach of human security suggests that more than only interstate conflict can lead to refugee flows. It is, of course, the latter point which makes it so convenient to include migration in all its forms into an enlarged security concept: failed governance, resource scarcity, intrastate and regional interstate differences in wealth, natural disasters, etc. can all encourage migration, either in a sudden outflow (namely as the result of a natural disaster) or in trickles of various degrees (namely the movements of 'economic refugees'). The security of refugees and migrants itself has similarly become an issue within the enlarged security concept. Secondly, the non-traditional security concerns represent migration not only as the result of traditional and non-traditional security concerns, but also as a threat to a non-traditional security concern such as the survival of societal identity and culture. Moreover, migration is often causally linked to domestic as well as transnational crime and terrorism which threatens domestic security and may even destabilize relations among states.

As we will discuss later, migration can threaten identities which are defined as a key part of societal security by authors such as Ole Wæver and Barry Buzan.

This securitization of migration has detractors not only with Realists, but also with Constructivists like Didier Bigo who discusses the domestic and transnational processes and structures of the securitization of migration. He critically analyses the utility of the security prism for politicians, for national and local police organizations, the military police, customs officers, border patrols, secret services, armies, judges, some social services private corporations, many journalists and a significant fraction of general public opinion.[25] The security prism, according to him, takes care of the rise of insecurity, crime, terrorism, and the negative aspects of globalization, but assists also those in charge of meeting these challenges to get legitimacy and a share of increasingly contested public resources. For him, the securitization of migration is part of a 'structural unease in the "risk society" framed by neoliberal discourses in which freedom is always associated at its limits with danger and (in)security'.[26] But rather than focusing on the political discourse of securitization of migration, he suggests that securitization 'works through everyday technologies, through the effects of power that are continuous rather than exceptional, through political struggles, and

---

[24] *Diplomatic Blue Book 1999* (Tokyo: Ministry of Foreign Affairs, 1999), p. 79.

[25] Didier Bigo, 'Security and Immigration: Toward a Critique of the Governmentality of Unease', in *Alternatives*, 27 (2002, Special Issue): 63.

[26] Ibid., p. 65.

especially rough institutional competition within the professional security field in which the most trivial interests are at stake'.[27]

## Migration and its Security Relevance in Asia

Migration in Asia deserves particular attention when looking at traditional and non-traditional security concerns because of the geographic and demographic dimensions of Asia, as well as its diversity in terms of political and economic development stages. Asia, if defined as stretching from the eastern rim of the Eurasian continent to the western rim formed by Myanmar, is home to about 40 per cent of the world's population. Non-traditional security concerns like human rights, economic deprivation, health problems and environmental degradation which potentially lead to refugee streams, have all been linked to this region. In the case of migration, there are strong links to threats to national identity, crime and economic welfare. Given the existence of many traditional security concerns like territorial disputes and arms races, there is a potentially explosive cocktail for conflict which may further aggravate the refugee situation. Differences of political and economic stages in this huge and diverse region demonstrate the degree of vulnerability of advanced and less advanced countries to security threats resulting from migration as well as the various origins and security-relevant results of migration. Not surprisingly therefore, Asia has the highest number of refugees today.[28]

The most massive Asian refugee streams were created during the third stage of the Vietnam War, leading to hundreds of thousands of Vietnamese refugees flooding into Southeast Asian countries (the so-called 'boat people'), later followed by Vietnamese of Chinese origin as a result of anti-Chinese policies by the Vietnamese Communist Party after reunification in 1975. These streams had a destabilizing effect on the delicate ethnic balance of many Southeast Asian countries as well as on their economic welfare which can still be felt today.

The most recent issues in Asian cross-border migration are related to illegal immigration among ASEAN member states, refugees from North Korea and illegal Chinese immigration into other Asian countries.

A surging influx of illegal workers, escaping from a stagnant economic situation at home, has become a major source of concern in Southeast Asia, especially in Thailand and Malaysia. Approximately one million illegal workers from Myanmar are said to be working in Thailand. This situation, in combination with armed incursions and drug smuggling, has led to a worsening of relations

---

[27] Ibid., p. 73. For the processes of the securitization and criminalization of immigrants in Europe see also Monica den Boer, 'Crime et immigration dans l'Union Européenne', in *Cultures & Conflits* (http://www.revues.org) (downloaded 9 March 2002).

[28] For a statistical comparison with other world regions see tables in *Gaikô Forum* (April 2002): 64-5.

among these two member states of ASEAN. Malaysia is said to have two million illegal workers, many of them from Indonesia.

North Korean migration is of particular concern to Northeast Asia because of its precursory message about the crumbling of the North Korean state which could even lead to the outbreak of another war on the peninsula, the threat to the delicate power balance in Northeast Asia, and the threat to the economies of at least South Korea and Japan. Stricken by famine and political repression, North Koreans are fleeing their country in increasing numbers. Their destination is mostly China (even if they later proceed to South Korea) because of its geographic proximity and the Korean ethnic composition of Yanbian, the Chinese area on the other side of the border. Estimates of these refugees vary from 10,000 by South Korean government organizations to as many as 400,000 by NGOs.[29] There were 1,141 arrivals in 2002, compared with 583 in 2001. Those in China are estimated to amount to 300 000 although not all want to leave North Korea permanently.[30] The South Korean government estimates that there are c. 75,000 Chinese of Korean ancestry illegally in South Korea.[31]

**Traditional and Non-Traditional Security Links**

The links between migration and traditional security are probably strongest on the volatile Korean peninsula but the transition to non-traditional security is fluid. The growing stream of refugees from North Korea to the countries around is destabilizing the North Korean regime as well as indicative of its decay, enhancing its international isolation, even towards friendly and sympathetic China, and upsetting relations among Northeast Asian countries. It has led to incidents of North Korean police and other state agents acting without proper permission in China and Russia, infringing on Chinese and Russian sovereignty. The intrusion of North Korean refugees into embassies of other countries in Beijing has strained relations among Northeast Asian countries which are often already difficult enough. Sending the refugees back to North Korea exposes China's human rights policy to even more international criticism. The transiting or relocating of North Korean refugees also has a destabilizing influence on China's Yanbian region which has a considerable percentage of Chinese of Korean ancestry, undermining public security. The illegal situation of these

---

[29] Shin-wha Lee, 'The UN and Low Politics: Environment and Human Security in East Asia', in *Global Economic Review*, 30/2 (2001): 62. For a general analysis of all kinds of migration related to the Korean peninsula see Martin Heisler, 'Cross-boundary Population Movements and Security in Korea: Gradual Rapprochement and Other Scenarios', in Miranda A. Schreurs and Dennis Pirages (eds), *Ecological Security in Northeast Asia* (Seoul: Yonsei University Press, 1998), pp. 171-93.

[30] *Comparative Connections*, 2nd quarter (2002): 97.

[31] *Comparative Connections*, 2nd quarter (2002): 106.

refugees is exposing them to smuggling and work place exploitation. Given the general tension on the Korean peninsula due to North Korea's brinkmanship policy, incidents related to this migratory phenomenon could contribute to the outbreak of at least local inter-state skirmishes.

In Japan's security policy planning, refugee flows as a result of interstate conflict (between North and South Korea) or state collapse in the North are considered more likely than any attack against Japan. The renewed outbreak of hostilities is considered to bring about hundreds of thousands of North Korean refugees. A 1993 report by the Japanese Defence Agency estimated that 270,000 refugees from North as well as South Korea would flee to Japan immediately after an emergency broke out in Korea, with the total number eventually rising to 2.7 million. The report said Japan's Self-Defense Forces would have to be called out to deal with the refugees since Japanese police are only capable of handling up to 35,000 of them.[32]

Non-conventional threats arising from migration have a direct negative impact on Japanese-Chinese security relations. Chinese immigration (particularly the illegal one) into Japan and Chinese-linked crimes in Japan (often linked to people-smuggling or the survival of illegal immigrants) aggravate the negative Japanese perceptions created by China's military developments since the beginning of the 1990s. Moreover, illegal Chinese immigration conjures in Japan the fear of the consequences of China failing economically which is seen as the more likely threat to Japan's security than a Chinese attack. It is obvious that the loosening of central and even regional control, combined with economic hardship and generational impatience, is contributing to illegal emigration and the regional expansion of China-based criminal syndicates. Satoshi Amako writes that if China's economy fails and the country disintegrates it is expected that this may lead to considerable refugee streams into China's immediate neighbouring countries. He also recalls that several thousand Chinese refugees landed in Okinawa and Kyushu after the massacre in Tiananmen in 1989.[33] The possibility of 100 million Chinese refugees destabilizing Asia is mentioned in a book co-edited by former Prime Minister Yasuhiro Nakasone.[34] The possibility of Chinese refugees in the aftermath of economic collapse threatening Japan's security is referred to in the revised Japan-US military cooperation guidelines of 1999, where the clause 'situations in areas surrounding Japan' also includes a scenario of

---

[32] 'Japan Estimates 2.7 Million Refugees in Korean War', in *Korea Times* (12 May 1998).

[33] Satoshi Amako (ed.), *Chûgoku wa kyôi ka* (Tokyo: Keisô Shobo, 1997), p. 9 and Chapter 7. See also Hideo Satô, 'Japan's China Perceptions and Its Policies in the Alliance with the United States', in *Journal of International Political Economy*, 2/1(March 1998): 11.

[34] Yasuhiro Nakasone, Seizaburô Satô, Yasusuke Murakami and Susumu Nishibe, *Kyôdô Kenkyû "Reisen igo"* (Tokyo: Bungei Shunju 1992), p. 281.

refugees coming to Japan.[35] As far fetched as the refugee scenario of some Japanese security specialists may seem now, increasing Chinese illegal immigration to foreign countries, including Japan, piracy in the South China Sea, and involvement of Chinese citizens in regional and domestic crime are seen as precursors of China's economic failure although these phenomena can also be interpreted as merely transitional and inherent in the modernization process of China's political and economic system. It is important to note for non-Japanese that Japanese China watchers give much more consideration to the likelihood of China failing, whereas in the West China's linear economic success seems to be granted and concerns are more linked to China becoming a military and/or economic challenge to the rest of the world on the basis of economic success.

Even without the above link between migration and conventional security concerns, non-traditional security concerns such as crime and national identity arising from migration deserve special attention because the perception of the latter concerns in some Asian states is much more critical in Asia than in Europe or North America despite the higher numbers in the latter two regions. In Asia Chinese migration is very much at the centre of attention. Even Taiwan, which has been experiencing the influx of mainland Chinese as a result of its democratization and economic development, feels its economic prosperity and social order threatened because many immigrants are seen as the source of much of Taiwan's growing crime and drug problems.[36]

Chinese illegal immigration into Japan may not be high in absolute figures nor in relation to Japan's population, but related links to internal security receive a lot of public attention.[37] Links between crimes committed by Chinese in Japan have a very high impact on the perception of a relatively crime-free and isolationist society like Japan since crime is much more widely reported in the media and touches the life or at the least the imagination of the individual Japanese in a much more tangible way than elsewhere in the world. Chinese immigration is caused by economic circumstances, namely the attraction of Japan's economic strength, the wide gap between the two countries' economies, educational opportunities and increasing Chinese unemployment due to the restructuring of China's state-owned enterprises.[38]

According to the Japanese police and the Maritime Safety Agency (now referred to in English as Coast Guard), about 90 per cent of people entering Japan illegally come from the People's Republic of China.[39] Until 1991, the number of Chinese nationals arrested for entering the country illegally remained in double

---

[35] *East Asian Strategic Review 2000* (Tokyo: The National Institute for Defense Studies, 2000): 129.

[36] Alagappa, *Asian Security Practice*, p. 302.

[37] The following is based on the author's book *Japan's security relations with China since 1989. From Balancing to Bandwagoning?* (London: Routledge, 2002).

[38] Yasushi Iguchi, *Gaikokujin rodosha shinjidai* (Tokyo: Chikuma Shobo, 2001), p. 62.

[39] *Kaijô Hôan Hakusho Heisei 11* (Tokyo: Finance Ministry Printing Office, 1999), p. 17.

digital figures, but it rose sharply to 1,209 in 1997, falling again to 824 in 1998. Between January-November 2000, 2,814 Chinese nationals were arrested, accounting for roughly half of all the arrests of foreigners. The number of Chinese being deported is increasing, and exceeded 11,000 in 1999.[40] According to Justice Ministry statistics, 33,000 illegal Chinese immigrants have been confirmed in the country, the third-largest group, following illegal immigrants from the Republic of Korea and the Philippines.[41] According to NPA statistics, in 1999, 45 per cent of all foreigners arrested were Chinese. Of that figure, about 35 per cent were residing illegally in Japan. Of 770 people apprehended in suspected human smuggling cases that year, 701 were Chinese citizens.[42] The number of officially registered Chinese residents in Japan and their share among foreign residents has been constantly rising from 40,000 (a share of 6.8 per cent) in 1950 to 252,164 (17 per cent) in 1997.[43] In view of the alarmist perception of Chinese immigration today it is useful to remember that the share of Chinese residents among foreign residents of Japan in 1890 was 56.6 per cent.[44]

The most important factor for the negative perception of Chinese immigration is crime. In 2000 54.2 per cent of crimes committed by foreign nationals were committed by Chinese, a 9 per cent increase from the previous year and the first time on record the figure has topped 50 per cent.[45] In 2000, 38 per cent of all prisoners in Japanese prisons of foreign nationality were Chinese.[46] In 1994 it was already reported that the Japanese *yakuza* and organized criminal syndicates in Taiwan, Hong Kong and China were helping illegal Chinese immigration into Japan.[47] There is considerable Chinese involvement in the smuggling of firearms and drugs into Japan. Hundreds of Chinese mobsters from more than 10 of Shanghai's 300 gangs are now active in Japan. The real figures may be several times as high. The governments of both countries started therefore in May 1998 talks on how to deal with this situation.[48] It is reported that almost 70 per cent of stimulants smuggled into Japan are produced in China's Fujian province. The trend marks a change from the 1980s when most illegal drugs brought in came

---

[40] *Asahi Shimbun* (24 February 2001). See also *Sentaku* (May 1999).
[41] *Keisatsu Hakusho Heisei 12* (Tokyo: Finance Ministry Printing Office, 2000), p. 246.
[42] *Asahi Shimbun* (26 August 2000).
[43] For a description of Chinese immigration and residency over the last centuries in Japan see Andrea Vasishth, 'A Model Minority: the Chinese Community in Japan', in Michael Weinter (ed.), *Japan's Minorities. The Illusion of Homogeneity* (London: Routledge, 1997), pp. 108-39.
[44] Yu Chunghsun (ed.), *Ethnic Chinese. Their Economy, Politics and Culture* (Tokyo: The Japan Times, 2000), pp. 147-9.
[45] *Mainichi Daily News* (23 March 2001).
[46] *Asahi Shimbun* (17 November 2001).
[47] *Far Eastern Economic Review* (4 August 1994).
[48] *The Daily Yomiuri* (20 June 1999). *Asahi Shimbun* (24 June 1999).

from Taiwan, and the 1970s when the Republic of Korea was the main source.[49] The Japan Coast Guard reported that the greatest amount of confiscated drugs in 1999, 48 per cent, came from China, followed by 34 per cent from North Korea.[50] The most recent crime involving Chinese includes 'cyber crimes'. In February 2000, the Japanese police reported that hackers behind a recent series of invasions of government-run web sites gained access to the sites through computers located in China, the United States and Tokyo University.[51] This year, reports about the import of Chinese slimming cures which resulted in injuries and even death in Japan have only heightened the general Japanese concern about China.

**Identity**

As we have seen the proponents of the enlarged security concept also include national identity in their catalogue of threats. For them, societal security 'can be threatened by whatever puts its "we" identity into jeopardy'.[52] A society's cultural and national identity can be threatened by migration and is therefore a central concern of the critical and constructivist school which puts societal security' next to 'national security'.[53] That it is very real and policy-relevant can be illustrated by reactions in Europe not only to immigration (legal or illegal) but also to efforts by governments which plan to offset Europe's sub-replacement fertility (the current UK and German positions) by some kind of legalized immigration. In order to achieve such an offset, a population of predominantly, eventually entirely, immigrant origin would be required. But this approach would change a country's original identity.[54] The problem is, according to Buzan, that societal identities are dynamic rather than static, and social communities are debating within themselves to what extent 'change has to be accepted as a natural process by which identities adjust and evolve to meet alterations in historical circumstances'.[55] The discussion of acceptability may vary according to different communities. According to Buzan, the 'main threats to security come from competing identities and migration (both inward and outward)'.[56] Further on he

---

[49] *Asahi Shimbun* (4 May 1998). For a brief mentioning of the role of Chinese see H. Richard Friman, 'Gaijinhanzai: Immigrants and Drugs in Contemporary Japan', in *Asian Survey*, 36/10 (October 1996): 965.

[50] *Kaijô Hôan no Genkyô 2000* (Tokyo: Finance Ministry Printing Office, 2000), p. 9.

[51] Yamada Hideki, '"Saiba kôgeki senryaku" no kaihatsu o hajimeta Jinmin Kaihôgun ni Nihon wa ippô okure o toru', in *Sapio* (22 March 2000).

[52] Buzan, in Wæver et al., *Identity*, p. 42.

[53] Krause, 'Broadening the Agenda', p. 245. Wæver et al., *Identity*.

[54] Christopher Coker, *Globalisation and Insecurity in the Twenty-first Century: NATO and the Management of Risk*, Adelphi Paper, No 345 (London: International Institute for Strategic Studies, 2002), p. 44.

[55] Buzan, in Wæver et al., *Identity*, p. 42.

[56] Ibid., p. 43.

states that 'the threat of migration is fundamentally a question of how relative numbers interact with the absorptive and adaptive capacities of society'.[57]

In Asia, the relationship between immigration and a perception of threat to national identity is indeed varied. India has a much higher tolerance level for immigrants than, for example, Japan and Korea which have a much higher emphasis on ethnic homogeneity due to their historical experience of seclusion. Malaysia with its goal of Malay political domination pursued by the Malay majority is more receptive to Malay-Muslim immigrants than to Chinese and Indian immigrants. The inflow in the 1970s and 1980s of Vietnamese boat people, predominantly of Chinese ancestry, was labeled as a security threat, but not the greater influx of Muslim Filipinos and Indonesians.[58]

Japan and South Korea have historically not experienced immigration and have a very strict notion of homogeneity, despite their close cultural links to China.[59] Immigration, which is negligible in comparison to what other Asian countries or even European countries today experience, is seen as a major threat to Japanese or Korean identity. Korea even had eliminated all China towns after the Second World War, and is now recreating them as a means to attract Asian (and particularly Chinese) tourists as well as to better integrate Chinese immigrants of Korean ancestry.

In Japan particularly Chinese immigration in conjunction with the rise of China's overall rise is perceived as a threat to the country's self identity of a homogeneous nation. Despite its considerable financial contribution for international efforts to deal with refugees and the ratification of the Refugee Convention in 1982, Japan has been extremely reluctant to accept refugees into its own country.[60] Japan's contradictory position was vividly illustrated in January 2002, when it refused political asylum to some Afghan refugees just while it was hosting the international conference for the reconstruction of Afghanistan for which Japan pledged 500 million US$. It is against this background that Japanese reactions to immigration-related crime, notably from its huge Chinese neighbour, become more understandable. Due to these close interlinkages and mutually reinforcing elements, it is difficult to analytically differentiate between concerns about national identity and other non-traditional and traditional security concerns related to migration.

---

[57] Ibid., p. 45.

[58] Alagappa, *Asian Security Practice*, p. 691.

[59] On Japan's reluctance to accept foreigners in any form see Mayumi Itoh, *Globalization of Japan. Japanese Sakoku Mentality and US Efforts to Open Japan* (New York: St. Martin's Press, 1998).

[60] On this situation see *Gaikô Forum* (April 2002): 52-9.

## Regional Approaches

In keeping with this book's interest in regional integration and human security, the latter being an essential operational device for regional approaches, I want to end with a brief look at regional approaches to security-related aspects of migration. Before, however, it is useful to explain the popularity of human security in Japan because the attitude of Asia's greatest aid donor towards this concept has an important impact on regional approaches.

'Human security' was started to be officially embraced in December 1998 when Prime Minister Obuchi spoke of his intention to make it an important element of Japan's diplomacy after he had mentioned the concept already in May of the same year in Singapore when he was still Foreign Minister.[61] The strong Japanese support for the broad developmentalist version of human security which plays down conventional security is, of course, related to the pacifism and the public's aloofness from international strife. Moreover, emphasis on a broad developmentalist approach allows the Japanese government to bridge the gap between the system of the Peace Constitution and the system of the Japan-US security alliance, to respond to international burdensharing demands, to materialize its ambition to be a regional leader (also competing against China's regional leadership aspirations) and to use as well as domestically justify ODA as Japan's greatest non-military foreign policy asset.[62] In order to respond in non-military ways to international demands for burdensharing after the exodus of Vietnamese boat people from 1975, Japan became the second largest contributor to the UNHCR (14.2 per cent in 2000, preceded only by the US with 34.8 per cent) and Professor Ogata Sadako was appointed the head of this organization. Due to Professor Ogata's influence, Japan increased its financially commitment to refugees substantially while at the same time, she pressed the government to become more open to accepting refugees on humanitarian grounds.[63] In February 2001, the Commission on Human Security, sponsored by the Japanese government

---

[61] For a short overview of the official and academic treatment of human security in Japan see Yusuke Dan, 'A Brief Review of Human Security', in *Human Security* (Hiratsuka: Tokai University, Heiwa Senryaku Kokusai Kenkyûsho), 4 (1999/2000): 325-9. For a listing of official Japanese statements and actions related to human security see *Ajia no anzenhosho 2002-2003* (Tokyo: Research Institute for Peace and Security, 2002), p. 310. See also a leaflet on the related Japanese-initiated UN Trust Fund for Human Security (Tokyo: The United Nations Information Centre, August 2002).

[62] For an explanation about the two conflicting systems see the author's *Japan's Foreign Policy for the 21$^{st}$ Century* (Basingstoke: Macmillan, 1998), pp. 25-7.

[63] For an account of Japan's refugee aid and policy see *Gaikô Forum* (April 2002), notably the article by Isami Takeda, 'Kachi totta 10 nen, Nihon no jindô enjô gaikô', pp. 23-9. See also an official presentation of Japan's refugee policy by Kôichi Takahashi, 'Nanmin mondai ni tai suru Nihon no torikumi', *Kokusai Mondai* (December 2002): 46-59.

and co-chaired by Sadako Ogata and Amartya Sen was established to prepare a document on human security within two years.[64]

Migration has the potential not only to threaten traditional security in the region, but it can also threaten the very security concept of the member states of ASEAN, that is national resilience.[65] It is obvious that no single state in Asia can tackle on its own the origins of migration and the required regional and global approaches. There are now some moves in Asia afoot to address these issues not only at the general global level through the relevant agencies of the UN, but also through multilateral regional approaches. Specific conditions and concerns in the region have shaped these multilateral responses. The difficulties encountered in doing so prove how strong the nation state still is particularly in Asia, and how limited the alleged sovereignty-reducing effects of transboundary non-traditional security threats are when it comes to dealing with them. Rather than establishing a comprehensive framework like the EU which serves as a framework to solve specific issues, the Asian countries have chosen to establish cooperative frameworks in individual and specific areas.[66] These endeavours are partly also driven by the perceived absence of regional organizations in Asia and the need to foster a 'security community'. Such endeavours are also seen as a more effective means to integrate China as a peaceful stakeholder into the region. In the case of migration we have seen that Chinese citizens are involved as victims as well as victimizers.

Smuggling of migrants and trafficking in persons is a particularly acute problem in the Asia-Pacific region. However, these issues do not yet seem to loom very high on the agenda of even the more developed countries in the region. Japan has still not ratified a UN protocol adopted in November 2000 on trafficking of women and children (U.N. Protocol to Prevent, Suppress and Punish Trafficking in Persons, Especially Women and Children) despite its considerable problem of trafficking.[67] In a report on human trafficking published the US Department of State in 2004, South Korea was out on the list of 'tier three' countries, indicating that it was not making sufficient efforts to meet minimum standards to curb trafficking in children and women. The Working Group on Transnational Crime of the Council for Security Cooperation in Asia-Pacific (CSCAP) has been allowed to study problems in human trafficking, but apparently only because

---

[64] *Asahi Shimbun* (19 February 2001).

[65] Amitav Acharya, 'The Association of Southeast Asian Nations: "Security Community" or "Defence Community"?', in *Pacific Affairs* (Summer 1991): 159-78.

[66] Quoted in *East Asian Strategic Review 2002* (Tokyo: National Institute of Defense Studies, 2002): 100. For a list of regional statements and institutions dealing with issues arising from migration in Asia see the paragraph 14 of the co-chairs' statement of the Regional Ministerial Conference on People Smuggling, Trafficking in Persons and Related Transnational Crime (26-28 February 2002) in
(http://dfat.gov.au/illegal_immigration/cochair.html).

[67] *Asahi Shimbun* (23 January 2003).

Asian governments do not give high priority to the issue.[68] The Indonesian and Australian governments agreed in late 2001 to jointly sponsor a Regional Ministerial Conference on People Smuggling, Trafficking in Persons and Related Transnational Crime. The resulting ministerial conference was hosted by Indonesia from 26-28 February 2002.[69] In the co-chairs' statement the link to security is clearly stated by saying that these flows of people 'were creating significant political, economic, social and security challenges, and that journeys were undertaken without respect for either national sovereignty or borders'. The latter clause (see also paragraph 9 on protecting national borders) is particularly important in the context of Asia's concern about sovereignty, appealing thus directly to links with traditional security concerns. The declaration is non-binding and contains only intentions rather than concrete commitments.

The limited and inchoate nature of regional cooperation and reliance on loose frameworks are also related to concerns which Asian states have with the concept of human security, despite the blessing it received from the UN. There is concern that the ever-growing agenda of human security has become a tool for the West to impose its values and political institutions on non-Western societies. This has only further enhanced their concern about sovereignty and noninterference into domestic affairs.[70] These suspicions cannot be denied since the very foundation of human security is that the violation of human rights and bad governance lead to many of the problems on the agenda of the enlarged security concept. It is ironic that we have here the situation that one concern, which is particularly but not exclusively linked to migration, namely national identity, arises also from one device of dealing with this concern. After all, the concept of human security is an appealing package device for a growing number of non-conventional security concerns, including migration, which is meant to mobilize a maximum number of governmental as well as non-governmental actors to deal with these concerns. Nowhere in the co-chairs' declaration mentioned above is therefore any mentioning of 'human security'. This Asian reluctance indicates yet another practical shortcoming of using the concept of human security, after we have already seen that this way of bundling all kinds of non-conventional threats creates considerable problems of prioritizing. This alone defeats attempts to deal with these threats which are often interlinked.

---

[68] Simon Sheldon, 'Evaluating Track II Approaches to Security Diplomacy in the Asia-Pacific: the CSCAP Experience, in *The Pacific Review*, 15/2 (2002), note 35.

[69] On this conference and for the co-chairs' statement see http://dfat.gov.au/illegal_immigration/cochair.html. See also Alexander Downer, 'Let's Stop the People-smugglers', in *International Herald Tribune* (27 February 2002).

[70] Mack, 'Human Security', p. 6.

## Conclusions

Migration is clearly on the list of non-traditional security concerns which has been proposed by academic as well as political practitioners. In the first part of my contribution I tried to explain, however, that the enlargement of security concerns is controversial because it raises practical as well as theoretical problems. More than any other non-traditional security concern, migration lends itself to securitization and it can be the result of threats to such concerns as well as cause for them, including even traditional security concerns.

This relevance of migration to traditional and non-traditional security concerns can be well illustrated in the case of Asia with its particular geographic and demographic dimensions. The linkages between migration and traditional and non-traditional security concerns as well as between these two categories of concerns are manifold and complex. The example of the security situation on the Korean peninsula and the Japanese-Chinese security relationship has clear linkages to traditional security concerns which are reinforced by non-traditional security concerns such as crime and national identity. The Japanese case shows how the highly emotive character of migration from China to Japan, linked to the relatively low but increasing crime rate, enhances the worsening Japanese security perception of China.

Regional approaches to these concerns are still very limited and provide one more example for the inchoate nature of regional cooperation in any area of common concern because of Asia's political and economic diversity. It is regrettable that Asian concerns about human security possibly being used by Western powers for interference into Asia's domestic affairs also negatively affect common approaches to migration.

# PART 2
# The Restructuration of Transnational Spaces

Chapter Five

# Migration and Geographical Distance

Leslie E. Bauzon[1]

**Geographical Distance and Geographical Space in Human History**

Two of the leading pillars in the study of the history of religion in the world, Mircea Eliade and Charles Long, give us in their respective works valuable insights into how people in earlier centuries viewed migratory movements. The eminent Eliade tells us, for example, that European immigrants in the sixteenth century who sailed across the Atlantic Ocean from Europe viewed and thought of America 'as the country where they might be born anew, that is, begin a new life'.[2] There was an expectation for a better and a beatific existence in the New World. For his part, the equally eminent Long says that the New World made an extraordinary impact on European consciousness, and European immigrants to America looked at their journey as a quest for Utopia and for a world with sacred meanings; in other words, a paradise where the pilgrims and the diaspora people from the Old World would be freed from the evils found in the homeland and

---

[1] I wish to express my deepest gratitude to Prof. Ma. Rosario P. Ballescas of the University of the Philippines in Cebu City, Prof. Francis A. Gealogo of Ateneo de Manila University, Mr. Benigno D. Tutor, Jr., Publisher of *Philippines Today* in Tsukuba City, Japan, and Prof. Ajit Singh Rye of the Asian Center of the University of the Philippines in Quezon City, for their extremely valuable comments and suggestions regarding the writing of this paper. Moreover, I am very grateful to Mr. Reynaldo Reyes of the University of Santo Tomas in Manila for his assistance in administering the questionnaire survey among prospective Filipino migrants in Manila and to my wife Dr. Aurora F. Bauzon of the Faculty of Medicine and Surgery of the University of Santo Tomas in Manila for help in the statistical analysis of the survey results. I am very profoundly grateful, and this study is dedicated, to my beloved Pampanga beauty for her inspiration, encouragement, patience and understanding. Last but not the least, I am highly indebted to my colleague in the University of Tsukuba faculty, Prof. Harald Kleinschmidt, for affording me this invaluable and irreplaceable opportunity to participate in his project on international migration. And I am thankful to the Doctoral Program in International Political Economy and the Graduate School of Area Studies of the University of Tsukuba for providing me the academic atmosphere that ennobles my spirit and provides me the freedom and opportunity to walk the way of my liking with joy, and for engendering my pursuit of the life of the mind.

[2] Mircea Eliade, *The Quest: History and Meaning in Religion* (Chicago and London: The University of Chicago Press, 1969), p. 98.

enjoy only blissful life in the Garden of Eden.³ It is clear from the writings of both Eliade and Long that geographical distance between Europe and America across the deep, blue waters of the Atlantic Ocean did not matter to the European immigrants in the sixteenth century. They were obviously willing to endure the hazards to life and limb they were sure to encounter along the way because they expected to find an Edenic quality of life on the other side of the Atlantic Ocean. This view would prevail in the European diaspora in America. And America is the product of this European diaspora.

However, in the nineteenth century, a European scholar named Ernest George Ravenstein would put forward his famous study based on the British Census of 1881 entitled 'The Laws of Migration'. He presented this study to the members of the British Royal Statistical Society on 17 March 1885. There are seven components of his 'Laws on Migration', namely (1) migration and distance, (2) migration by stages, (3) stream and counter-stream, (4) urban-rural differences in propensity to migrate, (5) predominance of females among short-distance migrants, (6) technology and migration and (7) dominance of the economic motive.⁴ Of the seven components, numbers 1 and 5 have to do with distance. For number 1 (Migration and distance), Ravenstein states that (a) '[t]he great body of our migrants only proceed a short distance and migrants enumerated in a certain center of absorption will ... grow less [as distance from the center increases]'; and (b) 'Migrants proceeding long distances generally go by preference to one of the great centers of commerce and industry'.⁵ And for number 5 (predominance of females among short distance migrants), Ravenstein says that 'females appear to predominate among short-journey migrants'.⁶

More than fifty years afterwards, Samuel A. Stouffer would do a theoretical construction of the mathematical relationship between migration and distance and published this theory in the 1940 volume of the *American Sociological Review*.⁷ Briefly and simply, Stouffer would look at distance as constantly present regardless of the number of kilometers existing between area of origin and area of destination. However, he advances his theory of intervening opportunities, by which he means the factors in the area of origin and the area of destination affecting a migrant's decision-making, and the intervening obstacles and difficulties migrants encounter in the process of movement between the two points.⁸

---

³ Charles H. Long, *Significations: Signs, Symbols, and Images in the Interpretation of Religion* (Philadelphia: Fortress Press, 1986), pp. 100-102.
⁴ Everett S. Lee, 'A Theory of Migration', in John A. Jackson (ed.), *Migration. Sociological Studies* (London: Cambridge University Press, 1969), p. 283.
⁵ Ibid.
⁶ Ibid.
⁷ Samuel Andrew Stouffer, 'Intervening Opportunities: A Theory Relating to Mobility and Distance', *American Sociological Review*, 3 (December 1940): 845-67.
⁸ Clifford Jansen, 'Some Sociological Aspects of Migration', in John A. Jackson (ed.), *Migration. Sociological Studies* (London: Cambridge University Press, 1969), pp. 60-70.

These are some views, ideas, interpretations and perspectives offered by a number of great scholars in their respective fields pertaining to the relationship between migration and distance. Eliade and Long, I believe, deal with the mindsets of European immigrants to America in the sixteenth century and thereafter, while Ravenstein and Stouffer are valuable for the contributions they have made toward theory-building with regard to migration. However, in this study, I understand that we are more concerned with perceptions, views, opinions and imaginings of the migrants themselves, so I shall deal with the perceptions, consciousness, opinions and imaginings of Filipino migrants primarily and Indian immigrants to the Philippines secondarily.

**The Study of Migration**

The topic of migration is becoming a popular one, with different scholars from different disciplines using their respective approaches – some are new and some are old – to the study of migration. The imperative of population moving en masse, from one region or country to the other, will be a subject that will be highly significant politically, diplomatically, culturally and of course in economic terms, too. In fact the Filipino scholarship must now pay attention to it. It will become a major issue in international economic, cultural and diplomatic relations. The Philippines will soon begin to feel the shortage of qualified manpower. The massive push of the factor of endemic poverty at home in the Philippines and the pull factor of reasonable opportunity of a good life abroad will hurt the country badly. Imagine that most of the graduates of the University of the Philippines where I was teaching prior to joining the University of Tsukuba will eventually end up working abroad. And it is not just the University of the Philippines that is involved here. At the venerable University of Santo Tomas, I know for a fact that a large number of its medical graduates immigrate to the United States and other industrialized Western countries where they can earn and are earning a higher income than in the Philippines. A highly placed Filipino educator said that one must not worry about it because it will somehow balance off. But I believe that a constant outflow of highly qualified professional Filipinos to the various parts of the world will eventually hurt the country's strategic interests.[9] The overseas workers will of course send in wealth to their families, and in fact Filipino overseas remittances annually reach up to over 7 billion US$, thereby providing a safety valve for the Philippine national economy, but the country I am afraid will be gradually bereft of their skills and expertise. The Filipino overseas migration's long-term impact is hard to imagine. I understand even now that there is a growing shortage of highly qualified and experienced nurses in the country due to their

---

[9] Mynardo Macaraig, More Middle-class Filipinos Seek Brighter Future in Canada (http://news.inq7.net/breaking/index.php?index=1&story_id=36836) May 13, 2005, pp. 1-3.

exodus to the United States.[10] Consequently, some big hospitals, I understand, have closed down some floors. One reason is the horrendously low salary offered by the hospitals to the nurses in the country. Often at about 5000 PHP as monthly starting salary, this amount is just enough for three changes of uniforms.[11] Besides hundreds of thousands of domestic caregivers and workers, we in the Philippines have the largest number of Filipino seamen, engineers, shipmasters and captains who now man the marine trade and transportation on the high seas![12]

**Asian Migration Factors**

The key concept that is at the center of discussion in this volume is the current concern of the advanced countries – the target destination of unwelcome migrants – about how to handle this rising flood of refugees sailing to these lands of affluence, opportunities and good life. In their risky effort to cross borders by sea and land to cover the distance from the lands of the poor to the prospective destination, I think that distance is not a very significant concern. In the olden days, when much of the migration within Asia took place, perhaps distance was a factor – inasmuch as oceanic travel was slow and took place on outmoded ships. But I believe that the push factor – misery and hopelessness at home was of much greater significance.[13]

Distance is an important consideration. Yet in Asia, the Chinese and others are risking lives by travelling through containers and many are dying on the way. It is clearly and basically the function of the push factor that is at work here. For the Chinese movements, lands much closer to their homeland, at present, have no strong pull factors such as opportunities for good life – say in the countries of Southeast Asia. I suggest to zero down as much as we could on the importance of these two significant factors – push and pull – in order to understand the comparative importance of distance between the perceived lands of opportunities like Japan, the United States and the European countries – and the homeland of the refugees.

---

[10] Veronica Uy, US to resume hiring of Filipino nurses – DOLE Law amended to 'recapture' 50,000 EB-3 visas (http://www.inq7.net/glbalnation/sec_new/2005/may/14-03.htm) 2005, pp. 1-2.

[11] Asami Nago, Filipino Nurses to the United States: Factors Affecting Their Decisions. Unpublished M.A. thesis presented to the Graduate School of Area Studies, University of Tsukuba (Tsukuba, 2005), pp. 99-101.

[12] Preciosa S. Soliven, 'The Social Costs of Being Filipino Migrants Abroad. In a Point of Awareness', *The Philippine Star* (3 July 2002): 1-6; forwarded message from Francis A. Gealogo, Thursday, 28 March 2002.

[13] Michael A. Bengwayan, There is no place like far away from home: An exodus, experienced nowhere else, is happening in the Philippines. Some 2,670 Filipinos are leaving daily, many with no intention of coming back (http://lw7fd.law7.hotmail.msn.com/cgi-bin/getmsg?curmbox= F000000001&a=18ca) 9 September 2002, pp. 1-6.

One factor that has, in my opinion, slowed down the smuggling of Chinese on a large-scale into the countries of Southeast Asia is the radical shift in the Chinese economy. The Chinese economy– both on the mainland and Taiwan – plus South Korea are now dominating much of the consumer markets in Southeast Asia. In manufactured consumer goods, Chinese, Taiwanese and South Korean consumer goods are now flooding the markets in the Philippines and other countries. This is not to mention vegetables from China like carrots, broccoli and garlic which have drastically affected the profitability of similar vegetables in Benguet province in the Cordillera region of Northern Luzon in the Philippines, to the point that protesters in my country are now demanding the pullout of the Philippines from the General Agreement on Tariffs and Trade (GATT).

For instance, Chinese ready-made garments have almost completely taken over the Philippine market. The supermarkets and department stores owned by Chinese-Filipinos like the SM Megamall of Henry Sy and Robinson's Galleria of the Gokongwei family have become the favorite distribution and sale centers, and they have destroyed or at least weakened the ready-made garment industry in the Philippines. This situation is equally true in the packed food that is now common in all big chain stores like Cherry Foodarama, SM Supersale and Robinson's Supermarket.

Why a Chinese or a Korean would venture into economies that they themselves have weakened, causing widespread unemployment is something that social scientists must look into. Near distance from China to Southeast Asian countries like the Philippines is no incentive for migration. Thus the risky destinations such as Australia, Europe, and the North American countries of Canada and the United States – not to mention Japan – even though far and risky are much preferred.

*Time Magazine* had a heartrending story in 2001 of a Chinese on its cover. He took many weeks of harrowing experience reaching the United States through many countries. He did reach his destination alive despite the distance because he was pushed by hardship at home and pulled by the prospect of a better life abroad.

There is relevance in this trend of thought and we can buttress it with some factual data on the gradual domination of the economies of Southeast Asia by the Chinese, Koreans and the Japanese. Japan in particular has an unassailable dominance in the market for industrial goods and services including the building of roads, highways and other infrastructure projects like the elevated Metro Rail Transit (MRT) in Metropolitan Manila. The World Trade Organization (WTO) regime is slowly revealing the plight of unplanned weaker and smaller economies like those in Southeast Asia and that of the Philippines in particular, so that these countries are not too attractive as destinations despite their proximity to China, and besides, their citizens are themselves leaving them for more attractive opportunities and better quality of life in the progressive and prosperous industrialized countries.

## Twentieth Century Filipino Migration

In the case of Filipino migrants during the twentieth century, the majority of them were seeking economic opportunities in more economically advanced societies. Economic and social mobility became a major impetus for migration, be it for the Ilocano migrants to Hawaii, the Cebuano tuna packers of Alaska, the plantation workers in California and Washington states in the USA, up to the postwar medical professionals who went to the USA, Canada and Europe. Even in the relatively recent phenomenon of Filipino blue collar workers in the Middle East, and the domestic helpers and entertainers in Hong Kong, Japan and elsewhere, most Filipino migrants imagine their lives to be economically and financially better if they migrate. Most of them, by the way, have the initial motivation of working temporarily in the migration-receiving country, only to find themselves semi-permanently or permanently settled in the country of destination. The realization of their cultural, linguistic and social distance to the migration-receiving country usually is a late one – bringing to the fore some social and psychological distress for most of them.

There lies the difference in geographic orientation. I think initially, most Filipino migrants still imagine their home to be the Philippines and that their being away from home is often regarded by them as a temporary condition. But some actually open themselves to the option of adopting the idea of permanently migrating to the country of destination, settling down there, thereby reorienting their geographical rootedness from the Philippines to their place of destination. In this regard, class, gender and racial conflict which emanate from this new sense of being rooted to a new geographical environment, after being uprooted from the Philippines and transplanted elsewhere, may be a common phenomenon. The diaspora of the Filipino migrant therefore is sure to develop new conflicts and contradictions, particularly from the way they regarded their new sense of geographical space.[14] The diaspora, by itself, can be regarded as a new space for contradictions and conflict. Such contradiction and conflict may be seen already in the case of Filipino–Americans, Asian-Americans and even Hispanic-Americans complaining about racial inequality, discrimination and prejudice they are experiencing in the USA as reflected in racial profiling by the American police forces, stereotyping and slurs they are subjected to in U.S. malls and shopping centers, segregation of communities of colour, and lack of participation in the process of governance.[15]

But of course, this sense of space is nothing but an expression of the material condition of alienation and multiple-rooted identities of Filipino diaspora labour.

---

[14] Dean Jorge Bocobo, Nationalism and the Filipino Diaspora (http://www.inq7.net/opi/ 20002/sep/09/opi_commentary1-1.htm), pp. 1-4.

[15] Kenneth E. Bauzon, 'Politics of Identity in the United States: The Emergence of the Hispanic American and the Asian American Communities in Comparative Perspective', in Tsuneo Ayabe (ed.), *A Comparative Study of Multiculturalism and Assimilation in Canada, the US and Australia* (Togane: Josai International University, 2001), pp. 89-111.

The phenomenon of Filipino migrant work abroad is characterized, based on the evidence, by this contradiction of wanting to adopt a new sense of space while not being completely uprooted from their nation. The evidence points to the attempt to establish national identities while the Philippine economic flow and the Philippine labour flow are already being thrust to international flows for capital. Globalization and nationalism thus find their logical space of conflict in the identity of Filipino labour diaspora.[16]

**Migration, Distance and Destination**

Destinations for migration can be viewed along two dimensions: the macroscopic and the microscopic level. Just as many view migration as a purely individual or household decision, there are also those who view migration destination as purely the migrant's personal or household choice. This can be considered as a valid view, considering that personal networks are the source of information about destination, the circumstances present in that destination like labour and living conditions, and so on. Most often, migrants go where others, particularly those they know like family members, relatives, friends and neighbours, have gone. A big factor in the choice of destination is whether anyone they know, preferably blood and kin relations is already at that destination. Microscopic factors may go beyond family and extend to community factors so that in Japan or elsewhere, migrants are observed to cluster in terms of geographical origins. At the destinations, one therefore finds pockets of communities of any given province or region in the Philippines like the Ilocos Region of Northern Luzon, the Bicol Region of Southeastern Luzon, Cebu and Central Visayas, and Zamboanga in Western Mindanao. Likewise, upon return to the sending country, one finds in the Philippines for example pockets of communities of returnees from Saudi Arabia, Hong Kong, Japan, Italy and so on. Those having the experience of working in the same country would tend to cluster together back in the homeland.

Microscopic factors, alone, however may not paint a complete picture of the factors affecting migration, destination decisions or choices. Why did it take Filipinos, for example, to go to Japan in large groups only in the 1970s? Why did they travel longer distances to the United States, Canada, Europe, Saudi Arabia and other Middle Eastern countries ahead of shorter distances as Singapore, Hong Kong, South Korea and Japan?

Macroscopic factors such as former and present historical and economic ties with countries of migrant destinations, loosening of migration policies at host countries, sprouting of migrant business networks that facilitate the movement of migrants from countries of source to destinations as well as other factors also provide the structural, global, more formal considerations affecting migrants' geographical destinations.

---

[16] Macaraig, 'Middle-class Filippinos', pp. 1-3.

The concept of geographical space regarding migration destination therefore can range from microscopic assessment (the expanded concept of family and community space) to macroscopic (global doors that are made available as a result of former or continuing historical, business, economic ties between sending and host countries, including global networks of telecommunications, advertising, multimedia coverage and dissemination).

**The Role of Geographic Distance in International Migration**

*Survey Results*

The Third World populations are leaving their respective countries in droves not so much to search for the proverbial pot of gold, as to just provide for the basic necessities of food, shelter and education.

Filipinos are no exception. They may be found anywhere in the globe, in any imaginable place so that in the event of any calamity, one would invariability find a Filipino among those affected, from the World Trade Center in New York, to the Palestinian suicide bombings in Israel.

Across the globe, there is a continuing economic slump. Many richer countries like Holland are tightening their visa regulations or labour laws, giving priority to their own residents in job opportunities.[17] The international job market has been shrinking. However, instead of choosing to come home, the poor people would rather extend their stay as illegal aliens and risk their safety and security.

There are many reasons for the feeling of hopelessness: lack of job opportunities, low salaries, unequal distribution of wealth, corruption, and deterioration of peace and order.

In a recent nation-wide survey by a private polling firm, Pulse Asia, Inc., of 1,200 people aged 18 and above from 22 March to 10April 2002, 19 per cent of Filipinos wanted to leave and migrate to another country; 20 per cent were undecided while 60 per cent wanted to stay. A bigger percentage of the upper class wanted to leave; 31 per cent wanted to migrate, apparently out of desperation.[18]

For the purpose of this paper, a survey was done in June–July 2002 among Filipinos attending to their migration papers at the Philippine Overseas Employment Administration (POEA) Office in Manila. On random sampling, a total of 94 prospective migrants were identified and requested to answer a questionnaire developed for the study of migration.

More than 75 per cent of the migrants are young, between 21-40 years old, the proportion of those aged 21-30 and 31-40 almost equal. This age group is the most eligible for employment. As shown in most studies, it is mostly the young who migrate because they have a longer expected work life and will serve better and

---

[17] BBC Headline News, 7:00 am, 26 May 2005.
[18] Bengwayan, There is no place, pp. 1-6. Macaraig, 'Middle-class Filippinos', p. 2.

longer. A small percentage (4 per cent) were above 50 years old, which confirms the observation of the elderly preferring to stay in their own place rather than having to adjust to a strange new place and environment. This is probably the group that would like to join their relatives, especially their children, who had earlier migrated.

*Sex and Civil Status*

As to sex, there were slightly more males (52 per cent) than females. Those married outnumbered the single, 52 per cent for the married, and 44 per cent for the single. A small percentage of 4 were either widows or separated from their partners.

*Place of Origin*

The migrants came from both Metropolitan Manila and the provinces in equal proportions.

*Education*

The migrants are highly educated, with 80 per cent having a college education, and would surely be a boost to the work force in their new place. This is also true of other studies because individuals with higher levels of attainment are more likely to move and will be more involved in national labour markets. There are many high school graduates, 18 per cent, while those who had elementary education were only 2 per cent.

*Economic Status*

Although highly educated, the respondents do not earn much because of the low wages. A very high 79% have a monthly income below 20,000 PHP. There are not enough job opportunities because many companies have either closed shop or streamlined their operations due to the economic crisis in the Philippines.

*Monthly Income in Philippine Pesos (US$=53 PHP)*

| | |
|---|---|
| 5,000 – 10,000 | 44.64% |
| 10,000 – 20,000 | 34.54% |
| 20,000 – 30,000 | 11.41% |
| 30,000 – 50,000 | 1.75% |

*Reasons for Migration*

As a result of their low income, 85 per cent of the would-be migrants are not happy and satisfied with their present jobs and/or income. A total of 22 per cent feel hopeless with the conditions prevailing in the country. A small percentage want to join their relatives abroad, a process of 'chain migration', or migration to where friends or relatives are located. This reduces the psychic and information costs associated with migration.

*Criteria for Choice of Place of Migration*

The most important criterion cited for choice of place of migration was the economic prospect (77 per cent). Others cited presence of relatives or friends as influencing factors. Only 5 per cent gave importance to distance, 3 per cent wanting a place far from their country, and 2 per cent wanting to move to a nearby place.

*Attitude towards Distance*

When asked about their attitude regarding distance, half said it was important to them. However, while they may initially view a place as far, staying in the area after sometime results in a change of this perception and they feel the distance does not matter anymore.

Comparing the group that thinks distance is important against the group that thinks it is not important, there was no significant difference as to age, sex, civil status and education.

However, further analysis of the group that thinks distance is not important revealed very significant findings: there were definitely more males, at 61 per cent. There were 18 females who deemed distance not important. Of these 10 were single, two were separated and one was a widow. These women did not have any families to worry about. Only five females were presently married. These five married females said they had to support their families. One was willing to 'sacrifice the relationship just to support the family'.

Earlier studies have shown that there is more likelihood of moving within a country than across countries. It is easier to acquire information of labour market opportunities locally. Moves over short distances also reduce the cost of leaving. More highly educated individuals are more likely to migrate over large distances.

Elaborating further on these results and using the preceding comprehensive analytical framework, for which I am indebted to Filipino colleague Ma. Rosario P. Ballescas and which is applicable to all visa categories, it is perhaps appropriate at this point to state that geographical distance and geographical space cannot be used interchangeably. Offhand, it seems clear to me that in a person's decision on migration destination, geographical distance – measured in kilometers between point of origin and point of destination – is not as important as geographical space, which I understand to mean the physical environment of the decision maker or the individual would-be migrant.

Interviews with Filipinos from various walks of life now working and living in Japan especially long-time Filipino resident, entrepreneur and publisher in Japan Benigno D. Tutor, Jr., show that geographic distance measured in kilometers is a minor factor in their migration decision. This is borne out by the results of the formal questionnaire interviews conducted among prospective migrant Filipinos in Manila. Informally queried on their overriding motive to come to a modern and industrialized country like Japan, those already in Japan as well as those intending to come replied overwhelmingly that they are attracted by the high value of the Japanese Yen. They said there were other significant variables, such as the presence of relatives, friends and acquaintances in the land of destination; the availability of specific opportunities like personal resources, invitation from company or relatives, scholarship and so on for entry; and expected favourableness of social and living conditions, including safety, security and a drug-free environment, not to mention disciplined public behaviour.

All these variables are of course interrelated. There have been chances of talking with people from the Philippines who have had a history of multiple migratory destinations like the Middle Eastern countries, Saipan, Hong Kong and others. Such persons have settled the longest in Japan because of the confluence of two or more of the variables identified and discussed above, the least significant of which is geographical distance. The most significant variable for them is the availability of economic opportunities, or more directly to the point, the Yen's high value.

While geographic distance itself is not a significant factor in the decision-making process of a would-be migrant concerning the target destination, geographical space on the other hand is a significant variable in migration choice in so far as it affects the abovementioned variables. For example, many Filipino entertainers come to Japan because of the information and opportunity afforded by local community networks consisting of relatives, neighbours or even remote acquaintances, who have had previous or are presently enjoying opportunities to come to Japan. Likewise, a significant number of housewives of Japanese men come from the same locality because the preferred mode now for would-be Japanese husbands to meet Filipinas is through the personal introductions made by present Filipina housewives in Japan. Today they met and are meeting their husbands through the introduction of other Filipinas married to Japanese or indirectly through the opportunity to come to Japan afforded by their respective local networks. Up to 7000 Filipino-Japanese marriages are taking place every year.[19]

Given the extreme geographical dispersion of the Filipinos in Japan, it is interesting to note the incidence of two or more people belonging to the same geographical space in their point of origin and point of destination is high. There

---

[19] Leslie E. Bauzon, 'Filipino-Japanese Marriages', *Philippine Studies*, 47/2 (2003): 206-23.

are clusters and pockets of Filipinos in Japan coming from the same geographical background in the Philippines because the members of such pockets of communities have a sense of belonging, identification and security common to one another. Such pockets of communities provide a social support system traceable to the Filipino tradition of mutual cooperation or 'bayanihan' in Tagalog, 'tagnawa' in Ilocano, and 'tinabangay' in the Cebuano-speaking provinces of the Visayas and Mindanao in Southern Philippines. Surprisingly, once in Japan, many Filipinos are practically illiterate in terms of geography. Try giving them a map test of Tokyo or the Kanto region. They have very limited knowledge of their immediate locality in relation to the total geographical space, although this may be due to the language barrier and to their lack of access to adequate guidebooks containing baseline information for their geographical orientation. And to tell the truth, this illiteracy in turn is not only true in relation to their localities where they come from in Japan but in relation to Philippine geography in general. Many of my students at the University of the Philippines could not tell what the prominent geographic features are of Luzon, Visayas and Mindanao, much less identify where Sarangani or Compostella Valley provinces are. They are in Southern Mindanao and Eastern Mindanao respectively.

Moreover, Filipino migrants as a whole are a highly mobile people – the informal sector composed of undocumented workers because of absence of legal, long-term employment; the formal sector composed mainly of spouses of Japanese nationals because of a high divorce rate of more than 50 per cent of Filipino-Japanese marriages. Filipino entrepreneurs, business and bankers catering to the overseas migrant Filipino workers in Japan like Nayon shop operating from Tsukuba City and the Philippine National Bank branch office in Tokyo must periodically update their respective client data bases through direct mail because up to 20 per cent of their data become dead files almost every month due to the trait of Filipino mobility for legal or illegal reasons.

It is therefore really doubtful if geography in its physical, dimensional sense indeed factors as a basis for rational decision-making on migration destination. Migrants will risk life and limb travelling vast distances across land and sea because of the lure of a better life and greener pastures in other countries where the standards of living and the quality of life are higher. Look at the recent case only in September 2002 of illegal immigrants who risked their lives sailing across the Mediterranean Sea to reach Italy and dying instead of realizing their dreams. It was a risk they took because they hoped to find the silver lining after encountering dark clouds along the way. Unfortunately, they died without attaining their goal to enjoy the good life.

But geography in its perceptual sense is significant: a place is either near or far depending on its distance from major community clusters (Visayan, Ilocano, Maguindanao, and so on) or centres such as Philippine food shops, Filipino markets, Filipino restaurants, Filipino churches like the Ibaraki Christian Center in Tsukuba City, and others. Thus overseas workers from the Philippines gravitate to places that are 'perceptually proximate' because of the convergence of the above mentioned variables – presence of relatives, friends, acquaintances and social support systems in the destinations: availability of specific opportunities like personal resources, invitation from company or relatives, scholarship and others for upward social and economic improvement; and expected favourableness of social and living conditions.

This trend to gravitate to pockets of communities and centres for Filipino activities may be related to the social environment in the host country wherein it is difficult to penetrate the tight and exclusive little circles of friends that the Japanese create for themselves, and so foreigners like the Filipinos are forced to find each other and hang around among themselves for social, psychological and even financial support for their psychic satisfaction and survival in the host country. Moreover, the Japanese tend to distinguish themselves as Japanese from foreigners, the Nihongo for which is *gaijin* that means 'monster'. This discriminatory attitude, reflected in the term *ainoko*[20] for offspring of mixed Japanese and foreign marriages, contributes towards breeding the absolute social division between the Japanese and foreigners like the Filipinos, thereby compelling the Filipinos, who have no choice, to cluster among themselves for comfort and security.

## A Word on Indian Immigration to the Philippines

Originally, I thought that I would focus my assignment for this volume on the Indian immigration to the Philippines. I soon realized though that the issue that has been assigned to me would need a well-designed case study of a selected group of people, who could be subjected to systematic interviews to find out their perceptions of this particular issue of space in their migration. The implication here is that I would take a study of a specific group of Indians at a given time and given situation and place. However, I must admit that it was difficult for me to gather data through interviews due to time constraints for a meaningful analysis. Besides, many of the pioneer Indian migrants to the Philippines have already died and there is a paucity of primary sources where their mindsets can be found. Nevertheless, I would like to say a few words here about Indian immigration to the Philippines, and suggest possible areas that scholars can go into for a deeper study.

Based on the available data that I have seen pertaining to Indian immigration to the Philippines as well as my contacts with a 78-year old naturalized Filipino citizen from India, retired Prof. Ajit Singh Rye of the University of the Philippines Asian Center, I would like to put in the clarification that in my view most of the Indian migrants into Southeast Asia moved from the British colony in India to other British colonies.[21] Many such immigrants had some familial contacts or links

---

[20] Colin E. Tweddel and Linda Amy Kimball. *Introduction to the Peoples and Cultures of Asia* (Englewood Cliffs, NJ: Prentice-Hall, 1985), pp. 240-241.

[21] Milton Osborne, *Southeast Asia: An Illustrated Introductory History* (St. Leonards, NSW: Allen & Unwin, 1988), pp. 99-114.

with people from their native areas who were living in the countries they were migrating to. Such societal links or knowing someone at the other end was a serious consideration. The distance of the destination was often subordinated to the fact that, at the other end, there were known people who would help and support them upon their arrival in the receiving country.

This was the general view of all migrants who came to the Philippines. There were clusters of migrants from the same district and sometimes from the same village in Punjab and or Sindh.[22] They migrated because of the kinship ties or some such links. The migrants arriving in the Philippines from these two linguistic groups in India were numerically insignificant. Yet their kinship at the destination played an important role in determining their migration. The expectation of social and financial support was also a major determinant.

During the colonial period, the British estate owners in places like Malaysia and Mauritius imported a large number of cheap labour from South India to these colonies. They worked as coolies and farm labourers on sugarcane fields in Mauritius, and as rubber estate workers in British Malaya, and as coolies in Singapore. They were all lured by the prospect of good jobs and better life, which, for many, turned out to be an illusion and a mirage of sorts. But they persisted nonetheless. This process of Indian migration was largely fuelled by the British imperial policy of securing manageable and cheap indentured labour from India. Most of the Indian indentured laborers came from South India and followed by those from the Northern and Eastern Indian areas. I can deduce that distance seemed to be a factor in their migration pattern, although once the indentured labor was no longer brought to these countries by the British colonial authorities, space in the sense of distance no longer mattered. Rather it was the existence of social links – such as the presence of relatives, friends, and the like that encouraged Indian migration to Malaysia, Singapore and Myanmar.

Here, I surmise that destination and distance were not primary considerations among the Indian migrants during the colonial period. The concept of space understood as distance was not always a primordial concern of most of the migrants. In fact, it was a combination of complex factors including the pull and push factors that determined their desire, impulse or compulsion for migration. In most cases, it was the push factor – homeland poverty that pushed people out, and the knowledge that the target country would have a better opportunity for a good life – that is the pull factor. In short, it was the search for security and opportunity for a better life that was the main concern.

In the actual case of Indian immigration to the Philippines, the evidence points to the early Indian migrants merely stumbling into the Islands. The Indian migrants to the Philippines were a very small number and they were accidental migrants settling down in the Philippines. Many of them were looking for the opportunity to migrate to Canada or the USA. The originally intended destination was North

---

[22] Anita Raina Thapan, *Sindhi Diaspora in Manila, Hongkong, and Jakarta* (Quezon City: Ateneo de Manila University Press, 2002).

America. However, in transit, there was relocation. But they could not make it because of strict entry restrictions for migrants from India imposed by both the Canadian and American governments. This was the factor causing the relocation of their destination. Instead they ended up in Manila having learned that the Philippines had become an American colony by 10 December 1898. There emerged a misconception among the Indian migrants regarding the assumption of overlordship over the Philippines by the USA. The Indian migrants thought that being in the Philippines would be just like being in America itself enjoying the benefits of direct American rule. A good number of the Indians really thought that Manila, having fallen under American control, would provide opportunities similar to what they were told were awaiting them in the American continent. So they decided to stay in the Philippines. From there on, the others followed in trickles as now there was someone to go to. There already emerged and existed a family or friendship linkage that would give them a sense of security, and this contributed to the gradual growth of the small but visible and economically successful immigrant community of Indians in the Philippines.[23]

**Concluding Reflections**

In the current surge of migration, prospective migrants plan carefully and systematically their migratory movements. In this case, considerations of destination and distance possibly play an important role in their final determination. These people, not all illegal migrants, target Australia, New Zealand, many European destinations, the United States, Canada and most certainly Japan. Here generally the pull and the push factors play a significant role in their decision-making. The pull factors connote the perceived better life and the opportunities of good work in the target destinations ahead. The push factor is the prevailing hopeless poor living conditions and circumstances at home. They push people to seek redemption abroad. For them leaving the homeland, in search for better lives, becomes imperative, irrespective of distance of the destination. In future research regarding the role of geographical space and geographical distance, I think that it is important to find out what is really meant by space. Is this physical, geographical space, or socio-psychological, cultural or economic space (opportunity)? This will give future researchers a chance to develop their own historical perspective too on migration within Asia, and to find out how keen early migrants away from home might have been on space, and whether they considered space as an essential part of their dream of building a new world for themselves – a new home and an opportunity to thrive. Then there is the need to compare outward migration with inner country migration and which would be more concerned with distance from

---

[23] Ajit Singh Rye, 'The Indian Community in the Philippines', in Kernial S. Sandhu and A. Mani (eds), *Indian Communities in Southeast Asia* (Singapore: Institute of Southeast Asian Studies and Times Academic Press, 1994), pp. 707-73.

the native space to the new one where one would go looking for work and opportunity. Tentatively, I would think that transitional migration is more influenced by the possibilities of realizing one's expectations through a given destination. Here distance appears to have only a minor relevance because it is the opportunity of a better or at least a good life that is the primary consideration, such as the Filipinos going to the USA for instance. It is opportunity or perceived opportunity for a better life that is the deciding factor.

For Mexicans, I think distance is important to make better wages by just crossing over the border to the USA. I leave it however to other scholars to look into this matter. In any case, let me reiterate my hypothesis that the concept of geographical distance is not always a primordial concern of most of the migrants. Rather, it is the combination of complex factors including the pull and push factors that determine their desire, impulse, or compulsion for migration. Homeland poverty pushes people out and the pull factor is the knowledge that the target destination country has a better opportunity to offer a good life. In short, it is for security and opportunity of a better life that appears to be the main concern.

Chapter Six

# Community Beyond the Border: An Ethnological Study of Chuukese Migration in Micronesia

Keiji Maegawa[1]

**Introduction: Migration**

The phenomenon of migration has previously been studied in terms of the migrants' adaptation to new social and cultural environments. These studies have focused on migrants' individual psychology or on their psychological adaptation to new socio-cultural settings, mainly, for example, through education, or migrants' political movement towards acquiring citizenship. Studies of ethnic groups, especially the second generation migrants downward within the USA represent this type of approach.

However, the majority of anthropologists have, until recently, concentrated on the so-called 'traditional' society. We tend to begin our studies with the traditional societies from which the migrants originate. From the viewpoint of the study of 'primitive' or 'traditional' society, the major anthropological approach has been structural-functionalism for which the unit of inquiry is a closed social group without external influences, maintaining an 'equilibrium' within itself.

A 'traditional' society might well maintain its fundamental norms and values even under prolonged external influences, such as the market economy, central government and Christianity. The phenomenon of emigration, however, clearly contradicts the postulate that traditional society is a closed unit. Emigration out from the community and also return migration to the community conflict with the assumption of the long prevalent structural and functionalist approach. Instead, the

---

[1] The fieldwork on which this paper is based was conducted several times from 1992 to 1997. The research project was supported financially by a Grant-in-aid for overseas scientific surveys (Project Representative, Ken'ichi Sudô) from the Japanese Ministry of Education, Science, Sports and Culture, and also by Tenroku Fund of University of Tsukuba. I would like to express my gratitude to the people of Parem and Weno Islands, Chuukese people, especially leaders in Guam and Saipan, the Chuuk State Government, and the Governments of the Federal States of Micronesia, Guam and CNMI.

open-system approach is advocated by some of the contemporary anthropologists such as John Comaroff.[2]

From the point of view of natal communities, emigration combines an outflow of population with an inflow of remittances. Emigration may have been ignited by the motivation of individuals but when growing it tends to have a great influence upon the natal community, which is still small-scaled and, until recently, was tradition-minded to a large extent. To their society at home, emigrants make various contributions, though often modest and minor from the point of view of the host society. These contributions cause unproportionately large changes in the economy, society and culture of the natal communities. Available statistical data indicate that in some countries such as Cook Island, as many as sixty percent of the total population is living abroad and the remittance of money from emigrants amounts to a half of the total gross domestic product.[3]

---

[2] John Comaroff, 'The Closed Society and its Critics: Historical Transformations in African Ethnography', *American Ethnologist*, 9 (1984): 571-83.

[3] For studies of these consequences see Richard P.C. Brown, *Consumption and Investments from Migrants Remittances in the South Pacific*, International Migration Papers 2, ILO working Paper (Geneva: International Labour Organization, 1995). L.J. Gorenflo and Michael J. Levin, 'Changing Migration Patterns in the Federated States of Micronesia', *ISLA: A Journal of Polynesian Studies*, 3/1 (1995): 29-71. John Connell, *Migration, Employment and Development in the South Pacific*, Country Report, No 3: Federated States of Micronesia (Noumea: International Labour Organization and South Pacific Commission, 1983). Connell, *Migration, Employment and Development in the South Pacific*. Country Report, No 6: Guam (Noumea: International Labour Organization and South Pacific Commission, 1983). Connell, *Migration, Employment and Development in the South Pacific* (Noumea: International Labour Organization and South Pacific Commission, 1987). Connell, 'Beyond the Reef: Migration and Agriculture in Micronesia', *ISLA: A Journal of Polynesian Studies*, 2/1(1994): 83-102. Connell et al. (eds.), *Migration from Rural Areas: The Evidence from Village Studies* (Delhi: Oxford University Press, 1976). Ward Hunt Goodenough, *Property, Kin, and Community on Truk* (New Haven: Yale University Press, 1951). J.R. Hagleglam, 'Problems of National Unity and Economic Development in the Federated States of Micronesia', *ISLA: A Journal of Polynesian Studies*, 1/1 (1992): 5-12. Geoffrey Hayes, 'Migration, Metascience, and Development Policy Island Polynesia', *The Contemporary Pacific*, 3 (1991): 1-58. Francis X. Hezel, *Reflections on Micronesia* (Honolulu: University of Hawaii, 1983). Keiji Maegawa, 'An Ethnological Study of Migration Movements. A Case Study of Oceanian Island Society' in Harald Kleinschmidt (ed.), *Europe and Japan* (Stuttgart: Helfant Edition, 1997), pp. 106-12. Peter Pirie, *Demographic Transition in the Pacific Islands: The Situation in the Early 1990s* (Honolulu: East-West Center 1994). Donald H. Rubinstein, Coming to America: Micronesian Newcomers in Guam. Paper presented at the 11th Annual U.O.G. College of Arts and Sciences Research Conference, University of Guam (5 March 1990). Rubinstein, *Micronesian Census: Guam* (Guam: Bureau of Planning, 1992). Rubinstein and Michael J. Levin, 'Micronesian Migration to Guam: Social and Economic Characteristics', *Asian and Pacific Migration Journal* 1/2 (1992): 350-85. Ken'ichi Sudô and Shûji Yoshida (eds), *Population Movement in the Modern World* (2 vols, Osaka: The Japan Center for Area Studies, 1997), vol. 1: Contemporary Migration in Oceania, Diaspora and Network.

## The Chuuk Islands[4]

In contradistinction to these long-term changes, large scale labour emigration from the Chuuk Islands in the Federated States of Micronesia (FSM) to urban centres such as Guam and Saipan is just at its outset. For the study of Chuukese migration, I began with the intensive work in natal communities from which a large number of people have emigrated to urban communities. Later I have shifted emphasis to the emergent migrant communities of the Chuukese people in the urban areas of the host societies: Guam and Saipan, Hawaii, and the US mainland. In so doing, I try to deal with interrelationship between the natal communities and the migrants' communities in host countries. I describe the phenomenon of Chuukese migration from the perspective of cultural continuity between the natal community in the 'traditional' society and the new community in the urban host society.

In Chuuk, a general decline of traditional culture, such as the abolishment of the men's house was recognizable in the 1960s but clan exogamy continues to be maintained until today. Chuukese people even in Weno, the administrative centre of the Chuuk State of the Federated States of Micronesia (FSM), where there are several supermarkets, live on subsistence food production and consumption while cash economy has largely permeated the lives of people in the islands. I did a short-term fieldwork study of a small island called Parem near Weno in July and August of 1992. There, the local food crops are banana, taro, breadfruit, watermelon, coconut, sugar cane and papaya Also fish is done by boats or with lines. Sea cucumbers are collected and occasionally exchanged for money in Weno thus becoming a source of income. The major source of income today is social security payment of various kinds ranging from 200 US$ to 300 US$ per month. These payments have already replaced the cash cropping of copra which had produced about 40 US$ per month in the 1980s. Some people who work as drivers or at the hospital in Weno earn 300-400 US$ per month. The average household consumption of money ranges from 30 US$ 100 US$ per month, depending on household size. A household is often composed of an extended large family. The income is usually used to buy foods such as rice, canned meat, coffee, cigarettes, kerosene, and gasoline for boats. The main property is land with houses valued

---

[4] For primary sources see Chuuk State, Compact Impact Assessment (Weno: Office of the Governor, 1992). Chuuk State, Chuuk State Five-Year Comprehensive Development Plan (3 vols, Weno: Department of Planning & Statistics, 1992-1996), vol. 1 (1992): the Overview. The Federated States of Micronesia, *Trade Bulletin*, No 3 (Noumea: Office of Planning and Statistics, 1991). The Federated States of Micronesia, *Trade Bulletin*, No 4 (Noumea: Office of Planning and Statistics, 1991). The Federated States of Micronesia, *U.S. Federal Programs Under the Compact of Free Association* (Noumea: Office of Budget, 1987). USA, Territory of Guam, *Impact of P.L. 99-239 on the Territory of Guam* (Guam: Office of the Governor, 1994). USA, Department of Commerce, *1990 Census of Population and Housing Guam* (Washington: Department of Commerce, 1992). USA, Department of Commerce, *1990 Census of Population and Housing. Commonwealth of the Northern Mariana Islands* (Washington: Department of Commerce, 1992).

between 2,000 US$ and 3,000 US$, boats valued at 1,000 US$ with outboard engines worth $2,000 and water tanks, most of which are obtained either by war claims, the Typhoon Aid Project Fund or the Fishing Project Fund in the 1980 s. The movement of people is mainly between Parem and the islands nearby, or Weno. The former movement is represented by occasional visits to mothers' relatives on the other islands, while the latter consists of visits to relatives or shopping in Weno on the average once or twice a month.

Soon, after the Second World War, people in the outer islands such as Mortlock in the Chuuk State of the FSM above all started to move to central islands, including Weno, either for education or medication, or for wage labour. At its beginning this migration was often circular.[5] Subsequently, movements converted into step migration to Weno (Moen), the centre of Chuuk for secondary education and wage labour. Eventually, migrants to Weno started to settle there. The basic push factor behind this migration was overpopulation in the outer islands. A household has seven to eight members on average, and some households have more than fifteen. A large family has been respected, as children have been regarded as a symbol of wealth. Therefore, abortion has not been traditionally practiced until today and as a result, the number of children has increased due to the improvement of the nutritional situation after the Second World War. Initially, only a limited number of people migrated from the outer islands. Then, many young people started to move into Weno and settled there in a small shanty area, called the ghetto. During the early phase of the migration to the area, young men from different outer islands were often fighting. But now the area is under better control, and in fact, outer-island people own some land there now. Moreover, some of the main entrepreneurs who are active in Chuuk originally came from the outer islands.

To move from Chuuk to more urban centres such as Guam and Saipan is another step migration. This long-distance movement to Guam and Saipan is labour migration. It has evolved into a major trend in Chuuk since 1985, when the Compact of Free Association was agreed upon. My field investigation on Parem reveals that at least one child, either a young man or a woman, of most households has worked either in Guam or Saipan, beginning in the early 1990s. Many families want some of their children to go and work in Guam or Saipan and earn money if only they can afford the airfare. There is apprehension that depopulation of families and as a result, of the island will be possible, if this trend continues and even spreads. However, hope persists that emigration will not constitute a big problem if there is at least one child who takes care of family property such as land and garden. In this matrilineal descent society, this person is usually one of the daughters.

Migration may be viewed as the result of an interaction between traditional

---

[5] M. Marshall, Beyond the Reef: Circular, Step, and "Permanent" Migration from Namoluk Atoll, FSM. Paper read at the 21st Annual Meeting of the Association for Social Anthropology in Oceania, New Orleans, LA (19-23 February 1992).

practice and external modern requests. In the early 1960s, the male initiation ceremony was abolished, which consisted in catching fish for boys. In the 1990s, young men after graduating from high school are expected to play adult roles to help their families in the form of providing money. If someone earns money which is to be shared by the family, he will be treated with some respect. If not, he is not made much of, especially in a matrilineal descent society. Because of overall rising expectations for better material life in Chuuk, fathers expect their sons to spend several months in Guam or Saipan and to contribute some of the money they earn to the family. The period of working abroad might the be functioning as their initiation in a different way; being away from their community and proving their ability to behave as a socially recognized adult by providing money to their family: a profane version of the previous initiation. However, many of the male migrants are not successful in this profane version of the initiation. Against their parents' expectation, young men tend to spend up their earnings for their own living expenses in the urban centres and do not to send any money to their families back in Chuuk. Or they often return without any money. The overall high cost of living in Guam and Saipan make them unable to send money to their families who expect the remittances. However, especially some women tend to send or bring money with them to their family, though the amount is small and ranges from 100 US$ to 200 US$ at a time. Also a small number of married men who stay and work in Guam regularly send money to their family. Some of them who stay in Guam or Saipan for several years come back once or twice a year, while many others only come back once in two to three years.

In Weno, public servants and teachers are high-salaried people and their kinsmen often come to ask for money on the day of the fortnightly payments of salary. Nowadays, these demands have become a heavy burden. However, they are difficult to avoid as only a limited number of low-wage jobs are available in Chuuk, so that people without paid jobs tend to rely on their well-paid kinsmen. It might be still better for jobless people to move to Guam and Saipan and earn money themselves rather than asking money of their kinsmen, especially as it has become easy to move to and work in Guam or Saipan. At the same time, however, it would be even better to expect that commercial fishing will develop locally.[6]

**Migration to Guam and Saipan**

One important condition of Chuukese migration is the enactment of laws influencing migration. A rapid increase of Chuukese migrants from the FSM to Guam has been triggered from 1985 Compact of Free Association between the USA and the FSM governments. Between 1986 and the beginning of the 1990s, the

---

[6] OFCF (Overseas Fishery Cooperation Foundation of Japan), *Report on Possibility Survey Project of Small Scale Commercial Fisheries Development for Demersal Fish in Federated States of Micronesia* (1992).

annual rate of increase of the number of migrants to Guam was at 50 per cent on average against the previous year. The motivation for migration is, of course, economic in kind as the actual per-hour wage is at least five times higher in Guam and Saipan than that of the central island of Chuuk. Moreover, having access to information about the unknown urban space through their network community, most of the younger, movable population is eager to experience the new urban life away from the 'traditional' community.

The Chuukese experience with staying in Guam started in the late 1940s. Then Guam and the current FSM were the US trust territories. With funds from the US government, about ten girls spent one year in Guam attending George Washington High School. Upon returning to Chuuk all of them became nurses. Later in the 1950s, the two Chuukese moved to Guam in order to receive education at a college in Guam on a two-year scholarship program. They became the first speaker of the legislative assembly of the FSM and a high school teacher in the FSM. In the 1960s, a limited number of Chuukese joined military service in Guam. And then, until the early 1970s, a series of students on federal scholarship moved to Guam. After finishing the programs or even without finishing them, most of these students have in fact remained in Guam, despite the expectation of local governments that they their would return and contribute to the improvement of educational, medical and administrative services in the local island society.[7] Some, however, started to work for the FSM government after returning to Chuuk. Later, some women who remained in Guam married white Americans and native Chamorros and became American citizens.

In the 1970s, relatives of the students who had remained in Guam started to come and stay with them. They were engaged in construction work or yard clearing. The number of immigrants from Chuuk was still limited at that time. It has increased substantially since the enforcement of the Compact of Free Association in 1986. Also, Continental Airlines launched half-price night flights for locals between Guam and the FSM. Before the Compact, more Chuukese migrants were found in Saipan than in Guam. The Carolinian minority residents of Saipan are ethnically and linguistically close to Chuukese. They even preserve the indigenous Chuukese language still nowadays, and there is no difficulty in communication between Chuukese and Carolinians. Migrants to Saipan were students who remained there. Some married the locals of Saipan. A number of women were also recruited for garment factories on a contract basis, being provided with airfare to Saipan and accommodation in dormitories. Under the Compact, Chuukese can migrate, stay and work freely without working permits or visas. In addition, they receive a US social security number. Of course, they can purchase land in Guam. Their choice of Guam or Saipan as their destinations depends on whether they have relatives in either island. The minimum hourly wage in Guam was 4.25 US$ in 1993 and 5.25 US$ in 1994, and 2.75 US$ in Saipan in 1993, while that it is 1.35

---

[7] Out of seven who earned their MAs, only two have returned to Chuuk in the mid 1990s. This is a so-called brain drain.

US$ in Pohnpei and is 1.25 US$ in Chuuk. In practice, 0.80 US$ is the actual average hourly payment for privately employed workers on Weno in Chuuk. This must motivate migration from rural areas to the urban centre. Some cases are reported of Chuukese who started to work in Saipan and later moved to Guam, attracted by the higher wages in Guam.

## Chuukese in Guam and Saipan

When our attention is directed to the emergent immigrant community, we have to deal with the relationship between the dominant resident population group and the emergent immigrant group and ask how the latter adapts to the former. The important matter here is to consider the relationship between several immigrant ethnic groups. For example, in Guam, the early immigrant groups, the Kosraeans and the Ponapeans of the FSM, have adapted somewhat more to urban life than the newly emergent immigrant group of the Chuukese of the FSM. Therefore, the former are a little more welcome among the majority of the resident population groups of the host society in Guam. Thus the relationship between the population groups in the urban host society is multiple; and comprises relations between the dominant resident population group and each immigrant minority group, and also among immigrant minority groups themselves.

Being short of places to stay in Guam in general, as many as ten to twenty immigrant Chuukese live in three-to-four-bedroom apartments or a house. Usually immigrants live with paternal or maternal relatives, and in some cases young friends who work together live in the same apartments. In these cases, many immigrants are in the same clans. In Saipan, however, Chuukese more often live in a nuclear-family situation, and the number of people staying together in one apartment or a house is smaller in Sapan than than in Guam. As more women than men have migrated to Saipan, Chuukese women have adapted better to the urban life style there, and as a result, some are married to local men.

The FSM people are mostly non- or semi-skilled workers in Guam. In the 1990s, it was common for Chuukese men to work on construction sites, as stewards or security staff of hotels, and Chuukese women worked as housekeepers or maids. Chuukese are the largest employees among the FSM people working in hotels in Guam, while Filipinos are the majority of employees and occupy more important jobs in these hotels. In Saipan where most of the US brand T-shirts are made, many women from the FSM are engaged in working in the local garment industry. Compared with other FSM people such as Kosraeans, Ponapeans, Yappees, the majority of Chuukese migrants are latecomers to Guam. Therefore, when newly incoming Micronesians work together in a group, other Micronesians with a little longer working experience tend to play supervising roles. Problems arise in their working context involving cultural elements. For example, an immigrant's mother's brother may want him or her to help with his work on week days, the immigrant tends to obey the uncles' request. This is so because honouring requests from relatives continues to be an overwhelmingly strong behavioural norm, as most Chuukese still maintain a kin-based community even in such an urban centre as Guam. As a result, though being aware of the working requirements at their places of work, Chuukese workers tend to take days off even without a prior notice cause their employers to lose trust.

In general, the native Chamorros' responses to immigrant Chuukese are more negative than positive. Among the people from the FSM, especially Chuukese appear to infringe upon public rules regarding drinking, fighting or driving. Some young people who know that they are perceived in this way even disguise their ethnic origin. For example, some cases are reported where people utilize the similarity of physical appearance. Thus some younger Chuukese pretend to be Kosraeans when in trouble or being interrogated. Under these pretenses, they behave freely as there are not many acquaintances in the streets of the urban centres. Since Palau became US territory in 1962, Palauans started to migrate to Saipan where they occupied a certain share of the immigrant population and became notorious for their behaviour in an early stage of their migration. Now, Chuukese are the dominant immigrant group in succession to Palauans in Guam. Palauans have become more adapted, like Filipinos have, while Chuukese have not had a sufficiently long experience to adapt to the more urban societies of Saipan and Guam. In addition, some differences in customs have also become a reason for the rise of negative feelings, such as the manner of the Chuukese disposal of fish and rubbish. However, a more institutional reason of a socioeconomic kind is that many of the FSM people, especially Chuukese, depend on welfare assistance, such as the Ghura Low Income Public Housing and the Section 8 Housing Assistance Program. These are programs to provide shelter for homeless people.[8] Actually Chuukese, as an ethnic group, are by far the highest number of homeless in Guam, and the local Chamorros have negative feelings toward Chuukese in this respect. This welfare problem, together with the problem of expansion of the number of students can be solved only by the increase of the flow of Federal funds to Guam.

In 1994, the leaders of Guam, the FSM, Marshall and Palau drew up a petition with several thousands of signatures asking for an increase of federal funds from four million US$ to 20 million US$. The Guamanian leaders are aware of the importance of their local indigenous culture which is up against the more powerful alien ethnic groups. However, their insistence on indigenous rights is neither formally nor politically incompatible with the presence of immigrants from neighbouring Micronesia. Here are the words of a Chamorro nationalist activist who became a senator: 'We don't really care about you [Micronesians] because you are sisters and brothers. We are Micronesians. I am against the people, Filipino, Koreans and Japanese because they came and they bought lands.' In fact, such

---

[8] K.D. Smith et al., 'Contemporary Micronesian Communities in Guam: Acculturation, Conflict and Economic Prospects', in Ken'ichi Sudô and Shûji Yoshida (eds), *Population Movement in the Modern World* (2 vols, Osaka: The Japan Center for Area Studies, 1997), vol. 1: Contemporary Migration in Oceania, Diaspora and Network, pp. 45-64.

activists were protesting the largest tourist group, the Japanese tourists, and accused them of violating the indigenous cultural heritage and the indigenous rights, instead of appealing to the Government of Guam. In 1995, Chuukese joined in the marching on Liberation Day for the first time. Also, in daily interactions, the leaders of the Chuukese Association make an effort to maintain a good relationship, for example, by giving fresh fish to Chamorro acquaintances. As such, responses to these minority problems have been made by Chuukese themselves. The leaders of the FSM have organized their own association following the idea of the Filipino association. In doing so they followed the advice given by the Compact Impact office in Guam in 1992. In Saipan also, they established the Chuukese Association in 1993.

The overall approach of dealing with the natal and the emergent immigrant communities includes a further aspect of migration. From a cultural point of view, it has been pointed out that the emergent immigrant may or may not group adapt to the host society while, in any case, maintaining their customs to a high degree. Not only kinship-based relationships but also group relationships through a religious organization, such as the Church, and through individual patron-client relationships continue at a high level in the emergent migrant communities. In general, the migration procedure itself is launched and mediated along the lines of these relationships. For first-generation immigrants (in some cases, second generation immigrants as well), cultural, social, economic and political relationships with their natal society are more important than the quest for citizenship or assimilated identity in the host society or country. New migrants come to stay with their relatives in Guam and Saipan. The immigrant community is formed based on kinship relations in this sense. At the same time, the migrant community is centred on the Church in Guam.

People, even Christians, believe in magic. This is certainly true for the Chuukese. To them, the Church has more meaning as a community than as a source of religious doctrine. The churchgoers keep the community values in Chuuk, and even after they move to Guam or Saipan, they tend to keep the Chuuk community values. People who do not obey social rules in Chuuk tend to neglect social rules also in urban centres as well. In this sense, the Church is the orthodox community space, both in the natal and the host society. Pastors sometimes come from Chuuk to provide Church service in Guam. Often they are also government officials. Members of the Chuukese Church Association occasionally visit Guam and Saipan. When visiting these urban places they stay for a time in their relatives' residence. In this sense, the Chuukese Church in Guam is the Guam parish of the Chuukese Church. In fact, their community in Guam is the extension of their natal community, along with this extension of their church community. The Church service is the time and space for their community announcements. For a wedding, for example, most of the church followers give donations, regardless of which island of Chuuk the family comes from. For Easter and Christmas, nearly nine hundred Chuukese gather together. Church service is a space to foster communication among Chuukese and to form ethnic identity in a positive way.

As the Chuukese did not have a Church building in Guam, they started services in one of their houses in 1989. Later, Chuukese were allowed to use an existing Salvation Army Church in Guam for their service. Palauans carry out the same kind of Church service as the Chuukese do in Guam. As many of Chuukese do not understand the English service, they prefer the service in the Chuukese language. Regardless of denomination and regardless of which part of Chuuk a person comes from, any Chuukese can participate in this service. In this sense, the community centred on the Church covers a wider area of the islands than in the homeland. Not only is daily and ceremonial cooperation carried out in Church but the new ethnic identity as a Chuukese, not, for example, as a Mortlocker or a Toll Islander is formed and fostered.

In contrast to the dominant urban population in Guam, Chuukese as a minority have become conscious of their common culture. Although it sounds contradictory, they are not assimilated in a simple linear way to the society and cultures but their ethnic identity as Chuukese is strengthened in the larger urban societies of Guam or Saipan. In Chuuk, they have a stronger identity as locals of each island. In fact, the structure of regional relationships in the natal society is seen as well maintained within the emergent immigrant community in Guam. Chuukese, being newcomers whose identity resides more in each island of Chuuk, maintain the structural relationships of their sub-groups in terms of centre-periphery, that is, between the central and the remote islands. For example, the historical relationship of alliance and hostility between local sub-groups in the natal society is often shown to be persisting. However, even if a general feeling of discrimination exists against outer-islanders among Chuukese in Guam and Saipan, the new overarching identity of Chuukese as a minority group weakens this structural dimension of discrimination. They even occasionally identify themselves as Micronesians in response to self-identification of Guamanians as non-Micronesians. Thus larger urban society provides an ambiguous three-dimensional space in which multiple ethnic identities and relationships are formed.

Most of the Chuukese migrants want to remain in Guam and Saipan and only occasionally visit their homeland. Especially outer-islanders such as Mortlockers in Guam have hardly ever returned to their natal island community, perhaps because they have the longer experience of migrating to the urban area within Chuuk itself, and have thus become accustomed to live in places other than their home island. They are also active in the emergent immigrant society. They are experiencing step migration to the centre of Chuuk, to Guam and Saipan, further to Hawaii and eventually to the West Coast of the US mainland. From Guam and Saipan they come back as far as to Weno where many of their relatives live, but not often back to their natal communities in the outer islands in Chuuk.

Some husbands who work in Guam or Saipan are preparing to bring their families there some day. Because of the implementation of the minimum-wage law in Guam, women can earn as much money as men, and on that economic basis, they can be a little more independent and released from the traditional behavioural norms for women. Therefore, they like to stay in Guam and Saipan. However, some couples who cannot find good housing, divorce in Guam and Saipan and often drink. The number of Chuukese arrested by the police is by far the highest, relative to the total number of FSM residents in Guam. The most frequent type of arrest is driving under the influence of alcohol. Disorderly conduct is found as the second most frequent reason for arrests of Chuukese, while this type of arrest is very rare among other FSM people.

## Continuity and Discontinuity

In the process of interaction between the natal and emergent immigrant communities, not only the remittance of money but also ceremonial gift exchange of money from the migrant side and on the side of frequent visitors, of ceremonial goods from the natal communities is observed. For example, the Samoan fine sago mat is an indispensable item for gift exchange, accompanied with the ceremony aiming at acquiring the chief title of the kin group.[9] This process of interaction is carried out in accordance with the behavioural norm of the natal society. This is what is termed 'cultural continuity', which is thoroughly maintained even in the new and totally different environment. We can interpret this as a symptom proving that the natal society extends itself into the emergent migrant communities in the urban areas of foreign countries. Within this extended and expanding society, not only population but also goods and information circulate regularly. 'Chain migration' is a regular process of extending this network community which is formed between various areas. 'Chain visits', that is step circular migration, is also another feature of consolidating the foundations of this network community.

The case of Samoa shows that the ceremonial exchange is realized at a larger scale in immigrant communities and can boost their identity in a new urban host society whose dominant population group has different ethnic and cultural origins. This phenomenon is explained in terms of Samoan 'conservatism'. As another example, the case of Cook Islanders shows that the second and the third generation immigrants to New Zealand continued to reconstruct their tradition as Polynesians. In the recent Festival of Pacific Arts in Cook Islands, NZ Cook Islanders designed and displayed Tahitian canoes as their original Polynesian culture.[10]

---

[9] M. Yamamoto, 'Urbanization of the Chiefly System: Multiplication and Role Differentiation of Titles in Western Samoa', *The Journal of the Polynesian Society*, 103/2 (1994): 171-202. Yamamoto, 'Samoan Diaspora and Ceremonial Exchange', in Ken'ichi Sudô and Shûji Yoshida (eds), *Population Movement in the Modern World* (2 vols, Osaka: The Japan Center for Area Studies, 1997), vol. 1: Contemporary Migration in Oceania, Diaspora and Network, pp. 65-76.

[10] S. Tanahashi, 'Cultural Policies and Renaissance of Tradition in a Polynesian MIRAB Society: a case analysis from the Cook Islands (MIRAB Shakainiokeru Bunnkano Aridokoro)', *The Japanese Journal of Ethnology (Minzokugaku-Kenkyû)*, 61/4 (1997): 567-85.

In Guam, two customary practices are obviously maintained around the marriage ceremony and its feast. Back in Chuuk, bridewealth is given to the bride's family and relatives, for example, as heaps of taros, and breadfruits. Similar ceremonial gift-giving is observed in wedding feasts in the Guam community centre. Heaps of sacks of rice and cases with chicken are displayed ceremonially in front of the attendants, and are later given to the bride's side from the bridegroom's side. They have now adapted to the urban life style of Guam using rice and frozen chicken as main staples. Yet the ethos of giving important staples to the bride's side is highly maintained so that the ceremonial gift-giving of rice and chicken replaces the gift-giving of taro and breadfruit at home in Chuuk. The process of adaptation to the new environment affects the type gifts given while maintaining the tradition of gift-giving at the same time.

Cultural innovation is also observed among Chuukese in Guam. In the feast, songs sung nowadays are not only those of the Chuukese tradition but some are also of Hawaiian origin. Being aware of the cultural affinity between Micronesians and Polynesians in comparison with the white urban culture, Chuukese prefer to encompass these cultural practices of adjacent regions which are not usually performed back in Chuuk. Clan exogamy is still kept or should be kept but second- and third-generation Chuukese immigrants in the urban society of Guam have not received knowledge of the traditional practices from their childhood. Chuukese acknowledge that the arranged marriage is not practiced among them in contemporary Guam society but a case was observed in which a Chuukese high school boy was discouraged from choosing his girl friend from the clan to which he also belonged and was not allowed to continue the relationship. Young second-generation Chuukese who were born and brought up in Guam and received their education with whites and urbanized Chamorros tend to feel as Guamanians. While maintaining their identity as Chuukese without their traditional knowledge and their additional identity as Guamanian at the same time, they will have to face this conflict from now on.

**Conclusion: Community beyond the Border**

Within the network community, further discrimination exists between the natal community and the migrant community and is also of great significance. The natal community tries to involve the emigrants in their community maintenance, such as shipping foods and other materials, and the remittance of money.[11] At the same time, however, elites among the immigrant group, now settled, tend to exercise their influence on the political structure of the natal society, instead. This is

---

[11] The opposite movement of money is seen only in the following case: For the dead of the FSM immigrants in Guam, the funeral is held in Guam Memorial Park. For this, the FSM government provides a coffin and a grave site worth more than 50 US$, which might become a burden to the future budget of the FSM.

attempted, with the background of 'modern' knowledge, by way of using economic resources now more available to them or by recovering their voting rights.

In 1993, 60 to 70 percent of the Chuukese population in Guam registered and voted in elections for the state governour of Chuuk. Candidates travelled to Guam to campaign among the voters there. As no political parties had yet been established in Chuuk, kinship and friendship and political views on particular matters were the determinants for the voters in terms of who to vote for. For that election, one candidate promised to purchase land for Chuukese in Guam in order to build their traditional meetinghouse like the Palauans and Kosraeans, and as a result, gained the most votes. In 1997 one of the leaders of the Chuukese in Guam ran for the governour's election of the Chuuk State of the FSM, and this was a topic of discussion among a small number of Chuukese attending a Church gathering in Oregon on the US West Coast. As Chuukese live in similar circumstances as immigrants there, these discussions might be indicative of distant nationalism as Benedict Anderson puts it.[12] Chuukese organize and maintain their Church service on the West Coast, as well as in Hawaii. For the immigrants on the West Coast, the Church is the place where they confirm their identity as Chuukese, even while they live somewhat more assimilated, individualistic daily lives there.

---

[12] Benedict Anderson, *The Spectre of Comparisons. Nationalism, Southeast Asia, and the World* (London: Verso Books, 1998).

Chapter Seven

# International Migration and Regional Integration: The Case of Central America

Wolfgang Hein

**Introduction: Migration, Transnational Social Spaces and Regional Integration**

Intuition suggests that there should be a close relationship between politics of regional integration and an intensification of migration between the national territories which form part of the integration process. Economic integration should further facilitate the movement of people between the participating countries. A closer look, however, reveals that things are different: Among the member countries of the European Union, the number of migrants has decreased with the progress of integration – in spite of the free mobility of the labour force – while in fact the number of immigrants from non-member countries has increased dramatically despite the continuing to existence of all kinds of obstacles to their migration.

In effect, from the vantage point of a push-pull perspective on migration, it makes sense to assume, on the one hand, that a process of regional integration which successfully contributes to an equalization of opportunities might in effect reduce the push-pull differential between different parts of this region. Nevertheless, at the same time this differential between the integrated region and external areas might increase. On the other hand, regional integration might lead to another dynamics of migration which one might call horizontal migration.[1] By this I understand a type of migration which does not result from push-pull effects on the macro-level of social development but from differences of opportunities due to specific individual interests or qualifications. Horizontal migration includes studying abroad because of better opportunities in a specific field of study or for learning a language, international research cooperation or an increased mobility of highly skilled employees.

---

[1] 'Horizontal migration' is seen in contrast to the vertical character of push-pull migration occurring predominantly between regions with different levels of economic development.

Obviously, if we look at Central America, there is one fundamental difference from migration patterns to or within the European Union, namely that the region as a whole does not attract people from neighbouring regions but rather 'pushes' people into migration to more attractive regions in the North. Thus the central question of this chapter will be whether we can detect any effect of Central American integration endeavours on migratory patterns at all. This could mean a partial diversion of push-pull migration from extra-regional to intra-regional destinations as well as an increase in horizontal migration as characterized above. As a starting point, I shall discuss some basic issues involved in the fields of analysis concerned, migration, regional integration and the particularities of Central America:

I shall start with migration. After some decades of internal rural-urban migration in developing countries, the last three decades saw an important rise of international periphery-centre-migration. While nineteenth-century migration theory had stressed the relief effects of emigration from overpopulated rural regions and the opportunities for immigrants in their 'new' home countries, be it in colonizing rural regions, be it as workers or entrepreneurs in the beginning of industrialization in their 'new' home countries, there has been a tendency towards a basically critical view of migration processes since the 1960s. They were then seen as an expression of structural underdevelopment in sending and as a cause of stress for the social systems in receiving countries, or, as in the case of the so-called 'brain drain', as a factor increasing the inequality between both groups of countries. Thus Arjan de Haan writes: 'Literature that usually departs critically from neo-classical models ... sees migration not as a choice for poor people, but as the only option for survival after alienation from the land, and highlights the exploitation of migrants in both destination and source areas.[2] The problem has to be solved by improving the employment and income situation 'at home'.[3]

In recent years, this perspective has changed in two ways: On the one hand, looking more realistically at the motivations and fate of emigrants, authors like de Haan stress the logic of poor migrants and the generally positive effects on their livelihoods, the role of remittances for countries of emigration and their positive impact on economic relations between sending and receiving regions. But even the flourishing of 'transnational enterprises' established by migrants, is basically seen as a form of the social integration of migrants and not as a phenomenon with an

---

[2] Arjan de Haan, 'Livelihoods and Poverty: The Role of Migration – A Critical Review of the Migration Literature', *Journal of Development Studies*, 36/2 (1999): 3.

[3] For example see Sarah Mahler, *Migration and Transnational Issues. Recent Trends and Prospects for 2020* (Hamburg: Institut für Iberoamerika-Kunde, 2000), p. 26. Armando di Filippo, Globalización, integración regional y migraciones, Contribution to the Symposium on International Migration in the Americas (San José, 4-6 Sept 2000).

important impact on economic development processes.[4] At least, there is a tendency to analyze migration not simply as an expression of structural imbalances to be overcome but to better understand new social structures which are developing.

On the other hand, writers on international migration have come to realize that migration today is neither really a finite movement of people from one society to another, from one distinct place to another nor related to far-reaching changes of identity. Instead, with the decreasing cost of international travel and communication, migrants have increasingly tended to produce transnational social spaces which encompass activities in their place of immigration as well as in their home countries.[5] The identities of migrants are increasingly being integrated into translocal networks which are frequently also trans-regional. This latter aspect is interesting as it points to the dialectics between the determinants of migration in a macroeconomic framework of analysis and the effective results of global integration in terms of communication, transport, and the polarizing tendencies of socio-economic development.

In macroeconomic terms we find a global liberalisation of the flows of goods and capital but not of the transnational mobility of labour. Nevertheless, in spite of many political obstacles to labour migration, we find an increase at least in specific migratory flows, particularly South-North, which can be seen as an extension of traditional rural-urban migration flows to the global scene. The flow of remittances becomes an important factor for setting off important trade deficits in many developing countries. Discussions about 'Global Cities' focus this phenomenon on the analysis of metropolitan spaces. This concept assumes a concentration of highly qualified personnel in cities like New York or Tokyo (thus also the in-migration of this type of people from other regions) but it explicitly discusses the immigration of poor people from Third World regions who find employment mostly in low-paid service jobs.[6]

---

[4] For example see Alejandro Portes, William Haller and Luis E. Guarnizo, *Transnational Entrepreneurs 2001: The Emergence and Determinants of an Alternative Form of Immigrant Economic Adaptation* (Davis, CA: University of California at Davis, 2001).

[5] Pioneers in the concept of 'Transnational social spaces' were Nina Glick Schiller, Linda. Basch and Cristina Szanton Blanc, *Towards a Transnational Perspective on Migration: Race, Class, Ethnicity, and Nationalism Reconsidered* (New York: New York Academy of Sciences, 1992). See also Ludger Pries, 'Transnationale soziale Räume. Theoretisch-empirische Skizze am Beispiel der Arbeitswanderungen Mexiko-USA', *Zeitschrift für Soziologie*, 25 (1996): 437-53. Pries (ed.), *New Transnational Social Spaces. International Migration and Transnational Companies* (London and New York: Routledge 2000).

[6] For the discussion on 'global cities' see Saskia Sassen, *The Global City* (Princeton: Princeton University Press, 1991). Sassen, 'The "Global City" – Einführung in ein Konzept und seine Geschichte', *Peripherie*, 81-82 (2001): 10-31. John Friedmann, 'Where We Stand: A Decade of World City Research', in Paul L. Know and Peter J. Taylor (eds), *World Cities in a World System* (Cambridge: Cambridge University Press, 1995), pp. 21-47.

Finally, and this is particularly important with respect to regional integration, we have to realize that there is another type of migration different from mass migration, that is, the migration of specific functional groups, such as entrepreneurs and intellectuals. This group is hardly documented in official statistics but might nevertheless be an important contributor to regional integration processes. This type of migrants represents at the core horizontal migration as defined above. There is some discussion now on the migration of highly qualified people, taking up the older discussion on 'brain drain' and to some degree the discussion on elite migration in history. Horizontal migration patterns within an expanded territory develop as a consequence of the removal of political obstacles to migration under the conditions of easier and cheaper communication and transport. In this respect, it is not just the number of migrants which counts but the specific role migrants take in the process of social change. While most quantitative research on migration concentrates on the dimensions of basic labour power, the poverty of and discrimination against migrants, we need a qualitative approach towards the analysis of specific migration patterns in order to understand the impacts of migration on the social and economic change of specific areas.

Taking these considerations as a starting-point, what are the resulting propositions on the relationship between regional integration and international migration? Regional integration normally refers to processes of political, economic and, to some degree, social integration of nations in a specific geographical area. I cannot summarize here the theoretical discussions on this topic but it seems fair to say that, to some degree, the dichotomy of 'form follows function' and 'function follows form' has characterised the discussion on the relationship between processes of economic and social integration on the one hand and the integration of political forms (as institutions) on the other hand.[7] Policy-based integration projects among economically hardly integrated developing countries are certainly based on the hope that formal political integration could in fact produce some conditions for functional integration with respect to socioeconomic development. Moreover, it seems obvious that these hopes could only be realized if some further conditions are regarded as givens, namely some kind of historically based regional identity and an economic imperative that there is no other chance of implementing

---

[7] 'Form follows function' characterizes the central idea of functionalist and neofunctionalist theories of integrations, going back to David Mitrany. See David Mitrany, *A Working Peace System: An Argument for the Functional Development of International Organizations* (London: Royal Institute of International Affairs, 1943). Mitrany, *The Functional Theory of Politics* (New York: St. Martin's Press, 1975), and the classical work of Ernst B. Haas on European integration. See Ernst B. Haas, *The Uniting of Europe: Political, Economic and Social Forces 1950 – 1957* (London, Stevens & Sons 1958). On the other hand, institutionalist authors tend to expect that 'functions follows form', at least that the development of institutional forms have a strong impact on functional changes. For example see Robert Owen Keohane, *International Institutions and State Power. Essays on International Relations Theory* (Boulder: Westview Press, 1989).

specific interests than through regional integration. For example, it may be feasible to develop the goal of creating a market large enough for the accomplishment of import substitution. In order to indicate potential relationships between regional integration and migration, I confine myself to pointing out a few effects integration processes might theoretically have on the push-pull mechanism and on horizontal migration.

## The Push-Pull Mechanism

Case (1) Integration creates or strengthens existing structures of uneven development within a region; migration to the more developed parts of the region will then intensify. If the resulting socio-political problems can be solved, migration may finally strengthen the support for regional integration.

Case (2) Integration strengthens economic development in the whole region in comparison with neighbouring regions and supports a tendency towards equalization of opportunities within the region: Under this condition there will be little incentives for internal migration but a growing pull effect on external migrants.

Case (3) Internal development remaining weak when compared to growth in surrounding areas will usher in an increasing push effect towards emigration. In this case, there might be a certain incentive to coordinate politics towards the main immigrant country or region in order to facilitate transfers of remittances and transnational businesses of migrants and to improve the situation of migrants there with respect to their social, economic and human rights situation. Whether these incentives alone could be strong enough to favour regional integration seems rather doubtful.

## Horizontal Migration

If political and economic integration is really successful in creating a certain equality of opportunities in formerly separated territories, there is – for large parts of the population – little need to migrate (case 2): Migration will probably be more specifically related to the differentiation of opportunities in specific economic sectors and to specific personal interests and qualifications. We can expect more migration of highly qualified personnel and more short-term and life-cycle related migration, such as migration of students or pensioners. Taking into account the increase in communication and travel within the region and the rise of social contacts, one can expect at least in the long run that this process will lead to a certain mix of people coming from different parts of the new regional union and to the development of a certain common identity.

In effect, if we look at Central America, we find a combination of case (1) with case (3) which, at first sight, seems to lead to more inequality, weak internal development rather than to a very sustainable process of integration. In order to correctly assess this situation, we have to take into account that in the age of globalization, regional integration does not simply imply the intensification of socioeconomic transactions within a region but also means a redefinition of the role of regional actors in the global context. The idea of an 'open regionalism'[8] – in short, regional cooperation without a high degree of protection towards the exterior – dominates actual concepts of regional integration. A regional centre can only arise if, among other things, it can authoritatively define the relations of the region with the rest of the world. In other words, a regional centre must offer learning opportunities for partners in the region to increase their competitiveness and must foster cooperation improves the region's prospects for gaining from international cooperation in the field of global governance. This demand requires a certain level of regional identity, that is, a trust in a positive outcome of a process which in the short run promises only limited progress for the less advanced members and may deprive the more developed centre of chances to profit from its competitiveness independently from any regional commitments.

The origin of the development of Costa Rica into a regional centre – or perhaps, a 'focal point of regional development' can be traced back to the historical development of positive preconditions for the evolution of specific locational factors, such as an early focus on education, social integration and political stability, whereas social polarization and militant conflicts characterized other Central American societies. In this context, national identity is a positive factor for national political and social integration and thus for supporting those factors which has come to define the Costa Rican position in regional development. Furthermore, specific patterns of migration emerged in the context of socio-political development, in particular the role of Costa Rica as a country of exile for intellectuals from other Central American countries and the attractiveness of the country for the temporary or definitive immigration of academics and entrepreneurs.

Whereas during the 1970s and early 1980s, these factors primarily strengthened the socioeconomic development of Costa Rica compared to its conflict-ridden Central American neighbours, the role of the country as a place of immigration particularly for intellectual refugees in the 1980s, in combination with the exemplary character of its own political institutions, has turned Costa Rica into an engine for a renewed effort for Central American integration since the second half of the 1980s.

I would suggest that the still existing close links between push- and pull-factors and migratory patterns would imply patterns of migration between Costa Rica and extra-regional areas different from those of other Central American countries. We should expect reduced extra-regional emigration and immigration from poorer countries in the region to Costa Rica and also expect some kind of horizontal migration due to regional integration processes. Processes of spatial differentiation in the developing world will therefore lead to quite distinct patterns of migration.

---

[8] See C. Fred Bergsten, *Open Regionalism*, Working Paper 97-3 (Washington, DC: Institute for International Economics, 1997).

Surprisingly, the current existing literature on migration and development ignores this issue but almost exclusively deals with the question of whether migration from the periphery to the centre has basically negative or positive impacts and in general ignores migratory flows which do fit into this pattern.[9]

These propositions are primarily based on nearly two decades of work on Costa Rica and in cooperation with Costa Rican academic institutions. Pursuing an analysis which follows this line of thought has turned out to be quite difficult basically because of a lack of data on specific groups of migrants. As mentioned before, migration statistics do not provide sufficiently detailed information and there are hardly any studies on refugees, students and immigrant entrepreneurs in Costa Rica. Therefore, this chapter will basically pave the ground for research waiting to be undertaken in the future.

**Migration: Tendencies in Central America**

Until the 1950s Latin America was a continent of immigration. Between 1821 and 1932 more than 12 million people migrated from Europe to Latin America, which was about 22 per cent of all transatlantic migration. Unlike the countries of the Southern Cone, Argentina, Brazil, Chile and Uruguay, and Cuba, Central America was not a favourite destination of European mass immigration in the late nineteenth and early twentieth centuries. Nevertheless, European immigrants played an important role as entrepreneurs, particularly in coffee production and trade. In addition, migrants from the Caribbean settled on the Central American Atlantic coast, most of them taking up work in the rapidly growing banana plantations, while Chinese and Italian workers played an important role in the construction of the Panama Canal and the railways in the region.[10]

Intra-Central American migration has always played a certain role, particularly in the form of the seasonal migration of agricultural workers across the borders of neighbouring countries. As late as in 1970, half of international emigrants from Central American countries moved to other countries in the region. However, already by 1980, 80 per cent of Central American emigrants moved to countries

---

[9] For example see Ninna Nyberg-Soerensen, Nicholas Van Hear and Poul Engberg-Pedersen, *The Migration-Development Nexus. Evidence and Policy Options* (Geneva: International Organization for Migration, 2002).

[10] For example see Boris Fausto (ed.), *Fazer a América. A Imigracão em Massa para a America Latina* (São Paulo: Fundação Alexandre de Gusmão, 1999). Thomas Fischer, 'Deutsche und schweizerische Massenauswanderung nach Lateinamerika 1819-1945', in Wolfgang Reinhard and Peter Waldmann (eds), *Nord und Süd in Amerika* (2 vols, Freiburg: Rombach, 1992), vol. 1, pp. 280-304. Fischer (ed.), *Ausländische Unternehmen und einheimische Eliten in Lateinamerika* (Frankfurt: Vervuert, 2001). Rita Bariatti, *Italianos en Costa Rica* (San José: Universidad Autónoma de Centro América, 2001). Roger Churnside, *Formación de la fuerza laboral costarricense* (San José: Editorial Costa Rica, 1985).

outside the region, basically the USA, but also to Canada and Mexico. In 1990 according to Mahler,[11] only per cent of all international migrants stayed in the region. This overstates the tendency – in effect, the percentage of intra-regional migration certainly is not that low – because Costa Rica, the most important regional immigration country, was simply ignored for a lack of census data. In 2000 about 2 million people born in Central America were living in the USA. Assuming that the percentage of Central Americans living in Mexico, Canada and in Central American countries other than Costa Rica did not change significantly from the data presented by the ECLA (see below, Table 7.1), we can assume that about 320,000 migrants are living in other Central American countries and 2.2 million in the North, making up 14.5 per cent

The data presented in the table can only be taken as approximations as they are based on censuses taken at some year between 1990 and 2000. As most countries do not publish migration data on the base of yearly cross-border flows, most studies on migration in Latin America have to rely on census data. Furthermore, I could not obtain the relevant data for Honduras as there has not been any census there after 1988. In that year we find an exceptionally high number of refugees present in Honduras (34,387). Because the number of refugees may subsequently have declined, the number of foreigners living there during the 1990s is probably significantly below the 1988 census data.[12] Therefore it is likely that the number of immigrants to Central American countries is probably about 15,000 to 20,000 higher than the one given in table 7.1.[13] There are also some data missing with respect to residents in Mexico being born in Costa Rica, El Salvador, Honduras and Panama, which also leads to an underestimate of the number of emigrants from these four countries to Mexico. Because of the large number of Central American immigrants who entered the USA undocumented in the 1990s. Central Americans are also considerably underrepresented in the table (their number in 2000 is about 2,066 million).

---

[11] Mahler, *Migration*, p. 9.

[12] See the IMILA/ECLA data base.

[13] Probably between 12,000 and 15,000 of them from other Central American countries but this is a pure guess.

**Table 7.1 Migration within Central America and between Central and North America**

| Country of residence (1) | Country of birth | | | | | | | | | | |
|---|---|---|---|---|---|---|---|---|---|---|---|
| | Costa Rica | El Salvador | Guatemala | Honduras | Nicaragua | Panamá | Immigrants Subtotal (2) | México | Canada | USA | Immigrants Total (3) |
| Costa Rica (2000) | --- | 8,714 | 1,996 | 2,946 | 226,374 | 10,270 | 250,300 | 2,327 | 1,057 | 9,511 | 263,193 |
| El Salvador (1992) | 856 | --- | 4,524 | 8,666 | 2,139 | 308 | 16,493 | 1,350 | 279 | 4,413 | 22,535 |
| Guatemala (1994) | 737 | 14,425 | --- | 4,634 | 3,621 | 245 | 23,662 | 5,250 | 145 | 2,873 | 31,930 |
| Nicaragua (1995) | 4,727 | 2,136 | 900 | 9,473 | --- | 351 | 17,587 | 734 | 147 | 2,952 | 21,420 |
| Panamá (1990) | 3,829 | 2,340 | 367 | 623 | 4,447 | --- | 11,606 | 1,361 | 137 | 3,242 | 16,346 |
| Emigrants (Subtotal) (4) | 10,149 | 27,615 | 7,787 | 26,342 | 236,581 | 11,174 | 319,648 | 11,022 | 1,765 | 22,991 | 355,424 |
| Mexico (1990) | n.d. | n.d. | 46,006 | n.d. | 2,566 | n.d. | 48,571 | --- | 3,011 | 194,619 | 246,201 |
| Canada (1991) | 1,305 | 28,295 | 8,920 | 2,245 | 6,460 | 1,170 | 48,395 | 19,400 | --- | 249,075 | 316,870 |
| USA (1990) | 43,530 | 465,433 | 225,739 | 108,923 | 168,659 | 85,737 | 1,098,021 | 4,298,014 | 744,830 | --- | 6,140,865 |
| Emigrants (Total) (5) | 54,984 | 521,343 | 288,451 | 137,510 | 414,266 | 98,081 | 1,514,635 | 4,328,436 | 749,606 | 466,685 | 7,059,360 |

(1) In parentheses the year is given in which the respective Census was taken.
(2) Subtotal of immigrants born in Central America and residents in another country in Central or North America.
(3) Total number of immigrants born in Central and North America and residents in another of these countries.
(4) Subtotal of emigrants residents in Central America and born in another country in Central or North America.
(5) Total number of emigrants born in Central and North America and residents in another of these countries.

Source: *Migración y desarrollo en América del Norte y Centroamérica: una vision sintética* (Santiago de Chile: CEPAL, 1999), p. 45; data from IMLA (Investigación de la Migración Internacional en América Latina, de CELADE/ECLA, supplemented by data from the Costa Rican Census of 2000).

In the early 1970s, the beginning of economic crises in most Central American countries (after two decades of relatively rapid economic growth), was responsible for the change of migratory patterns towards migration to the North. Subsequently, the increasing political conflicts in Nicaragua, Guatemala and El Salvador pushed many citizens into exile. Again, there are contradictory data but on the whole one can assume that about 600,000 Central American refugees left their countries between 1980 and 1989 and settled in other countries of the region (among them 237,000 in Honduras, 183,000 in Guatemala and 120,000 in Costa Rica), in addition approximately 240,000 in Mexico. Out of those only 91,000 were officially recognised as refugees (37,000 in Honduras, 3,000 in Guatemala and 40,000 in Costa Rica), an additional 42,000 in Mexico.[14] Vargas et al. assumed that furthermore 217,000 Central Americans migrated for economic reasons within the region in the same decade, with 170,000 of them going to Costa Rica. The peace processes of the 1990s were accompanied by a large repatriation programme coordinated by the UNHCR. Yet still on 1 January 1996, there were still 24,266 recognised refugees in Costa Rica, wheile tere were only 63 in Honduras. From January 1995 to 1 May 1996, 263 refugees were assisted in repatriating but by 1 May 1996, 10,500 were granted resident status in Costa Rica.[15] Studies usually discuss social problems and economic costs of exile but there are hardly any references to possible effects on Central American integration.

After processes of reconciliation in the civil war countries in the 1990s, emigration continued to grow, basically for economic reasons. The flow of migrants from Central America to the USA increased from 31,814 in 1995 to 66,443 in 2000;[16] the number of US residents born in Central American countries including Belize and Panama increased from 1.124 million in 1990 to 1.504 million in 1995 and 2.066 million in 2000.[17] Remittances are of increasing importance for Central American economies, with their total amount for all countries together increasing from 206 million US$ in 1984 to 1.225 billion US$ in 1992 and 2.344 billion US$ in 1998.[18] In the case of El Salvador remittances contribute about one third of all foreign exchange earnings.[19] The emerging structures of transnational spaces between immigrants in the USA and their home communities constitute a growing theme in migration literature, including the rise

---

[14] Juan Rafael Vargas et al., 'El impacto económico y social de las migraciones en Centroamérica (1980-1989)', *Anuario de Estudios Centroamericanos*, 21/1-2 (1995): 39-81.

[15] UNHCR, Update on Regional Developments in the Americas and the Caribbean, 19 Aug 1996, Doc. EC/46/SC/CRP.43 (New York: UNHCR, 1996).

[16] (www.migrationinformation.org), based on U.S. Census Bureau, Current Population Survey, March Supplement, 1995 to 2001.

[17] US Census Bureau, for 1990: IMILA data base; Census population born in Latin America and Caribbean by country of residence according country of birth.

[18] See Mahler, *Migration*, p. 28.

[19] The World Bank, *World Development Report 2000/01* (Washington, DC: The World Bank, 2000).

of transnational business in the hands of migrants, the growing number of immigrant 'home town associations' in the USA and the perspectives of a 'brain gain' through the use of human capital acquired by migrants in their home countries in consequence of re-migration.

Costa Rica is a fundamental exception, not only with respect to its rather low number of emigrants (1,324 in 2000 compared to 22,578 from El Salvador and 24,029 from Nicaragua entering the USA according to US census data) but also as the only country with an important immigration from Central America (basically Nicaraguans). I will go more into details on Costa Rica in the following section. Besides that, one should take into account that a sizable number of Central Americans, basically from Guatemala and El Salvador, have migrated to Belize. Though the absolute number of these migrants is considerably smaller as in the Costa Rican case (estimates range from 24,000 to 60,000 compared to 250,000 registered by the Costa Rican census), their percentage in the total population of Belize is considerably higher, growing from 8 per cent in 1980 to 13 per cent in the 1991 census. At the same time, a considerable number of Belizeans has migrated to the USA.[20] The Afro-Belizean population dropped from 48 per cent in 1980 to 36 per cent in 1991 while during the same period, the Mestizo population grew from 33 per cent to 44 per cent. These recent trends suggest a change of the ethnic composition in Belize and can be seen as an aspect of Central American integration, though hardly a central one.

Taking into account the tendency of global migration of becoming more and more similar to traditional patterns of periphery-centre migration within national territories, I should ask whether we can find this pattern among Central American countries as well. Within separate countries, rural-urban migration is going on to play a significant role. The proportion of urban populations in El Salvador, Honduras, Panama, and Nicaragua is expected to reach two thirds of the total population in 2020, 10 per cent higher than in 1995.[21] Nicaraguan migration to Costa Rica is to a large degree traditional and seasonal rural-rural migration even though the number of Nicaraguans living in Costa Rican cities is increasing. So, to a very limited degree, the San José metropolitan region may come closer to the role of a small 'global city' with a polarized service sector including, on the one hand, relatively highly paid employees in financial services, the software and other sectors and, on the other hand, poorly paid immigrant labour in domestic and other services requiring few specific skills.

Little attention appears to be paid to the contribution of migration to regional integration as nearly all publications on migration and Central America concentrate on the analysis of emigration to the North with the exception of some wok that focuses on the migration of Nicaraguans to Costa Rica. Even if part of the intra-regional immigration documented in Table 7.1 can be traced back to refugees of

---

[20] In 2001, 53,000 immigrants born in Belize were living there. The total population of Belize in 1999 was 247,000.

[21] Mahler, *Migration*, p. 14.

the 1980s, there are no studies which try to take a closer look at the characteristics of other migrants within Central America – though their number of about 90,000 is not altogether insignificant. In effect, there is some discussion on migration and regional integration, but this discussion concentrates on the development of regional approaches to coordinate policies with respect to migration.[22] I shall return to this point later.

With respect to the potential of migration to contribute to regional integration, I would assume that quantitative migratory flows and legal provisions have to be taken into account but that they alone do not allow more far-reaching conclusions. There is no doubt that general migration data do not indicate any process of socio-economic integration in Central America – with the exception of the movement of Nicaraguans to Costa Rica, which, however, links traditional patterns of seasonal migration with the modern pattern of periphery-centre migration and is comparable to emigration to North America. In order to detect an interrelationship between the two processes, my next step will be to look more closely at two questions. The first question is about the specific migratory pattern of Costa Rica. This pattern may be related to the transformation of the country into a regional centre or it may just indicate a semi-developed enclave in a 'sea of underdevelopment'. The second question asks whether it is possible to determine the relative importance of specific groups of migrants as actors in the process of regional integration. While some statistical information is available regarding the first question, we can only rely on a few propositions for answers to the second question, serving as a base for future research. After a look at these questions I will return to the effective processes of regional integration in Central America and their actual and potential relationship to migratory processes.

### The Migratory Pattern of a Regional Sub-centre: the Example of Costa Rica

*Costa Rica: Structures of Migration*

Costa Rica has been the only country in Central America with a continuously positive net migration balance. Until the 1950s one can observe the traditional immigration pattern from Europe to America, supplemented by a certain flow of immigrants from China beginning with the railroad construction in the 1870s and from the Caribbean islands basically to the banana plantations on the Caribbean coast. Like in other Central American countries, immigrants, particularly from Germany, played an important role in the development of the production, processing and export of coffee, whereas Italian immigrant workers played a role in railway construction and agricultural colonization.

---

[22] See Mahler, *Migration*, pp. 43-53. Dora Celton, Hervé Domenach and Alejandro Giusti (eds), *Migraciones y Procesos de Integración Regional* (Nueva Córdoba: Editorial Copiar, 1999).

Costa Rica neither significantly participated in the onset of economically motivated emigration from Latin American countries to the United States nor, of course, in the outflow of political refugees seeking asylum in European countries or the USA. As we have seen, the country itself became an important destination of regional migration for asylum seekers, intellectuals and students as political refugees or simply looking for a stimulating place to work and to study, and, particularly since the 1980s, for a rapidly growing number of poor labour migrants, basically from Nicaragua.

Interestingly enough, Costa Rica distinguishes itself from most other Latin American countries by its pattern of centre-periphery-migration: On the one hand, we find an immigration of qualified personnel, entrepreneurs as well as scientists, who constituted a kind of a positive 'brain drain'. On the other hand – as has already been pointed out – there is immigration of poor people mostly from neighbouring countries taking over low-paid jobs for which the local labour market offers but scarce supply.

*Costa Rica: Immigration*

The analysis of migration statistics has already made it clear that the labour migration of Nicaraguans to Costa Rica constitutes the quantitatively outstanding fact in intra-Central American migration (see table 7.1). To some degree these immigrants have also come to Costa Rica in an attempt to obtain access to the much more extensive social benefits offered here than in their home country. A lack of interest in very low paid work in coffee and other plantations by Costa Ricans has led to a high demand for immigrant seasonal agricultural workers. But also the construction industry, particularly projects related to tourism in areas with little administrative control by the central government, and finally, household services in the San José area have attracted many immigrants, among the latter mostly women. Many of these immigrants enter the country illegally, so the effective number of them is considerably higher than those caught by census data. Most recent studies on migration within Central America concentrate on this specific aspect; here we find the typical push-pull-structure of migration.

Minimum wages for agricultural workers in Nicaragua amounted in 1993 to 23.8 US$ per month, in Costa Rica to 109.3 US$; for transport workers 35.7 US$ in Nicaragua and 116.1 US$ in Costa Rica.[23] The World Bank's key indicators of development point to the large gap between the two countries.[24]

---

[23] Proyecto Estado de la nación, *Estado de la región en desarrollo humano sostenible. Primer Informe* (San José: s.n., 1999), chapter 14.

[24] The World Bank, *World Development Report 2002*, Table 1, p. 232.

**Table 7.2 Key Indicators of Development for Central American Countries**

|  | GNI per capita (PPP)* | Life expectancy at birth | Under-5 mortality rate (per 1,000) | Adult illiteracy (% of people 15+) |
|---|---|---|---|---|
| Costa Rica | 8,250 | 77 | 14 | 5 |
| Nicaragua | 2,100 | 69 | 43 | 32 |
| Honduras | 2,390 | 70 | 46 | 26 |
| El Salvador | 4,390 | 70 | 36 | 22 |
| Guatemala | 3,770 | 65 | 52 | 32 |
| Panama | 5,700 | 74 | 25 | 8 |

*Gross national income in Purchasing Power Parity (in US $)
*Source*: World Development Report 2002, Table 1, p. 232.

It is interesting to note as an anecdote that in 1998 the Nicaraguan township (*municipio*) of Cárdenas demanded to leave Nicaragua and to be annexed to Costa Rica with the argument that it was being systematically neglected by the Nicaraguan government and better linked in terms of infrastructure to the neighbouring Costa Rican town of La Cruz there having access to free medical services and the labour market.[25]

We have already seen that statistical data on Central American migration are far from being reliable. Certainly immigration to Costa Rica has considerably increased during recent years, particularly of illegal immigrants from Nicaragua. Former studies probably underestimated the immigrant population,[26] while the 2000 census arrives at 296,461 inhabitants born in a foreign country (inclusive of 226,374 in Nicaragua) in a total population of 3.8 million people. Considering a continuing flow of immigrants and, in addition, an important number of illegal workers, there are estimates of over 400,000 foreigners actually living in the country. Besides the problem of estimating the number of illegal immigrants, there are further difficulties arising from the seasonality not only of agricultural work but also of work in the tourism sector. All foreigners who have the status of residents also have access to all social services and should be insured through their employers. This is different in the case of migrant workers, entering Costa Rica with a '*tarjeta laboral*' (worker's card) and, of course, in the case of illegal immigrants. Yet even illegal immigrants have access to basic local health services (provided at 'health centres') and to primary schooling for their children.[27] In some

---

[25] Christina Bollin, *Der zentralamerikanische Integrationsprozess* (Frankfurt and New York: Lang, 2000), p. 141. *La Prensa* on the Web, Honduras (15 June 1998).

[26] Estimate for 1997: c. 120,000 foreigners, among them 87,000 Nicaraguans, in a total population of approximately 3.3 million.

[27] Guillermo Acuña González and Edith Olivares Ferreto, *La población migrante Nicaraguense en Costa Rica. Realidades y Respuestas* (San José: Universidad de Costa Rica, Cuadernos de Trabajo, 2000), pp. 12-13.

basic programmes for the assistance of children, more than half of the beneficiaries in the Northern Region are believed to be Nicaraguans. Though there is some reservation with respect to Nicaraguan immigrants in the country there seem to be no severe social and/or political tensions, as in general the need for their work is acknowledged.

As table 7.2 shows, Central American countries other than Panama display differences in wages and other social indicators against Costa Rica. However, there are few labour migrants from those countries to Costa Rica. Instead, Guatemaltecan and Salvadorian workers tend to migrate to Mexico or the USA. To some degree this is a matter of geographical distance but also an indicator of one weakness of Costa Rica's role as a regional centre: the country is too small to effect a spill-over to the other Central American economies (Costa Rica: 3.8 million inhabitants; other countries together c. 23 million). With respect not only to migration but also to other aspects of regional integration, Costa Ricans are still afraid of being stripped of their own achievements by the weight of the other countries' problems.

In addition to intra-regional migration, migration flows to and from other regions remained important particularly as a source for strengthening the national base of qualified personnel. This includes small and medium entrepreneurs, researchers in academic institutions; personnel of international corporations and institutions and also the so-called pensionados (pensioners) who can acquire resident status by proving that they receive a monthly minimum of transfer payments from a foreign country of 600 US$ or 1,000 US$, pending specific conditions. The number of people who benefit from the pensionados status probably ranges from 10,000 to 15,000.[28]

There are two groups of immigrants or refugees which I assume to be of great importance for the Costa Rican position in regional development, although it is hardly possible to obtain more than sketchy evidence. These groups are intellectual refugees during the 1980s and small and medium entrepreneurs born in foreign countries.

Elite immigration played a significant role in the history of Central American societies. In large part due to its political stability and its liberal political and legal system as well as its positive economic and social development, Costa Rica succeeded in adapting this tradition to the needs of the socio-economic modernization of the country. At the beginning was a colonization project led by retired Italian officers in the early 1950s. They developed themselves into successful agricultural colonizers and turned the remote forest-covered area of San

---

[28] I could not obtain statistics on *pensionados* but would assume by a very rough guess that about one third of residents born in North America (table 7.1) and Europe and one fifth of migrants from Asia, South America and the Caribbean (Cubans) and a very low percentage of migrants from Central America have benefited from this status. By this count I would estimate a number of 12,000 *pensionados* (data on those born in outside North and Central America are taken from the 2000 Costa Rican census).

Vito in the extreme south into a dynamic agricultural region. In 1951 they concluded a contract and committed themselves to settling between 250 and 300 families within ten years (at least 20 per cent of them Costa Ricans); in 1959 there 1,100 people were living in the area (among them 59 per cent Costa Ricans); in 1987 40,000 people had their homes around the well developed town of San Vito.[29] In the 1950s and later, religious minority groups settled in Costa Rica and developed small centres of successful agroindustrial development, like a group of Quakers in Monteverde and other groups in the Northern Zone of the country (Mennonites, engaging in poultry raising now for a chain of fast-food stores in San José and other Costa Rican towns, the production of jam and other fruit and vegetable preserves). In the 1980s many of the successful non-traditional agricultural enterprises (export of non-traditional fruits and ornamental plants) were founded by foreigners settling in Costa Rica.

Regrettably, there are no general studies on 'immigrant entrepreneurs' in Costa Rica. This term now seems to be reserved for immigrants from the South to the North.[30] While working on studies on agro-industrial development and tourism in Costa Rica, I was surprised at the importance of immigrant entrepreneurs (not transnational corporations) mostly from industrial countries for the development of small business in the country. Reviewing the information obtained on these occasions, I can report a few estimated numbers.[31] Out of 22 enterprises interviewed, which were selected to cover all agro-industrial enterprises in three peripheral regions in the country, two were owned by large Transnational Corporations, four or five by small US-Transnational Enterprises, seven or eight by immigrants and eight by Costa Ricans. Out of 11 enterprises in agro-industry related machinery production, two were owned by immigrant families. Out of 24 hotels visited in two micro-regions (all larger and a sample of the smaller hotels), three belonged to international hotel chains, 14 to immigrants and only seven to Costa Ricans.

This suggests that the country can build on an important middle class immigration which includes social scientists and entrepreneurs in the machinery industry, agro-industries and tourism. The entrepreneurs' contacts to their home countries constitute constituted an important factor of market access, related to imports of important inputs and above all to opportunities for selling products, and thus boosted competitiveness. Structures are in some ways similar to those of

---

[29] See Bariatti, *Italianos*.

[30] For example see Michael Peter Smith and Luis Eduardo Guarnizo (eds), *Transnationalism From Below* (New Brunswick: Rutgers University Press, 1998).

[31] The data are extracted from interview records collected within research projects in which I participated but they are not included in the project publications. Tilman Altenburg, Wolfgang Hein and Jürgen Weller, *El desafío económico de Costa Rica. Desarrollo agroindustrial autocentrado come alternativa* (San José: Editorial DEI, 1990). Edgar Fürst and Wolfgang Hein (eds), *Turismo de Larga Distancia y Desarrollo Regional en Costa Rica* (San José: Editorial DEI, 2002).

'transnational enterprises' analysed by Portes et al.[32] but obviously with reversed signs and most of the Costa immigrant entrepreneurs migrated with the outright intention of building up businesses. They are people from industrialised countries, usually well-off, who for one reason or another found it attractive to settle in Costa Rica. Some of them came into the country as experts in development cooperation projects. Relations to their home countries are important for economic success. Moreover, in many cases the demonstration effects for local entrepreneurs have also been significant. Of course, the non-traditional export sector, basically so-called 'ethnic foods' have also profited from the demand among Central American emigrants to the U.S. and contacts to the Portes-type entrepreneurs.

Costa Rica has been attractive to some kind of a reversed brain drain because of natural attractions, political stability, being a competitive location for certain activities and, finally, a lack of entrepreneurial spirit among Costa Ricans themselves. The latter factor has made it easier for immigrant entrepreneurs to establish themselves in the country. Some data on the immigration of professionals are available which also include the immigrants found in the above-mentioned studies.[33] Regrettably they are not comparable to the comparative data presented by Pellegrino/ Martínez Pizarro[34] because the latter data only refer to migrants from other Latin American countries.

By far the largest number of immigrants is from Central America (250.300; see table 7.1) and has generally low levels of qualification. I suppose that at most 1,000 of the 9,031 professionals reported in table 7.3 come from other Central American countries. So we can assume that about 8,000 of the remaining 30,000 to 35,000 [35] economically active immigrants from outside Central America are professionals, which is probably a rather high percentage for immigrants in a developing country. The large group of people in the economic category of 'others' (see table 7.3, right hand column) contains an important number of entrepreneurs and independent professionals (architects, lawyers, medical doctors, private language schools and others).

---

[32] Portes, 'Transnational Entrepreneurs'.

[33] CELADE, Banco de Datos, Proyecto IMLA, 'Costa Rica 2000', cf. table 7.3.

[34] Adela Pellegrino and Jorge Martínez Pizarro, *Una aproximación al diseño de políticas sobre la migración internacional calificada en América Latina* (Santiago de Chile: CEPAL, 2001).

[35] This estimate is based on the Costa Rican 2000 census (total number of immigrants: 296,461; see above), deducting the number of 250,300 immigrants from Central America (data presented in table 7.1) and the estimate on *pensionados* (see above, footnote 30), who do not enter into the labour force.

**Table 7.3  Foreign-born Professionals and Technicians in Costa Rica, according to Occupational Groups and Area of Work**

| Occupational Groups | Total number | Chemical Industry, machinery construction | Teaching | Research | Medical services | Communal social services | Other |
|---|---|---|---|---|---|---|---|
| Total | 9031 | 260 | 2630 | 66 | 1322 | 1037 | 3716 |
| Architects, engineers | 878 | 122 | 9 | - | 2 | 9 | 736 |
| Chemists, physicists | 63 | 12 | 2 | 5 | 4 | - | 40 |
| Biologists, agronomists | 398 | 12 | 23 | 37 | 50 | 22 | 254 |
| Medical doctors, dentists, veterinarians | 1175 | 4 | 19 | 3 | 1043 | 5 | 91 |
| Paramedical personnel | 232 | 14 | 1 | 2 | 138 | 1 | 70 |
| Teachers | 2547 | - | 2396 | - | - | 7 | 144 |
| Lawyers | 425 | 3 | 3 | - | - | 11 | 408 |
| Writers, artists | 409 | 1 | 5 | - | - | 294 | 109 |
| Priests/monks/nuns | 612 | - | 16 | - | 2 | 562 | 32 |
| Others, technicians | 2292 | 72 | 160 | 19 | 83 | 126 | 1832 |

*Source*: CELADO, Banco de Datos, Proyecto IMILA, 'Costa Rica 2000'. (www.eclac.cl/celade/noticias/noticias/9/9869/COSTA RICA mig2000.xls), visited on 28 June 2005.

It is also noteworthy that Costa Rica is among the top ten host countries for U.S. students studying abroad. In the academic year 1999/2000 there were 3,421 U.S. students in Costa Rica, in Latin America topped only by Mexico with 7,374 students.[36] Furthermore, the country's democratic tradition and the importance of local civil society has favoured the development of a strong presence of international NGOs In fact, it has become increasingly difficult to distinguish between immigrants and academics or activists having worked in Costa Rica for some time.

*Costa Rica: Emigration*

It is difficult to find recent statistics on Costa Rican emigration in general, as emigrants are not specified in the national census and immigration data from other countries available to me are mostly from the early 1990s. Nevertheless, there is no great risk assuming that there are few Costa Rican labour emigrants of the typical Third-World type looking for low-qualified jobs in industrialised countries and transferring money to their families back home. Many Costa Ricans are leaving their country temporarily for the purposes of studying abroad or improving their professional careers. Certainly, there are poor or also middle-class Costa Ricans looking for a better future abroad and certainly, in the crisis years of the early 1980s larger numbers of Costa Ricans left their country for the United States and have stayed there since then. Thus in 1990, there were 43,530 people living in the USA born in Costa Rica – rather few compared to 465,433 from El Salvador, 168,659 from Nicaragua and 108,923 from Honduras (Table 7.1). This number has increased to 68,000 until 2001 (compared to 830,000 from El Salvador, 250,000 from Nicaragua and 301,000 from Honduras in the same year).[37]

Recent US migration statistics suggest that a large part of Costa Ricans entering the US are students and scholars. In 2000, there were just 1,324 Costa Ricans 'inflowing' to the USA,[38] while at the same time, during the Academic Year 2000/01, there were 928 Costa Rican students enrolled in US universities and 71 Costa Rican scholars working there. Even if most of them spend more than a year in the USA, it is safe to assume that they account for a considerable part of immigrants. Though the absolute number of students from other Central American countries is at a similar level, which means it is relatively low compared to the larger population of these countries, the statistics show that the percentage of graduate students among Costa Ricans is considerably higher than that of neighbouring countries (Costa Rica: 38.1 per cent, Guatemala: 21.3 per cent, Honduras 15.4 per cent). It corresponds to this pattern that the number of visiting scholars from these countries is considerably lower (Guatemala: 35, Honduras: 19).[39]

---

[36] (www.opendoorsweb.org/Press/Americans_Studying_Abroad.htm), visited 13 November 2001.
[37] See U.S. Census Bureau, Current Population Survey, March Supplement 2001.
[38] U.S. Immigration and Naturalization Service, *Statistical Yearbook* (2000), Table 3.
[39] Statistics from (www.opendoorsweb.org).

It is even more difficult to find empirical material on the importance of the qualifications that Costa Ricans acquired while studying or acquiring work experience in industrialized countries and that they may devote to fostering local development processes at home. During my field work in Costa Rica during the 1980s, I found some evidence about the importance of a combination of a fairly well developed local higher education and an experience of studying abroad for the development of high-tech sectors. Stimulated by Intel's construction of a processor manufacturing plant in Costa Rica, there has been a rapid increase of software production in Costa Rica since the late 1990s. The Costa Rican chamber of Software Producers now counts 79 member firms and the country seems to be the second largest exporter of software among Third-World countries, surpassed only by India. There appears to be some similarity to Indian and East Asian computer specialists studying in the USA, working there for some time, then returning to their home countries and becoming entrepreneurs there.

**Migration and Central American Integration**

What do the data presented so far tell about the development of the Central American integration and Costa Rica's specific role in this process? Migration statistics and some qualitative data reveal that Costa Rica has a pattern of migration which, compared to the rest of Central America, corresponds to that of a more developed country. In addition there is some kind of labour market integration at least between Costa Rica and Nicaragua. This pivotal role supports the ranking of the country as a developing regional sub-centre. Furthermore Costa Rica was also important as a haven for political refugees from other Central American countries during the 1990s. Because of that, it is quite difficult to interpret the apparent stagnation of numbers of immigrants from some other Central American countries between the censuses of 1984 and 2000 (between 2,000 and 8,000 depending on the country of origin). While in 1984 many migrants were refugees, it seems that, at present, it is Costa Rica's leading role in the region that is having some importance in attracting migrants and keeping the numbers approximately at the level of the 1980s. The rise of the number of migrants from Panama might support this interpretation (4,794 in 1984; 10,270 in 2000). On the whole, however, what seems to matter more for processes of regional integration is what kind of people are the migrants rather than how many people are migrating.

**Political Asylum as a Factor of Political Integration: Costa Rica's Role as a Catalyst for Peace in Central America and a New Phase of Central American Integration**

Costa Rica has traditionally been a country granting political asylum at least since the 1930s: Many famous Latin American politicians spent some time of their exile in Costa Rica: the later Venezuelan president Rómulo Betancourt, the Peruvian Haya de la Torre, later Carlos Fonseca, one of the founders of the Sandinist movement in Nicaragua, and Violeta Chamorro, the Nicaraguan president from 1990 to 1997.

During the 1970s and the 1980s, not only did large numbers of refugees flow out from the war-torn countries in Central America but also many prominent intellectuals from Guatemala, El Salvador and Nicaragua spent some years in exile Many of them spent at least part of the time of their exile in Costa Rica where they had a greater chance to have some impact on politics in their home countries and later on Central American integration than outside the region. Among them are well-known social scientists and writers, namely Edelberto Torres Rivas and Gabriel Aguilera from Guatemala, Rafael Menjivar and José Roberto López from El Salvador, Sergio Ramírez from Nicaragua. The Central American University Council (CSUCA) and the central secretariat of FLACSO, a Latin American social science research institution, are located in Costa Rica as well as important agricultural research centres, such as CATIE (Centro Agrónomo Tropical de Investigación y Enseñanza) and IICA (Instituto Interamericano de Cooperación para la Agricultura). In the 1980s and early 90s a number of regional graduate study programmes (Maestrías Centroamericanas) were initiated in Costa Rica and resulted in many Central American students receiving their Master's degrees from Costa Rican universities. Thus, the country could uphold the attractiveness it acquired at times of crisis in the region.

It would be interesting to study the catalytic role of these people in the Central American peace process (Esquipulas), which was initiated by the Costa Rican president and later Nobel Peace Laureate Oscar Arías, and the revival of the Central American integration process in the 1990s. Many of those who worked in one of the many institutions which proliferated with the development of the Central American Integration System (SICA: Sistema de Integración Centroamericana) during the 1990s or participated in expert studies for these institutions, have probably known each other since the time of exile or from spending some time together at institutions in Costa Rica. This, I think, is quite an interesting proposition but very difficult one to provide something close to convincing evidence without further original research work.

**Regional Integration in the 1990s: Institutional Aspects**

Under the Spanish crown Central America (exclusive of Panama that until 1903, belonged to Colombia and before independence to the Spanish Vice-Kingdom of Nueva Granada) formed one administrative unit as the Capitanía General de Guatemala. After independence and a short episode as part of Mexico, the region formed the 'República Federal de Centroamérica' from 1823 to 1839 which then broke apart because of the resistance of the regional units against Guatemalan dominance in a situation of little administrative integration and few venues of communication. Various attempts to renew political integration failed so that each of the five countries in the region developed their own political histories and national identities.

The need for socio-economic modernization and a larger internal market at a time dominated by the strategy of 'industrialization through import substitution' led to renewed endeavours towards regional integration in the 1950s and eventually in 1958, to the foundation of the Central American Common Market (CACM) with a Permanent Secretariat (SIECA), a Bank of Central American Integration and the creation of the Peso Centroaméricana (pegged to the US$) as an accounting unit for intra-regional payments. This project was rather successful: a common external tariff was accomplished and until 1971, a free trade regime for 96 per cent of all regional products was established. Industrial production grew considerably on the basis of import substitution for a medium-size market and the volume of intra regional trade soared from 33 million US$ in 1960 to 299 million US$ in 1970. But it was just this success which created new problems: on the one hand industrial production was very unequally distributed, with rapid growth first in Guatemala and El Salvador and then in Costa Rica as well and little development in Honduras and Nicaragua (in 1971 Honduras left the Common Market for some years); whereas on the other hand, the modernization process created internal tensions within member countries leading to civil wars in Guatemala, El Salvador and Nicaragua. In the 1970s intraregional trade stagnated and declined considerably during the 1980s. Nevertheless, the institutional structure did not break down and continues to constitute one base of the renewed integration effort that has emerged from the late 1980s.[40]

The revival of political activities for Central American integration was a consequence of the peace process initiated by the second Esquipulas conference in 1987, when Central American governments agreed to a common concept for ending the civil wars in their countries – against objections from the USA. The first result was the signing of the Protocol of Tegucigalpa to the Charter of the Organization of Central American States (ODECA, founded in 1951) in December 1991 by the five CACM member states and Panama. The Protocol included provisions for a broad new institutional development to be put into practice during the 1990s consisting of the Assembly of Presidents, which is scheduled to meet at least once a year, a Council of Ministers, an Executive Committee and a General Secretariat. In summary, as a result of this process during the last ten years the Assembly of Presidents has evolved into an effective gathering that takes place more than once a year and is keeping up a continuous process of consultations. Furthermore the General Secretariat has developed a complicated network of Central American institutions in charge of an increasing range of issues. The General Secretariat comprises a number of technical secretariats and about 30 institutes which are attached to one of the following five sectoral subsystems: the political, economic, social, cultural and environmental subsystems. These

---

[40] For a good summary of these processes see Bollin, *Integrationsprozess*.

institutions differ with respect to their tasks and relevance: SIECA as the central organization of economic integration is more or less the heart of the whole integration process, while other institutions are important for the coordination of external help in different respects. Among them are CEPREDENAC, the Coordination Committee for the Prevention of Natural Disasters in Central America and SE-CCAD, the Executive Secretariat for the Central American Commission for Environment and Development. Others are important in academic life, like CSUCA, the Central American University Federation, ICAP, the Central Institute for Public Administration, ICAITI, the Central American Institute for Research and Industrial Technology, while still further institutions are more or less dormant. Most of them, however, are quite busy commissioning studies, organizing conferences and other events and thereby at least contribute to communication among Central American countries and to the coordination of their positions in international affairs.

In the 1990s further central institutions beyond those included in the Tegucigalpa Protocol were founded, most of them with great names but, so far, little relevance for the integration process, like PARLACEN (Parlamento Centroamericano) and CCJ (Corte Centroamericana de Justicia). Nevertheless, the Consultative Committee (Comité Consultativo), founded late in 1995, constitutes an interesting attempt to integrate civil society in the process of regional policy making. It consists of members from 21 organizations who are supposed to represent different sectors of society, such as labour unions, farmers' organizations, chambers of industry, human rights organizations.

Migration does not play an important role in these institutional networks but it is not totally absent either. In reaction to the crisis of the 1980s and the resulting refugee problems, a Commission of Central American Directors of Migration was established in 1990 to improve regional monitoring of migration and migration facilities and to allow transit of Central American citizens throughout the region. One result was the formation of an integrated migration policy among El Salvador, Guatemala, Honduras, and Nicaragua (CA-4) together with the introduction of control cards for nationals of these countries which allowed them to pass freely from one country to another. Costa Rica is not taking part because it fears a further increase of immigration. Finally, the Regional Conference on Migration (or Proceso Puebla) was created in Puebla, Mexico in 1996. The Conference includes regular meetings of foreign affairs officials and directors of migration from North and Central America. It represents a multilateral approach to the problem and identifies five main areas of concern, namely migration policies, migration and development, combatting human smuggling and international cooperation for return migrants and human rights.[41]

Economically, the effects of this new phase of Central American cooperation are less spectacular than those in the decade following the foundation of the CACM. Due to the globalization process the economic and social conditions have changed

---

[41] See Mahler, *Migration*, pp. 42-3.

at the very bottom. The debt crisis and structural adjustment policies have subjected the Central American countries to pressures for economic liberalisation and political deregulation. This new environment has compelled regional cooperation to assume a different shape, frequently referred to as 'open regionalism'. At present, the basic reason for regional cooperation is to allow a better integration in the global market, through cooperation to the end of improving the competitiveness of regional production while reducing common external tariffs. The new pattern of migration and remittances as a form of effectively employing surplus labour and alleviating foreign-exchange deficits – supported by negotiations between Central American countries and the USA – seems to harmonize with this concept of 'open regionalism'.

Nevertheless, the Central American market continues to have a certain importance for a number of industries and the growth of intra-regional trade is at least keeping up with the general development of trade. In effect, the share of intra-Central American trade of the total trade of the five CACM countries slightly increased from 14.3 per cent in 1991 to 16.0 per cent in 1997. While Costa Rica and Guatemala had high export surpluses, Nicaragua and Honduras had high deficits and El Salvador a balanced regional trade structure. Costa Rica and Honduras were least dependent on intra-regional trade but for opposite reasons, Honduras because of its low level of industrialization and the ongoing dependence on traditional agricultural exports, Costa Rica because of the competitiveness of its industrial and non-traditional agricultural exports on the world market.

The same pattern of unequal development which led to conflict in the 1970s seems to reappear. In a perspective of 'open regionalism', however, these imbalances may be less important than in strategies aimed at the development of the internal market. In this new context, the coordination of politics in international affairs might play a more important role. Hence, rather than promoting unilateral measure for the growth of internal markets it has become more salient to negotiate with one voice in the various fields of global governance like development cooperation, disaster relief, trade negotiations, among them the WTO negotiations with the EU about the banana conflict, about the Annex on Tourism in GATS, on free trade in the Americas or perhaps even about the rights of immigrants in the USA.

Mass migration does not play such an important role although, needless to say, settling the issue of the migration of Nicaraguans to Costa Rica is seen as an issue in the process of regional cooperation. The rapid increase of employment opportunities in Costa Rica might lead to the certain re-direction of migration flows from other Central American countries to Costa Rica and away from their current destinations in the North, although this may seem unlikely at the moment. Yet there is no doubt that the proliferation of Central American institutions has itself contributed to an increasing mobility of elites in the region and thus to communication among the elites. The enhancement of communication among elites plays a role for students and academics in the institutions referred to. However, in other cases, mobility will remain at a level below the accepted social-science definition of migration as moving to a new place of residents and staying there for at least a year. This includes movements within the limited projects of SICA-institutions. We also should not forget the intensifying activities at the level of civil society organizations.

## Costa Rica's Reluctance of Assuming Leadership in Central American Integration – Economic Structures and National Identities

While in the 1960s Costa Rica still showed little interest in joining the process of regional economic integration, during the 1980s and the 1990s the country has developed into a political and economic pivot of regional development without which the process of regional integration in Central America has no chance to succeed. Costa Rica has gained an important economic advance over the other countries in the region and has developed into an intellectual centre and a birthplace of new political concepts respected far beyond the Central American region, particularly in the field of environmental politics.

The voluntary and involuntary migratory experiences of the new professional elites provide an important base for the processes of regional cooperation in close connection with economic pressures to improve the competitiveness of the region. In fact, as we have seen, the position of Costa Rica is ambiguous: On the one hand, implicitly, it serves as a social and political model for the other Central American countries, and does so implicitly. Costa Rica is the only country which, due to its economic, political and diplomatic position, can play a leading role in regional integration. On the other hand, Costa Ricans themselves are afraid of the burden of leadership in an economically and socially much less developed region – particularly because of the relative small size of the Costa Rican economy. One example of this reluctance has been the country's reluctance to integrate into the recently established Central American Customs Union.

Against the backdrop of the objective difficulties of a small country like Costa Rica to become the engine of economic development in the whole region, this reluctance to become tied into a close regional integration process seems rational. It is not just the experience of recent decades but that of centuries which has become a central element of Costa Rica's national myth and national pride and has entailed a feeling of superiority and caution with respect to its Central American neighbours. Consuelo Cruz, assistant professor at Tufts University, paraphrases the position held by Juan Mora Fernández, the first Costa Rican chief of state (still within the Central American Federation), in the 1820s:

> The Chief of State himself, in his effort to keep Costa Rica at a prudent distance from her Central American "sisters", promised to "draw" on the "virtues, morality, and good judgment" of his compatriots. Only distance, he told them, would allow their small and weak country to maintain "public peace". Only peace, he added, could afford them "the

time" to devote themselves to "business". And only in distant peace he concluded, could they enjoy the "fruits of their labor and investments".[42]

The pride of their peaceful country, devoted to business and not to violent conflicts, and the distance kept to the conflicts of the others, certainly was an important determinant for local development and migratory behaviour, but of course, it also has been an obstacle to regional integration. Maybe, now in a situation where Costa Rica is – compared to its neighbours – not any more a 'weak' country (at least economically) and the global situation demands primarily a mediating role as a manifestation of regional leadership, this might begin to change. On the other hand, of course, we also find a strong national identity in each country, particularly in the traditional elites, which makes it quite difficult for the cooperative politics of new elites really to prevail.

## Summary and Short Comparison with the Role of Migration in the Unification of Europe

I want to conclude with some short observations regarding the relationship between migration and regional integration in the Central American and European integration processes. Both processes have been accompanied by some important experiences of migration where the processes of periphery-centre migration have received much political and academic attention. By contrast, another form of migration which I have proposed to call horizontal migration has been going on without much notice although it may actually be more important for the processes of social integration in a region.

With respect to the first type of migration there is a fundamental difference between Europe and Central America: The European Community is one of the great players in the world economy and as such, a centre of attraction to neighbouring regions. Migration is an indicator for that attraction. Membership in the EU means profiting from its internal expansion effects. With the increase of local opportunities, these effects slow down the push-pull mechanism and, in turn, lead to a slowdown of mass migration from countries which have been admitted to the Community. In the 1950s, the 'economic miracle' in Western Europe first began to redirect migratory flows that had until then been targeted at external areas, namely the Americas and Australia, to the core industrial areas of Europe itself. Migrants came from Italy and then from countries which later-on joined the then EC, such as Spain, Portugal and Greece. The six founding countries were economically strong enough to pull up those countries which later became members, particularly as they had a smaller population than the economically

---

[42] Consuelo Cruz, Constructed Realisms: Distinction and Development in Central America. Paper presented at the Ideas, Culture and Political Analysis Workshop (Princeton University, 15-16 May 1998).

strong core countries. The sources of labour migration then moved again outside the Community, attracting migrants from Turkey, North Africa and in the 1990s, the former socialist countries. Obviously, the situation in Central America has been thoroughly different, the region being peripheral itself with surplus labour aiming to migrate to the dynamic regions in North America. In Central America, Costa Rica has assumed a leading position with respect to economic development, technology, environmental politics and representation in global governance. But effectively, because of its small size and some problems of national identity, it is improbable that Costa Rica will become a growth engine in the Central American region. Costa Rica will go on to attract a considerable number of migrants but the country alone will not be in a position to create a dynamics of Central American economic growth that could re-direct migratory flows from North America to regional growth centres.

On the other hand, horizontal migration may also have a certain periphery-centre bias but, in addition, develops between countries of a similar level of development. 'Horizontal migration' even includes people who migrate from the centre to more peripheral countries because there they find specific opportunities related to their personal qualifications or preferences. Specific situations like that of political refugees might intensify this type of migratory flows. In effect, these types of migration might be more important in binding a region together as they lead to an exchange of ideas and a rapprochement of political strategies creating common identities. And probably it is in this respect that we can find a lot of parallels between European and Central American integration.

Furthermore, we have to take into account that regional cooperation does not imply a form of collective protectionism at present but is closely linked to strengthened market-based integration into global markets. In this context we should take into account the importance of a small- and medium-enterprise export sector which attracts migrants from outside the region as we have seen in the case of Costa Rica. In the context of globalisation, strengthening the competitive base of the region becomes increasingly important and in that respect, Costa Rica can tap human resources from other Central American countries. At the same time, we find close links between the new professional elites and global-governance processes through which regional elites try to find improved opportunities for utilizing new resources to fuel regional development. This has been so particularly in the field of global environmental politics enshrined in the Biodiversity Convention, the Kyoto process where the 'selling' of environmental services of tropical forests has emerged as an important issue, or in efforts to strengthen the Central American position in global trade negotiations.

Chapter Eight

# The Kurdish Movement: Ethnic Mobilization and Europeanization

Andreas Blätte[1]

**Introduction**

The Kurdish question has always been an intricate one for the international system of nation-states. As Kurdish minorities are spread throughout Turkey, Iraq, Iran, and Syria, the issue cuts across existing borders within the Middle East. As a result of labour migration and refugee flows, a Kurdish minority and a Kurdish movement have evolved in Member States of the European Union. And as there has recently been protest directed at European institutions, the Kurdish movement may perform yet another leap beyond the confines of the nation-state – a Europeanization.

A Europeanization of the Kurdish movement would challenge the view that social movements, including migrant groups hardly respond to political opportunities created by European integration.[2] Ruud Koopmans and Paul Statham have noted the 'almost complete absence of claims-making related to the EU' among migrants.[3] Adrian Favell and Andrew Geddes find an absence of ethnic

---

[1] I should like to thank the *Central Archive for Empirical Social Research, University of Cologne* (ZA) for the permission to use the dataset *Protestereignisse in der Bundesrepublik Deutschland 1950-1993* (Study No. 2971). Interviews with Nikolas Brauns, Haydar Isik and Ciler Firtina have contributed to my understanding of the concerns of the Kurdish movement. Most importantly, I should like to thank Prof. Harald Kleinschmidt for the opportunity to present a first version of the paper at the Tokyo Migration Conference and for his patient and kind support.

[2] Gary Marks and Doug McAdam, 'Social Movements and the Changing Structure of Political Opportunity in the European Union', in Gary Marks et al. (eds), *Governance in the European Union* (London: Sage, 1996), pp. 95-120.

[3] Ruud Koopmans and Paul Statham, 'Challenging the Liberal Nation-State? Postnationalism, Multiculturalism, and the Collective Claims Making of Migrants and Ethnic Minorities in Britain and Germany', *American Journal of Sociology*, 105/3 (1999), pp. 652-693, p. 689.

mobilization directed at EU institutions,[4] and Hans-Jörg Trenz basically concurs by pointing out that migrants' representatives in Brussels are usually without contact to their social base.[5]

The possibility of a Europeanization of the Kurdish movement was discussed first by Vera Eccarius-Kelly.[6] Noting that supranational political opportunities for the Kurdish movement nowadays exist both in the institutional setting of the European Union as well as in the context of the Council of Europe, Eccarius-Kelly concludes: 'The Kurdish Diaspora's most immediate challenge is to take full advantage of the convoluted European bureaucracy. In utilizing the supranational system to encourage reforms in Turkey, the challenger group has gained access to powerful mechanisms'.[7] However, Eccarius-Kelly's discussion of Kurdish activists' European-level activities focuses on lobbyism rather than movement activity and protest. But as will be argued here, a Europeanization of the Kurdish movement has begun to occur in a fuller sense, including European-level Kurdish protest activity. This phenomenon first appeared in the period after the arrest of the PKK's leader Abdullah Öcalan in 1999. In particular, there have been several demonstrations in Strasbourg, seat of the European Parliament and the European Court of Human Rights.

The perspective of the subsequent analysis is to account for the rise and the repertoires of the Kurdish movement by examining the political opportunities it has encountered.[8] According to Sidney Tarrow,[9] 'political opportunities' can be defined as 'consistent – but not necessarily formal, permanent, or national –

---

[4] Adrian Favell and Andrew Geddes, 'Immigration and European Integration. New Opportunities for Transnational Mobilization?', in Ruud Koopmans and Paul Statham (eds), *Challenging Immigration and Ethnic Relations Politics* (Oxford: Oxford University Press 2000), pp. 407-28.

[5] Hans-Jörg Trenz, '"Lokal Denken – Global Handeln". Zur Mobilisier Adrian Favell and Andrew Geddes, 'Immigration and European Integration. New Opportunities ungslogik von Migranteninteressen in Europa', in Ansgar Klein, Ruud Koopmans and Heiko Geiling (eds), *Globalisierung – Partizipation – Protest* (Opladen: Leske + Budrich, 2001), pp. 177-203.

[6] Vera Eccarius-Kelly, 'Political Movements and Leverage Points: Kurdish Activism in the European Diaspora', *Journal of Muslim Minority Affairs*, 22/1 (2002), pp. 91-118.

[7] Ibid.: 114.

[8] Dieter Rucht, 'Komplexe Phänomene – komplexe Erklärungen. Die politischen Gelegenheitsstrukturen neuer sozialer Bewegungen', in Kai-Uwe Hellmann and Ruud Koopmans (eds), *Paradigmen der Bewegungsforschung* (Opladen: Westdeutscher Verlag, 1998), pp. 109-27.

[9] Sidney Tarrow, *Power in Movement. Social Movements and Contentious Politics*, second edn (Cambridge: Cambridge University Press, 1998), p. 20.

dimensions of the political struggle that encourage people to engage in contentious politics'. Other perspectives common in social movement research stress, for instance, discursive factors such as the 'framing' of issues for mobilization,[10] or the characteristics of social movement organizations.[11] Accepting that these perspectives would contribute to a fuller understanding of the Kurdish movement, the presumption is here that the 'political opportunity'-perspective is a reasonable perspective for explaining Kurdish mass mobilization and the alleged Europeanization.

It should be noted that the purpose of this article is not theory development. Sophisticated conceptual models have been developed to analyze transnational movements,[12] and variants have been applied to the Kurdish movement.[13] The intention here is rather to analytically describe an empirical instance that might inspire further theoretical or conceptual elaboration – such as an effort to add a supranational component to conceptualizations of transnational movements – than to present a conceptualization of this kind already.

Assuming that it is necessary for an understanding of the sources and the context of the alleged Europeanization, the first part of the article will trace the rise of the Kurdish movement within the national context of a European nation-state. Here, the analysis will focus on developments in Germany, as Germany has the largest Kurdish population in Europe by far[14] and has seen the strongest Kurdish movement activity. The second part, devoted to Europeanization, will first take a closer look at European-level political opportunities. Then, Kurdish protests aimed at European institutions shall be reported and discussed.

---

[10] David A. Snow and Robert D. Benford, 'Master Frames and Cycles of Protest', in A. Morris and C. Mueller (eds), *Frontiers in Social Movement Theory* (New Haven: Yale University Press, 1992), pp. 133-55.

[11] John D. McCarthy and Nayer N. Zald, 'Resource Mobilization and Social Movements: A Partial Theory', *American Journal of Sociology*, 82 (1977), pp. 1212-41.

[12] Donatella della Porta (ed.), *Social Movements in a Globalizing World* (New York: St. Martin's Press, 1999).

[13] Alynna J. Lyon and Emek M. Uçarer, 'Mobilizing Ethnic Conflict. Kurdish Separatism in Germany and the PKK', *Ethnic and Racial Studies*, 24/6 (2001), pp. 925-48.

[14] Based on a comparison of different publications, expert interviews, an analysis of press coverage and her own research, Birgit Ammann gives the following estimate for the number of Kurds in different European countries: Germany 600,000; France 70,000; Netherlands 60,000; Switzerland 30,000; United Kingdom 40,000; Austria 40,000; Denmark 15,000; Sweden 30,000; Belgium 40,000; Greece and Cyprus 2,000; Italy 8,000; Finland 3,000; Norway 4,000; Eastern Europe 10,000. The total number of Kurds in Europe is estimated to be about one million. Birgit Ammann, *Kurden in Europa. Ethnizität und Diaspora* (Munster and Hamburg: Lit., 2001), p. 138.

## Ethnic Mobilization of Kurds in Germany

The beginning Europeanization of the Kurdish Movement is an interesting case for social movement research but there are also extraordinary aspects of the preceding development of the Kurdish movement in a (trans-) national context. Considering the Kurdish movement in Germany, the proportion of the Kurds mobilized is amazing. From 1993 onwards, up to 80,000 protesters attended Kurds' demonstrations. Accepting 600,000 as an estimate [15] for the total Kurdish population in Germany,[16] every eighth Kurd in Germany has attended these protest events. If the mobilization rate had been as high at any 'German' protest event, 10 million people would have attended that demonstration.

With respect to Kurdish protest in Germany, public discourse has primarily been concerned with the political violence committed by a number of radical Kurds. There is no denying that this was a political problem. However, the point here is that the sheer extent of mass mobilization among Kurds in the diaspora has often been overlooked. But before proceeding to an account of the rise of the movement, I shall present a method that allows the extent of Kurdish protest to be displayed more systematically.

### A Protest Event Data Analysis of Kurdish Protest in Germany

The development of Kurdish mass protest can be measured using a method called 'protest event data analysis'. The essence of the method, developed in the so-called Prodat Project, is to gather information about protest events by means of a systematic analysis of newspaper reports.[17]

A list of Kurdish protest events produced with the methods of the Prodat Project certainly could not claim to reproduce exactly how many Kurds attended the protest events recorded. A first caveat concerns the representativeness of the data. The data does not include *all* protest events, as the Prodat Project only examined the newspapers' Monday issues. Also, Kurdish protest events may have taken place that have not been reported at all by newspapers. Second, concerning validity, there is some uncertainty as to whether the numbers reported in the newspapers are correct. Giving estimates for the attendance at demonstrations is

---

[15] As there is no Kurdish state, most ethnic Kurds have Turkish, Iraqi, Iranian or Syrian nationality. As official procedures in Germany only ask for nationality but not for ethnicity, official statistics do not give information on ethnicity, and there are no numbers of Kurds in Germany apart from estimates.

[16] Ammann, *Kurden in Europa*, p. 138.

[17] Dieter Rucht, Ruud Koopmans and Friedhelm Neidhardt (eds), *Acts of Dissent. New Developments in the Study of Protest* (Berlin: Ed. Sigma, 1998).

generally difficult, and estimates usually vary considerably between organizers', reporters' and police estimates. Accordingly, the numbers that will be reported here may not be absolutely correct and some protest events may even be missing. Still, protest event data analysis is considered a powerful method to show how protest in general or the ethnic mobilization of a particular group has developed.

Applying protest event data analysis to Kurdish protests, Table 8.1 visualizes how attendance at Kurdish demonstrations in Germany developed in the 1980s and 1990s. The data basis for the figure presented here is an extract from the data of the Prodat Project (1950 to 1993) and an analysis that I carried out of the *Süddeutsche Zeitung* for the time from 1993 onwards.[18]

One point is particularly noteworthy about the development of Kurdish protest, as presented in Table 8.1: A huge Kurdish protest potential manifested itself from 1992 onwards. An initial wave of Kurdish mass protest in 1993 and 1994 followed the ban of the PKK (the Kurdistan Worker's Party) by German authorities in November 1993; a second wave was triggered by the kidnapping and arrest of PKK leader Abdullah Öcalan in January 1999. The question is, however, why did Kurdish mass protest occur that late? Kurds have been present in Germany since the 1960s and there were mobilizing events earlier on. One might recall the breakdown of Kurdish resistance in Iraq in 1975, the disastrous consequences of the 1980 military coup in Turkey for Kurds and the chemical weapons attack on Kurds in Halabja in Iraq in 1988. To understand mobilization in the 1990s requires tracing the development of the Kurdish group in Germany. Again, the focus will be on Germany, as Germany has the largest Kurdish minority in Europe.

---

[18] In the Prodat Project, one variable was the characterization of the group of persons participating at a protest event. Among those protest events carried out by 'foreigners', Kurdish protest events could be identified by looking at the purpose of the protest event, enabling me to produce an extract with Kurdish protest from the Prodat database. Concerning my own analysis carried out for the period from 1993 to 2003, three remarks are in order: (a) The Prodat Project examined reports both in the *Süddeutsche Zeitung* as well as in the *Frankfurter Rundschau*. As I could not organize access to an archive of the *Frankfurter Rundschau*, my analysis is limited to the *Süddeutsche Zeitung*. (b) The Prodat Project only recorded protest events that took place on weekends as it only examined the newspapers' Monday issues. In my analysis, which used the possibilities to query CD-ROMs with all issues of the *Süddeutsche Zeitung* from 1993 to 2003 electronically, all issues were included. (c) Although it would have been desirable to avoid the differences between the procedures of the Prodat Project and my own analysis, it is assumed here that these differences are of minor importance and do certainly not lead to a distorted picture when comparing mobilization levels in the 1980s and 1990s. Practically all larger protest events took place on weekends and a random comparison between a couple of reports in the *Süddeutsche Zeitung* and the *Frankfurter Rundschau* shows that the numbers given for attendance at protest events usually concur.

**Table 8.1** Attendance at Kurdish Protests in Germany 1980-2002

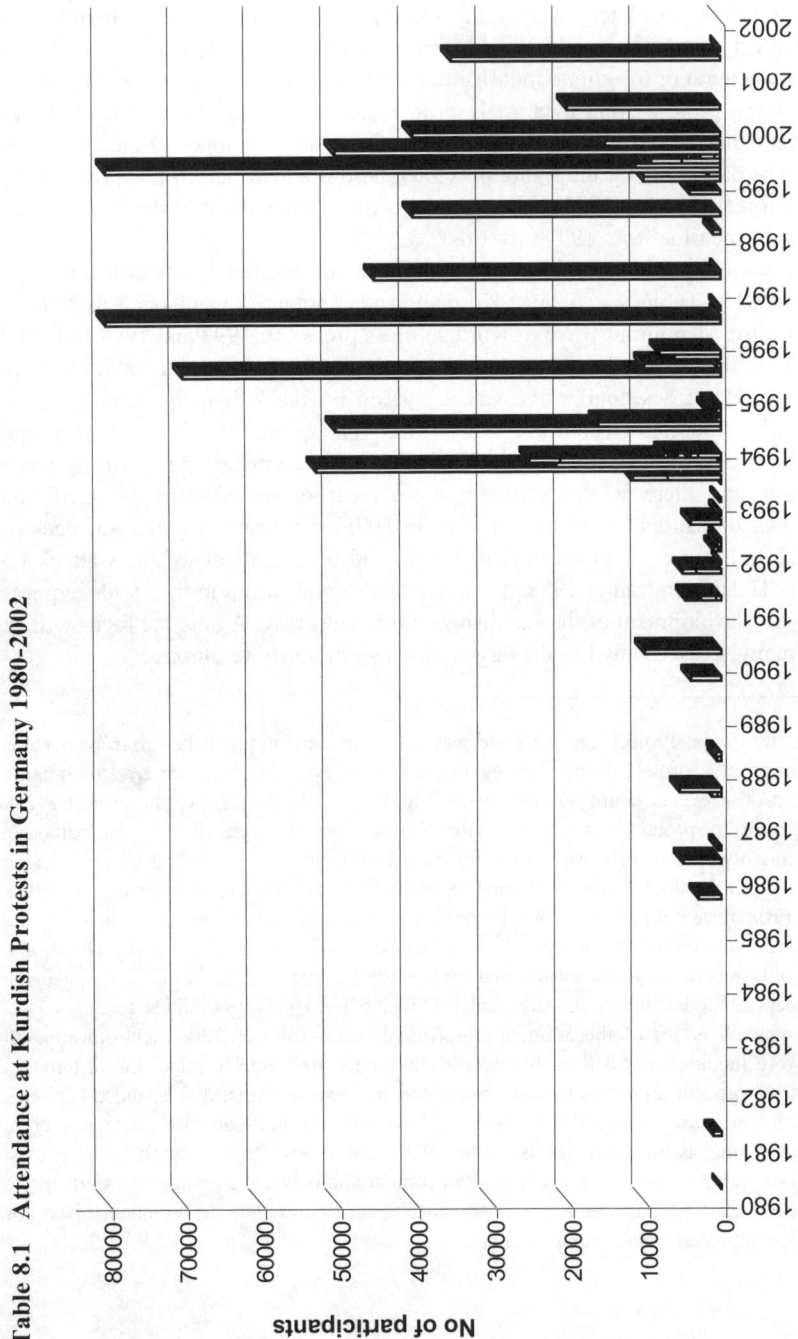

*The Rise of the Kurdish Movement in Europe: The Case of Germany Labour Migrants and early Ethnicization (1961-1980)*

Throughout the twentieth century, there have always been students from different Kurdish settlement areas attending German universities. However, the first large group of Kurds that came to Germany was among the labour migrants from Turkey. An estimated 20 to 25 per cent[19] of the 900,000 Turkish 'guest workers', people recruited between 1961 and 1973 to work in the German manufacturing sector, were of Kurdish origin. But as most of them came from urban areas, where Kurdish traditions and ethnicity had given way to the Kemalist Turkish mainstream, Kurdish labour migrants generally had a weak ethnic consciousness.

Germany's policies certainly did not further the development of a Kurdish ethnic consciousness. Kurds, like all migrants in Germany, were in a situation of political exclusion. Pursuing a policy that was to become a severe strain for the German-Kurdish relationship later on, the German state accepted the official Kemalist Turkish doctrine of not considering Kurds as a distinct ethnic minority. Kurds with Turkish nationality could not give their children Kurdish names as German authorities would only accept (ethnically Turkish) names found on lists that were provided by Turkish consulates.[20] There were programmes of mother-tongue education for Turkish labour migrants' children; Kurdish children with Turkish nationality had to attend classes given in Turkish even if their native language was Kurdish. Generally speaking, Germany's effort to maintain good relations with the Turkish government resulted in policies that were far from supporting a distinctive Kurdish ethnic identity.

Nevertheless, liberal constitutional guarantees allowed for and protected the expression and development of a Kurdish ethnic self-understanding. Among other things, it was possible to found Kurdish associations. Concurring with developments among other immigrant groups, Kurdish associations were founded from the 1960s onwards. There were self-help organizations with no political purpose and political clubs as well but many associations offered cultural activities that would foster migrants' sense of belonging. In most other ethnic groups, cultural activities were a means to maintain ethnic identity; among the Kurds, their organizations and activities were instrumental for *recovering* an ethnic identity that had been eroded. In 1974, the Kurdish festival of the New Year, Newroz, was celebrated for the first time in Germany. It was to become the special cultural manifestation of Kurdish identity. Kurdish language courses organized by Kurdish

---

[19] Ammann, *Kurden in Europa*, p. 121.
[20] This policy has begun to change and several German *Länder* nowadays accept Kurdish names.

organizations were another important aspect of ethnicity formation. Many Kurdish labour migrants from Turkey only learned the Kurdish language in the diaspora.[21] In fact, ethnicity itself was only rediscovered in the diaspora.[22]

Kurdish labour migrants, like all labour migrants of the 1960s and 70s, worked in poorly paid jobs. Not surprisingly, most Kurds tended to lean more toward the left. Building on the formation of associations on the local level, Komkar, the 'Federation of Kurdish Workers' Association' was founded in 1979. An organization with a social democratic outlook, it had two distinctive aims. First, it supported the struggle of the Kurdish people in Kurdistan and organized activities to generate a respective public awareness in Germany; second, it furthered the integration of Kurds in Germany and represented its members' social, cultural, and political interests to German authorities and German political parties.[23]

## Refugees and Mobilization (1980-1993)

Ethnic consciousness formation was accelerated in the 1980s, as events in Turkey reverberated in the Kurdish community in Europe. Following the military coup in Turkey on September 12, 1980, the Turkish state cracked down on forms of the expression of Kurdish identity. To combat Kurdish separatism, Kurdish organizations and parties – moderate ones included – were banned. Around 81,000 Kurds were detained between September 1980 and September 1982. Two-thirds of the Turkish army were deployed in Kurdish areas to 'pacify' the situation.[24]

Military repression and human rights violations in Turkey roused the solidarity of Kurdish migrant labourers in Germany.[25] But the consequences of the situation in Turkey were still more immediate. Between 1979 and 1999, around 330,000 asylum seekers came to Germany from Turkey, between 60 and 80 per cent of them Kurds.[26] Most of them came from Kurdish settlement areas in the southeast of Turkey, a region where Kurdish traditions were much stronger than in the west of the country. In a study on the situation of Kurdish refugees in Sweden, Östen Wahlbeck remarks that 'refugee communities ... often contain large resources for ethnic or political mobilization because of all refugees' similar backgrounds and

---

[21] Ammann, *Kurden in Europa*, p. 290.
[22] Martin van Bruinessen, *Transnational Aspects of the Kurdish Question* (San Domenico: European University Institute, 2000), p. 10.
[23] Şengül Şenol, *Kurden in Deutschland. Fremde unter Fremden* (Frankfurt a.M.: Haag + Herchen, 1992), p. 213.
[24] David McDowall, *A Modern History of the Kurds* (London: Tauris, 2000), p. 414.
[25] Bruinessen, *Transnational Aspects*, p. 6.
[26] Ammann, *Kurden in Europa*, p. 135.

life stories'.[27] This observation applies to Germany as well, and refugees began to drive the consciousness formation of the Kurdish community in Germany.[28]

Changes in the group composition altered predominant attitudes and resulted in changes in the organizational field. In the 1980s, the PKK emerged as an organization. It had been founded in 1978 by Abdullah Öcalan and took up an armed struggle against the Turkish state in 1984. The PKK's activities in Germany were exclusively homeland-oriented: they focused on the struggle for the independence of Kurdistan, and the use of force was accepted as a means in this struggle. Unlike Komkar, the PKK rejected furthering the integration of Kurdish migrants into German society – it was not considered conducive to the fight of the Kurdish people for independence. Instead, the diaspora was considered primarily as a source of financial resources and young men willing to fight in Kurdistan.

The deteriorating situation in Kurdish settlement areas induced other Kurdish organizations such as Komkar to shift the focus to country-of-origin-oriented activities. However, their moderate political stance increasingly failed to withstand the point of view that Kurds' chances to influence politics by conventional ways of political participation were marginal. Initially, the PKK had found its social base among refugees but the PKK's radical way now found more and more adherents among labour migrants as well. A reorientation away from Komkar and toward the PKK began.

*PKK prohibited and Öcalan arrested (1993-1999)*

The vector of change of the attitudes of Kurds in Germany was enhanced anew by the civil war between the Turkish central government and the PKK beginning in 1992. That situation was very much felt in Germany. Factions within the PKK sought to bring their struggle to Germany. From 1991 onwards, there were several series of occupations of German broadcasting agencies and party offices as well as of Turkish consulates and Turkish-run banks and travel agencies. But what is more, Turkish institutions in different German cities were the targets of violent attacks and the PKK was suspected to be behind these attacks.

After some hesitation, German authorities decided to ban the PKK as a terrorist organization in November 1993. Yet the violence of the reaction was unanticipated. There were hunger strikes in various German cities and – what gained most attention among the German public– blockades on German highways accompanied by violent riots. Particularly the latter forms of protest provoked overwhelmingly

---

[27] Östen Wahlbeck, *Kurdish Diasporas. A Comparative Study of Kurdish Refugee Communities* (Basingstoke: Macmillan, 2000), p. 11.

[28] Ammann, *Kurden in Europa*, p. 136.

negative reactions from the German public. However, and most importantly for the argument here, there were mass demonstrations with an attendance of up to 50,000 people. Building on developments in the Kurdish community that had begun in the 1980s, a huge Kurdish protest potential erupted for the first time.

A consolidated ethnic consciousness and orientation toward country-of-origin politics had successively increased the protest potential among Kurds. But the ban on the PKK did not only trigger the protest potential, it further deepened the basis for Kurdish protest. As the PKK had increasingly served as a focal point for Kurdish identity, the ban on PKK was perceived as a hostile affront by most Kurds – and not only by those that had been adherents of the PKK before.

The ban deepened a sense of Kurdish ethnicity. Thomas Brieden recorded that the number of those of Kurdish origin claiming that their exclusive identity was 'Kurdish' (and not 'Turkish-Kurdish', for instance) rose from 20 per cent in 1984-1986 to 76 per cent in 1994.[29] More importantly, the social base of the PKK was extended. In two sets of qualitative interviews with Kurds – the first between 1986 and 1990, the second between 1997 and 1999 – Birgit Ammann found a substantial growth of the approval for the PKK. This particularly applies to first-generation labour migrants not initially inclined to the PKK. As one respondent of Ammann put it, 'Former guest workers were somehow truly educated by the PKK. Before, they said: "We won't quarrel as long as we are left in peace." Then the PKK came and said: "You have slept long enough; now wake up!"'.[30] German security agencies reported that PKK membership in Germany rose from 5000 in 1993 to around 9000 in 1999. Despite the ban and criminal proceedings, there continued to be coordinated violent attacks on Turkish consulates, banks, and shops as well as occupations of German institutions until 1996.

But again, the acts of political violence that have occurred should not conceal the extent of mass protest. In January 1999, the arrest of Abdullah Öcalan – the founder and leader of the PKK – triggered a wave of protest even larger than the first one. Most Kurds felt personally affected by the kidnapping and the arrest of Öcalan.[31] Again, there were occupations of and attacks on Turkish and other institutions. Following Öcalan's arrest, 1999 was a year of demonstrations attended by up to 80,000 persons. There was an almost comprehensive identification of Kurds with the PKK's struggle in Germany. In 1993 and 1994, it was primarily

---

[29] Thomas Brieden, *Konfliktimport durch Immigration. Auswirkungen ethnischer Konflikte im Herkunftsland auf die Integrations- und Identitätsentwicklung von Immigranten in der Bundesrepublik Deutschland* (Hamburg: Verlag Dr. Kovač, 1996), p.111.

[30] Ammann, *Kurden in Europa*, p. 338.

[31] Ammann, *Kurden in Europa*, p. 392.

refugees who attended protests but in 1999, it was first-generation Kurds who had managed to enter the middle classes as well.

In *Power in Movement*, Sidney Tarrow remarks: 'If we were to elevate political opportunity structure into a general covering law, we would always find movements it cannot "explain" and those that arise as opportunities are closing'.[32] Political opportunities were closing for Kurds in Germany in the 1990s. The PKK, the focal organization for most Kurds, was forbidden and the PKK's leader arrested. These negative developments induced Kurds to go protesting.

**The Europeanization of the Kurdish Movement**

After the 1999 wave of protest, the situation changed in Turkey as well as in Europe. The Öcalan arrest was a blow for the military struggle of the PKK. In 2002, the PKK was dissolved and founded anew as 'Kadek', claiming to now be committed to peace and democracy. The mass protest of Kurds across Europe recessed as well. But a new phenomenon emerged: protest directed at European-level institutions.

From 1999 onwards, a perspective for Turkish accession to the European Union – real for the first time – meant a new political opportunity for change in Turkey. Membership in the European Union had been an aim of Turkey since the late 1950s. But besides Turkish instabilities and hesitations, Turkey also persistently met an unwilling or ambiguous Europe. Membership in the European Union was mentioned in the EC-Turkey association project of 1963 but it was never really on the table. Yet in 1999, the European Council of Helsinki affirmed Turkey's status as an accession candidate, stating: 'Turkey is a candidate State destined to join the Union on the basis of the same criteria as applied to the other candidate States.' The membership of Turkey in the European Union would not be discussed in terms of cultural belonging but in terms of the fulfillment of the so-called Copenhagen criteria of 1993. If certain economic and political criteria were met, Turkey could become a member of the European Union.

---

[32] Tarrow, *Power in Movement*, p. 200.

**Table 8.2   Kurdish European-level Protest Activity 1999-2003**

| Date | Description of Event | Claim(s) | Attendance | Area of Mobilization | Source |
|---|---|---|---|---|---|
| 12 Feb. 2000 | Demonstration at Strasbourg | Freedom for Öcalan | 15 000 | Germany, Belgium, Italy, UK, Switzerland | SZ, 14 Feb. 2000, p. 6 |
| 21 Nov. 2000 | Demonstration at Strasbourg | (no information available) | 15 000 | Predominantly Germany | AFP, 21 Nov. 2000 |
| 29 Jun. 2001 – 11 Jul. 2001 | Protest march from Mannheim (Germany) to Strasbourg – Council of Europe | Recognition of the Kurds' political and cultural rights | 150 | Germany | AZADI Press Release, 3 Jul. 2001 |
| 16 Feb. 2002 | Demonstration at Strasbourg | Freedom for Öcalan | 6 000 | France, Germany, Switzerland, Belgium, Netherlands, Luxemburg | AFP, 16 Feb. 2002 |
| 4 May 2002 | Demonstration at Brussels | Against inclusion of the PKK on EU list of terrorist organizations | 150 | (no information available) | AFP, 4 May 2002 |
| 22 Aug. 2002 | Protest march from Strasbourg to Brussels | Against inclusion of the PKK on EU list of terrorist organizations | 100 | (no information available) | AFP, 22 Aug. 2002 |
| 15 Feb. 2003 | Demonstration at Strasbourg | Freedom for Öcalan | 20 000 | France, Belgium, Germany | La Croix, 16 Feb. 2003, p. 10 |
| 8 Mar. 2003 | Demonstration at Brussels | No Turkish intervention in Northern Iraq | 4 000 | (no information available) | FR, 10 Mar. 2003, p. 6 |

**Table 8.2 Continued**

| 14 Feb. 2004 | Demonstration at Strasbourg | Freedom for Öcalan | 15 000 | France, Germany, Belgium, Netherlands, Luxembourg | AFP, 14 Feb. 2004 |
|---|---|---|---|---|---|
| 9 Jun. 2004 | Demonstration at Strasbourg | Freedom for Öcalan | 7 000 | (no information available) | taz, 10 Jun. 2004, p. 9 |
| 11 Dec. 2004 | Demonstration at Brussels | Recognition of the Kurds' rights in Turkey | 7 000 | (no information available) | AFP, 11 Dec. 2004 |

Abbreviations:
AFP = *Agence France Press*      SZ = *Süddeutsche Zeitung*
FR = *Frankfurter Rundschau*      taz = *die tageszeitung*
AZADI = *Rechtshilfefonds für Kurdinnen und Kurden in Deutschland e.V.*
(www.nadir.org/nadir/initiativ/azadi/presse, press release retrieved on 23 Jul. 2005)

Turkey's active longing to obtain membership in the European Union tremendously changed the capacities of the European Union to have an impact on the situation of Kurds in Turkey. Traditionally, Turkey had rejected any foreign discussion about the Kurdish question as interference in its internal affairs. But the desire of Turkey to be a member of the European Union transformed the EU's issuing of concerns to a self-imposed process of monitoring and criticism. The conditionality entailed in the Copenhagen criteria was a powerful instrument in the hands of the European Union with respect to the Kurdish issue.

This was a new political opportunity for the Kurdish movement in Europe. If Kurds in Europe managed to call European policy-makers' attention to the situation of Kurds in Turkey, the European lever could be used to induce Turkey to change. That possibility arose in 1999 when the European Council decided to consider Turkey a candidate country, and it will continue as long as accession negotiations are still in progress. However, this analysis here will be limited to the situation between the announcement to consider Turkey a candidate country and the decision made in December 2004 to assume accession negotiations.

## The Political Opportunity Structure

A strategy of Kurdish movement activists to use the EU-Turkish accession nexus would actually have met favorable circumstances. Among those European institutions relevant for Turkish accession, especially the Commission and the European Parliament had paid considerable attention to the situation of Kurds in Turkey.

### European Parliament

The European Parliament has always shown sympathy for the Kurds' cause. On the one hand, there are individual parliamentarians' initiatives. Feleknas Uca (GUE/NGL), a Kurdish-origin parliamentarian, is an important contact for Kurdish organizations. She is a member of the EU-Turkey Joint Parliamentary Committee and has started various initiatives to highlight the situation of Kurds. For instance, she collected 93 signatures of members of the European Parliament in the spring of 2000 to protest against the Turkish government's action against the Diyarbakir Branch of the Human Rights Association, which was closed several times without explanation. Other parliamentarians were fairly active in using oral and written questions and 'Question Time' to inquire about the Commission's and the Council's stance on issues such as the 'Imprisonment of Leyla Zana and Turkey's accession to the EU', the 'Ban on political parties in Turkey', or the EU ban of the PKK.

But the EP's sympathy with Kurds goes beyond individual parliamentarians' initiatives and is shared by a grand coalition across all parties in the EP. Two quotations may serve to illustrate this point. In a debate on 'Democratic rights in Turkey, in particular the situation of HADEP' on 27 February 2002, Johannes Swoboda (PSE) proclaimed: 'What Parliament stands by is this: We campaign for the cultural rights of the Kurds – rights that are inalienable, that do not amount to separatism or terrorism, that do not create difficulties for Turkey, but which could be the salvation of Turkey as a European country.' The statement of the speaker of the PPE-DE, Lennart Sacrédeus was equally emphatic. Commenting on the trial against the ethnic Kurdish party HADEP, he promised 'that we in the European Parliament will show no lack of vigor, energy and persistence in monitoring this judicial process in Turkey. Within the framework of an ad hoc delegation, we intend to act in such a way as to protect democratic rights, the multiparty system and, of course, the rights of the Kurdish minority too in Turkey.'

The European Parliament has a record of taking strong positions on the Kurdish issue. In 1995, the Sakharov Freedom Award of the European Parliament went to the Kurdish politician Leyla Zana. In September 1996, an EP resolution called on the Commission to block financial aid for Turkey because of human rights violations. In its annual follow-up resolutions to the Commission's reports on

Turkey's progress towards accession, the EP regularly called for improvements of the Kurds' situation. In 1999, three resolutions were passed on the arrest, trial, and death sentence of Abdullah Öcalan and in February 2002, it adopted a resolution asking for the trial in Turkey against the ethnic Kurdish party HADEP to be dropped.

*European Commission*

The European Parliament has been more outspoken for the Kurdish movement's concerns than any other European institution But the Commission has also continuously displayed concern for the Kurdish issue. It also has a considerable say in the accession process. In preparation for the decision to begin accession negotiations, the Commission prepared annual reports that evaluated Turkey's progress towards accession. A negative evaluation being extremely difficult to override, the power to define the situation vested in the European Commission was a tremendous one.

Generally, the Commission has been fairly critical about the human rights and minority rights situation in Kurdish settlement areas. As the 1998 report, which set the stage for the following reports, put it:

The constitution does not recognize Kurds as a national, racial or ethnic minority. There are no legal barriers to ethnic Kurds' participation in political and economic affairs but Kurds who publicly or politically assert their Kurdish ethnic identity risk harassment or prosecution. Most of the Kurdish population lives in the South-East of the country. In this region, the Turkish authorities have engaged for over a decade in armed conflict with the Kurdistan Workers Party (PKK), whose goal is to create an independent state of Kurdistan in south-eastern Turkey, and which employs terrorist methods. As a direct consequence of this situation, there is evidence of large-scale forced evacuation and destruction of villages accompanied by abuses of human rights perpetrated by the Turkish security forces.[33]

Different points critically dealt with in the Commission's reports were the death sentence for Abdullah Öcalan, bans on Kurdish newspapers and magazines and on radio or TV broadcasting in Kurdish, limitations to the possibility to give children Kurdish names, a lack of educational opportunities in the Kurdish language and infringements on the work of human rights associations.[34] These concerns led the

---

[33] European Commission, *Regular Report from the Commission on Turkey's Progress towards Accession* (Brussels: European Commission, 1998), 19.

[34] European Commission, *Regular Report from the Commission on Turkey's Progress Towards Accession* (Brussels: European Commission, 1999). European Commission, *Regular Report from the Commission on Turkey's Progress Towards Accession* (Brussels:

Commission from 1998 to 2002 to the conclusion that Turkey did not yet meet the Copenhagen criteria. In 2002, there was a positive acknowledgement of the constitutional reforms of August of that year that expanded Kurds' cultural rights. Nevertheless, the Commission indicated that it would continue to monitor the situation in southeast Turkey.[35] Finally, in the 2004 Recommendation on Turkey, the Commission stated with tentative optimism: 'Cultural rights for the Kurds have started to be recognized. The state of emergency has been lifted everywhere; although the situation is still difficult, the process of normalization has begun in the Southeast.'[36] But in the longer 2004 *Regular Report on Turkey*, several points concerning the situation in the Kurdish areas were still critically mentioned.

## Council of the European Union

During time period under consideration, the Commission had an important preparatory role in the accession process and it would have been difficult to reject serious objections of the EP. Ultimately, however, the decision to assume accession negotiations is made by the Member States of the European Union. Thus, the final task is to discuss the stance of the European Council and the Council of Ministers towards the Kurdish issue.

The Council of the European Union plays an important role in the accession procedure of Article 49 TEU and oversees the EU's pre-accession strategy towards Turkey. According to the EU-Turkey Partnership Agreement decided by the Council in 2001, the allocation of pre-accession financial assistance (176 million EUR in 2000 and 152 million EUR in 2001) is conditional on progress toward fulfillment of the Copenhagen Criteria and on specific points to which the Partnership Agreement refers; financial aid may be suspended by the Council. The Kurds' situation might have been a reason for this. Two demands in the Partnership Agreement address their situation: 'Remove any legal provisions forbidding the use by Turkish citizens of their mother tongue in TV/radio broadcasting', and 'Develop a comprehensive approach to reduce regional disparities, and in particular to improve the situation in the south-east, with a view to enhancing economic, social and cultural opportunities for all citizens.'

---

European Commission, 2000). European Commission, *Regular Report from the Commission on Turkey's Progress Towards Accession* (Brussels: European Commission, 2002).

[35] European Commission, *Regular Report* (2002), p. 42.

[36] European Commission, *Communication from the Commission to the Council and the European Parliament. Recommendation of the European Commission on Turkey's progress towards accession*, Brussels, COM (2004) 656, p. 3.

The Council is important in the accession process but there are considerable difficulties to determine what the strategy of the Council vis-à-vis Turkey and the Kurdish issue actually is. One might muse that the relationship is strained because of a matter that took place in 2002: The Council decided on 2 May 2002 to put the PKK on the European Union's list of terrorist organizations. The step was rather symbolic, as the PKK had transformed itself into Kadek, and it was the PKK – the dissolved organization, not Kadek – that was put on the list. Nevertheless, there was harsh Kurdish criticism. In a letter addressed to the Council, the Kurdish National Congress (KNC), a Brussels-based congregation of Kurdish intellectuals and politicians in exile, demanded the revision of this decision or, by default, the publication of the evidence that had guided the Council. That demand was renewed by the KNC in a letter dating 28 October 2002 but then it was rejected. As a reaction, the KNC filed a case at the Court of First Instance (C-206/02).

In the end, not too much can be concluded from this incident. It is the Member States of the European Union that are represented in the Council and views differ greatly between these states. Council meetings are not public, making it difficult to know where states stand during debates. Certain governments and even certain politicians are more attentive to Kurds' problems, while others are less so. Generally speaking, it is simply not possible to determine a position of 'the Council' in general.

The same consideration applies to the European Council. The European Council decides whether accession negotiations are assumed or not, making it in practice much more important than the Council. The European Council was instrumental in opening and maintaining the perspective of Turkish accession to the European Union. In its conclusions, the European Council repeatedly and emphatically pointed to the Copenhagen criteria and their relevance for the situation of Kurds in Turkey. However, it has never referred to the Kurdish issue explicitly in any of its conclusions. Thus, one has always been left to guess how much importance the European Council would assign to the situation in the Kurdish areas. Other politically relevant factors might override remaining questions or the Kurdish issue might serve as a pretext if other considerations make Turkish membership undesirable.

Influencing the heads of government assembled at European Council meetings is difficult and such attempts are rare. However, there is one interesting exception. On the occasion of the Copenhagen European Council in December 2002, the Kurdistan Human Rights Project (KHRP), a London-based organization fighting for Kurds' human rights, sent a 13-page briefing paper on the situation in Turkey to the Danish EU presidency, the Permanent Representatives of all the member states and the European Commission. The paper contained a detailed evaluation of the Kurds' situation in Turkey and highlighted that Turkey's constitutional reform packages had not yet been sufficiently implemented into ordinary law.[37]

**Assessment**

Among the bodies discussed, the Commission and the European Council were most central for the decision on opening accession negotiations with Turkey. Here, a quote ascribed to the Turkish President Sezer describes the situation quite well. Commenting on the Commission's position – and its progress reports in particular – he stated a few days before the Copenhagen Summit in December 2002: 'The Progress Report and the Strategy Paper is the product of technical work carried out by the Commission. However, the decision that is going to be taken by the 15 member states at the Copenhagen European Council will be beyond the technical and will carry a political connotation.'

The Commission assembled data and information relevant to the Copenhagen criteria and gave – depending on whether the balance sheet is positive or negative – an evaluation of their fulfillment. Statesmen convened at a European Council meeting will be more inclined to consider the long-term strategic dimension of their decision or be prone to issue-linkage, that is, to include broader or short-term political considerations that may not be directly linked to the issue at hand into a decision. The political nature of the decision of the European Council left considerable uncertainty as to what the positions of heads of state would be.

But that challenge was the prime opportunity for a purposeful strategy of the Kurdish movement. Movement activity such as protest could draw public attention and thus ensure that the European Council and other European bodies would assign

---

[37] To illustrate the perceived value of the EU's pressure on Turkey, it is instructive to quote from the briefing paper: '... If the EU does not ensure that changes in theory are matched by equivalent changes in practice, it risks irreparable damage to its credibility and integrity. It also risks compounding rather than alleviating the systematic violations to which the Kurdish citizens of Turkey have been subjected for decades, and thereby reigniting the bloody conflict which wracked the southeast for nearly two decades. The Kurdish Human Rights Project therefore urges the representatives of the European Union meeting in Copenhagen this week not to submit to irrelevant and unfair external political pressure, and to consider in detail whether Turkey's reforms are sufficiently proven and established to grant a definite date for the start of accession talks. To offer rewards for work not yet done is to set a precedent which imperils rather than expedites the utterly desperate need for genuine human rights reform in Turkey. We trust that such rewards will only be made on merit.'

political importance to the state of affairs in southeast Turkey. So the question is whether and how the Kurdish movement has reacted to this political opportunity.

*European-level Activities of the Kurdish Movement*

One aspect of the Europeanization of the Kurdish movement is a respective organizational development. The Kurdish National Congress and the European Federation of National Kurdish Federations (Kon-kurd) have their offices in Brussels. A campaign in the summer of 2001 illustrates that the Kurdish movement is very well linked in Europe: Kon-kurd organized, as a part of its 'identity campaign', a collection of signatures with the self-declarations 'I am the PKK' and 'I Support the New Line of PKK'. The signatures were finally handed over to official authorities. According to Kon-kurd, almost 100,000 signatures were gathered until 19 July 2001, pointing to a remarkable ability to organize a cross-European campaign.

Anyway, the issue at stake here is not organizational developments but protest activities that purposefully exploit European opportunities. However, one encounters certain difficulties in using 'protest event data analysis' to capture Kurdish European-level protest. The newspapers scanned for protests in Germany (*Süddeutsche Zeitung, Frankfurter Rundschau*) do not report consistently on protests outside of Germany. Drawing on French newspapers (for instance, *Le Monde, Le Figaro*) for protests in Strasbourg and Belgian newspapers (*Le Soir, Le Belgie libre*) for protests in Brussels would deliver a mixed set of sources with different reporting standards.[38] A pragmatic problem beyond these methodological issues is that coverage of Kurdish protests in these newspapers was limited. Thus, as a second-best solution – though not an entirely satisfactory one – different and, in fact, mixed sources have been used to gather information about Kurdish European-level protest. The results are reported in Table 8.2.

From early 1999 until December 2004, there were ten Kurdish protest events aimed at a European institution – if the term 'European institution' is not limited to institutions of the European Union but understood in such a manner as to also include the Council of Europe and the European Court of Human Rights. Six protest events were demonstrations related to the appeals procedure of Abdullah Öcalan before the European Court of Human Rights. Looking at the other protest events, there was one protest march from Mannheim to Strasbourg (it did not reach

---

[38] Compare Ruud Koopmans, 'The Use of Protest Event Data in Comparative Research: Cross-National Comparability, Sampling Methods and Robustness', in Dieter Rucht, Ruud Koopmans and Friedhelm Neidhardt (eds), *Acts of Dissent. New Developments in the Study of Protest* (Berlin: Ed. Sigma, 1998), pp. 90-110.

its aim, as it was stopped before the end by German police) which demanded an end of the bans on the PKK and a recognition of the Kurds' political and cultural rights. Its aim was the Council of Europe. Finally, there were three protests that aimed at European Union institutions.[39]

All in all, there has been a Europeanization of the Kurdish movement in a sense. Yet at first sight, because of the preponderance of protest aiming at the European Court of Human Rights (ECHR), there seems to be a slight mismatch between the political opportunities as they were analyzed before and the protest events that actually occurred. Maybe from the perspective of a 'rank-and-file' Kurdish protester, the ECHR is the institution where their leader's fate is on trial. Perhaps a clear distinction between the political opportunities offered by the European Union and the Council of Europe or ECHR was not made. An interesting respective imprecision can be found in the eight-volume defense Öcalan has written for the trial in Strasbourg, which includes a part on the Kurdish question and European Law. The text identifies quite clearly the importance of a solution of the Kurdish issue for the ability of Turkey to comply with the Copenhagen criteria. But there is also a strange twist in the argument. Considering the European Convention of Human Rights as the solution to the Kurdish problem and the Council of Europe as the agency enforcing this law, Öcalan ultimately assigns supreme importance to

---

[39] Another new element in the repertoire of the Kurdish movement in Europe is the use of the European Court of Human Rights (ECHR) to raise complaints because of human rights violations against Kurds in Turkey. The London-based Kurdistan Human Rights Project is an organization dedicated to supporting the filing of cases before the ECHR. In January 2001, the KHRP celebrated its twenty-sixth successful judgment before the ECHR (Eccarius-Kelly, 'Political Movements': 111). As the European Commission noted 1874 applications at the ECHR concerning Turkey from October 2001 through June 2002 (European Commission, *Regular Report* 2002, p. 26), this may appear to be a relatively small number. But the cases supported by the KHRP were usually politically salient ones. Among other things, they were related to Turkish policy to destroy Kurdish villages and to disappearances, for instance. The activity of the KHRP can be related to the political opportunities analyzed before, though indirectly. Cases decided by the ECHR are considered by the European Commission in its reports on Turkey and thus they become a factor that increases pressure on Turkey. Most of the cases that have recently been decided were filed at a time when Turkey's accession perspective to the EU did not yet rank high on the agenda; the original intention behind the proceedings has not been to pressure Turkey using its aspirations to enter the EU. Nevertheless, this is a function the cases before the ECHR have assumed.

these Europeans institutions.[40] This seems to misjudge the reality in which the European Union is the far more important institution.

Perhaps, however, a clear distinction between the European Union and the ECHR/Council of Europe is not that important in a political sense. Protests addressing the ECHR at Strasbourg point out to the public the fact that Turkey is at trial because of an alleged human rights violation. If reported, that would make it more difficult for European institutions to neglect the Kurdish issue. It may be questioned whether that was really the purpose protest organizers had in mind, as Kurdish protests may have been exploiting European opportunities without doing so intentionally. However, there have also been three protest events that explicitly addressed European Union institutions.

Two smaller protest events that complained against the inclusion of the PKK on the EU list of terrorist organizations, and – more relevant for the argument here – a demonstration with 7000 participants in December 2004 demanding the incoming European Council to consider the situation of Kurds when deciding upon beginning accession negotiations with Turkey. Admittedly, proving a general reorientation of the Kurdish movement towards the European Union because of political opportunities it offers would require more evidence. But still, these are initial indicators of a purposive Europeanization. In fact, the hesitant Europeanization is in so far surprising as the perception that 'Turkey's way to the European Union leads over Diyarbakir' is fairly prominent. In the following conclusion, some factors shall be discussed that might explain why European-level opportunities have not been exploited in a fashion that might have been expected.

## Discussion

It has been argued here that a perspective capable of explaining the ethnic mobilization of Kurds in Germany is the political-opportunity perspective. Though it was the closing of political opportunities – the ban of the PKK and the arrest of Öcalan – that spurred Kurdish mobilization in the 1990s, those factors explain the rise of the Kurdish movement in Germany. Then, in the period from 1999 to 2004, new and genuine political opportunities have arisen for the Kurdish movement, as Turkey pushed to become a member of the European Union. The political-opportunity approach would predict a transformation of the movement's repertoire in response to these changed political opportunities.

---

[40] Abdullah Öcalan, *Kurdische Frage und Europäisches Recht. Extract from the Complaint of Öcalan at the European Court of Human Rights* (2002) (www.freedom-for-ocalan.com).

The Kurdish protest that has taken place warrants saying that there has been a Europeanization of the Kurdish movement. However, as much of it was directed at the ECHR and related to the Öcalan case, the claim that a Europeanization intentionally exploiting new political opportunities in the European Union had taken place must be made on a tentative basis. The protests at Brussels – in particular the December 2004 demonstration – are relevant evidence but it is not yet a sufficient foundation for an emphatic judgment.

One reason that a decisive turn to a Europeanized strategy has not yet occurred may be the underdevelopment of a European public sphere.[41] Doing the research for this paper and finding newspaper reports about protests addressing European institutions – about some of which I had learned in interviews – proved to be extremely difficult. No newspaper offers continuous coverage on Kurdish European-level protest. As the efficacy of protest depends essentially on the public attention paid to it, protest organizers may consider protests aiming at European institutions ineffective.

The case of the Europeanization of the Kurdish movement deserves more inquiry and further attention. 'Water makes noise when the river gets narrow' – keeping in mind this Kurdish saying and that the Kurdish issue is still pending, it is not to be expected that the Kurdish movement will disappear. Thus, it will be possible to monitor whether a strategy of Europeanization will be pursued indeed.

---

[41] Friedhelm Neidhardt, Ruud Koopmans and Barbara Pfetsch, 'Konstitutionsbedingungen politischer Öffentlichkeit: Der Fall Europa', in Friedhelm Neidhardt (ed.), *Zur Zukunft der Demokratie* (Berlin: Ed. Sigma, 2000), pp. 263-93.

# PART 3
# Regional Approaches to Migrants' Security Concerns

Chapter Nine

# Labour Migration and Human Security in East and Southeast Asia

Motoko Shuto

**Introduction**

Labour migration constitutes the majority of migration flows in Asia. The primary purpose of migrants is to work for a certain period and send remittances back to their countries. Labour migration per se is not a new phenomenon in international relations. But the patterns of current labour migration in East and Southeast Asia, involve a transnational structure of labour flows and a gendered division of labour at an unprecedented scale.

Behind this transnational structure there are three assumptions related to labour migration in East and Southeast Asia. First, although the states in the region have been accelerating efforts to liberalize trade through the World Trade Organization (WTO) or bilateral Free Trade Agreements, it is neither likely nor possible for them to agree on the liberalization of labour migration. Second, in spite of that and due to existing inequalities of wages, economic opportunities and population pressure, labour migration in East and Southeast Asia has produced typical labour-receiving economies and labour-sending countries in the past two decades. East Asia, except China, is a mainly labour-receiving region where labour is in shortage and skilled professional workers are accepted. In Southeast Asia, there are both labour-sending countries where there is surplus of unskilled labour such as Indonesia and the Philippines, and labour-receiving countries such as Malaysia and Singapore. To a lesser extent, Myanmar, Cambodia and Vietnam are also sending labour migrants abroad. As long as there exist structural inequalities of wages, job opportunities and labour surpluses, labor migration is likely to continue. Third, particularly because of vast and porous land or sea borders, it is practically difficult to monitor undocumented labour migrants crossing the borders. Unless the quality of governance is improved particularly in labour-sending countries, any efforts to stop irregular labour migration are likely to fail and even bilateral agreements do not seem to be sufficient. Consequently it is such irregular migrants who have often suffered from exploitation or other tragic incidents.

In other words, labour migration is a dynamic social process related to the liberalization of market economies, the transnational supply of labour, ever-changing immigration policies in the labour-receiving states and issues of the human dignity of migrant workers. In this on-going process, this chapter focuses on issues of unskilled migrant workers because they are the predominant majority of labour migrants in the region and, unlike skilled workers who have resources to protect themselves, they are directly affected by policy changes in labour-recipient states. In a sense, the issues of unskilled labour migration cover the dilemma between the growing transnational labour market and the traditional systems of labour policy under strict state control.

From the aspect of unskilled migrant workers this chapter examines two major patterns of the migration flows of unskilled workers in East and Southeast Asia. One pattern emerges from the case of Malaysia. As the largest majority of unskilled migrant workers come to Malaysia from Indonesia, migration is primarily a bilateral issue between Malaysia and Indonesia. The other case is Japan to which there are several dominant migration flows of unskilled workers largely from East and Southeast Asia. By discussing the issues of labour migration of these cases, this chapter examines whether such ad hoc and state-based responses can be effective enough in monitoring the migration flows and protecting the rights of unskilled migrant workers at their work places. While labour migration has been, and will be, handled in the context of development strategies of individual states, this chapter intends to suggest that the current transnational flows of labour migration in East and Southeast Asia contain new policy implications not only at the state level but also at the regional level for protection of the rights and dignity of migrant workers.

## Major Patterns of Labour Migration in East and Southeast Asia

The increase in population mobility including labour migration has been a striking feature in East and Southeast Asia particularly since the 1980s. In addition to the quantitative increase, outstanding aspects of transnational labour migration in East and Southeast Asia are feminization and the dominant share of unskilled labour. Unskilled workers often become undocumented labour migrants without or with expired immigration permits.

For example, it is estimated for the Philippines, one of the world's largest sources of international labour migration, that about 4.2 to 6.4 million women are working abroad as domestic helpers or entertainers, constituting 60 to 80 per cent of the estimated number of Filipino migrant workers.[1] The labour share in service sectors by Filipino female workers has been as high as 92 per cent.[2] This means

---

[1] Vivienne Wee and Amy Sim, 'Transnational Networks in Female Labour Migration', in A. Ananta and Evi Nurdidyaya Arifin (eds), *International Migration in Southeast Asia* (Singapore: Institute of Southeast Asian Studies, 2005), p. 167.

[2] The figures in 1999 and 2000, respectively from *Overseas Employment Statistics, 1982-2000*, unpublished files of statistics at the library of the Philippine Overseas Employment Administration (POEA), Manila.

predominant feminization of Filipino migrant workers in service sector. Their major destinations are Hong Kong, Singapore and Japan. Not only in the Philippines but also in Indonesia, female workers abroad made up a share of 68 to 75 per cent of its documented migrant workers during the years of 2000 and 2002.[3] Indonesians working abroad in service sectors as housemaids, nurses or hotel service workers are mostly females. Their top destinations are the Middle East (mostly Saudi Arabia or the United Arab Emirates) and Malaysia. To a lesser extent, Singapore and Taiwan are also important destinations of Indonesian unskilled workers due to the geographical and linguistic proximity. The top five destinations for Thai migrant workers are Taiwan, Singapore, Brunei, Israel and Japan. Among them the majority of Thai female workers go to Japan and Hong Kong, while male migrant workers mostly go to the Middle East or Taiwan. Thai female labour migrants are largely unskilled workers employed as domestic helpers in Hong Kong or in the service sectors in Japan.[4]

On the other hand, in Japan, one of the major hubs of labour migration in East Asia, 78 per cent of those who obtained work visas are categorized as 'entertainers', and roughly 70 per cent of those who obtained visas as 'entertainers' come from Asia, especially from Southeast Asia.[5] The major pattern of migrant workers in Japan is that male workers are mostly engaged in construction or metalwork, while female migrants work mostly as entertainers or factory workers. Moreover, 90 per cent of undocumented workers in Japan came from East and Southeast Asia, especially from Korea, China (Taiwan and Hong Kong excluded), the Philippines and Thailand. In this way there has been close interaction of labour migration in East and Southeast Asia at the regional level.

In terms of the population of foreign registered workers, Malaysia is by far the largest labour-receiving country. It has constantly received about 1,500,000 of registered workers. The number of registered foreign unskilled and semi-skilled workers has increased in the 1990s and reached about 1,500,000 in 1997.[6] Early in 2005 Vice Prime Minister Tun Razak stated that Malaysia will continue to need 1,500,000 foreign workers for the time being.[7] However, the real number including undocumented workers was estimated to be 2 million or more even before the currency crisis in 1998. Migrant workers in Malaysia, as of July 2002, are said to be 2,860,000, and Indonesian workers in Malaysia represent almost 80

---

[3] Ministry of Manpower and Transmigration, from the data compiled by Solidaritas Prempuan, at the office of Solidaritas Prempuan, Jakarta, March 2003.

[4] Yongyuth Chalamwong, 'Recent Trends in Migration Flows and Policies in Thailand', in *International Migration in Asia* (Paris: OECD, 2001), p. 319.

[5] Ministry of Foreign Affairs, *Blue Book of Diplomacy 2002*, (Tokyo: Ministry of Foreign Affairs, 2003), p. 336.

[6] Machiko Watanabe, 'Economic Development and International Labour Migration in Malaysia', in Yasuko Hayase (ed.), *International Migration in APEC Member Economies: Its Relations with Trade, Investment and Economic Development* (Tokyo: APEC Study Center, Institute of Developing Economies, 2003), p.180.

[7] *Suara Pembaruan* (18 February 2005).

per cent of them. In 2002 Prime Minister Mahathir Mohamad pointed out in his meeting with President Megawati of Indonesia that the number of Indonesians working in Malaysia stood at 2 million.[8] As the total workforce of Malaysia is about 10 million, roughly one-fifth consist of foreign workers. It is not an exaggeration to say that most construction projects of high-rise buildings would not have been completed without foreign workers. Malaysia's economy heavily depends on unskilled foreign labour, particularly from Indonesia. On the other hand, Filipino workers in Malaysia are less than 2 per cent and they are concentrated in Sabah or the Federal Territory of Labuan, not in Peninsula Malaysia.

Thailand is also a net labour-receiving country, having about 2 million foreign workers. Foreign workers have immigrated to Thailand largely from countries in the region, namely Myanmar, Laos, Cambodia, southern China and Bangladesh. This has been so because it is difficult to control the thousands of kilometres of borders between Thailand and its neighbours. The number of undocumented migrants in Thailand once reached 1 million in 1998, with 80 per cent of them coming from Myanmar. The remaining came from Cambodia, Laos or others. Because labour-intensive industries in the border areas needed cheap labour, the Thai government had taken a laissez-faire policy to employ undocumented migrants. At the time of the currency crisis in 1998, almost 1 million undocumented workers were estimated to stay in the country, and about 300,000 (less than 30 per cent) of them were said to have received permission to stay as 'registered illegal workers'.[9]

What are the implications of such rapid feminization and massive flow of unskilled, often undocumented, labour migrants for the current political economy in East and Southeast Asia? The feminization of labour migration, particularly as domestic helpers, means that labour participation of women in the labour-receiving areas has produced a vacuum of labour in the private sphere. This labour vacuum has been filled by the insertion of migrant women workers who prefer to come for work. Ironically, however, there is a survey in the Philippines showing that mothers' absences as migrant workers have a strong psychological effect on children left behind.[10] This ironical labour relationship reveals that a transnational gendered hierarchy, extended from private to public dimension as a result of job participation of women in the labor-receiving areas, has caused distortions of gendered contribution to private sphere in the labor-sending side.

There exists a similar pattern of the migration of unskilled labour. Better educated young people in the major labour-receiving countries are shunning so-called 3D (dirty, demanding, and dangerous) jobs, even if they are unemployed.

---

[8] *Daily Express* (9 August 2002).

[9] Yongyuth Chalamwong, 'Recent Trends', p. 307. The category of 'registered workers' means those from Myanmar, Laos and Cambodia.

[10] Nimfa B. Ogena, 'Policies on International Migration: Philippine Issues and Challenges', in Ananta and Arifin, *International Migration*, pp. 302-3.

This has created jobs for migrant workers in small and medium-sized firms. A transnational and hierarchical division of labour has emerged in East and Southeast Asia.

Where push-and-pull factors of labour migration exist, migrants do not go as individual travellers but the migration process is facilitated by public institutions, private recruitment brokers or personal networks. Once such migration networks are established, they tend to evolve into a self-perpetuating process. These networks then provide an infrastructure for transnational labour migration. In this sense, the increase in labour migration in East and Southeast Asia is the output of a multiple infrastructure of recruitment and supply relations. In these conditions, migrant workers, particularly unskilled workers, are exposed to multiple vulnerabilities at every stage of their migration processes.

The economic impacts of remittances are recognized as a positive aspect of labour migration. It is often said that female migration contributes to the empowerment of women and their upward social mobility. Although this chapter does not intend to discuss these points in depth, its finding support doubts that as far as unskilled migrant workers are concerned, their remittances can contribute to macroeconomic growth of labor-sending countries to a significant extent.[11] This appears to be so because remittances are largely spent to fulfill personal subsistent needs and private consumption. In fact, according to a recent survey, remittances played a very small role, less than 1.5 per cent, in Indonesian GDP and consequently, the report concludes that 'sending labor abroad is not a substitute for sound macroeconomic policies'.[12] In reality though there is no reliable relevant statistics, it seems that the remittances of unskilled migrant workers can hardly be converted into sustainable investment for macroeconomic development.

However, it is true, although not in all cases, that remittances have raised the welfare of the families who sent migrant workers abroad. Particularly in the cases of Filipina women migrant workers, 'overseas migration has become a recent vehicle for upward social mobility within communities' and 'can cause a redefinition of traditional bases for status and facilitate the emergence of migrant-related social classes'.[13] Another survey says that female migrant workers responded saying that it had largely been their own decision to work abroad.[14] It is

---

[11] According to the *World Economic Outlook* (WEO) published by the IMF in April 2005, the total amount of remittances by migrant workers reached 100 billion US$ in 2003. The largest amount of remittances goes to Mexico, India, the Philippines, China and Pakistan. IMF analyses that remittances have contributed to economic growth and poverty alleviation in recipient countries.

[12] Elan Satriwan Sukamdi and Abdul Haris, 'Impact of Remittances on the Indonesian Economy', in Ananta and Arifin, *International Migration*, pp. 137-65. The quotation is at p. 138.

[13] Maria Rosario Piquero-Ballescas, Multi-level Consequences of Female Migration: The Philippine Case. Unpublished paper (January 2003).

[14] Supang Chantavanich (ed.), *Female Labour Migration in South-East Asia* (Bangkok: Asian Research Center for Migration, 2001), pp. 253-8.

clear that there are cases that labour migration enhances women's status in family and local community. Especially Filipina migrant women are not the poorest among labour migrants, and they can expect institutional protection by the Philippine government to a much higher degree than any other nationals in the region. They have also established strong human networks which can generate cycles of migration including care for returnees from abroad.

The situation is different in other areas. No other countries in East and Southeast Asia have so far generated such well-established state organizations to support migrant workers and strong human networks as the Philippine migrant workers have at their disposal. Basic issues such as public heath care and legal protection in cases of need are out of question for many migrant workers. Unskilled migrant workers are generally left in vulnerable positions which can be easily affected by economic fluctuations and policy changes of a labour-receiving country. However, there is no formal institution for monitoring the migration flows of unskilled workers across state borders at the regional level.

## Migration Policies and Unskilled Workers in East Asia

### Overview of Migration Policies

There is something common in the immigration policies of labour-receiving countries and areas in East and Southeast Asia, though there are variations as well. The main strategies of Japan, Taiwan, South Korea, Malaysia, Singapore and Hong Kong to tackle their labour shortage problem have consisted in shifting towards higher technology-intensive industries or labor-intensive production offshore by means of foreign direct investment. Particularly Japan, South Korea and Taiwan did not allow migrant workers to play an important role before the 1980s and still now their acceptance of migrant workers is selective. Although they have started to open the labour market by establishing new categories of immigration, except Taiwan which has accepted foreign unskilled labor since 1991, they have not formally accepted the immigration of foreign unskilled labour.

Among them, Hong Kong and Singapore have traditionally depended on migrant workers from their neighbours. In addition, as mentioned earlier, female migrant workers have been injected to their labour markets largely from the Philippines or Indonesia. However, because of its dependence on foreign human resources Singapore has tightly controlled the labour market, having a tax of employing foreigners and imposing various conditions for the employment of migrant workers including housemaids. Singapore, where one resident in every four is foreign, is strict in punishing illegal migrant workers. In comparison, Malaysia is less tight in regulating migration than Singapore. In Malaysia and Thailand as well, migrant workers have played a central role in the agricultural sector, then in the last decade construction, services and export-oriented industries have been added as further sectors. In Singapore, on the other hand, more than half of the foreign workers are skilled professionals and in addition a new IT-related labour permit was introduced in July 2004.

The inflow of unskilled migrant workers has increased particularly in Malaysia, Thailand and South Korea. Therefore governments have made efforts to establish regulations and to conclude agreements with major labour-sending countries in the region. In South Korea, a new law enacted in August 2004 allows the employment of foreign unskilled workers for three years at most on condition that both governments conclude memoranda of understanding. Subsequently South Korea has concluded agreements with the Philippines, Indonesia, Thailand, China, Mongolia and Sri Lanka. This new system has been in operation since 2004. The target number for the first year was 25,000 but less than half have obtained work permits.[15] Malaysia, too, has since May 2004 operated a similar labour permit system based on bilateral agreements and has concluded similar labour agreements with seven countries. One of them is the memorandum of understanding with Indonesia, to which more detailed reference shall be made later.

In case of Japan, immigration policies have been frequently amended but it is difficult to expect that the labor market will radically accept more unskilled foreign workers. Though it has not been designed for unskilled workers, the currently existing Technical Intern Traineeship Program has started in 1993 as a recruitment system for foreign workers. This programme was introduced to remedy the labour shortage in certain labour-intensive sectors, though there are about 3 million unemployed in Japan. Shortly after the programme started foreign workers complained about the wide gap between its declared purpose and the reality of its implementation. Influential business associations of Japan, such as Nippon Keidanren, and NGOs working for labour migrants, particularly unskilled workers, have made efforts to submit policy recommendations to improve the system. The case of Japan will be discussed later in more detail.

From this brief comparison, it becomes clear that labour migration in East and Southeast Asia is closely related to the industrialization patterns in the region. Whether or not related labour-intensive sectors, labour migration is regulated by individual governments as part of their strategies to supply human resources to the domestic labour markets. However, the labour markets of the industrialized countries have become tighter since the 1990s. Also, the human rights of migrant workers have become a matter of international concern since the early 1990s, following the adoption of the International Convention on the Protection of the Rights of All Migrant Workers and Members of their Families (often called 'Migrant Workers Convention') by the UN General Assembly in December 1990. However, only a few countries in Asia have so far ratified it.[16]

---

[15] Only 3,167 out of 10,823 who obtained the work permit really came to South Korea for work. Report of International Workshop 'Migration and Labor Market in Asia', organized by The Japan Institute for Labor Policy and Training (2005), p. 3 (http://www.jil.go.jp/institute/kokusai).

[16] In the Asia Pacific area, only the Philippines (July, 1995) and Sri Lanka (March, 1996)

Will the current manner of regulating migration policies by individual governments in East and Southeast Asia work well and effectively in the on-going process of the regionalization of market economies? Will bilateral agreements be sufficient to control or monitor irregular labour migration? Fluctuating policies regarding migrant workers in labour-receiving countries and administrative inefficiency in labour-sending countries have caused tragic troubles for migrant workers who are usually deported or turned into the scapegoats at times of economic downturn. Policies, problems and recent changes related to unskilled migrant workers shall be examined below.

*Unskilled Indonesian Labour Migration to Malaysia*

Labour migration has repeatedly become a source of friction between Malaysia and Indonesia since the early 1980s, because, as mentioned earlier, unskilled foreign workers in Malaysia come mostly from Indonesia. Once there emerged demand for unskilled labour in Malaysia, push factors in Indonesia sustained labour migration to Malaysia. Both countries have complementary relations and share psychological and cultural closeness based on language, common ethnicity and religion between Malay and Indonesian locals. Their borders are easy to cross. This proximity reduces the cost and pressure to move. Consequently labour recruitment brokers emerged as mediators on either side.

With regard to Indonesia's push factor, the current 90 million workforce is increasing at an annual rate of 2 per cent. Indonesia has an abundant supply of unskilled labour with the majority having scarcely more than primary education. Up to early 1980s the prime concern of the Suharto regime was to overcome uneven population distribution in the country. Consequently while the government promoted internal transmigration from Java to outer islands, labour migration abroad did not attract attention. It was since early 1980s that sending labour migrants abroad became recognized as a means of easing the labour supply pressure. At the same time, the Indonesian media began to report abuses against Indonesian migrant workers, mostly against women, in the Middle East. As, however, the political basis of the labour movement was totally destroyed and social groups were depoliticized under the Suharto regime, labour problems were negligible issues for the government and the parliament. Instead, maintaining good relations with Saudi Arabia was the diplomatic priority. The then Minister of Labor, Retired Admiral Sudomo, issued a ministerial decree in 1985 ordering that the migrant workers should not to talk to the press about their experiences abroad.[17]

For Malaysia, on the contrary, the demand for and existence of foreign workers has always been a keen political matter. At the outset of the New Economic Policy (NEP), which was in force for two decades from 1971, it is said that there was a

---

ratified the convention.

[17] Riwanto Tirtosudaarmo, 'Cross-Border Migration in Indonesia', in Ananta and Arifin, *International Migration*, p. 318.

political motivation of accepting Indonesian immigration after the ethnic riots on 13 May 1969, in a vague hope that creating good relations with Indonesia might help Malaysia get support from Indonesians in case a clash with Chinese should happen.[18]

More practically, the Malaysian economy has needed foreign labour to sustain its development projects, and the government officially accepted workers from five countries, namely Indonesia, Thailand, the Philippines, Bangladesh and Pakistan. The largest sector of their employment is manufacturing (29.2 per cent), followed by plantations (22.3 per cent) and construction (21.6 per cent).[19] The manufacturing sector was once a domain of female workers in Malaysia, but Malaysian women have changed to enter into higher income jobs. Consequently, the government began to allow employers to recruit foreign workers in the manufacturing sector up to 30 per cent of the total workforce. Among them, Indonesians are by far the most numerous both in the Peninsula and Eastern Malaysia, followed by Bangladeshis in the Peninsula and the Filipinos in Sabah.

The strong pull factor is higher wages in the Peninsula. Over years a noticeable job distribution has been made based on nationalities. There were two factors of this job distribution, difference of labour quality due to educational attainment and due to recruitment pattern among the same nationalities. Indonesian male labour migrants used to work mostly in plantations since the 1980s but they have shifted to the construction sector. Now Indonesians accounted for up to 70 per cent of construction workers in Malaysia, and 80 per cent of them are said to be undocumented workers, including those with expired permits.[20]

The other pressing pragmatic reason is the cost and the existence of brokers who facilitate irregular flow of labour migration.[21] For Indonesians, the irregular entry through irregular brokers is cheaper and faster than taking time-consuming process of getting certificates from such institutions as police, a village exit permit and so on. In Malaysia the cost of legal recruitment is high, because the employer and employee have to pay various costs for the agencies, including the cost of passage, medical examinations, annual levy, travel documents. Also, it is mandatory for

---

[18] Record of the Australia High Commission, quoted by Joseph Liow, 'Malaysia's Illegal Indonesian Migrant Labour Problems', in *Contemporary Southeast Asia,* 25/1 (April 2003), p. 46.

[19] Azizah Kassim, 'Recent Trends', p. 267.

[20] 'Southeast Asia – Malaysia', in *Migration News*, 9-10 (October 2002). Bangladeshis work mainly in manufacturing. Filipino men work in agriculture, logging and fisheries, almost all in Sabah in Eastern Malaysia. According to Mantra, there is a strong correlation between sectors in which Indonesian migrants were employed in Malaysia and Indonesia. Also only 10 per cent of them have gone more than senior high school education, and 78 per cent of the returning migrants from Malaysia were between 20 and 39 years of age. I.B. Mantra, Kasto and Y.T. Keban, *Mobilitas Tenaga Kerja Indonesia ke Malaysia: Studi Kasus Flores Timur, Lombok Tengah dan Pulau Bawean* (Pusaat Penelitian Kependudukan Yogyakarta: Univesitas Gadjah Mada, 1999), p. 217.

[21] They are called *calo* in Indonesia and *taikong* in Malaysia.

foreign workers to contribute 9 per cent of their basic pay to the Malaysian Employees Provident Fund. Consequently, for Malaysian employers it is cheaper to recruit Indonesian undocumented workers. In addition, brokers recruit undocumented workers who tend to accept poor working conditions with lower wages than locals.

However, needless to say, not all of Indonesian workers in Malaysia are undocumented workers. According to the recent research by Wong and Afrizal, there are three Indonesian migration streams to Malaysia, the Aceh pattern related to migrants coming from Sumatra legally and work mostly in ethnic business, the Lombok pattern related to coming from Eastern Indonesia usually through irregular brokers and working in plantations, and the Bawean pattern related to migrants coming from East Java legally, usually through brokers and working in the construction sector.[22] There are different figures about illegal workers in Malaysia. Malaysian Immigration Director-General Mohamad Jamal Kamdi was quoted by The Star newspaper as saying that some 300,000 illegal immigrants had left under the four-month amnesty which began on 22 March 2002 and ended on 31 July 2002.[23] Another source says that there were 800,000 Indonesian migrant workers in Malaysia, half of them illegal, working in plantations or factories.[24] On the other hand, an Indonesian NGO gives the figure of 2.26 million Indonesians working in Malaysia as of March in 2002, among them 1.67 million being undocumented migrants.[25]

Under such conditions, Malaysia has restricted the immigration of foreign unskilled workers. The regulations have been fluctuating unilaterally and have often been enforced abruptly. For instance, in March 1997, before the financial crisis, there was a regularization attempt giving a chance to Indonesian workers to obtain legal status. Approximately 300,000 undocumented workers were registered. However, during the currency crisis, a total freeze on new recruitment was imposed in August 1997, and the annual levy for foreign workers was suddenly increased. For another example, the maximum stay of foreign unskilled workers had been once six years, except seven years for plantation workers, until a new regulation was approved by parliament in October 2001. The new regulation restricted the validity of those work permits to three years. It meant that many foreign workers who had carried six-year permits and had worked for more than three years would be categorized suddenly as 'illegal' workers. Under this new law, both illegal

---

[22] Diana Wong and Teuku Afrizal Teuku Anwar, '*Migran Gelap*: Irregular Migrants in Malaysia's Shadow Economy', in Graziano Battistella and Maruja M.B. Asis (eds), *Unauthorised Migration in Southeast Asia* (Zuaexon City: Scalabrini Migration Center, 2003), pp. 169-228.

[23] 'Malaysia Detains Suspected Illegal Immigrants', *Tapol* (3 August 2002) [aceh] (Internet news).

[24] *The Asahi Shimbun* (9 August 2002).

[25] 'Indonesia Watching', *Asiaconsult Associates Newsletter*, No 213 (19 August 2002) (Internet monthly media).

foreign workers and their employers faced fines, mandatory prison terms of up to five years and six strokes with a cane together with their employers. This controversial new regulation came to effect on 1 August 2002.

In mid-summer 2002, thousands of desperate undocumented migrants flooded in ports and other exit points to return home ahead of the expiry of the amnesty. The governments of Indonesia and the Philippines expressed concern at the speed of the exodus and said that they would have problems in absorbing the returning masses of unemployed people. Malaysia, in response, blamed such undocumented migrants for causing crimes or security problems. In fact there occurred riots by 400 Indonesian workers in the suburbs of Kuala Lumpur in January 2002 and frustrated Indonesian workers resorted to violence in detention centres. It is said that the death of 71 detainees at a detention camp in 1995 was a result of the shortage of water, food and lack of proper sanitation.[26] At Nunukan, a point of entry for Indonesian migrants to Sabah, in the continuing flood of returning Indonesians, 79 people died due to inadequate shelter, lack of food or medical facilities in the summer of 2002.

The Nunukan tragedy has called for the state to pay more serious attention to the unskilled migrant workers who have been vulnerable to policy changes in Malaysia and the inefficiency of Indonesian bureaucracies. In fact there have been remarkable changes since the tragedy, though NGOs had actually been appealing to the government for the diplomatic, administrative and legal protection of migrant workers even before. Among the newly implemented changes, the Department of Social Affairs, after consultation with NGOs, decided to set up crisis centres for migrant workers both in foreign countries and at home. A new law on the 'Placement and Protection of Indonesian Migrant Workers Abroad' was enacted on 18 October 2004. This bill which was based on three drafts[27] and had been under discussion from 2002 in Parliament, stipulated that the pre-sending procedure and protection of migrant workers abroad is primarily the responsibility of the government. Article 4 prohibits private recruitment business dealing with migrant workers.[28]

Another important progress is the bilateral agreement in the form of the Memorandum of Understanding between Malaysia and Indonesia signed on 10 May 2004.[29] This specifies terms for and obligations of Indonesian migrant

---

[26] Joseph Liow, 'Migrant Labour Problems', p. 57.

[27] The three drafts were made by the Parliament, Brawijyaya Univeristy and KOPBUMI. KOPBUMI (Consortium in defence of migrant workers), which was established in 1997 by NGOs concerned with the improvement of conditions of Indonesian migrant workers and submitted its draft bill on labour in 1997. Komnas Peremuan, Solidaritas Perempuan dan Caram Indonesia, *Buruh Migran Pekerja Ruman Tangga(TKW-PRT) Indonesia* (Jakarta: Komnas Perempuan, 2003), pp. 46-7.

[28] *Undang-Undang*, No 39 (2004)
(http://www.nakertrans.go.id/perundangan/undang-undang/uu_39_2004.php).

[29] As of May 2005, Indonesia has a Memorandum of Understanding related to migrant workers with Jordan, South Korea, Kuwait and Taiwan, in addition to Malaysia.

workers and their Malaysian employers. It also allows Malaysia to suspend the acceptance of migrant workers for the reasons of threats to security and public order after notifying the Indonesian side thirty days in advance.[30] Subsequently the Malaysian government urged undocumented foreign workers to leave the country between 29 October and 14 November 2004. The Indonesian government requested to extend the period, and it was eventually extended till the end of January 2005, partly due to the huge Tsunami disaster of December 2004.[31] Thereafter, the two governments concluded 'Minutes of Implementation' in February 2005. In the 'Minutes', the two governments agreed to open eleven places of immigration and to introduce a joint immigration system staffed with Malaysian immigration officials and Indonesian counterparts at these entry ports in Indonesia for three months from March till May 2005. To accompany this procedure the Indonesian side has launched the One Roof System which is a joint team consisting of representatives of departments related to labour migration issues.[32]

On the other hand, shortly after the massive deportation of undocumented foreign workers in the summer of 2002, the resulting sudden labour shortage had knock-on effects on the manufacturing and construction industries in Malaysia. Consequently the Master Builders Association in Malaysia proposed to set up an employment exchange where foreign labour can be hired for short terms, and subsequently the government agreed to the proposal in principle. Though Indonesian labour has played a crucial role in the expansion of the Malaysian economy, communication and cooperation between the two governments have been conspicuously missing until recently.

*Unskilled Labour Migration to Japan*

In Japan unskilled labour migration has no such dominant source of origin as the case of Malaysia. Therefore labour migration does not easily turn to tense bilateral diplomatic rows. Nevertheless, since mid-1980s labour migration has become a social issue in Japan, both in terms of immigration policies and settlement problems. The bubble economy created job vacancies, especially for unskilled labour in the so-called 3D (Dirty, Dangerous and Demanding) jobs. Japan has

---

[30] This memorandum is unpublished. By courtesy of the Department of Foreign Affairs of Indonesia in Jakarta, this writer could inspect the document.

[31] About 280,000 undocumented workers returned from Malaysia during this period. 'Media Indonesia On Line' (14 January 2005).

[32] They are the Departments of Foreign Affairs, Home Affairs, Justice and Human Rights, Manpower and Transmigration and the National Police. The Director for Socialization and Guidance for Indonesian Overseas Placement, Ms Fifi Arianti Pancawedha, said to this writer that 'This One Roof system has just started, but the government intends to institutionalize this system' on 28 March 2005, at the office of Directorate General of Overseas Placement, Ministry of Manpower and Transmigration in Jakarta.

rapidly become a country where many foreigners live. Their number was 850,000 in 1985 but has doubled within 15 years, reaching 1,680,000 in 2000.

Along with this sharp rise in the total number of foreigners, the number of undocumented foreigners has also increased. With the population aging and the fertility rate continually declining labour shortage in Japan is becoming an acute problem in a longer term, though at present there are three million unemployed and the unemployment rate is worsening. The distribution of legal and illegal workers by industrial sector is complementary because foreign workers fill vacancies in certain jobs, which young Japanese do not want to take because of low wages, poor working conditions and irregular working time.

The basic policies of Japan can be summed up in the following three points. First, since the Immigration Control and Refugees Recognition Act of 1989 (implemented in 1990), the legal entry of unskilled workers to Japan has been admitted to people of Japanese descent (*Nikkeijin*) from Latin America, provided they have been employed. While foreign workers had previously been employed illegally in small and medium firms, the enactment of this law has induced big manufacturing factories to hire foreign workers for unskilled jobs.

Second, the Immigration Control and Refugees Recognition Act has frequently been amended since its enactment in 1989. The amendments in 1999 have imposed severe penalties, namely fines of up to 300,000 yen and/or prison terms of up to three years for illegal entrants, fines of up to 2 million yen and/or prison terms of three years for employers employing illegal migrants and fines of up to 3 million yen or prison terms of five years for brokers of illegal migration.[33] This policy seems to be informed by the goal of preventing overpopulation. The act was most recently amended in 2004 when the conditions of fines, refusal of entry and forced deportation were tightened due to security concerns. However, as to the entry of skilled and professional workers, the minimum visa duration was extended from six months to one year in 1999. For those skilled workers the maximum period of the initial renewable visa was also extended to three years. In the case of 'entertainers', the minimum period of visa is three months, the maximum non-renewable duration is one year.

Third, the Technical Intern Traineeship Program[34] has been introduced in 1993 in response to employers' pressures. This was meant to be a preventive measure against illegal employment, controlling the number of foreign workers, and alleviating the labour-shortage in the manufacturing sectors in Japan. Problems related to unskilled foreign workers belong to the much-criticized issues in Japan. The Japan International Training Cooperation Organization (JITCO) was established as a liaison office between Japanese companies and the foreign governments which select and send trainees to Japan under the auspices of the

---

[33] Articles 70, 73, and 74 of the Immigration Control and Refugee Recognition Act, amended in August 1999 and come into force in February 2000.

[34] A training system for foreigners started in the late 1960s but it was only in 1981 that a new entry category for 'trainees' was established by the immigration law.

Traineeship Program. Since 1993, approximately 50,000 trainees have come to Japan each year, about one- fourth of them are trainees at government organizations and the other trainees have been accepted by private firms.[35] Officially Technical Intern Trainees are foreign trainees who have passed a test and are allowed to work for one year in Japan after a training period of at most two years. Hence a maximum of three years stay is legal. After the expiration of this period, trainees are expected to return equipped with skills useful to economic development of their countries.

In reality, however, this Technical Intern System has systemic ambiguities that have caused human rights abuses. It is only from NGOs' surveys that the real situation of the trainees has come to the surface. According to NGO reports, there were cases, to mention only a few, where trainees had their passports taken away by employers upon arrival at the airport, where they were forced to do unskilled work and were paid less than Japanese workers doing the same job, or where injuries from accidents at work were not covered by insurances. According to a survey report, 70 per cent of those who answered questionnaires noted that 'they do not think [trainees] are mastering technology'.[36]

NGOs concerned with unskilled foreign workers and Nippon Keidanren, Japan's leading employers organization, have made policy recommendations to the end of improving this system. Their argument is that while it contributes to providing labour for small and medium enterprises in Japan, the 'system itself is still imperfect and has problems which the parties concerned should tackle to find solutions in sincerity'.[37] Fearful of the potential impacts of a rapid increase in the number of foreign workers the government has reacted to migration issues in a defensive and ad hoc manner. Nationalists, not in favor of dependence on foreign workers, have expressed concerns that Japan as a homogeneous society may be eroded even though the notion of a homogeneous society is more or less an illusion. When compared with the defensive stance of the government and nationalists, the straightforward argument of this report on unskilled foreign workers is remarkable. NGOs in Japan have made efforts to deal with these issues.

---

[35] In 2000, among 54,049 trainees who entered Japan, 12,030 were trainees at government organizations. The rest trainees are accepted in private firms largely through JITCO. Trainees from China make up 51 per cent, from Indonesia 11 per cent, the Philippines 6.9 per cent, Thailand 5.5 per cent and Vietnam 5.1 per cent. Japan NGO Network on Indonesia (JANNI), Evaluations and Proposals on Technical Intern Traineeship Program. Unpublished report (March 2002), p. 51. As of 2002, the total number increased to 63,000. The share of Chinese increased to 78.9 per cent, Indonesia 10 per cent, Vietnam 7.0 per cent, the Philippines 2.7 per cent and Thailand 0.6 per cent in Nippon Keidanren, Policy Proposals on Acceptance of Foreign Workers. Unpublished report (April 2004), p. 26.

[36] JANNI, Evaluations and Proposals, p. 7.

[37] Nippon Keidanren, Policy Proposals, pp. 27-9.

## Roles of NGOs for Migrant Workers

There are two types of NGOs concerned with migrant workers. One is network of support systems for workers seeking employment. This network is often drawn on former migrants themselves, their family members, neighbours or recruitment agencies. This type of network is even involved in human trafficking. The other type of NGOs is made up of agents of humanitarian support systems for migrant workers. There are a number of such NGOs working for humanitarian support of migrant workers in Japan, East and Southeast Asia as well. This in itself reveals the neglect by or inefficiency of formal institutions dealing with issues of migrant workers.

The success of such NGOs depends on the degree by which the authorities are cooperative to their appeals. On the one hand, there are countries where the authorities perceive the increase of foreign migrants as a potential threat. In these countries NGOs are not active to support migrant workers. Singapore and, to the lesser extent, Malaysia represent such cases. On the other hand, where the state is actively promoting labour migration like the Philippines, there are numerous active NGOs and advocacy groups to support migrant workers. It so seems that there are fewer NGOs in Thailand, although there are about two million foreign workers there. In academic research, however, the Asian Research Center for Migration based at Chulalongkorn University has participated in the Asia Pacific Migration Research Network (APMRN).

When the Labor Minister announced a plan to deport 300,000 undocumented foreign workers within three months after the currency crisis, the Migration Center of Chulalongkorn University made a survey and demanded that the government should allow approximately 90,000 undocumented migrants to work in 18 kinds of jobs in 37 provinces.[38] The National Committee on Employment concurred with the observation that there were even higher demands for over 300,000 undocumented migrant workers, especially in fishery, agriculture, construction and clothing industries. The Chamber of Commerce petitioned the Labor Ministry to remove the ban on the employment of undocumented migrant workers, saying that Thai locals did not wish to accept jobs in agricultural, construction and some manufacturing sectors. Consequently the government revoked its stance and allowed the employment of undocumented workers in ten border provinces on condition that they pay a registration fee. At the same time the government was reported to have given permits to 106,000 unskilled workers from Cambodia, Laos and Myanmar to work in 37 provinces.

In Indonesia, there have emerged many advocacy groups and NGOs supporting migrants especially since the end of the 1990s. While labour was not a major political agenda in the early 1980s, as mentioned before, the Middle East

---

[38] S. Chantavanich, *Alien Workers: Why Granted Permission only to 100,000?* (Bangkok: Asian Research Center for Migration, Institute of Asian Studies, Chulalongkorn University, 1999).

Indonesian Manpower Supply Association (APJATI) was formed for the purpose of regulating the flow of workers in 1981. It was a consortium of labour-recruiting agencies, officially licensed by the Ministry of Manpower. Subsequently the fourth Five Year Development Plan (1984-89) identified overseas employment as a useful tool to solve the problem of surplus labour. However, only since late 1990s have NGOs become active in humanitarian assistance and policy advocacy in Indonesia. KOPBUMI,[39] FOBMI (Federation of Indonesian Migrant Workers' Organizations), Solidaritas Perempuan (Women's Solidarity), to mention only a few, have been active in collecting data of cases of victimized migrants and making policy proposals. The National Commission on Women (Komnas Perempuan), which is a commission supported from the state budget but whose activities are independent of the state, has worked in cooperation with those NGOs in making surveys of victims, holding workshops, and submitting proposals to departments concerned or to UN agencies. It can be said that the new law on migrant workers abroad was a joint-product of the involved departments and those NGOs. One of the reports says that in Indonesia 'governmental agencies which are committed to sending labor migration abroad have other channels established due to corruption, collusion and manipulation. They were created in the New Order era and in the era of reformation it is not changed'.[40]

Interestingly Filipino migrant workers in Hong Kong are supported by active groups and migrants' social networks, such as the Asia Pacific Mission for Migrant Filipinos (APMMF), the Mission for Filipino Migrant Workers (MFMW), the Asian Migrant Center (AMC), all of which are based in Hong Kong and they are expanding their activities to also provide for the basic needs of other foreign migrant workers such as Bangladeshis, Thais and Indonesians.[41] Indonesian domestic helpers used to have less access to such supporting networks abroad, but Indonesian networks in Hong Kong have been increasing.

In Japan a further major concern related to migrant workers, in addition to undocumented workers and the operation of the Technical Intern Traineeship Program, is women workers engaged in entertainment businesses, mostly from Thailand and the Philippines, although some came from Colombia and Eastern Europe in the past several years. Groups of lawyers and Catholic Church organizations in Japan have worked for the empowerment of migrant workers since the mid 1980s. They have asked labour unions for help to campaign for the legal rights of migrant workers who are at the mercy of employers' wage-cutting and overwork policies. Also some Catholic Church organizations have worked to

---

[39] Ibid.

[40] Komnas Perempuan et al., *Buruh Migran Indonesia: Penyiksaan Sistematis di dalam dan Luar Negeri,* (Jakarta: Komnas Perempuan, 2003), p. 5.

[41] Jorge V. Tigno, 'Migration, Security and Development: The Politics of Undocumented Labor Migration in Southeast Asia', in David Dewitt and Carolina Hernandez (eds), *Development and Security in Southeast Asia* (2 vols, Aldershot: Ashgate, 2003), vol. 2, pp. 49-50.

provide migrants, particularly female migrants, with shelter to escape from employers who often belong to gang groups.

These women are often in heavy debt which was fabricated by brokers, are deprived of their passports by brokers or employers on arrival at the airport and do not receive full remuneration. There are several women shelters in Japan. Among them the earliest and one of the largest shelters is the 'HELP Asian Women's Shelter' in Tokyo. From the start of its activities in 1986 up to March 2002, female migrants from Thailand were the most numerous among those protected by HELP.[42] The number of Thai female workers asking HELP for protection has drastically decreased in recent years. This is primarily due to the efforts of public education by the Thai government, according to the director of HELP.[43]

After having worked to help migrant workers in Japan for 15 years, the National Network in Solidarity with Migrant Workers (NNSMW) was established in Tokyo in 1997. The main activities are policy advocacy, lobbying to the government and the National Diet and networking by holding national meetings. The organization also has an Asian network.[44] In May 2002, NNSMW presented its first comprehensive policy-proposals regarding foreign residents in Japan. With regard to migrant workers, it demands new legislation to protect human rights, including labour rights such as the right to join social security insurance and labour unions. It also insists that the Technical Intern Training Program should be fundamentally improved in many respects so that trainees can obtain the technology training that is really needed by the sending organizations and that their human rights are respected by employers in Japan.[45] Interestingly, so the policy proposals of NNSMW concerning this program have much in common with the policy recommendations of Keidanren.

## Agendas of Regional Cooperation on Migrant Workers in Asia-Pacific

With regard to unskilled labour migration it is the common concern to curb undocumented migration. For that purpose negotiations have taken place mostly at the bilateral level. One of the earliest cases is the series of bilateral talks between Malaysia on the one hand and on the other, the countries sending labour to

---

[42] The top five countries since the start of HELP's activities are: 1,544 (Thailand), 442 (Philippines), 72 (Columbia), 60 (Peru) and 43 (Korea). *Fujin Shinpo (New Journal for Women), Christian Women's New Wind Association of Japan)*, No 1221 (June 2002), p. 15.

[43] Interview with Ms Keiko Ôtsu, Director of HELP Asian Women's Shelter (29 August 2002).

[44] It affiliates with the Migrant Forum in Asia, which was founded in 1996, and other Asian regional NGOs such as the Asian Migrant Center and the Joint Committee of Migrant workers in Korea.

[45] National Network in Solidarity with Migrant Workers, Toward Multi-ethnic and Multicultural Co-existing Society: comprehensive policy-proposals on foreign residents. Unpublished report in Japanese (May 2002), pp. 85-100.

Malaysia, namely Indonesia, the Philippines, Bangladesh and Thailand. The result was the Medan Agreement with Indonesia in 1985. The main agenda in the negotiations evolved around the question of who should pay the cost of rounding up undocumented labour migrants and deporting them. So far Indonesia and the Philippines have shown their readiness to help repatriating their nationals from Malaysia.

However, a multilateral forum on migrant workers, especially unskilled workers, would be helpful for the exchange of information about and experiences related to other successful policies in managing foreign workers or protecting workers abroad. So far there was one regional official meeting of this kind at Bangkok in April 1999. In cooperation with the International Organization for Migration the Thai government organized this international symposium focusing on the regional coordination of efforts to reduce irregular or undocumented migration. As a result ministers and representatives of 18 participating countries and one Special Administrative Region[46] unanimously adopted the 'Bangkok Declaration on Irregular Migration'. Some passages of the declaration suggested that regional migration arrangements should be established to provide technical assistance, capacity-building and policy support on migration issues, including research and analysis of the causes and consequences of irregular migration.[47] The 'Bangkok Declaration' was significant in the sense that it declared the necessity of regional cooperation on irregular migration issues in the Asia Pacific.

Subsequently, in February 2002, the Asia-Pacific Ministerial Meeting on People-Smuggling was held in Bali. It was the first official meeting on this agenda at the regional level. 37 countries participated and shared a sense of urgency to deal with the migration issues in the region. As a result participants agreed to establish ad-hoc groups of experts with New Zealand and Thailand as coordinators.[48] Beyond these gatherings, there has been little progress in regional cooperation for migration issues. Even though the ASEAN Plan of Action for Cooperation on Immigration Matters mentions that it is one of ASEAN's objectives 'to cooperate amongst Member Countries in the movement of labor both skilled and unskilled',[49] no such cooperation has yet come into existence at the ASEAN level.

Nevertheless, an interesting international workshop on migration and labour markets in East Asia has been held in Tokyo every year since 1995. The workshop

---

[46] They represented Australia, Bangladesh, Brunei, Cambodia, China, Indonesia, Japan, Korea, Laos, Malaysia, Myanmar, New Zealand, Papua New Guinea, the Philippines, Singapore, Sri Lanka, Thailand, Vietnam, and Hong Kong.

[47] Annuska Derks, *Combating Trafficking in Southeast Asia: A Review of Policy and Programme Responses,* IOM Migration Research Series, No 2 (Geneva: International Organization for Migration, 2000), quoted by C.P.F. Luhulima, 'People Smuggling as an Increasingly Crucial Factor in Transnational Organized Crime', in *The Indonesian Quarterly*, 30/2 (2002), p. 156.

[48] *The Asahi Shimbun* (1 March 2002).

[49] ASEAN Plan of Action for Cooperation on Immigration Matters (http://www.aseanse.org/16572.htm).

is organized by the Japan Institute for Labor Policy and Training (JILPT), which is closely connected with the Ministry of Health, Labor and Welfare. Participants are mostly high officials of Ministries involved, but the main purpose of this international workshop is to exchange information about the migration policies of each participating country or area and to discuss prospects and policy matters with experts.[50] Though the workshop does not intend to formulate policy proposals, it is an interesting track II approach to such transnational issues as labour migration in East and Southeast Asia.

What is missing in the regional context is a formal scheme for discussions on labour migration policies and the monitoring of irregular flows of labour migration or human trafficking. There is no government cooperation to combat illegal practices related to migration in the region. Exchange of information and regional cooperation would be important and for that purpose some more concrete joint programs are needed. For example, it is said that notorious smugglers in Fujian province in China, known as Snake Heads, have global networks and professional technology of falsifying documents and faking passports of any country.[51] Smugglers change tactics in order to minimize the risk of detection. However, diplomatic and legal approaches are not enough because problems are rooted in a lack of political will to control brokers and to enhance the quality of governance to sever the corruption of the officials or bureaucracies linked to brokers.

## Conclusion

The major aspects of labour migration in East and Southeast Asia are feminization and the migration flow of unskilled workers. These two patterns were dominant during the past two decades as a consequence of the different rate of economic growth, geography, state policies and human networks. Feminization is double-edged. One the one hand, it may bring about economic and social empowerment for female migrants and their families. On the other hand, female unskilled migrants often find themselves vulnerable to various abuses. Efforts to monitor the movement of unskilled workers have been made so far by NGOs. There is no formal framework to monitor the flow of unskilled workers, much less to provide protection when they need. Particularly issues of domestic helpers, who are the majority of labour migrants in the region, lie outside the capacity for any kind of monitoring and legal protection at the present time.

---

[50] Participants of the workshop in January 2005 came from China, Malaysia, Indonesia, Thailand, South Korea, the Philippines, Singapore, Hong Kong, Vietnam, Taiwan and Australia in addition to those from the host country, Japan.

[51] David Kyle and Zai Liang, 'Migration merchants: Human smuggling from Ecuador and China to the United States', in Virginie Guiraudon and Christian Joppke (eds), *Controlling a New Migration World* (London and New York: Routledge, 2001), p. 211. The smuggling fee has risen from 28,000 US$ in the early 1990s to 60,000 US$. Ibid., p. 215.

In principle as well as in reality a labour-receiving country as a sovereign state has the right to regulate its immigration policy. Migration policies in East and Southeast Asia have been reactive, made through individual decisions by each government. This has been so primarily because migration policy has been considered strictly as a domestic issue in Asian countries. Even bilateral problems are decided unilaterally, such as the recent cases in Malaysia mentioned earlier. However, the increase in the numbers and the never-ending flow of undocumented migrants show that state borders are becoming porous and people will move by whatever means, when they want or need to move.

The issue of labour migrants involves many neighbouring countries. In this sense, any effort to limit irregular labour migration to a bilateral level will not be sufficiently effective. For the purpose of promoting economic benefits through market convergence, various visions have been launched at the government level, such as the 'ASEAN Community', especially after the Asian currency crisis in 1997. There has been no regional approach to labour migration issues, however. What is missing in East and Southeast Asia is political cooperation and coordination at the formal level with regard to procedures for the placement, recruitment, training and protection of migrant workers.

An urgent agenda among others at the multilateral consultation would be to establish and exchange databases of migrant workers in the region. This has already been suggested in the ILO Action Plan of Migrant Worker of 2004. Based on such databases, a regional approach particularly to unskilled labour migration should be created in East and Southeast Asia. However, the legal approach alone is not sufficient for the improvement of the social conditions of migrant workers. Efficiency and transparency of the public organizations whose activities are related to labour migration need to be enhanced. If wider aspects of 'security' should have primacy, in the advancement of human dignity, over the conventional concept of national security, issues of labour migration, particularly of unskilled labour migration, should be regarded as one of the core issues of human security.

Chapter Ten

# European Immigration and Asylum Policy: Scope and Limits of Intergovernmental Europeanization

Dietmar Herz[1]

**Introduction**

The European Union's migration policy has evolved rapidly over the past two decades. This should actually have come as a surprise to many observers. Migration policy – understood here to encompass asylum, refugee and immigration policy – is generally seen as an essential matter of national sovereignty. This is reflected by the intergovernmental policy-making procedures of European migration policy. But whereas intergovernmentalism is usually associated with stagnating European integration, migration policy – as a common European policy – has evolved nonetheless.

It shall be argued here that the unlikely development of a European migration policy has resulted from a process of 'intergovernmental Europeanization' and that a dense intergovernmental cooperation between various levels of government provides an important mechanism of intergovernmental Europeanization. Dense intergovernmental cooperation is assumed to create shared identities and problem definitions among administrators and members of executive agencies. That way, it facilitates the issuance of harmonized policies and European solutions – even if supranational governance is absent.

In order to develop this argument, the following account will follow a framework of analysis suggested by John Peterson[2] and deal consecutively with (a)

---

[1] More than anybody else, I need to thank Andreas Blätte for many thoughtful comments on different versions of this article. In particular, he suggested to conceptualize dense intergovernmental cooperation as a mechanism of intergovernmental Europeanization.

[2] John Peterson, 'Decision-Making in the European Union: Towards a Framework of Analysis', *Journal of European Public Policy*, 2/1 (1995), pp. 69-93. Peterson and Elizabeth Bomberg, *Decision-Making in the European Union* (Basingstoke: Macmillan, 1999).

the big intergovernmental bargains setting the 'constitutional' framework of migration policy-making, (b) the regular policy-making within this frame, and (c) the intergovernmental cooperation that takes place below the ministerial level. The latter level of interaction prepares (d) the argument about the sources of intergovernmental Europeanization that shall finally (e) be highlighted by looking at recent cases of decision-making.

**The Constitutional Framework of Migration Policy**

European migration policy is essentially a by-product of the elimination of border controls between EU Member States. Eliminating border controls was a vision deeply rooted in the project of European integration: The tearing down of border gates was a symbolic act of the European movement in the immediate aftermath of World War II and is a common starting point of narratives on European unification. Yet although various measures were taken to facilitate migration within the European Community, free movement policies did not include lifting border controls until the 1980s.[3]

The issue re-emerged on the European policy agenda in the mid-1980s. To revive stagnating European integration, plans for lifting border controls between the Member States of the European Community were considered. The project had as its proponents two powerful heads of state: German chancellor Helmut Kohl and French president François Mitterrand pushed for it from 1984 onwards. Both were concerned that citizens in Europe increasingly lacked emotional attachment to the idea of a united Europe. A symbolic and at the same time tangible step such as doing away with bothersome waiting times and controls at borders was seen as a way to convince European citizens that 'Brussels' could provide immediate benefits to them.

Due to staunch opposition from Great Britain and Ireland, the plan was only vaguely mentioned in the Single European Act of 1986, without any indication of a European Community policy. But Germany and France stuck to their plans, and as an alternative to a Community policy, an international treaty, the Schengen Agreement of 1985, was concluded outside the framework of the European

---

[3] For a general overview, see also: Andrew Geddes, *The Politics of Migration and Immigration in Europe*, (London: SAGE, 2003). Andrew Geddes, *Immigration and European Integration. Towards a Fortress Europe?* (Manchester: Manchester UP, 2000). Alfredo Märker, 'Zuwanderungspolitik in der Europäischen Union: Europäisierte Lösungen oder Politik des kleinsten Nenners?', *Aus Politik und Zeitgeschichte*, B 8 (2001): 3-10.

Community. Envisaging the 'gradual abolition of controls at the common frontiers', it was signed by Belgium, the Netherlands, Luxembourg, France and Germany.[4]

The signatories of the agreement pledged to eliminate border controls and to allow citizens to travel freely within their common territory. At the same time, so-called flanking measures were foreseen to coordinate and strengthen control of the common external borders. The signatory states considered this a necessary correlate to the loss of control (i.e. reduced security) the elimination of their borders would entail. These flanking measures turned out to be the nucleus for the European migration policy (understood to be a policy dealing with migration across external borders) that has emerged since.

The 1985 Schengen Agreement did not yet spell out concrete measures for enforcing the common boundary and was indeed rather a declaration of will. To implement the Schengen project, the path of international negotiations was pursued further, leading to the so-called Schengen Convention on Implementation in 1990. It entailed (a) intensified controls of the external borders, in accordance with uniform standards (Art. 3-8); (b) a harmonization of visa and entry regulations (Art. 9-27); (c) the creation of a 'Schengen Information System', containing data on persons; and (d) a coordination of asylum policies by laying down rules for the responsibility for asylum claims (Art. 28-38). As many technical points still had to be clarified among the governments of the signatory states, it took until 1995 before border controls between the initial signatories of the Schengen Agreement and of the Convention, and the states that had acceded in the meantime (Spain and Portugal) were abolished.

There was yet another process pointing towards a European migration policy that followed the road of concluding international agreements external to the Community framework. As indicated, the Single European Act mentioned migration affairs only in the most general language. Nevertheless, an intergovernmental ad hoc committee associated with the Council of the European Union was established. In the so-called 'High-Level Working Group on Asylum and Migration', there was agreement on the need to reduce the political and social burdens that asylum seekers were said to incur. Negotiations on an international agreement with rules for reaching this aim were taken up.

The result was the so-called 'Agreement on the State Responsible for Examining Applications for Asylum Lodged in One of the Member States of the European Communities' – the 'Dublin Agreement', for short – which was signed in June 1990. Its central provision was that any asylum claim should be dealt with only by the European state first entered by an asylum-seeker. When the Dublin Agreement came into effect in September 1997, its rules supplanted the provisions

---

[4] Klaus-Peter Nanz, 'Das Schengener Übereinkommen. Personenfreizügigkeit in integrationspolitischer Perspektive', *Integration*, 17 (1994): 92-108.

of the Schengen Convention concerning the state responsible for dealing with asylum claims.

The Schengen and Dublin Agreements, being the result of international negotiations and having been reached without the involvement of supranational actors, were concluded in an intergovernmental fashion. An ad hoc cooperation of a group of European states on asylum and on the control of external borders was instituted. Very soon, this cooperation was to be integrated into the framework of the European Union, as this issue was included at the request of Germany in the agenda of the Intergovernmental Conference (IGC) negotiating the Treaty of Maastricht of 1992.

European states agreed that the ad hoc cooperation they had begun should be done on a more continuous basis in order to prevent inefficiency. In addition, Germany hoped that an integration of asylum affairs into the European Union framework might lead to a shared responsibility for asylum-seekers; that is, to a more equal distribution of perceived burdens. Pushing for a full supranationalization of migration affairs, it gained the support of Belgium, Italy, Greece, the Netherlands, Spain and Ireland. However, Great Britain strongly insisted on migration remaining an intergovernmental matter.

Due to the need for consensus, only the lowest common denominator was achieved, which was the Justice and Home Affairs pillar of the European Union with its intergovernmental decision procedures. The competences included into the Treaty on the European Union were not much more than an inclusion of what had already been dealt with external to the European Union framework before: asylum policy, the control of the external borders, and policies regarding third-country nationals. The only new issue inserted was that of combating unauthorized immigration (Art. 62, ex Art. 73j). The result of Maastricht thus reflects the Member States' desire to create a greater continuity of cooperation without conferring sovereign powers on supranational institutions.

During negotiations at the next IGC, when preparing the 1997 Treaty of Amsterdam, two issues were at the core of negotiations. Pro-European federalists – Belgium, the Netherlands and Luxembourg, in particular – wanted to overcome intergovernmentalism and to fully integrate asylum and immigration matters into the supranational first pillar of the European Union, which meant to communitarize it and to introduce qualified majority voting (QMV). Second, there was a need to prepare the European Union for eastern enlargement. Thus the proposal was made to incorporate the Schengen legislation into European Union law, so that accession candidates would have to adopt and implement that body of law upon accession.

Great Britain, Ireland and Denmark rejected these proposals, insisting on their sovereign control over borders. Due to the need for unanimity, an agreement had to be reached with these persistent objectors. As a result, 'flexible integration' was necessary to make treaty reform possible at all. Britain, Ireland and Denmark reserved the privilege of withholding themselves from the communitarization of EU migration policy and of opting in when they wished. This opened the way for the inclusion of the Schengen *acquis* into EU law, requiring accession candidates to accept this body of law.

When negotiations went beyond this point and dealt with the communitarization of migration policy and QMV, it became clear that other states were not the outright federalists they had appeared to be when more reluctant states were still involved. Most importantly, Germany resisted QMV in immigration and asylum policies, fearing that European decisions taken without its consent might increase the number of asylum-seekers arriving in Germany.

Nevertheless, the 1997 Treaty of Amsterdam achieved the transfer of asylum, visa and immigration affairs from the third and intergovernmental pillar of the European Union to the first pillar with its community method. The formula of creating 'an area of freedom, security and justice' was introduced as a keyword, indicating that security and restriction were at the heart of the EU's migration policies. The EC Treaty now projected far-reaching measures in the field of asylum and migration policy, including minimum standards for the acceptance of asylum-seekers and refugees, as well as for issuing permanent visas and maintaining family integrity.[5] As was acknowledged by the Working Group on Freedom, Security and Justice at the European Convention, in immigration policy, 'the current legal bases [...] in principle cover the full breadth of the immigration domain'.[6]

At first glance, there seems to have been a bold transfer of powers. Yet when looking at provisions in more detail, the changes appear more modest. The EC Treaty includes several safeguards that allow European governments to resist unwanted developments. In general, there was a time limit of five years ending in May 2004 during which policies in the various fields detailed in the treaty needed to be adopted. But issues of particular concern to national sovereignty or ones that might incur burdens — distribution of refugees, permanent immigration, non-EU nationals' rights — are excluded from the five-year period (Art. 64). In addition, a clause was inserted stating that 'the exercise of the responsibilities incumbent upon Member States with regard to the maintenance of law and order and the safeguarding of internal security' (Article 64, 1) shall be untouched. Most importantly, there are fairly complex provisions concerning voting requirements, which shall be discussed in the next section.

---

[5] Kay Hailbronner and Claus Thiery, 'Amsterdam – Vergemeinschaftung der Sachbereiche Freier Personenverkehr, Asylrecht und Einwanderung sowie Überführung des Schengen-Besitzstandes auf EU-Ebene', *Europarecht*, 5 (1998): 583-615.

[6] European Convention, *Final report of Working Group X 'Freedom, Security and Justice'*. CONV 426/02. Brussels, 2 December 2002.

To sum up the development of the framework of European migration policy, it quite clearly corresponds to an intergovernmental pattern so far. Every step of integration has quite deliberately been made by the states involved. This does not, however, preclude the possibility that regular decision-making during the big intergovernmental bargaining sessions would entail mechanisms pointing to a further Europeanization of this policy domain.

**Regular Decision-Making**

As early as during the negotiations concerning the 1990 Schengen Implementation Convention, there was an awareness that decisions would have to be taken on a continual basis. At the same time, the states involved shared a concern that the issue at stake – the control of the external borders – was crucial to their sovereignty. To maintain leverage, it was not a supranational decision-making body that was instituted, but rather a strictly intergovernmental one operating under a rule of unanimity, the 'Schengen Executive Committee', made up of the representatives of Member States (Art. 131 and 132 of the Convention). The Schengen Executive Committee continued to operate independently of the European Union after the introduction of competences on migration affairs in the Treaty of Maastricht but was integrated into the Community structure with the Treaty of Amsterdam.

The Justice and Home Affairs pillar of the European Union worked in an intergovernmental fashion as well. The decision-making body for migration policy was the Council of Ministers, representing Member States' interests. The European Commission was deliberately assigned only a very limited role in the policy-making process. As one European Commission official put it: 'Some of [the Member States] are almost pathological in their determination to keep the Community institutions out of the process ...'[7] The European Parliament's role was limited to information rights and the European Court of Justice did not obtain jurisdiction.

Qualified majority voting was planned for only very limited areas of a more technical nature. As the unanimity requirement generally remained, states retained a dominant position in decision-making, so that decision-making in fact remained intergovernmental. This was celebrated by Britain's prime minister at the time, John Major: 'At Maastricht we developed a new way, and one much more

---

[7] Quoted from: Verónica Tomei, *Europäisierung nationaler Migrationspolitik. Eine Studie zur Veränderung von Regieren in Europa* (Stuttgart: Lucius & Lucius, 2001), p. 56.

amenable to the institutions of this country – co-operation by agreement between governments, but not under the Treaty of Rome'.[8]

Maastricht retained intergovernmental decision-making in general, though with one qualification: Article 100c was inserted into the European Community Treaty, which established the regular community procedure for 'issuing a list of countries whose nationals must be in possession of a visa when crossing the external borders': The list was to be prepared by the European Commission, to be discussed in the European Parliament and to be decided upon by the Council of Ministers, thus giving supranational actors a say in this field of the policy-making process. Beyond that, Article 100c (6) would have contained the possibility to transfer further issues to Community decision-making by a unanimous Council vote, but this chance was not exploited.[9]

It was the Treaty of Amsterdam that brought about major changes by integrating issues of migration policy into the European Community Treaty. With the transfer of areas of jurisdiction into the first pillar of the European Union, supranational actors entered the field. The European Commission was assigned its usual role to initiate policies, the European Parliament gained the right to be heard in the policy-making process and the European Court of Justice obtained jurisdiction, albeit limited in certain respects. As mentioned earlier, voting provisions were fairly complex and required, on a case-to-case basis, unanimity, QMV, or the cooperation procedure of Article 251 ECT (table 1). In due course, QMV will apply for most issues in European migration policy apart from legal economic integration.

But for the period under consideration here, intergovernmental procedures requiring unanimity were predominant and left the European Commission in a weak position vis-à-vis the Council. That circumstance affects the shape of Community policy. The Commission is inclined to a liberal and inclusive immigration policy. Its open standpoint is founded on the assumption that immigration is an economic and demographic necessity. In its Communication on immigration policy presented in 2000, the Commission expressed the conviction that migration will generally have positive effects, if properly regulated, and that it 'believes that channels for legal immigration to the Union should now be made available for labor migrants'.[10]

---

[8] Quoted from: Andrew Geddes, *Immigration and European Integration*, p. 93.
[9] Monica den Boer and William Wallace, 'Justice and Home Affairs', in Helen Wallace and William Wallace (eds), *Policy-Making in the European Union* (Oxford: Oxford University Press, 2000), pp. 499-500.
[10] European Commission, *Communication from the Commission to the Council and the European Parliament on a Community immigration policy.* COM(2000)757 final of 22 November 2000.

Apart from economic considerations, the Commission's positive approach to immigration is also based on an acceptance of multiculturalism. As António Vitorino, the EU's Justice and Home Affairs Commissioner from September 1999 to November 2004 put it: 'It is essential to create a welcoming society and to recognize that integration is a two-way process involving adaptation on the part of both the immigrant and of the host society. The European Union is by its very nature a pluralist society enriched by a variety of cultural and societal traditions [...]. There must, therefore, be respect for cultural and social differences'.[11] Generally speaking the Commission pursues an open immigration policy aiming at making the European Union attractive to highly skilled immigrants.

The Member States in the Council of the European Union usually do not share the Commission's liberal standpoint. Due to unanimity requirements, a frequent pattern of migration policy-making has been that the standards of a fairly liberal proposal by the Commission are lowered during negotiations in the Council of Ministers. The Member States' preferences, by simplifying matters, often appear to converge towards using European Union policy-making to maximize security and minimize social and economic burdens. This is not to be confused with a position of Euroscepticism. In some subfields of European migration policy, EU Member States are quite happy to use European legislation, but then as an instrument for restricting migration.

## Dense Intergovernmental Cooperation

Along with and extending beyond meetings of heads of states at European Council summits and those of ministers in the Justice and Home Affairs-Council, a dense web of intergovernmental cooperation on migration policy has evolved. High-ranking officials from national ministries meet regularly within the substructure of the Council, there is a constant exchange of information among national administrations and practitioners from executive agencies meet on various occasions.

Similar to other policy domains, the decision-making of the Council of Ministers on migration affairs is prepared by meetings of the Committee of Permanent Representatives (COREPER). Operating under COREPER, the 'Strategic Committee on Immigration, Frontiers, and Asylum' prepares Council decisions. Most of its substantial work is done by seven working parties (on Migration, Expulsion, Visa, Asylum, the 'Centre for Information, Reflection and

---

[11] António Vitorino, 'Interview with António Vitorino', *Schweizerische Monatshefte*, 81/11 (2001): 34.

Exchange on Asylum' – Cirea, the 'Centre for Information, Discussion and Exchange on the Crossing of Frontiers and Immigration' – Cirefi, and Frontiers). Except for COREPER, where members of the Member States' foreign ministries are present, it is members of the national ministries of the interior who are present at meetings dealing with migration policy.[12]

As a part of these intergovernmental dealings within the substructure of the Council, national administrations and executive agencies have institutionalized contacts in several additional ways. From 1992 onwards, several instruments for information exchange and personal contacts between national administrations have been created. As their existence may have repercussions for policy formulation, 'Cirea' and 'Cirefi' shall be described briefly.

To gather exchange and disseminate information and to compile documentation on all matters relating to asylum, the 'Centre for Information, Reflection and Exchange on Asylum' (Cirea) was founded by a Council decision in June 1992. More than just providing information services, it issues joint reports on countries of origin of asylum-seekers and is a forum for the exchange of information on asylum-seekers' travel routes and national asylum law. The overall aim is a harmonization of asylum practice through an exchange of information. As was said in the Council's directive on guidelines on joint reports on third countries: 'The ministers responsible for immigration have on several occasions spoken of the desirability of drawing up joint situation reports on certain third countries of origin of asylum-seekers. They believe this to be essential if a convergent and eventually harmonized analysis of asylum applications is to be obtained'.[13] Cirea assembles members from national ministries and executive agencies eight to ten times a year in Brussels.

The 'Centre for Information, Discussion and Exchange on the Crossing of Frontiers and Immigration' (Cirefi), founded in 1992 as well, serves a similar purpose. It collects and analyses information on legal and illegal immigration, on unlawful residency, the entry of aliens through facilitator networks, the use of false or falsified documents and the executives' decisions. Since May 1999, Cirefi offers an early-warning system for the transmission of information on illegal immigration and facilitator networks. The Centre assembles experts from the Member States and meets every month.

The contacts that have emerged between national administrators go beyond the structure of the Council of the European Union. For instance, in March 1998, the EU Council of Ministers adopted 'Odysseus', a program of training, exchange and cooperation in the field of asylum, immigration and the crossing of external borders. The program's general objective was to extend and strengthen cooperation.

---

[12] Monica den Boer, William Wallace, 'Justice and Home Affairs', p. 515.
[13] Council of the EU, *Guidelines for joint reports on third countries adopted by the Council on 20 June 1994*. OJ C 274/52 of 19 September 1996.

Public or private institutions, non-governmental organizations, research institutes, universities and training bodies could take part in the program. The Odysseus program was continued in 2002 under the name ARGO ('Action Programme for Administrative Cooperation in the Fields of External Borders, Visas, Asylum and Immigration'). Major objectives are to promote cooperation among national administrations responsible for implementing Community rules and to ensure that proper account is taken of the Community dimension in their actions. The program includes training measures such as the elaboration of harmonized curricula, staff exchanges, the exchange of best practice and the organization of conferences and seminars.[14]

In addition, two Community-wide information systems have been established. To facilitate an effective control over the external borders of the signatory states of the Schengen Convention, the 'Schengen Information System' (SIS) was created. It is a database used by the police and by consular agents to obtain information on individuals who are checked at borders or who apply for a visa, as well as on goods thought to be lost or stolen. Another information system, Eurodac, is related to the Dublin Convention. The Dublin Convention contains rules for determining the state responsible for examining an asylum application. Thus a mechanism for the comparison of the fingerprints of asylum applicants needed to be established to identify persons who have already applied for asylum in another member state. Eurodac's central unit is a computerized central database that became operational on 15 January 2003.[15]

The instruments described here lead to continuous contact and discussion among administrators and practitioners in the field of asylum, visa and border-control affairs on the one hand. On the other hand, officials concerned with regular immigration are as yet seldom involved in networks of dense intergovernmental cooperation. However, the Commission has presented respective proposals in its statement on an 'open method of coordination'.

To promote 'co-operation, exchange of best practice, evaluation and monitoring', the Commission intended to make arrangements including the setting up of committees and working groups – with senior officials, experts in immigration matters from the Member States, representatives of the social partners and of local and regional authorities, experts on particular topics under review and with other representatives of civil society.' This was considered conducive to

---

[14] Council of the EU, *Council Decision of 13 June 2002 adopting an action programme for administrative cooperation in the fields of external borders, visas, asylum and immigration (ARGO programme)*. OJ L 161 of 19 June 2002, pp. 11-5.

[15] Council of the EU, *Council Regulation (EC) No 2725/2000 of 11 December 2000 concerning the establishment of 'Eurodac' for the comparison of fingerprints for the effective application of the Dublin Convention*. OJ L 316 of 15 December 2000, pp. 1-10.

achieving convergence of practice and procedure and 'to achieve a gradual approach to the development of an EU policy, based, in a first stage at least, on the identification and development of common objectives to which it is agreed that a European response is necessary'.[16] The open method of coordination is a part of a two-tiered approach towards a European immigration policy and was meant to supplement the legislative development of a European immigration policy. However, only very limited steps have been taken so far to implement the open method of coordination and to create continued contacts among officials in the field of regular immigration.

To sum up, European migration policy in general follows a policy mode of intergovernmental cooperation. However, while there is 'dense intergovernmental cooperation' on visa, asylum and border-control affairs, cooperation among national officials on regular immigration remains sporadic to date. It shall be suggested in the next section that the differences in the degree of cooperation among national governments in these subfields of European migration policy may account for variations in the integration process.

## Dense Intergovernmental Cooperation and Intergovernmental Europeanization

With respect to the manifold contacts among national administrators that have emerged in certain subfields of European migration policy, an argument can be made about the impact of these patterns of cooperation on the dynamics of the integration process in European migration policy: Once initiated, continual cooperation of national administrators in the field of migration policy or its subfields leads to shared knowledge, problem definitions and shared identities. The sharing of knowledge, problem definitions and identities facilitates the finding of European solutions. As administrators are a major source of input for the policy-makers responsible, their cooperation will facilitate European decision-making. A dense cooperation of governments at various levels will contribute to the issuing of further policies.

Verónica Tomei has in fact acknowledged in her analysis of European migration policy that due to an 'intrusion of the European discourse in the national formulation of policies'[17], there is a 'creeping communitarization'.[18] Among those concerned with migration policy, there are cross-national networks of officials

---

[16] European Commission, *Communication from the Commission to the Council and the European Parliament on an open method of coordination for the community immigration policy*. COM(2001)387 of 9 July 2001.
[17] Tomei, *Europäisierung*, p. 135.
[18] Ibid., p. 137.

where professional interests dominate national interests.[19] As a result, migration policies that have traditionally been formulated independently have increasingly converged.[20]

One aspect of this mechanism, considered important in a process of 'intergovernmental Europeanization', is its implication that progress in a policy domain is not exclusively dependent on supranational actors' entrepreneurship and on relaxed voting requirements in the Council like QMV. There is a mechanism pointing to a convergence of national policies towards a Europeanized policy, even if the mode of governance is intergovernmental and voting operates under unanimity.

In order to explore this hypothesis, two cases of migration policy-making shall be examined. Intergovernmental Europeanization would predict that progress will be more continuous in areas with dense intergovernmental cooperation while it is expected to stagnate in the absence of it. The two cases looked at here – presented without a claim to offer a systematic test of the hypothesis but rather to explore it – concern a directive on temporary protection and a directive on family reunification. Both directives were the first to be decided in their respective fields.[21] The following account will lay a stress on the decision-making process and the interplay between the Commission and the Member States in the Council in order to show how steps towards integration were taken and what they entailed. This will result in an estimate of the progress in integration achieved. It will then be necessary to relate these outcomes to differences in the density of cooperation.

*Asylum and Refugee Policy: The Directive on Temporary Protection*

'Temporary protection' is a new instrument for dealing with mass flows of refugees as they appeared in the 1990s, most importantly during the Kosovo crisis. Traditional mechanisms of refugee protection proved incapable of coping sufficiently fast with these situations of mass influx, as they deal with refugees' claims on an individual basis. In order to be better equipped for dealing with huge migratory flows in crisis situations, there were negotiations for creating a European instrument for a coordinated response of European states.

---

[19] Ibid., p. 127.

[20] For a related argument see Penelope Turnbull and Wayne Sandholtz, 'Policing and Immigration: The Creation of New Policy Spaces', in Alec Stone Sweet, Wayne Sandholtz and Neil Fligstein (eds), *The Institutionalization of Europe* (Oxford: Oxford University Press, 2001), pp. 194-220.

[21] Jan Niessen, 'Overlapping Interests and Conflicting Agendas: The Knocking into Shape of EU Immigration Policies', *European Journal of Migration and Law*, 3 (2001), pp. 419-34.

In May 2000 the Commission presented a proposal regarding temporary protection which was decided upon by the Council in July 2001.[22] It is difficult to reconstruct in detail how changes to the proposal were effectuated, as transcripts of negotiations in the Council of Ministers are not publicly available. However, by way of a comparison of the Commission proposal and the directive finally adopted, one may recognize the influence of politics in the Council and get an impression of what was actually achieved.

First of all, the Council broadened the scope of applicability of temporary protection. The Commission proposal limited temporary protection to two years, and it was meant to apply to situations when there was indeed a mass influx and the asylum system was unable to process the number of applications. The final directive extended temporary protection to three years, to situations with an imminent influx, and it was modified in order to apply to situations without an overburdening of asylum systems. This broadening of scope reduces states' burdens to engage in the more demanding refugee protection procedures under the Geneva Convention.

Major changes were made concerning family reunion. The Commission proposal foresaw family reunification (a) with the extended family and (b) with family members who were dependent, (c) had undergone traumatic experiences or (d) who needed special medical treatment. If scattered across Member States, families would have had the choice to reunify in any member state. The final directive narrowed this down to a reunification of the nuclear family and left the choice of the place of reunification to Member States' discretion.

With respect to return to the country of origin at the end of temporary protection, the Commission proposal referred to the European Convention on Human Rights and to Art. 33 of the Geneva Convention. A 'long-term, safe and dignified return' was mentioned as a condition. The Council deleted the reference to those international instruments and used the scaled-down formulation 'safe and durable return'. A clause mentioning enforced return *expressis verbis* was inserted and discretion granted, whether children would be allowed to complete their school year before a family's return.

Other provisions inserted into the directive by the Council, none of which had been contained in the original proposal, permitted (a) charging for issuing visas, (b) allowed for discrimination of persons under temporary protection vis-à-vis refugees concerning access to employment, and (c) entailed the provision that access to asylum procedures should be granted only after the expiration of temporary protection.

---

[22] Council of the EU, *Council Directive 2001/55/EC of 20 July 2001 on minimum standards for giving temporary protection in the event of a mass influx of displaced persons and on measures promoting a balance of efforts between Member States in receiving such persons and bearing the consequences thereof.* OJ L 212 of 7 August 2001, pp. 12 – 23.

Modifications of the Council made the directive much more restrictive. It left more discretion to the Member States but potentially lowered standards of protection. Human rights organizations' suspicions that 'temporary protection' may undermine standards of refugee protection were fed and, as one commentator remarked, the final directive 'does not show a commitment to high standards among the Member States'.[23] On the one hand, the case shows that the Commission is a relatively weak actor vis-à-vis the Council and that Europeanization was government-driven, as far-reaching changes have been made to its proposal. But more importantly, there has been a convergence towards certain – albeit limited – standards among Member States. They were able to reach a substantial result, even if the issue was controversial.

*Immigration Policy: The Directive on Family Reunification*

The Treaty of Amsterdam envisaged legislative work relating to long-term visa and residence permits, family reunion and rights of third-country nationals. After protracted negotiations including the rejection of a first version of a Commission proposal by the Council, a directive on family reunification was finally adopted in September 2003.[24] It deals with the question of which family members are eligible for family reunion with a citizen of a non-EU state living in the EU and under what conditions his relatives may enter.[25] Comparing the original proposal of December 1999, the amended proposal of May 2002 and the final regulation points to a very diluted result.

In the explanatory memorandum to the first proposal for the regulation on family reunion, the Commission put the proposed legislation in the wider context of the emerging immigration policy of the European Union. The Commission expressed the conviction that harmonizing immigration policies must entail the restriction of 'the possibility that the choice of the Member State in which a third-country national decides to reside will be based on the more generous terms offered there'.[26] Due to some Member States' resistance in the Council, most staunchly advocated by Germany, the directive had to be modified substantially. Acknowledging that 'negotiations in the Council particularly in May 2000 and

---

[23] Steve Peers, 'Key Legislative Developments on Migration in the European Union', *European Journal of Migration and Law*, 4 (2002): 90.

[24] Council of the EU, *Council Directive 2003/86/EC of 22 September 2003 on the right to family reunification*, OJ L251/12 of 3 October 2003.

[25] Kay Hailbronner, 'Migrationspolitik und Rechte der Drittstaatsangehörigen in der Europäischen Union', *Zeitschrift für Ausländerrecht und Ausländerpolitik*, 3 (2002): 83-9.

[26] European Commission, *Proposal for a Council Directive on the right to family reunification*. COM(2000)624 final of 10 October 2000, p. 9.

May and September 2001 were tricky and success did not ensue',[27] the amended proposal the Commission presented was watered down in many respects.

The regulation concerns third-country nationals; that means, immigrants who are not nationals of a member state of the European Union and who want to be reunified with relatives at their place of residence in the EU. A crucial point in need of regulation is the question of which family members of a third-country national are eligible for family reunification. The Commission's original proposal obliged Member States to permit the entry and residence of an applicant's spouse, the family's minor children and the materially dependent relatives in the ascending line of the applicant (Art. 5). In the amended proposal, the obligatory authorization of entry and residence was restricted to an applicant's spouse and children; the admission of a materially dependent applicant's parents and of dependent adult unmarried children was left to the discretion of the Member States (Art. 4). But due to a provision leaving it to the Member States 'to adopt or retain more favorable provisions for persons to whom it applies' (Art. 3, 5), it is basically up to the Member States to decide whom to admit.

The question whether an applicant's minor children may be denied family reunification if a certain age is exceeded was particularly contested. Under pressure from Germany, the derogation was inserted that 'where a child is aged over 12 years, the Member State may [...] verify whether he or she meets a condition for integration', thus giving room for the German migration law debated at that time to restrict possibilities for children older than 12 years to reunify with their family. Before political agreement was reached during the meeting of a Justice and Home Affairs Council of Ministers in March 2003, a further derogation was inserted. Now, Member States may request that 'applications concerning family reunification of minor children have to be submitted before the age of 15, as provided for by its existing legislation on the date of the implementation of this Directive. If the application is submitted after the age of 15, the Member States which decide to apply this derogation shall authorise the entry and residence of such children on grounds other than family reunification.'

Other points not contained in the Commission's original proposal were that a member state 'may provide for a waiting period of no more than three years between submission of the application for family reunification and the issue of a residence permit to the family members' (Art. 8, 2) and permission to charge a fee for issuing visas for family reunion (Art. 13). Certain parts of the directive have maintained their binding character, in particular as far as family reunification of refugees and access to employment and education are concerned. But the flexibility and derogations introduced into the proposal imply that the Commission's original

---

[27] European Commission, *Amended proposal for a Council Directive on the right to family reunification.* COM(2002)225 final of 2 May 2002, p. 2.

intention to harmonize family reunification and to establish a first building block of genuine European immigration legislation has not been reached.

Acknowledging this implicitly, the Commission adopted a strategy to prevent Member States from moving still further away from common standards. First, there is a standstill clause that ensures that Member States do not use the derogations if their legislation at the time of adoption of the Directive did not already provide for them (Art. 3, 6). The objective is to ensure that the Directive does not operate paradoxically as a source of fresh divergences between the Member States. Second, to keep the harmonization process going, a review of the regulation was envisaged (Art. 19).

The case of the directive on family reunification demonstrates that European Union Member States have retained a dominant position over migration policy-making. But unlike the directive on temporary protection, Member States' preferences did not converge towards shared, albeit low, standards. In the case of family reunification, divergences among Member States' positions made so many derogations and exemptions necessary that the aim to create the first part of a harmonized immigration policy was ultimately missed.

## Intergovernmental Europeanization and the Face of European Migration Policy

It was hypothesized here that in a process of intergovernmental Europeanization, attaining substantial results is more probable in fields with dense intergovernmental cooperation and that stagnation is more probable when dense intergovernmental cooperation is absent. Of course, this argument just highlights one source of progress in a European policy field. Other variables need to be taken into account for a full explanation. But the point here is that dense intergovernmental cooperation is a constitutive mechanism in a process of intergovernmental Europeanization. With respect to the two cases at hand, there is clearly variation concerning the density of intergovernmental cooperation. As has been noted in the discussion of the formal structures bringing about manifold contacts among national policy-makers, administrators and practitioners, there is dense intergovernmental cooperation on asylum affairs but hardly any on immigration policy. Further systematic empirical research could deliver a much more nuanced picture of the workings of networks in asylum as well as in immigration affairs and would be desirable indeed. But relating the analysis of the formal structures for cooperation to the discussion of differential progress in the two legislative processes presented already supports the presumption that policy would proceed towards substantial results in asylum and refugee affairs (where dense intergovernmental cooperation has come about) but not in immigration policy (where dense intergovernmental cooperation is absent).

At a more general level, the mechanism of intergovernmental Europeanization pointed out sheds light on the ways priorities have been set and shifted in migration policy. Intergovernmental Europeanization suggests a certain degree of path dependency. Areas of action with far-reaching institutionalized cooperation are likely to prosper, while in the absence of dense cooperation, stagnation cannot be prevented. A comparison of the outlook of European migration policy today with the profile of the Treaty of Amsterdam and the conclusions of the Tampere European Council points to two significant shifts in European migration policy.[28]

First of all, the perspective of a development of a genuine European immigration policy has been dropped almost entirely. This is reflected, for instance, by the report of the Working Group on 'Freedom, Security and Justice' at the European Convention. It states that despite the far-reaching competences included in the European Community Treaty, 'Member States will in practice, according to a generally shared understanding, remain responsible for the volumes of admission of third-country nationals and of their integration into the host country'. The report recognizes that the Union will play but a supportive role, namely: 'the Union could provide added value to national integration efforts mainly through incentive and support measures, rather than through harmonizing legislation'.[29] An outright rejection of a determination of admission levels by European institutions was uttered before by German minister Otto Schily: 'The admission of labor migrants has to be geared to the genuine needs of the national, regional, and local labor markets. Decisions on this need are to remain within the jurisdiction of the Member States.'

Second, fighting illegal immigration has emerged as a new top priority of European migration policy. Included in the Amsterdam Treaty as a matter of secondary concern, it was at the heart of the European Council of Seville in June 2002, adding the joint management of external borders as a new issue on Europe's migration policy agenda. The European Convention Working Group acknowledged that 'there is a stronger call in practice for common Union action regarding the fight against illegal immigration, including criminal sanctions, given the evident ineffectiveness of purely national policies.'

Without a doubt, the shifting focus from regulating legal economic immigration and asylum to combating illegal immigration reflects the events of September 11th and a new concern for security matters. But the securitization of migration policy can also be accounted for by drawing on dense cooperation as a mechanism driving intergovernmental Europeanization. Progress in the management of external borders could be achieved quickly by building on the cooperation of the interior and justice ministries and, more particularly, of the police forces, customs and

---

[28] European Council, *Tampere European Council – Presidency Conclusions*. 15 and 16 October 1999.
[29] European Convention, *Final report*, p. 5.

immigration services that had existed before. Quite the opposite is true for cooperation on legal immigration. A take-off of this field of policy has never taken place, one reason being that national policy-makers were never really integrated into trans-European networks that would have had the potential to create shared perspectives and an appreciation that European solutions may be appropriate for immigration.

The discussion of the way European migration policy has evolved has suggested that one core feature was intergovernmentalism. Intergovernmentalism does not, however, necessarily imply – as is often said to be the case – stagnating European integration. Certain fields of migration policy have evolved in a steadfast way; the factor driving intergovernmental Europeanization singled out was dense intergovernmental cooperation. A dense intergovernmental cooperation that includes institutionalized contacts of administrators and members of executive agencies at different levels is assumed to have facilitated the Europeanization of certain fields of migration policy.

This notion allows two points to be made concerning the future of European migration policy.[30] First of all, one question is whether intergovernmental Europeanization will continue in the years ahead. In this respect, the consequences of the enlargement of the European Union are still unknown. It will introduce new groups of officials and practitioners concerned with migration policy. As the continuity of actors is a precondition for the pattern of intergovernmental Europeanization highlighted here, migration policy-making may sputter due to the accession of new countries to the European Union. Insecurity over whether the Europeanization of the policy domain will continue if unanimity requirements are maintained was recognized during the negotiations on the Amsterdam Treaty revision. On visa affairs, automatic moves to QMV were foreseen, though with a delay of five years on certain policy matters (Art. 67, 3 & 4). For the remaining fields of migration policy, a move to QMV was envisaged pending a unanimous decision of the Council (Art. 67, 2). Expanding on this approach to extend QMV, the Treaty of Nice introduced QMV in further areas. The European Convention's Working Group on 'Freedom, Security and Justice' proposed an outright extension of QMV to asylum policy and combating illegal immigration. While there are efforts to integrate the personnel of accession candidates into the existing networks at an early stage, QMV may be an appropriate response to the limits of intergovernmental Europeanization ahead.

---

[30] The recent state of affairs is discussed in Petra Bendel, 'Immigration Policy in the European Union. Still Bringing up the walls for fortress Europe?', *Migration Letters*, 2/1 (2005), pp. 20-31.

**Table 10.1 Voting Requirements in Selected Fields of European Migration Policy**

| Treaty Provision | Field of Action | Voting until May 2004 | Voting after May 2004 |
|---|---|---|---|
| **Visa Policy** | | | |
| Art. 62(2)(b)(i) | list of third countries whose nationals must be in possession of visas when crossing the external borders | QMV | QMV |
| Art. 62(2)(b)(ii) | procedures and conditions for issuing visas | unanimity | QMV / Art. 251 |
| Art. 62(2)(b)(iii) | uniform format for visas | QMV | QMV |
| Art. 62(2(b)(iv) | rules on a uniform visa | unanimity | QMV / Art. 251 |
| **Asylum and Refugee Policy** | | | |
| Art. 63(1)(a) | responsibility for asylum claims | unanimity | QMV / Art. 251 |
| Art. 63(1)(b) | minimum standards – reception of asylum seekers | unanimity | QMV / Art. 251 |
| Art. 63(1)(c) | minimum standards – qualification as a refugee | unanimity | QMV / Art. 251 |
| Art. 63(1)(d) | minimum standards - granting or withdrawing refugee status | unanimity | QMV / Art. 251 |
| Art. 63(2)(a) | temporary protection to displaced persons | unanimity | QMV / Art. 251 |
| Art. 63(2)(b) | burden-sharing between Member States | unanimity | unanimity |
| **Immigration Policy** | | | |
| Art. 63(3)(a) | long term visas and residence permits | unanimity | move to QMV & Art. 251- procedure after unanimous vote |
| Art. 63(3)(a) | family reunification | unanimity | move to QMV & Art. 251- procedure after unanimous vote |
| Art. 63(4) | third countries' nationals' rights | unanimity | move to QMV & Art. 251- procedure after unanimous vote |
| Art. 63(3)(b) | illegal immigration | unanimity | move to QMV & Art. 251- procedure after unanimous vote |

QMV: Qualified Majority Voting; Art. 251: Codecision Procedure

The second point concerns the profile of European migration policy. Its 'Fortress Europe' image would be fundamentally changed if the restrictive measures that dominate at present were counterbalanced by opening opportunities for legal immigration. If the argument made here is correct, a deliberate creation of dense intergovernmental cooperation in integration and immigration affairs would prepare the ground for further Europeanization. The Community's proposed open method of coordination for national migration policies might therefore be, in the long term and if properly implemented, an appropriate strategy to start a process that might give Europe's migration policy another face.

# Chapter Eleven

# Migration and Cross-border Cooperation in Central and East European Countries

Kazu Takahashi

**Introduction**

Since the end of the Second World War Western Europe has actively accepted asylum-seekers and immigrants for economic or political reasons. On the one hand, immigrants have contributed towards Europe's economic development but on the other hand, this increase in the number of immigrants from the former colonies of Great Britain and France and the *Gastarbeiter* (guest workers) from Turkey has provoked racial prejudice and social tension in European society. As a consequence, negative feeling against the migration has arisen. At the same time immigrants' civil status became the subject of controversy. The issue of whether or not immigrants should be accepted with a civil status equal to that of the European population has been a concern in Western Europe for a long time.

The situation has changed since the middle of the 1980's due to a steady flow of people from Eastern into Western Europe. These people asserted that they were not immigrants but political refugees and the asylum-seekers. Under the political situation of the Cold War West Germany accepted these people on her own initiative and treated them as political refugees or asylum-seekers. But the number of refugees increased year after year along with the economic burden for West Germany.

When the socialist regimes in East European countries collapsed simultaneously in 1989 moving restrictions to Western Europe were abolished reducing the threshold for migration to the West. West European countries, especially Germany, were afraid that the numbers of refugees or immigrants would increase rapidly. As expected, the numbers of the refugees reached almost half a million in Germany during the year 1992.[1] In response to the increase Germany changed its asylum policy and denied refugee status to migrants from East European countries. The decision was informed by the view that East European countries were 'safe third countries' and that, therefore, there was no need to grant asylum to migrants from these countries.

---

[1] Statistisches Bundesamt (ed.), *Statistisches Jahrbuch 1993 für die Bundesrepublik Deutschland* (Wiesbaden: Statistisches Bundesamt, 1993).

The number of refugees from Eastern Europe peaked in 1992 and came down again later. But this situation entailed a further problem for East Central European countries. As 'safe third countries' they were asked to conclude agreements with the 'Schengen countries' about the readmission of persons who had crossed borders and entered the EU illegally. East Central European countries, namely, Poland, the Czech Republic, Slovakia and Hungary, became obliged to readmit immigrants who had come from other countries and had transited East European countries on their way into the EU without proper documents. It had been easy for the people from former socialist countries to enter the East Central European countries because of the policy visa-free entry common among socialist countries. Therefore people who intended to immigrate to the EU first entered East Central European countries and then attempted to reach the country of their final destination. But they were often caught at the border and deported to their home countries or continued to stay in East Central European countries if they did not have proper documents to certify their country of origin. Apparently EU member states have managed to prevent refugees or immigrants from settling in because of the Schengen Agreements and the readmission policy. However, East Central European countries have had to take the role of a buffer zone for the waves of refugees or immigrants from the East.[2]

Generally speaking, the reason for the enforcement of restrictive regulations concerning the movements of asylum-seekers, refugees and immigrants is the fear of social unrest that might arise from the increase of crime rates related to smuggling, prostitution and human trafficking etc. The social cost of receiving refugees, asylum-seekers and immigrants as well as cultural friction have been further reasons. However, these anxieties were drawn on the perception of migrants as a social encumbrance and reflect a negative assessment of the consequences of migration.[3] Even a more appreciative standpoint merely rests on the utilitarian assumption that immigrants supply a low-wage workforce to receiving societies in the branches unpopular among the population of the EU countries. With a declining and ageing population in the EU, immigrants appear to be more acceptable to take up work in EU countries. Nevertheless, some researchers have criticized the discriminatory treatment of immigrants.[4] In fact, the entire discussion does not display much difference of views because it focuses on problems of the acceptance of refugees, asylum-seekers and immigrant workers, while their common point of departure are efforts to distinguish migrants from EU nationals.

However, when we deal with migration problems from the point of view of

---

[2] Kumiko Haba, 'EU no Kabe, Schengen no Kabe', *Kokusai Seiji,* 129 (2002): 78.

[3] Robert Miles and Dietrich Thränhardt (eds), *Migration and European Integration: the Dynamics of Inclusion and Exclusion* (London: Pinter, 1994). Solon Adrittis (ed.), *The Politics of East-West Migration* (Basingstoke: Macmillan, 1993).

[4] Barbara Marshall, *The New Germany and Migration in Europe* (Manchester and New York: Manchester University Press, 2000).

regional integration, we should consider another type of migration. Usually international migration refers to a movement through which people leave their country of origin and resettle in other countries. Conventional explanations of migration have usually adduced push-and-pull factors. But nowadays many researchers are pointing out that the more acute problem of migration in East Central Europe is one of sub-migration. This means short-term and short-distance migration by people who keep their residences in their country of origin. These migrants either leave their own country temporarily or commute to another country across the border every day. This category of migration to which Dariusz Stola refers as 'quasi-migration',[5] looms largest among all categories of migration in East Central Europe, thereby playing an important role for integration in the border regions.

Now, I shall examine the role of sub-migration in the process of integration in the border regions. The hitherto existing discussion on migration in Central and Eastern European countries has focused on the Schengen Agreements and the readmission policy. The Schengen Agreements have been viewed as measures to build the 'Fortress Europe' or 'a European Nation-State'.[6] Therefore the Schengen Agreements have been criticized for enhancing closer cooperation among the Schengen countries while, at the same time, posing obstacles against the cross-border movement of the people from neighbouring Central and Eastern European countries.[7]

However, the EU has launched cross-border cooperation schemes as elements of its regional policy and has contributed to the promotion sub-migration as a factor of regional integration. Sub-migration is basically a process of dismantling borders. Therefore, it seems that the EU has taken contradictory attitudes towards its migration problems. Which direction does the EU intend to take?

Before examining the EU regional policy for cross-border cooperation, I shall describe the background to the migration situation in Central and Eastern European countries.

---

[5] Concerning to 'quasi-Migration', Dariusz Stola, 'Two Kinds of quasi-Migration in the Middle Zone:Central Europe as a Space for Transit Migration and Mobility for Profit,' in Claire Wallace and Dariusz Stola (eds), *The Pattern of Migration in Central Europe* (London: Palgrave, 2001), p. 85.

[6] Dietmar Herz pointed out that 'the European migration policy reproduced patterns of nation-building characteristic for the formation of nation state.' Dietmar Herz, 'The European Union's Asylum and Immigration Policy', Chapter Ten of the present volume.

[7] Elena Jileva, 'Larger than the European Union: The Emerging EU Migaraion Regime and Enlargement', in Sandra Lavenex and Emek M. Ucarer (eds), *Migration and the Externalities of European Integration* (New York: Lexington Books, 2002), p. 85.

## The Types of Migration after the Collapse of the Socialist Regime

There were four categories of migration in Central and Eastern European countries during the 1990s. First, emigration to EU member states, especially Germany and Austria, increased from the middle of 1980's, peaked in 1992 and declined gradually thereafter. The number of emigrants from Central and Eastern European countries to EU member states amounted to 642,105 in total between 1990 and 1997 and this figure represents 0.3 per cent of the EU population.[8] Poland sent most emigrants numbering about 300,000 in 1990, 140,000 in 1991 and 80,000 in 1993. The numbers of emigrants from the Czech Republic and Hungary increased until 1992 and later declined as well. The figure was around 20,000 for each year.[9] This trend is estimated to have continued even after the enlargement of the EU when the borders between the EU and East Central European countries were dismantled.[10]

Second, immigration across the Eastern borders of the Central and Eastern European countries increased rapidly. In 1990, the number of immigrants from areas east of Poland to the EU surpassed that of immigrants from Poland. Whereas, until then, Poland had been notorious for being a country of emigration the situation has changed and Poland has become an immigrant receiving country.[11] The country of origin of most immigrants is Ukraine. The situation is almost the same in the Czech Republic. There were 4,809 Ukrainians who held permanent resident status in 1993 in the Czech Republic but their number increased to 46,444 by 1998.[12] In each Central and Eastern European country, Ukrainians are the largest group among all immigrants holding working permits, that is, 14 per cent in Poland, 41 per cent in the Czech Republic and 18 per cent in Slovakia. Only in Hungary the situation is different. Here, immigrants from Rumania make up for 47 per cent of this category.[13]

The third category consists of refugees and asylum-seekers. Most of them came from former Yugoslavia. Because of the civil war in Bosnia and the Kosovo, a large number of refugees flowed into East Central European countries. Hungary accepted most of these refugees and asylum-seekers. But they have started to return home so that their number has decreased. More recently asylum-seekers have come from Rumania, Bulgaria (almost all of them Roma), Afghanistan, India, Sri Lanka and elsewhere. This category does not comprise high figures for each country. For example, the figures were under 2000 per year in the Czech Republic

---

[8] Christian Weise, John Bachtler, Ruth Dowernes, Irene Mcmaster and Kathleen Toepel, *The Impact of EU Enlargement on Cohesion, Final Report* (Berlin and Glasgow: German Institute for Economic Research, March 2001), p. 108.
[9] Wallace, *Pattern of Migration*, p. 108.
[10] Weise, *Impact of EU Enlargement*, pp. 109-10.
[11] Wallace, *Pattern of Migration*, p. 178.
[12] Ibid., p. 203.
[13] Ibid., p. 32.

until 1997 and have increased gradually since then, while admission as asylum-seeker has become very strict. Therefore, this category is estimated not to increase rapidly as long as no large conflict occurs in the world.[14]

The fourth category is most important here. It relates to sub-migration as short-term and short-distance migration. The EU report *Enlargement and Cohesion – Background Study for the 2nd Cohesion Report* has stressed the importance of sub-migration:

> Migration between the CEECs [Central and Eastern European countries] and the EU member states is characterized by a relatively high gap of per capita incomes over a short geographical distance. This changes the potential for different types of migration and significantly increases the option for short-term, temporary migration as well as cross-border commuting which almost exclusively affects Germany and Austria. Temporary migration is already very significant, and has risen at the expense of permanent migration and full post-enlargement integration is likely to increase the potential for this type of activity even further.[15]

But this type of migration is very difficult to grasp exactly because there is much daily movement. Some persons have short-term visas for sightseeing or study, while others do not need visas at all. In addition, statistics are not standardized among Central and Eastern European countries and EU member states. However, scholars working on migration in these countries agree that sub-migration accounts for the largest number of migrants in these states. For example, it is assumed that there are more than 400,000 migrants of this category in the Czech Republic, while it is estimated that 130,000 migrants of this type have been flowing into the EU from 2004.[16]

Sub-migration does not only take place from east to west within the EU. Instead, the same kind of sub-migration is occurring across the eastern border of East Central European countries, too.

Another problem resulting from migration concerns the maintenance of border control. As we have seen above, the figures for sub-migration are far larger than the number of persons arrested at the border for illegal entry. Sub-migration has thus become the most important issue in East Central Europe. When we consider this situation, it does not make much sense to continue discussions on the problem of whether the Schengen Agreements and readmission policies are effective or not. Instead we should focus on EU regional policy, which tries to promote regional integration through cross-border cooperation. Cross-border cooperation schemes were set up for the purpose of integration across borders among internal regions within the EU and its neighbouring countries during the post-Cold War era.

---

[14] Rosemary Byrne, Gregor Nor and Jens Vedsted-Hansen (eds), *New Asylum Countries?* (The Hague: Kluwer, 2002), p. 78.
[15] Weise, *Impact of EU Enlargement*, p. 113.
[16] Dusan Drhohlav, 'The Czech Republic,' in Wallace, *Pattern of Migration*, p. 203.

Sub-migration has emerged as one of the important factors launching regional integration at the micro level.

I shall proceed with a discussion of cross-border cooperation between the EU and its neighbouring countries up to the admission of ten new member states in May 2004.

**Cross-Border Cooperation as the Promoter of Sub-migration up to 2004**

Here, I examine cross-border cooperation between the EU and its neighbouring countries, especially emphasizing the activities of Euroregions.

In general, the term 'Euroregion' refers to a region in Europe. But its technical meaning is cooperation among communities which share a common international border. The first Euroregion was organized between the German community of Gronau and the Dutch community of Enschede in 1958. Its purpose was to resolve problems that arose from the region being divided by the Dutch-German border. This cross-border organization received the name 'Euregio' which has become an appellative. Euregio tried to harmonize traffic and telecommunication between the two communities. Both communities are located on the periphery of their states so that access to the centre has been difficult. In addition, the central governments did not pay much attention to such peripheral communities. As a consequence, Euregio remained in a disadvantaged position. Communities sharing a common international border thus discovered that they had common problems, and decided to cooperate across the border.

There has been a further reason to launch cross-border cooperation. For example, the Euroregion Neiße/Nisa/Nysa was established in 1990 among the communities which are located at the intersection between former East Germany, Poland and former Czechoslovakia, with the River Neiße/Nisa/Nysa flowing across the borders of the region. The most important and urgent problems of the region were environmental in kind, namely advancing protection against acid rain caused by air pollution and purifying the river. In order to deal with these environmental problems the communities had to cooperate across the border that divided them. They could not expect that their central governments would take measures to improve the local conditions. Therefore, cross-border cooperation was essential and Euroregion Neiße/Nisa/Nysa started its activities from community initiatives. From its start the Euroregion has been expected to deal not only with environmental problems but also to develop the regional economy, which was suffering from poor economic conditions.[17]

Does cross-border cooperation in the Euroregion Neiße/Nisa/Nysa contribute to

---

[17] Kazu Takahashi, 'Ôshû ni okeru Kai-chiiki Kyôryoku – Cheko Seibu ni okeru Yûro-rijyon no Katsudô wo Chûshin', *Kan Nihonkai Kenkyû*, 4 (1998): 34-5. Takahashi, 'Kai-chiiki Kyôryoku ni okeru Chiikiteki Rigai Jitsugen no tameno Mekanizumu', Yamagata Daigaku Hô Gakkai (ed.), *Hôsei Ronsô*, 16 (1999): 51-80.

the enhancement of integration? It is very difficult to measure this impact. However, we can confirm an increase of the number of cooperation projects. According to the *Information der Euroregion Neiße*, the number of applications for INTERREG projects, to which reference will be made in the next section, tripled between 1993 and 1995.[18] The activities of the Euroregion have continued for more ten years since its inception in 1991. The range of its activities has been expanded beyond economic cooperation and cooperation for the protection of the environment and now including programs for the exchange of children and young people, cooperative research projects and joint lending systems among university libraries in the region. These cooperation schemes have not only eased the coming and going of people in the region but have also improved communication among people through the cooperative implementation of the projects.

If such sub-regional cooperation was intended to promote the exchange of people at a time when the Euroregion was located between an EU member state and its neighbours, did the migration restrictions of the Schengen Agreements disturb cross-border movements in the region? In the case of the Czech Republic and Germany, there was in effect a bilateral agreement that people residing within 50km of the border could commute and work on the other side. Likewise, people in a Euroregion could seek employment across borders. More importantly, Euroregions usually established a system of consultation for workers employed on the other side of the border. It was the purpose of this system of consultation to provide the information about taxes, social security and other issues. Hence the argument is tenable that the Schengen Agreements did not always disturb cross-border cooperation before 2004.

**Regional Policy of the EU: Support for the Cross-Border Cooperation**

From 1990 to 2004 Euroregions rapidly spread as actors promoting cross-border cooperation along the border between the EU and its neighbouring countries. Nowadays Euroregions exist not only between EU countries and their neighbours but also among the non-EU countries in Europe.

One of the reasons for the spreading of Euroregions has been the regional policy of the EU that supports cross-border cooperation through the establishment of Euroregions. Especially, the 'INTERREG Initiative' has supplied financial assistance to support cross-border cooperation.

INTERREG started in 1990. Its first stage continued until 1993. The EU approved of a total budget of 800 million ECU and distributed the funds not via central governments but directly to local communities. There were four types of projects for which applications were possible. The first type of projects was designed to remedy the poor economic condition resulting from peripheral location and alienation from the centres of the national economies. The second type of

---

[18] *Information der Euroregion Neiße*, Ausgabe 12 (July/August 1996).

projects focused on the enlargement of cross-border cooperation networks. The third type of projects aimed at preparing the establishment of a Single Market within the process of admitting new member states to the EU. And the fourth type of projects was concerned with cooperation between the EU and external countries.

At the beginning of the first stage of the INTERREG initiative, the EU expected that applicants would come from the peripheral regions of Greece, Spain and Portugal after their accession to the EC in the 1980s. However, because of the financial assistance, cross-border cooperation spread not only in the internal regions of the EU but also along the borders between the EU and its neighbours and even to external regions. For example, the Carpatia region – the Euroregion Carpatia – is organized among local communities in Poland, Ukraine, Slovakia, Rumania and Hungary.[19]

The rapid increase of the number of Euroregions or cross-border cooperation schemes forced the EU to step up its financial assistance. The first stage of the INTEREG initiative expired in 1993, and the second stage was in existence as INTERREG II from 1994 until 1999. Its six-year budget was 2.9 billion ECU. This was 4 times the budget of the first stage. When Sweden, Finland and Austria entered the EU in 1995, the budget increased to 3.065 billion ECU. The purpose of INTERREG II was to improve communication between EU member states and the candidate countries and it placed special emphasis on infrastructure improvement. At the same time, many projects were begun in order to launch the exchange of personnel, for example, through such programs as Erasmus, Leonard, and Youth.

Generally speaking, INTERREG selected regions for infrastructure improvement which the EU regarded as important for its integration. It channelled more financial assistance into these regions than into others, while assistance for the exchange of personnel was distributed to every region.

Whereas the initial INTERREG initiative had merely provided financial assistance for cross-border cooperation, financial assistance was limited to internal regions of the EU the second stage of INTERREG. Before the 2004 EU enlargement external regions which organized Euroregions together with internal regions, could not apply to INTERREG III. However, these external regions, especially in Central and Eastern European countries, did not have sufficient financial resources to carry out projects for cross-border cooperation together with the German side. To overcome this gap, the Regional Committee of the EU, which was established in 1994 for the purpose of implementing the regional policy of the EU and is not an intergovernmental organization, decided to provide financial assistance for cross-border cooperation with Central and Eastern European countries under the PHARE (or PHARE/CBC) program. As a result, the Euroregions which were located astride the border of Germany and Central and Eastern European countries, were able to obtain financial assistance from

---

[19] Kazu Takahashi, 'Cheko to Surobakia ni okeru Yûro-rîjon no Kokoromi', in Hiroshi Momose (ed.), *Kai-chiiki Kyôryoku to Tenkanki Kokusai Kankei* (Tokyo: Yushindô-Kôbunsha, 1996).

INTERREG for the internal regions of the EU and from PHARE/CBC for the external regions.

At the same time, two further systems were introduced to INTERREG and PHARE/CBC in order to preserve the identities of regions. One is the 'Mirror Project', the other is 'JPMCs'. The 'Mirror Project' demands that each set of projects for which Euroregions apply within INTERREG and PHARE/CBC should be identical or totally coordinated as one set composed of both projects. 'JPMCs' stands for 'Joint Programming and Monitoring Committees'. The system requires that when local communities apply for a project within PHARE/CBC to the Regional Committee, representatives from other communities and advisors from the involved central governments should participate in the assessment of the application. Through these two systems, the EU tried to secure regional identification.[20]

Assessments of INTERREG have shown that the activities of the Euroregions which had intended to improve their economic situation through cross-border cooperation at the beginning, shifted to projects for the exchange of personnel. From the standpoint of economic development, cross-border cooperation did not necessarily improve the economic situation and the unemployment rate did not decrease.[21]

However, we can see that migration in the region has become more active year after year and we should be remindful of the fact that migration is not unidirectional from East to West but goes both ways in regions with cross-border cooperation schemes. Now, cross border cooperation is becoming more common. Euroregions have spread all over Europe. Hence further reasons have to be taken into account to explain why cross border cooperation has spread so widely and why the EU has supplied financial assistance even to the external region.

The Presidency Conclusion of the European Council of Berlin asserted in 2000 that due attention had been given to cross-border activities through the INTERREG initiative, in particular regarding member states with extensive borders to applicant countries. Consequently, INTERREG III was established for the period from 2000 to 2006. Its budget was 4.875 billion EUR.[22] Compared with that of INTERREG, II the budget for INTERREG increased by almost 150 per cent.

INTERREG III was composed of three categories: INTERREG A for cross-border cooperation; INTERREG B for transnational cooperation intended to contribute to the territorial integration between the EU and the candidate countries; INTERREG C for interregional cooperation.

---

[20] Takahashi, 'Kai-chiiki Kyôryoku', pp. 24-5.
[21] European Commission, *Information Note. The Free Movement of Workers in the Context of Enlargement* (6 March 2001), p. 10.
[22] 'Communication on the Impact of Enlargement on Regions Bordering on Candidate Countries: Community Action for Border Regions' (http://europa.eu.int/comm/regionalpolicy/sources/docoffic/official/communic/pdf/borden.pdf, 30/07/2002), p. 19.

INTERREG A allocated some 627 million EUR to the cross-border cooperation program in Germany for the period between 2000 and 2006. Compared to the approximately 419 million ECU spent for INTERREG in the period of 1994-1999, the increase was considerable. 67 per cent of the German INTERREG A funds were allocated to eligible regions bordering Poland and the Czech Republic. This means that cross-border cooperation contributed to the preparation of the candidate countries for EU membership.

Next to Germany, the Austrian INTERREG A programs with the Czech Republic, Slovakia, Hungary and Slovenia, witnessed an even more striking increase making available some 110 million EUR. This amount was three times in excess of that for the period 1995-1999. At the same time, cooperation projects of Italy with Slovenia and Greece with Bulgaria and Cyprus increased their funds by more than 200 per cent.[23]

In total, the EU regions bordering on Central and East European countries have so far received 818 million EUR within the framework of INTERREG A. The priorities for these programs are infrastructure improvement, training human resources and enhancing economic cross-border cooperation.

It is often said that INTERREG was designed for the preparation of the enlargement of the EU. However, INTERREG is a program only for the internal regions of the EU and needs to be assessed in conjunction with PHARE/CBC or TACIS/CBC for regions belonging to CIS. Projects for PHARE/CBC must be a coordinated or operated on a joint plan with INTERREG projects. Concerning the INTERREG III, EU documents make it clear that since 2000, the EU has focused on regions straddling across international borders while forming single geographical and socio-economic entities. Further to this, in order to lump together PHARE/CBC and INTERREG, the EU decentralized the implementation of PHARE/CBC projects and demanded that PHARE/CBC projects should be similar in size and nature to INTERREG projects.[24]

INTERREG III has just been launched in 2000 so that it remains difficult to assess. However, when tracing the institutional development of INTERREG and PHARE/CBC, we can say that the EU has gradually recognized the importance of cross-border cooperation. *Inter alia*, cross-border cooperation schemes among local communities like Euroregions have taken on an important role in the enlargement of the EU. Eventually, the EU concluded that Euroregions play an increasing role in fostering integration among communities on either sides of international borders.[25]

---

[23] Ibid., p. 12.
[24] Ibid., p. 34.
[25] Ibid., p. 19.

## Cross-border Cooperation as a Bottom-up Initiative against International Politics

Beyond financial assistance from the EU, there was a further factor that launched cross-border cooperation in East and Central European countries. Until the end of World War I this area had been under the Habsburg Empire, the German Empire, the Russian Empire and the Ottoman Empire and the people living there were moving about relatively freely. But after World War I several national states arose and borders were drawn in accordance with the so called 'nationality lines'. In East Central Europe these borders ignored the spaces which the people had enjoyed until then. At the end of World War II these borders were restored. Some people were compelled to move to other countries while others had to change their citizenship because of border rectification. Under the dynamics of international relations, the spaces which people had been building up until then, were destroyed in a moment.

After World War II the region along the eastern border of West Germany was the most rigidly controlled frontier in Europe due to the Cold War. When in 1989, US President George Bush and General Secretary of the Communist Party of the USSR Mikhail Gorbachev declared that the dividing line between the West and the East no longer existed, there were still no substantial relations between Germany and her eastern neighbours. There were no highways for transportation and no traffic communications between neighbouring cities just across the border. On the other hand, this new situation resulted in many people commuting across the borders daily. Then the main purposes of the establishment of Euroregions were reestablishing the lost connections and improving relationships with Western Europe at the level of daily life.

From this I conclude that the rapid spreading of cross-border cooperation at the level of the micro-regions signifies an objection against concept of the international politics according to which nation-states should enjoy absolute superiority.

## Migration and Cross-border Cooperation: the View of the EU

Euroregions as organizations for cross-border cooperation supply an important framework to launch inter-migration within regions. In order to foster the common identity between an internal region of the EU and an external one, the EU followed the policies of financial assistance for cross-border cooperation, that is, INTERREG and PHARE/CBC. In consequence of these policies, the border between the EU and its neighbouring countries was gradually dismantled already before 2004. From the time of the initialization of these programs, the EU has, however, been fearful that the gradual dismantling of the border would allow people from Central and East European countries to immigrate into the EU and take up work at lower wages than the resident population, with a rising unemployment rate being the result. Although EU documents show that cross-border cooperation activated inter-regional migration, there have not been any negative consequences of the dismantling of the border. It has even been reported that the border regions in Austria have experienced an increase in income due to tourism. In Bavaria, short-term migration and seasonal migration have grown without significant effects on the unemployment rate. In the agricultural sector, the workforce in Germany and Austria was already composed of short-term and short-distance migrants.[26]

Reportedly the possibility of the access to various forms of financial assistance has reduced the income disparity in border regions. But, at the same time, we cannot say that cross-border cooperation has contributed to improving the economic situation.

Contrary to some positive assessments, there are some negative side effects due to migration as well. It has been assumed that migrants engaged in prostitution, the smuggling of drugs and the organized crimes of human trafficking, thereby increasing social unrest. Some researchers have emphasized against these negative assessments the difficulty of proving that the crime rate is higher for migrants than for ordinary citizens, if crimes, such as violations of immigration regulations, are excluded from the count because only migrants can commit these violations. Hence, as long as research has not yielded conclusive results on this matter, it seems difficult to assume that the migration is responsible for crimes and rising social unrest.

Another negative assessment is that migrants have less access to information about job contracts and social services, whence they may be induced to work for lower wages and under worse working conditions than the resident population and may thereby be exploited.

Generally speaking, the EU has supported cross-border cooperation with an awareness that sub-migration would be the result. For example, the EU established the 'Consultative Council of Regional and Local Authorities' which was given the task of providing information about taxes and social security to migrant workers. Euroregions can consult with this council. And the EU has introduced the specific category of 'frontier workers' and ruled that 'under the Regulations on social security for migrant workers, frontier workers enjoy certain benefits which do not apply to other migrant workers. As regards sickness insurance, frontier workers may claim benefits in kinds in the country of residence or the country of employment'.[27]

Why then has the EU supported cross-border cooperation? There are some merits to sub-migration for recipient countries and migrants. First, migrants can maintain their accustomed daily lifestyle and neither need to change their place of

---

[26] Ibid., pp. 9-10.
[27] 'Living and Working Conditions of Frontier Workers,' Activities of the European Union Summaries of Legislation
(file://C:Docume~1OwnerLocals~1Temptr4iNOIAE.htm, 15/01/2003).

residence nor bother about the education of their children or the care of members of their families. Recipient countries do not need to worry about migrants' social security and nor bear the expenses of social services. Of course, even if the EU mentioned a privileged position for the 'frontier workers', the problems of migrants suffering from the lack of equality of incomes for the same jobs or exclusion from social security remain. In addition, as some researchers have shown, migrants take jobs that are unpopular in recipient countries. So it is impossible to say that the dismantling of the border immediately guarantees the equality of civil status to the migrants. But the Euroregions being composed of the representatives from both sides have contributed to facilitating consultation with migrants and improving the situation.

Cross-border cooperation schemes have launched sub-migration. Euroregions have played the role of improving the relationship between EU internal regions and external ones so as to establish common identities through cross-border cooperation activities. They must offer a plurality of occasions to consult if the cooperating parties want to obtain financial assistance from the EU. Consultation is to be accomplished not only among persons from the local communities in the region but also with advisors from each involved central government. Through these consultations Euroregions have promoted mutual understanding and fostered regional identity. Boosting common identity within the region can contribute to the mitigation of regional conflicts that might otherwise evolve into national conflicts in the long run. Therefore it is possible to say that cross-border cooperation can even contribute to national security.

The EU has supported Euroregions where regional conflicts were expected to occur, for example, in the Carpatia Euroregion. Moreover, on 7 March 2000, the Former Yugoslav Republic of Macedonia and UNMIK (UN Interim Administration Mission in Kosovo) signed a joint program to enhance cross-border cooperation in the Skopje-Pristina corridor. On this occasion, the European Commissioner for External Relations Christopher Patten observed that cross-border cooperation was an excellent example of the Stability Pact in action.[28]

When only considering the costs and benefits of cross-border cooperation, I cannot find any reason to launch such schemes in the short run. But, as Patten said, cross-border cooperation is able to contribute to regional stability in the long run, whence the EU has taken a positive stance towards it.

## Conclusion

When we try to understand migration problems from the vantage point of border

---

[28] 'Signature of the Joint Statement on Cross-Border Cooperation between the Former Yugoslav Republic of Macedonia and UNMIK' (http://europa.eu.int/comm/external relations/news/03_00/ip_00_126.htm, 30/07/2002).

control, Central and East European countries seem to have been pressured by the EU to accept its readmission policy as a condition for gaining EU membership. However, when we consider migration problems from the point of view of regional cooperation, especially at the micro level, Euroregions as cross-border cooperation actors have tried to dismantle borders and to promote migration by way of joint projects and the fostering of common identity in regions which had been divided for a long time. Therefore, migration is one of the measures advancing regional integration.

The EU has recognized the importance of cross-border cooperation year after year. Consequently, the EU has increased its financial assistance for INTERREG. At the same time, it has emphasized the coordination of INTERREG with the external programs of PHARE/CBC and TACIS/CBC.

We can thus glean the importance of and the expectations for cross-border cooperation from the spreading of the Euroregions. Euroregions which started in 1990 in Central and East European countries, have disseminated throughout Europe until today. Even in the Kosovo, where local government has not been functioning, a cross-border cooperation agreement has been signed between Macedonia and UNMIK. These facts suggest that the EU and its neighbouring countries take a positive stance towards the role of cross-border cooperation for confidence- and security-building measures and consequently, for the enhancement of regional stability.

In the Euroregions, there is no strained relationship similar to that between the EU and the external countries regarding border control. By contrast Euroregions have developed positive attitudes towards sub-migration because launching mutual sub-migration is a measure of regional integration. Although these cross-border cooperation schemes follow from community initiatives, Euroregions stand against neither central governments nor the EU. This is so because it is mandatory for applicants from local communities to obtain the approval by the EU and all involved central governments for INTERREG and PHARE/CBC or TACIS/CBC projects. In other words, central governments have the ability to forestall cross-border cooperation projects. However, instead of doing so governments have actively supported them.

As long as we confine discussions about migration in Europe to the national dimension or to the Schengen Agreements, we lose sight of sub-migration that affects the highest number of migrants in any category. Regional policy in favour of cross-border cooperation pursues the goal of encouraging sub-migration. Not only the EU but also central governments in East Central Europe share the perspective that cross-border cooperation contributes to establishing common identities for regions, to promoting regional integration and consequently to enhancing confidence- and security-building measures. Therefore cross-border cooperation receives support from all involved institutions. To conclude with regard to sub-migration in East Central Europe, I suggest that migration does not entail negative but positive and essential consequences for regional integration and regional stabilization.

## Chapter Twelve

# People on the Move: The Theoretical Challenge of Migratory Movement

### Henning Eichberg

Where there are people, there is migration.

Migration is so fundamental and broad a phenomenon in popular life that one may wonder why people's movement across the borders in political theory has normally only found so narrow attention: as being a 'problem' (for the involved states) and mainly a question of institutional control. Migration is more, and its significance for social and political theory goes deeper.

This is the nub of this present volume, which is trying to transcend the established limits. Its collected contributions open up towards the deeper anthropological dimensions of migration and movement. At the horizon, one can see a theory of the people – as migrating people. An important political implication of migration, if understood in this way, is civil security.

**Pride and Shame, Tradition and Modernity: Some Cases of Migration**

Migration is not just one phenomenon. When talking about migration, one talks about a large diversity of migratory phenomena. Let us enter by some cases.

*The Danish Jews*

During World War II, the Danish Jewry succeeded in emigrating to Sweden and was thus rescued from the German Nazi holocaust. The fate of the Danish Jews is regarded as unique among the occupied countries of that time. When German authorities prepared an Anti-Jewish raid in 1943, a danger-signal coming from a German official was via a network of Social Democrats forwarded to the Mosaic community in Copenhagen. The Jewish people left their homes and found shelter among 'Aryan' Danish people so that the German Nazi round-up some days later became a fiasco. The majority of the Danish Jews could subsequently escape to Sweden by small boats, helped by friends and fishermen, the latter sometimes taking high prices for their service. 7,220 Danish Jews survived in Sweden, whilst 472 persons were arrested by the occupants and 100 were murdered.

The rescue of the Danish Jews had its background in the well-integrated life of the Jews in Danish society. This made Nazi Anti-Semitism especially unpopular in the country. Furthermore, the action of rescue became a matter of Danish national activism against the German occupants. In fact, the resistance movement in Denmark had been rather weak during the years before. The action of pro-Jewish solidarity, mobilizing a broad spectrum of initiatives, now made the Danish resistance movement an important factor in peoples' conscience and brought forth its organizational break-through.

The glory of the rescue action shadowed through longer time that the Danish state had not shown the same solidarity against Jews who tried to escape from Nazi Germany to Denmark. During the years 1940-1942, at least 21 Jews were expelled by Danish state officials, and most of these died in Nazi extermination camps. After this has been documented by recent research, a strong critical debate arose in the Danish media. In May 2005, at the occasion of the sixtieth anniversary of the liberation of Denmark, the state minister apologized in public for this treatment. The migration of Danish Jews under World War II has, thus, dimensions of both Danish pride and shame.

*The Minangkabau of West Sumatra*

The main people of West Sumatra, the Minangkabau, are known by their matrilineal kin structure and their vigorous migration. Both features are connected with each other. The social life of the Minangkabau is characterized by matrilineal clans and the tradition of matrilocal housing. The mother owns the land, she owns the house where the husband moves in, and she forwards her clan name to her children. With their five or six million people, the Minangkabau are said to be the largest 'matriarchy' of the world. The particular life form of *adat*, the customary law of Minangkabau, is the background for a traditional form of migration, which is called *merantau*. Merantau has through centuries brought a remarkable part of the male population – often the most energetic and enterprising young Minang man – out into the border regions of Minangkabau, called rantau, but also into other parts of Indonesia and Malaysia and even as far as East Africa.

In the course of *merantau*, the man was expected to make his fortune. This traditional migration was characterized by strong bonds between the migrant and his home kin relatives. After having made his fortune, the migrant would return to his village in order to take over the role as uncle and administrator of the property of his sister (in the mother clan) and by marriage enter into his wife's clan. This classical pattern has been supplied and varied by forms of economic emigration under colonial rule in the nineteenth and twentieth centuries, and more recently by educational and labour migration to Jakarta and other centres of 'development'.[1]

---

[1] Mochtar Naim, *Merantau: Causes and Effects of Minangkabau Voluntary Migration*, second edn (Singapore: Institute of Southeast Asian Studies, 1974). Also: Henning

## Kenyan Sport Migrants

Modern top athletes are on the move. In some sports, athletes assume an almost nomadic migratory life style, constantly moving from one sport competition to the other. And in some sports this involves more permanent labour movement from one country to another, even between continents. A well-known case is the 'brawn drain' of talented elite runners from Kenya to Western metropolis. Among these migrants, the new-Danish Wilson Kipketer is a prominent profile.

At a closer look, the case of the Kenyan runners' international success reveals relevant ethnic differentiations inside Kenyan society. The elite runners do not come from Kenya in general, but from certain ethnic minorities, Kalenjin, Nandi and Gusii.[2] Existing ethnic cultural patterns play together with pull-effects of the modern market, leading to surprising new streams of migration. Sports migration thus constitutes a special variation of modern labour migration, based on cultural unbalances of ethnic and colonial character and answering to the call of the international entertainment industry.[3]

## The Normality of Moving

The diverse cases underline one main point of the present book, namely that migration is a question of people's lives and thus requires a critical approach towards state-centrism. Methodological etatism dominates actual policies as well as sociological theory. Political theory and social theory are often hampered by an implicit identification between people and state. This deep-rooted intellectual custom is critically called in question by the phenomenon of migration, by those living pictures and stories of people on the move. As in the named cases, migrating people often meet the state not as a partner or assistant of their migratory practice, but as a system of reactions, regulations and barriers: authorities controlling the German-Danish border, officials expelling 'unwanted' migrants etc. The wall in Berlin 1961-1989 against emigration from the German Democratic Republic and the wall protecting the United States against unwanted immigration from Mexico expressed, in stone and high tech this intention of control – and its failure. The pro-immigration policies of some absolutist states in early modern Europe and of

---

Eichberg, *Sozialverhalten und Regionalentwicklungsplanung. Modernisierung in der indonesischen Relationsgesellschaft (West Sumatra)* (Berlin: Duncker & Humblot, 1981).

[2] John Bale and Joe Sang, *Kenyan Running. Movement Culture, Geography and Global Change* (London: Cass, 1996), p. 149.

[3] John Bale, *The Brawn Drain. Foreign Student-Athletes in American Universities* (Urbana and Chicago: University of Illinois Press, 1991). Bale and Joseph Maguire (eds), *The Global Sports Arena. Athletic Talent Migration in an Interdependent World* (London: Cass, 1994).

some industrial countries during the 1960s were more positive expressions of the etatistic will to control.

That is why theoretical attempts are needed to question beyond or underneath state-border thinking, state-security thinking and state-control thinking. This is the challenge of the present volume. The matter of security, which is normally colonized by state imaginations – military, border, control – appears in a new perspective: as a matter of civil security.

A further lesson is that migration, that is, the geographical movements of people across borders, is not unusual or 'non-normal'. Whether traditional as in the case of the Minangkabau of West Sumatra or modern as in the case of labour and sports migration: migratory movement is normal practice. It is neither exceptional nor at all deviant.

However, this normal practice is political, that is, it leads into a world of contradictions and conflicts. This political quality is not necessarily created by the political intention of the migrant – for instance by the oppositional escaping from repression – but by action. The migratory movement in itself is political.

Therefore it is not sufficient to treat the migratory practice and its contradictory implications only on the surface of management logic and demographic policy, as neo-functionalism does. The phenomenon of migration poses anthropological questions of fundamental significance.[4] Who is the human being on the move? More exactly: who are the human beings (in plural) on the move, who are the people in motion, the moving folk?

That is why our initial sentence – where there are people, there is migration – must also be read the other way round: Where there is migration, there are people, there are folk on the move.

It is not possible to understand the implied questions by a theory on the purely institutional level, that is, on the level of superstructure. What is required is a basic social theory of 'the people'. In this connection, the term of 'movement' includes a special challenge. This has so far been discussed in relation to the theory of democracy and social movements[5] more than in relation to migratory movements. A rough outline of the demos problem may, however, help to some deeper understanding of migration, too.

## People as Substance, Construction and Movement

Traditionally, scholars have quarrelled about whether 'the people' was something 'substantial' or merely an ideological concept. This dualism has hampered a deeper understanding.

---

[4] Also for anthropology it took long time to discover this challenge, see the self-critical reviews in the Danish *Tidsskriftet Antropologi*, No 28 (Copenhagen, 1993), special issue: Migration.
[5] Henning Eichberg, *The People of Democracy. Understanding Self-Determination on the Basis of Body and Movement* (Århus: Klim, 2004).

Since the dawn of modern democracy and industrial society, researchers as well as political ideologists have tried to define a given people by a certain substance, often using the metaphor of 'organism'.[6] The 'people' was treated like a material object. Folk were objectified by means of language, history (understood as common origin or ancient roots), territory, religion, customs, national character and inner psychic disposition, state and constitution, common economy, community of communication or whatever. In an extreme case of objectification, Nazi theorists attempted to identify the people (*folk*, *Volk*) on the basis of race and genetic heritage, thus searching for a certain biological materiality, which could be measured. But this naturalization of 'folk' was only one case in the long series of objectifications: 'Danes are those who speak Danish', 'the French people has Gallo-Celtic ancestors', 'Irish identity is Roman Catholic', 'Israel is the people of God', 'the people of the Federal Republic of Germany are all those who accept the constitution', etc.

The substantialist view of the people always focuses on what the people 'is', not how it has emerged. The people or folk are seen as static, not in dynamic terms of historical change and are defined in relation to certain borders: 'The people' reaches 'so far and no further'. No wonder, that migration is troublesome and disquieting for this view.

The substantialist view of the people was again and again opposed by interpretations of the people as an idea. A forerunner of this idealism can be seen in early modern contractualism which tried to understand human sociality as resulting from an imagined contract between imagined individuals (Thomas Hobbes). Classical idealistic thinking at the dawn of the modern revolutions democratised and nationalised this imagination by assuming that the 'people' as political unity was created by the idea of the nation. The propagandistic actions of leaders or intellectuals made the nation-people. This had typically elitist connotations: The 'people' cannot find itself, it is made from above. Rousseau, Montesquieu, Herder, Jefferson, Napoleon, Hegel – 'men invent traditions', and 'avant-gardes make history'.

This top-down concept has more recently been reproduced by theories of social constructivism: There is no really existing 'people', there are only individuals, and these are artificially constructed into peoples and nations in the form of 'imagined communities'.[7] A nation-people is built by print media, by Protestantism and the centralized state, by schools and a common language – and by leaders and theorists. The Third World, it is said, has reproduced this Western pattern by constructing nations – in prolongation of the colonial project – by 'census, map and museum'. Or if one sharpens the point: The 'people' is merely an ideology, postulated with

---

[6] For instance Max Hildebert Boehm, *Das eigenständige Volk. Grundlegung der Elemente einer europäischen Völkersoziologie* (Darmstadt: Wissenschaftliche Buchgesellschaft, 1965).

[7] Benedict Anderson, *Imagined Communities. Reflections on the Origin and Spread of Nationalism* (London and New York: Verso, 1983; second, revised edn, 1991).

the help of some 'invented tradition'.⁸ As a 'false consciousness', the identity of 'the people' is imposed on human beings in accordance with the interests of political and economical power.

Though social constructivism may look like a critical theory, it continues older traditions of elitist idealism. It does not answer to the fundamental question of how people move towards identity in the context of democracy and revolution, from 'below'. And it tends to conceal the fact that people move over the borders without ceasing to be people.

Evidently, the concept of movement disturbs the dual pattern of substance vs. social construction in a fundamental way.⁹ 'Movement' destabilizes both the 'organism' and the 'idea' of the fortified nation. By thinking 'movement', one can avoid the traditional dead-end philosophical quarrel between objectivism and subjectivism. If the 'people' is understood as inter-personal movement, the question is neither how to define the 'real' people – 'what is really Danish?' – nor to limit the question to the disclosure of manipulative ideology.

In the historical rise of democracy, the term 'movement' has mainly appeared in the form of social movements. Social movements are the modern dynamics of civil

---

⁸ Eric John Hobsbawm and Terence Osborne Ranger (eds), *The Invention of Tradition* (Cambridge: Cambridge University Press, 1983).

⁹ The analytical dualism between 'the people' as substance and 'the people' as construction, the insufficiency of this dualism and the tricky question of movement is discussed more detailed in Eichberg, *The People*, pp. 121-9. Simultaneously, Peter Sloterdijk, *Sphären* (3 vols, Frankfurt: Suhrkamp, 1998-2004), vol. 3, pp. 261-308, has developed a parallel critique of the dualism between 'society' as contract and 'society' as organism. He proposed the picture of 'foam' as the third, the associations of associations. This is illustrative and challenging, indeed, but it tends to obscure the relation to movement.

About the term 'people' in critical social (and socialist) theory beyond constructivism see Raphael Samuel (ed.), *People's History and Socialist Theory* (London: Routledge & Kegan Paul, 1981).

The methodological approach from body and movement [Henning Eichberg, *Body Cultures. Essays on Sport, Space and Identity* (London and New York: Routledge, 1998) and Henning Eichberg, 'Wandering, Winding, Wondering: The Subject in the Labyrinth', in Anindita Banerjee (ed.), *Wandering Subjects* (in press, 2005)] can be seen in connection with the classical philosophical program, which was launched one and a half centuries ago, but which was never really followed up in its radical consequences: 'The first condition of all human history is of course the existence of living human individuals. The first matter of fact, which has to be stated, is the bodily organization of these individuals and their thereby established relation to the rest of the nature'. Karl Marx and Friedrich Engels: *Die deutsche Ideologie* [1845], Marx/Engels, *Werke*, vol. 3 (Berlin: Dietz, 1962), p. 16.

More specifically this could be translated here as: The first matter of fact, which has to be stated, is the bodily movement of these human beings in relation to each other and to the rest of the nature.

society, and typically visible as bodily movements in the street.[10] In certain situations of social tension, people join together, demonstrating in the streets and assembling on public places. This may escalate towards revolutionary events. By song, dance and festivity, folk utter the call 'We are the people!' This democratic call has been documented since the age of early revolutions 1789/1848[11] and obtained again a central significance during the uprisings of 1989/91 in Eastern Europe. The rhythmic call neither expresses the objective substance of a people, such as something like 'We are the blood!' or 'We are the race!', nor does it express an ideological construction such as 'We are an idea!' or 'We are an imagined community!' But it expresses a movement. By saying 'We are the people!' the revolutionary folk says: We are on the move, we are in motion!

The move makes up the difference between 'people' and 'population'. While 'population' exists in stasis, 'people' is human beings in movement.

## Epistemological Solipsism and Thinking the 'Between'

It requires some deeper reflections how migratory movement is related to the term of democratic movement or social movement. Migration is, like social movement, more than a matter of population. While 'population' has connotations of demography, cartography and administration – 'people' as object, seen 'from above', from the state – migration concerns the people as active subjects in plural, people on the move.

What is common to migratory movement and democratic movement is also the deeper anthropological and humanistic dimension: The human being is not only what is inside the individual skin bag. People's movement has its material basis not in the static and individual physical body, which is taken as granted by epistemological solipsism. The methodological solipsism knows quite well that the human being is not alone in the world but constructs theory as if it was. From out the monadic assumption of the lonely individual, the mainstream of Western philosophy step by step constructs the larger units of 'the house' (with its walls), the town (with its fortifications), the nation state (with its borders and frontiers), and the multinational empire.[12] Migration disquiets this pattern of hierarchical

---

[10] John Keane, *Civil Society. Old Images and New Visions* (Cambridge: Polity Press, 1998), pp. 1-2. Rebecca Solnit, *Wanderlust. A History of Walking* (New York: Penguin/Viking, 2000), pp. 218-25.

[11] Probably for first time, this call found a literary form in Georg Büchner's drama *Danton's Death*, 1835. The young author, democratic revolutionary himself, wrote this play about the French Revolution and its fundamental human conflict between Robbespierre's will of virtue and purge on one hand and Danton's love to life on the other. In this conflict, the people of the streets steps on to the scene crying: 'We are the people!'

[12] Critically: Sloterdijk, *Sphären*.

construction. Migration is a human practice between and among human beings in plural, between the houses, between the towns and across the state demarcations.

For an anthropological understanding of this 'between', one may find some help in the philosophy of the I-Thou relation as developed by Martin Buber.[13] It is not the monadic subject ('I'), from which we can reconstruct the world, and it is not the reification of beings, relations and processes ('it'). But human knowledge as well as human practice develops in the encounter (*Begegnung*) with 'the other', and by the dialogical principle between 'me and you'. 'The fundamental fact of human existence is the human being with the human being'.[14] It is in the intermediary space of this relation that movement develops.

People are, thus, in contrast to states as structures, characterized by movement – and these people-to-people movements are quite 'normal'. The normality of migratory movements is, however, diverse, and each of the manifold forms of migratory practice calls for different responses from the side of state and security. Migratory movements include nomadic life of different types, from the wandering of the Australian Aborigines[15] to the nomadic life of Gipsy tradition, which for centuries has disquieted the European territorial states. Migration may be voluntary or forced movement – including many intermediary forms. Migration may concern minor groups or whole ethnic peoples (in German *Völkerwanderung*). Migratory practice includes modern locomotion, where sedentary life is combined with huge financial and temporal investment into the means and ways of locomotion and tourism.[16] Migration may be life cycle migration as in the case of Minangkabau, seasonal migration as the Polish harvest workers in early twentieth century's Denmark, labour migration (*Gastarbeiter* in Germany) or permanent emigration as nineteenth century's Irish and Scandinavians migrations to America.[17]

Migratory movement must be seen in relation to the broader term of movement. There is a deeper wisdom in many languages that they refer to 'movement' – French *le mouvement*, German *Bewegung*, Italian *movimento*, Danish *bevægelse*, Swedish *rörelse* – at the same time on social, emotional and bodily levels.

People unite in social movements. This is what the sociology of people and democracy is about. Social movements are the dynamic side of civil society or what in Scandinavian languages is called *folk*.

---

[13] Martin Buber, *Ich und Du* [1923]. English version: *I and Thou* (New York: Collier 1986).

[14] Martin Buber, *Das Problem des Menschen* (Heidelberg: Lambert Schneider, 1948), p. 164. First published in Hebrew in 1942.

[15] Bruce Chatwin, *The Songlines* (London: Penguin, 1988).

[16] Wolfgang Sachs, *Die Liebe zum Automobil. Ein Rückblick in die Geschichte unserer Wünsche* (Reinbek: Rowohlt, 1984). Rainer Schönhammer, *In Bewegung. Zur Psychologie der Fortbewegung* (Munich: Quintessenz, 1991). Peter Borscheid, *Das Tempo-Virus. Eine Kulturgeschichte der Beschleunigung* (Frankfurt and New York: Campus, 2004).

[17] More in Harald Kleinschmidt, *People on the Move. Attitudes toward and Perceptions of Migration in Medieval and Modern Europe* (Westport, CT, and London: Praeger, 2003).

People are moved by feelings, affects and humour. Emotions as e-motions, motives and motivations demonstrate that there is emotional movement. This is what the psychology of social interactions and inter-human relations, of togetherness and difference is about, revealing mechanisms of building of or quest for identity.

People move in concrete bodily activities like sports and dance, play and games, gymnastics and festivals, wandering and tourism. Bodily movement is what the theory of body culture or praxeology is about, casting light on the culture of inter-bodily situations and relations.[18]

The challenge is to find the theoretical place of migration in this interdisciplinary pattern. The present volume can be read as a step into this direction – representing a shift of paradigm from state-centric residentialism to studies in civil society and movement.

## Movement in Contradictions – Contradictions in Movement

When we say 'people in movement', however, the analytical process is only beginning. It demands a dialectical thinking of contradictions. What we need is a theory of contradictions inside 'the people' and their 'move'. This is illustrated by the contributions of the present volume, where the words 'popular', 'people (moving)' and 'population' appear in different and sometimes contradictory contexts. The phenomenon of migration calls to our attention a rich world of people in contradicting relations.

People are, on one hand, migrant people. People move, while states rather try to inhibit the popular migration: this is the main story of the volume. The contradiction – people in migration vs. states hindering migration – is relevant, indeed, but at a closer examination it is more complex.

One additional aspect lies in the more or less intense connections, which migrant people often retain with their home people. They become double-home people as in the cases of the Minangkabau *merantau* and the Filipino emigrants with their persisting kin relations but also in the life of European labour migrants.[19] The double-home existence and the implied movements to-and-fro have enriching

---

[18] Schönhammer, *In Bewegung*. Eichberg, *Body Cultures*. Maxine Sheets-Johnstone, *The Primacy of Movement* (Amsterdam: Benjamins, 1999). Knut Dietrich (ed.), *How Societies Create Movement Culture and Sport* (Copenhagen: University of Copenhagen, Institute of Exercise and Sport Sciences, 2001). Klaus Moegling, *Integrative Bewegungslehre* (3 vols, Immenhausen: Prolog, 2001), vol. 3. Monika Fikus and Volker Schürmann (eds), *Die Sprache der Bewegung. Sportwissenschaft als Kulturwissenschaft* (Bielefeld: transcript, 2004).

[19] An illustrative novel about the Greek labour worker in Germany was written by Dimitris Chatzis, *Das doppelte Buch* (Cologne: Romiosini, 1983). It describes the double-home situation from below.

aspects, not only at the linguistic level. But they are not only 'idyllic'. They may also imply that conflicts are exported from the country of origin to the host country. Conflicts between Turks and Kurds may rise in Berlin, tensions between Muslim fundamentalism and secularism are sharpened in Copenhagen.

Another complexity lies in the encounter of the migrant people with the home people of the host country. There are people who want 'to be at home' among 'their own' people, with their own national language and habits. At the level of human rights, this means a clash between the right to migrate and the right to be at home (among one's own people). Anti-Chinese riots in Indonesia under shifting circumstances, sometimes instrumentalized by the power, but sometimes also in connection with anti-regime riots, have shown violent expressions of this conflict.

This means that one does not only find states as opponents of migration. Some home people may feel threatened and develop a sort of anti-immigration populism. Populist opposition against migration appears under certain circumstances in violent and racist forms. And sometimes it is expressed by shocking electoral results, turning political patterns upside-down even in well-established social democracies as in the Netherlands and in Denmark. Anti-immigration populism may drive much farther than established state control.

Paradoxically, the 'anti-immigrant' people – being anti-migrant by attitude and vote – may de facto be migrant people by their own life practice at the same time. This is one of the typical contradictions inside civil society. The states, however, often use the populist movements for their actions of control and prohibition, thus functioning as superstructures above anti-migrant populism.

What is often neglected are the welcoming people. From pre-modern societies one knows practices of 'adopting' foreigners to one's own kin group. Often, the foreigner obtained a lower status inside the clan but he or she was recognized. Nowadays, NGOs are active in civil society pursuing aims of 'welcoming' and recognition. But important initiatives are also going on beneath the level of formal organization. Refugees who are threatened to be expelled, find shelter in churches, and local initiatives constitute an underground of solidarity. The rescue of the Danish Jews is not only a story from past history. Among the actual popular movements like 'the people of Seattle', Attac and World Social Forum, there are strong elements of 'welcoming people' and multi-culturalism, while these movements at the same time are strongly opposing globalization.

**Civil Security and the Region**

All together, this panorama characterizes the people of democracy, i.e. the contradictory relations inside the *demos* (*folk*) of civil society. Democracy when seen 'from below' concerns the people as actors – as migrant people, home people, populist people, welcoming people, double-home people, people in movement ... . These people in their diversity are, again, more and different from the 'population' of state demography and administrative control. And migration is more than a geographical displacement.

This is fundamentally relevant for the question of security. It is the people of civil society who are the actors and subjects of civil security. Civil security can be advocated and supported by the state – but it can also be counter-acted by state authorities. Civil security is fundamental at another level.

The perspective of the civil people is also crucial for an understanding of the region in this game of contradictions. If the people's perspective is lacking, the 'region' will be thought as a quasi-state, a supra-state or a state ersatz. This is a problem in the actual state-building process of the European Union and similar supra-state structures, where there is lacking popular support. The region as 'nation state of Europe' or 'Europe as fortification' is continuing the logics of the classical national state.

A contrast can be found in the Nordic region. During the last two centuries, there have now and then also been initiatives to build a Nordic union as a larger quasi-state. But these attempts failed. The result of democracy building was that Nordic welfare societies, quite the reverse, tended towards smaller units. Besides the two classical Scandinavian states from early modernity, Denmark and Sweden, there appeared during the twentieth century at first Norway and Finland, then Iceland, Åland, Faeroe Islands, and Greenland. The Sami people have obtained their own parliaments, too. Similar tendencies of decoupling have developed in Canada during recent decades where French Quebec and Inuit Nunavut have appeared as autonomous units. All this was based on the peoples' right of self-determination.

Decoupling must not mean a mere reproduction of the national state on a minor scale. The smaller units of Northern Europe cooperate across the borders, forming a region of quite another type than the 'Nation of Europe'. Nordic cooperation includes not at least ways of facilitating migration between the countries.

The question of migration and civil security is, thus, related to the culture of democracy. At the political level, it cannot be handled separately from welfare and self-determination 'from below'. And at the theoretical level, migration demands attention to the basis of social life – the people and their (bodily, emotional, social) movement.

# Epilogue

## Harald Kleinschmidt

Contextualizing Migration with regional integration and human security reveals the paradigm shift through which research about migration, the making and implementation of migration policy have gone for about 25 years. Up until the end of the 1970s, most scholars as well as lawmakers, political decision-makers and administrators habitually perceived migration as a social phenomenon which they strove to understand and handle as a process of collective action. Sociologists were placed in charge of research, and welfare provision considerations to the benefit of allegedly poor immigrants fuelled the making and implementation of migration policy. On the one side, migration researchers took it as their prime task to determine collective migration motives and to establish categories for the prediction of mass migration movements. Most commonly they identified economic hardship as the core motive triggering emigration. On the other side, lawmakers, political decision-makers and administrators classed migrants as deviant people, construed migration as a unidirectional and finite process, seemingly pushing people out from unfavourable habitats and pulling them to the lands of their dreams.

Controversies over migration policy were few, as convictions underlying migration research and policy-making were undisputed and inherited from nineteenth-century social theory. These convictions suggested, first, that emigrants should be regarded as 'undesirables' and 'uprooted' people lost to the societies of their origin and, second, that immigrants should be authoritatively surveyed and selected in accordance with administrative and political expectations about their 'usefulness' in their future host societies. The convictions converged on categorizing migration as the process of the factual disintegration of migrants from the societies of their origin, combined with no more than the possibility of reintegration into their future host societies. Liberal migration policies seemed to consist in accepting the human right to emigrate, whereas governments of states appeared as agents legitimately placed in charge of determining the possibility of reintegration.

This simple world has fallen into the competence of historians.

While migration has not ceased to be a social phenomenon, it has become politicized. Political scientists, historians, geographers and anthropologists have placed migration on their research agendas. Push-and-pull factors continue to be at work but have moved under the control of migrants. Governments of sovereign states continue to exercise control over immigration policy and border surveillance but have had to learn to deal with self-assertive, well informed and well connected people determined to accomplish their set goals sooner or later. Moreover, the societies over which government are entrusted to rule, are no longer conceivable as territorialized 'political bodies'. Instead, the notion of transnational social spaces has obtained wide currency and is often merely another word for bottom-up regional integration. Controversies over migration policy are looming large, with residents' social security concerns often militating against migrants' human security interests.

One set of controversies ranges between liberalism and conservatism. Liberal migration policy has moved from a scheme of regulating the disintegration of emigrants and has become equivalent to a design for setting fair conditions for the cultural, social and political integration of immigrants. Conservatives often rally demonstrations of discontent against these liberal creeds and paint grim scenarios of waning national identity and declining political stability. Ever more often, governments of sovereign states have to strike an uneasy balance between respecting, on the one side, international human rights concerns together with human security interests of migrants and, on the other, the political will of their domestic constituencies. The making and implementation of migration policy has been levelled up to a touchstone of the liberalism of policy-making in democratic states.

Another set of controversies is more fundamental and touches on the very nature of the migration process. 'New migration' has begun to focus on the personhood of individual migrants rather than social factors of disintegration and reintegration, to demand respect for migrants' livelihood strategies and to deplore the imbalance between the recognition of the human right to emigrate and the denial of a human right to immigrate. 'New migration' thereby suggests that migration is a normal process that people choose whenever their motivation to move is becoming stronger than their motivation to stay, acknowledges that migration motivations as most persons' collective identities may be multiple, and admits that migration research remains inconclusive unless it investigates motivations to move together with motivations to stay.

Saying that migration is a normal process is another way of saying that borders connect rather than divide. It is at this point that 'new migration' clashes with state interests informing the decisions of lawmakers, political decision-makers and administrators. It is a clash over security broadly understood as human security, far more fundamental than the previous quibbles over the degree of necessary or welcome welfare provision extendable to immigrants. While some migrants may wish to become integrated into their host society, others may not as they may prefer to develop a multicultural social setting with multiple collective identities concurring. Insisting on their right to opt for integration or multiculturalism migrants are now demanding a far higher degree of autonomy than governments of sovereign states are commonly willing to grant. Enforcing restrictive immigration policies and developing a liberal integration policy may both militate against the security interests of migrants without alleviating the security concerns of residents.

Lawmakers, political decision-makers and administrators have begun to recognize that one way out of the dilemma is cooperation across international borders. It is one of the most striking policy twists at the turn of the twenty-first century that some institutions of regional integration have enhanced their migration policy-making capacity, namely ASEAN, CACM, ECOWAS and the EU. Migration policy has thus become a regional issue, whether by legal stipulation a or by intergovernmental bargaining. The rationale behind this development is easy to find, once recognition is made of the fact that most migration takes place within regions. Migration as a normal process thus is a definitional element of regional integration and turns regional integration into a democratically controlled bottom-up process that receives its legitimacy from the security-providing competences of the involved institutions of governance.

Perhaps, our past will be our future, when governments of sovereign states will compete for people on a global migration market. In this market the capability of institutions of governance for the provision of security, broadly understood as human security at the regional level, could well evolve as the decisive factor attracting migrants, boosting the legitimacy of institutions of governance and enhancing popular consent as the act of voting by the feet.

# Bibliography

Acharya, Amitav, *The Quest for Identity. International Relations of Southeast Asia* (Singapore: Institute of Southeast Asian Studies, 2000).
Acharya, Amitav, *Constructing a Security Community in Southeast Asia. ASEAN and the Problem of Regional Order* (London and New York: Routledge, 2001).
Adler, Emanuel, and Michael Barnett (eds), *Security Communities* (Cambridge: Cambridge University Press, 1998).
Adrittis, Solon (ed.), *The Politics of East-West Migration* (Basingstoke: Macmillan, 1993).
Ajibewa, Aderemi, *From Regional Security to Regional Integration in West Africa. Lessons from the ASEAN Experience* (London: Cass, 2002).
Alagappa, Muthiah, *Asian Security Order* (Stanford: Stanford University Press, 2003).
Ammann, Birgit, *Kurden in Europa. Ethnizität und Diaspora* (Munster and Hamburg: Lit., 2001).
Ammassari, Savina, and Richard Black, *Harnessing the Potential of Migration and Return to Promote Development: Applying Concepts to West Africa* (Brighton: Sussex Centre for Migration Research, 2001).
Ananta, A, and Evi Nurdidyaya Arifin (eds), *International Migration in Southeast Asia* (Singapore: Institute of Southeast Asian Studies, 2005).
Anderson, Benedict, *Imagined Communities. Reflections on the Origin and Spread of Nationalism* (London and New York: Verso, 1983; second, revised edn, 1991).
Anderson, Benedict, *The Spectre of Comparisons. Nationalism, Southeast Asia, and the World* (London: Verso Books, 1998).
Bach, Daniel C. (ed.), *Regionalisation in Africa. Integration and Disintegration* (Oxford and Bloomington, IN: Indiana University Press, 2000).
Bale, John, *The Brawn Drain. Foreign Student-Athletes in American Universities* (Urbana and Chicago: University of Illinois Press, 1991).
Bale, John, and Joseph Maguire (eds), *The Global Sports Arena. Athletic Talent Migration in an Interdependent World* (London: Cass, 1994).
Battistella, Graziano, and Maruja M.B. Asis (eds), *Unauthorised Migration in Southeast Asia* (Zuaexon City: Scalabrini Migration Center, 2003).
Bergsten, C. Fred, *Open Regionalism*, Working Paper 97-3 (Washington, DC: Institute for International Economics, 1997).
Bevilacqua, Piero, Andreina de Clementi and Emilio Franzina (eds), *Storia dell'emigrazione Italiana* (Rome and-Bari: Laterza, 2001).

Bollin, Christina, *Der zentralamerikanische Integrationsprozess* (Frankfurt and New York: Lang, 2000).
Bommes, Michael, and Andrew Geddes (eds), *Immigration and Welfare. Challenging the Borders of the Welfare State* (London and New York: Routledge, 2000).
Booth, Ken (ed.), *Statecraft and Security* (Cambridge: Cambridge University Press, 1998).
Bottin, Jacques, and Donatella Calabi (eds), *Les étrangers dans la ville* (Paris: Maison des Sciences de l'Homme, 1999).
Brieden, Thomas, *Konfliktimport durch Immigration. Auswirkungen ethnischer Konflikte im Herkunftsland auf die Integrations- und Identitätsentwicklung von Immigranten in der Bundesrepublik Deutschland* (Hamburg: Verlag Dr. Kovač, 1996).
Bruinessen, Martin van, *Transnational Aspects of the Kurdish Question* (San Domenico: European University Institute, 2000).
Buzan, Barry, Ole Wæver and Jaap de Wilde, *Security: A New Framework for Analysis* (Boulder: Lynne Rienner, 1998).
Byrne, Rosemary, Gregor Nor and Jens Vedsted-Hansen (eds), *New Asylum Countries?* (The Hague: Kluwer, 2002).
Celton, Dora, Hervé Domenach and Alejandro Giusti (eds), *Migraciones y Procesos de Integración Regional* (Nueva Córdoba: Editorial Copiar, 1999).
Chantavanich, Supang (ed.), *Female Labour Migration in South-East Asia* (Bangkok: Asian Research Center for Migration, 2001).
Chirot, Daniel, and Anthony Reid (eds), *Essential Outsiders: Chinese and Jews in the Modern Transformation of Southeast Asia and Central Europe* (Seattle: University of Washington Press, 1997).
Ciprut, Jose V. (ed.), *Of Fears and Foes. Security and Insecurity in an Evolving Global Political Economy* (Westport, CT, and London: Praeger, 2000).
Clark, Peter, 'The Migrant in Kentish Towns, 1580-1640', in Peter Clark and Peter Slack (eds), *Crisis and Order in English Towns, 1500-1700: Essays in Urban History* (Toronto: University of Toronto Press, 1972), pp. 117-63.
Coker, Christopher, *Globalisation and Insecurity in the Twenty-first Century: NATO and the Management of Risk*, Adelphi Paper, No 345 (London: International Institute for Strategic Studies, 2002).
Cole, Philip, *Philosophies of Exclusion* (Edinburgh: Edinburgh University Press, 2000).
Collignon, Stefan, *Regionale Integration und Entwicklung in Ostafrika* (Hamburg: Institut für Afrikakunde, 1990).
Comaroff, John, 'The Closed Society and its Critics: Historical Transformations in African Ethnography', *American Ethnologist*, 9 (1984): 571-83.
Comba, Rinaldo, Gabriella Piccinni and Giuliano Pinto (eds), *Strutture familiari, epidemie, migrazioni nell'Italia medievale* (Naples: Edizioni Scientifiche Italiane, 1984).

Curi, Umberto, and Bruna Giacomini (eds), *Xenos. Filosofia dello straniero* (Padua: Il Polifilo, 2002).

Dewitt, David, and Carolina Hernandez (eds), *Development and Security in Southeast Asia* (2 vols, Aldershot: Ashgate, 2003).

Eccarius-Kelly, Vera, 'Political Movements and Leverage Points: Kurdish Activism in the European Diaspora', *Journal of Muslim Minority Affairs*, 22/1 (2002): 91-118.

Ehrenreich, Barbara, and Arlie Russell Hochschild (eds), *Global Woman – Nannies, Maids and Sex Workers in the New Economy* (London: Granta Books, 2003).

Etzioni, Amitai, *Political Unification* (New York: Holt, Rinehart and Winston, 1965) [revised version (Huntington, NY: Krieger, 1974)]. Etzioni, *Political Unification Revisited* (Lanham, MD: Lexington Books, 2001).

Fahrmeir, Andreas, *Citizens and Aliens. Foreigners and the Law in Britain and the German States. 1789-1870* (Oxford and New York: Berghahn, 2000).

Faist, Thomas, *The Volume and Dynamics of International Migration and Transnational Social Spaces* (Oxford: Clarendon Press, 2000).

Favell, Adrian, *Philosophies of Integration. Immigration and the Idea of Citizenship in France and Britain* (Basingstoke: Macmillan; and New York: St. Martin's Press, 1998).

Fielding, Anthony, 'Migration and Culture', in Tony Champion Fielding (ed.), *Migration Processes and Patterns* (2 vols, London: Belhaven Press, 1992), vol. 1, pp. 201-14.

Foner, Nancy, Ruben G. Rumbaut and Steven J. Gold (eds), *Immigration Research for a New Century* (New York: Russell Sage Foundation, 2000).

Gabaccia, Donna R., and Fraser M. Ottanelli (eds), *Italian Workers of the World: Labor Migration and the Formation of Multiethnic States* (Urbana and Chicago: University of Illinois Press, 2001).

Gardner, Katy, *Global Migrants, Local Lives. Travel and Transformation in Rural Bangladesh* (Oxford: Clarendon Press, 1995).

Geddes, Andrew, *Immigration and European Integration. Towards Fortress Europe?* (Manchester: Manchester University Press, 2000).

Geddes, Andrew, *The Politics of Migration and Immigration in Europe*, (London: Sage, 2003).

Gorenflo, L.J., and Michael J. Levin, 'Changing Migration Patterns in the Federated States of Micronesia', *ISLA: A Journal of Polynesian Studies*, 3/1 (1995): 29-71.

Graham, David T., and Nana K. Poku (eds), *Migration, Globalisation and Human Security* (London and New York: Routledge, 2000).

Guiraudon, Virginie, and Christian Joppke (eds), *Controlling a New Migration World* (London and New York: Routledge, 2001).

Haan, Arjan de, et al., *Migration and Livelihoods: Case Studies in Bangladesh, Ethiopia and Mali*, IDS Research Report 46 (Brighton: Institute of Development Studies, 2000).

Hayase, Yasuko (ed.), *International Migration in APEC Member Economies: Its Relations with Trade, Investment and Economic Development* (Tokyo: APEC Study Center, Institute of Developing Economies, 2003).

Hellmann, Kai-Uwe, and Ruud Koopmans (eds), *Paradigmen der Bewegungsforschung* (Opladen: Westdeutscher Verlag, 1998).

Hettne, Björn, András Inotai and Osvaldo Sunkel (eds), *Globalism and the New Regionalism* (Basingstoke: Macmillan; and New York: St Martin's Press, 1998).

Hettne, Björn, András Inotai, and Osvaldo Sunkel (eds), *The New Regionalism and the Future of Security and Development* (New York: St. Martin's Press, 2000).

Hettne, Björn, András Inotai, and Osvaldo Sunkel (eds), *Competing Regionalisms* (Basingstoke: Palgrave, 2001).

Hobsbawm, Eric John, and Terence Osborne Ranger (eds), *The Invention of Tradition* (Cambridge: Cambridge University Press, 1983).

Jessen, Anneke, and Ennio Rodriguez, *The Caribbean Community* (Kingston: Institute for the Integration of Latin America and the Caribbean, 1999).

Keane, John, *Civil Society. Old Images and New Visions* (Cambridge: Polity Press, 1998).

King, Russell (ed.), *Mass Migrations in Europe. The Legacy and the Future* (London: Belhaven Press, 1993).

Klein, Ansgar, Ruud Koopmans and Heiko Geiling (eds), *Globalisierung – Partizipation – Protest* (Opladen: Leske + Budrich, 2001).

Koopmans, Ruud, and Paul Statham (eds), *Challenging Immigration and Ethnic Relations Politics* (Oxford: Oxford University Press, 2000).

Krause, Keith, and Michael C. Williams (eds), *Critical Security Studies. Concepts and Cases* (London and New York: UCL Press, 1997).

Kubat, Daniel, and Hans-Joachim Hoffmann-Nowotny, 'Migrations. Vers un nouveau paradigme', *Revue internationale des sciences sociales*, 33 (1981): 335-59.

Lavenex, Sandra, and Emek M. Ucarer (eds), *Migration and the Externalities of European Integration* (New York: Lexington Books, 2002).

McNeill, William Hardy, and Ruth S. Adams (eds), *Human Migration* (Bloomington, IN and London: Indiana University Press, 1978).

Mahler, Sarah, *Migration and Transnational Issues. Recent Trends and Prospects for 2020* (Hamburg: Institut für Iberoamerika-Kunde, 2000).

Marshall, Barbara, *The New Germany and Migration in Europe* (Manchester and New York: Manchester University Press, 2000).

Mattli, Walter, *The Logic of Regional Integration* (Cambridge: Cambridge University Press, 1999).

Miles, Robert, and Dietrich Thränhardt (eds), *Migration and European Integration: the Dynamics of Inclusion and Exclusion* (London: Pinter, 1994).

Mokyr, Joel, *The Lever of Riches: Technological Creativity and Economic Progress* (New York and London: Oxford University Press, 1990).

Moravcsik, Andrew, *The Choice for Europe. Social Purpose and State Power from Messina to Maastricht* (Ithaca, NY, and London: Cornell University Press, 1998).
Moses, W., and B. Letnes, *If People Were Money: Estimating the Potential Gains from Increased International Migration* (Helsinki: World Institute for Development Economics Research / UNU-WIDER, 2003).
Naim, Mochtar, *Merantau: Causes and Effects of Minangkabau Voluntary Migration*, second edn (Singapore: Institute of Southeast Asian Studies, 1974).
Niemann, Michael, *A Spatial Approach to Regionalism in the Global Economy* (Basingstoke: Macmillan; and New York: St Martin's Press, 2000).
Niessen, Jan, and Yongmi Schibel, *EU and US Approaches to the Management of Immigration. Comparative Perspectives* (Brussels: Migration Policy Group, May 2003).
Page, Sheila, *Regionalism among Developing Countries* (Basingstoke: Macmillan; and New York: St Martin's Press, 2000).
Papastergiadis, Nikos, *The Turbulence of Migration. Globalization, Deterritorialization and Hybridity* (Cambridge: Polity Press, 2000).
Poku, Nana K., and David T. Graham (eds), *Redefining Security. Population Movements and National Security* (Westport, CT: Greenwood Press, 1998).
Porta, Donatella della (ed.), *Social Movements in a Globalizing World* (New York: St. Martin's Press, 1999).
Portes, Alejandro, William Haller and Luis E. Guarnizo, *Transnational Entrepreneurs 2001: The Emergence and Determinants of an Alternative Form of Immigrant Economic Adaptation* (Davis, CA: University of California at Davis, 2001).
Pries, Ludger (ed.), *New Transnational Social Spaces. International Migration and Transnational Companies* (London and New York: Routledge 2000).
Rucht, Dieter. Ruud Koopmans and Friedhelm Neidhardt (eds), *Acts of Dissent. New Developments in the Study of Protest* (Berlin: Ed. Sigma, 1998).
Sandhu, Kernial S., and A. Mani (eds), *Indian Communities in Southeast Asia* (Singapore: Institute of Southeast Asian Studies and Times Academic Press, 1994).
Sassen, Saskia, *Losing Control? Sovereignty in an Age of Globalization* (New York: Columbia University Press, 1996).
Schiller, Nina Glick, Linda. Basch and Cristina Szanton Blanc, *Towards a Transnational Perspective on Migration: Race, Class, Ethnicity, and Nationalism Reconsidered* (New York: New York Academy of Sciences, 1992).
Schiller, Nina Glick, and Georges Eugene Fouron, *Georges Woke Up Laughing: Long-Distance Nationalism and the Search for Home* (Durham and London: Duke University Press, 2001).

Schilling, Heinz, 'Innovation through Migration: the Settlements of Calvinistic Netherlanders in Sixteenth- and Seventeenth-Century Central and Western Europe', in *Histoire sociale – Social History*, 16/31 (May 1983): 7-33.

Schreurs, Miranda A., and Dennis Pirages (eds), *Ecological Security in Northeast Asia* (Seoul: Yonsei University Press, 1998).

Şenol, Şengül, *Kurden in Deutschland. Fremde unter Fremden* (Frankfurt a.M.: Haag + Herchen, 1992).

Smith, Michael Peter, and Luis Eduardo Guarnizo (eds), *Transnationalism From Below* (New Brunswick: Rutgers University Press, 1998).

Soerensen, Ninna Nyberg, Nicholas Van Heer, and Poul Engberg-Pedersen, *The Migration-Development Nexus: Evidence and Policy Options: Policy Study* (Copenhagen: Centre for Development Research, April 2002).

Soysal, Yasemin Nuhoğlu, *Limits of Citizenship. Migrants and Postnational Membership of Europe* (Chicago and London: University of Chicago Press, 1994).

Stalker, Peter, *International Migration* (London: New Internationalist Publications, 2001).

Sudô, Ken'ichi, and Shûji Yoshida (eds), *Population Movement in the Modern World* (2 vols, Osaka: The Japan Center for Area Studies, 1997).

Sweet, Alec Stone, Wayne Sandholtz, and Neil Fligstein (eds), *The Institutionalization of Europe* (Oxford: Oxford University Press, 2001).

Tarrow, Sidney, *Power in Movement. Social Movements and Contentious Politics*, second edn (Cambridge: Cambridge University Press, 1998).

Tay, Simon S.C., Jesus P. Estanislao and Hadi Soesastro (eds), *Reinventing ASEAN* (Singapore: Institute of Southeast Asian Studies, 2001).

Thapan, Anita Raina, *Sindhi Diaspora in Manila, Hongkong, and Jakarta* (Quezon City: Ateneo de Manila University Press, 2002).

Tomei, Verónica, *Europäisierung nationaler Migrationspolitik. Eine Studie zur Veränderung von Regieren in Europa* (Stuttgart: Lucius & Lucius, 2001).

ul-Haq, Mahbub, 'Global Governance for Human Security', in Majid Tehranian (ed.), *Worlds Apart. Human Security and Global Governance* (London and New York: Tauris, 1999), pp. 79-94.

Wæver, Ole, Barry Buzan, Morton Kelstrup, and Pierre Lemaitre, I*dentity, Migration and the New Security Agenda in Europe* (London: Pinter Publishers, 1993).

Wahlbeck, Östen, *Kurdish Diasporas. A Comparative Study of Kurdish Refugee Communities* (Basingstoke: Macmillan, 2000).

Wallace, Claire, and Dariusz Stola (eds), *The Pattern of Migration in Central Europe* (London: Palgrave, 2001).

Wallace, Helen, and William Wallace (eds), *Policy-Making in the European Union* (Oxford: Oxford University Press, 2000).

Weiner, Myron, *The Global Migration Crisis. Challenge to States and to Human Rights* (New York: HarperCollins, 1995).

Yamamoto, M., 'Urbanization of the Chiefly System: Multiplication and Role Differentiation of Titles in Western Samoa', *The Journal of the Polynesian Society*, 103/2 (1994): 171-202.

Yans-MacLaughlin, Virginia (ed.), *Immigration Reconsidered. History, Sociology, and Politics* (Oxford: Oxford University Press, 1990).

Zolberg, Aristide R., and Peter M. Benda (eds), *Global Migrants Global Refugees* (New York and Oxford: Berghahn Books, 2001).

# Index

Aceh pattern 214
Action Programme for
    Administrative Cooperation
    in the Fields of External
    Borders [EU] 236-7
Afghanistan, emigration from 37,
    115, 246
aging population 30, 32
Aguilera, Gabriel 173
Amish 50
Amsterdam, Treaty of (1997) 2, 55,
    228-9, 231, 238
Anabaptists 52
Antwerp, emigration from 52
Antwerpenaar 53
apprenticeship migration 47
ARGO [EU] 234
Arías, Oscar 173
Armenians 50, 58
ASEAN, migration policy of 5, 62,
    117-8, 222
Ashanti 89
Asia Pacific Migration Research
    Network 219
Asia Pacific Mission for Migrant
    Filipinos 220
Asian Migrant Center 220
Asian Research Center for
    Migration [Bangkok] 217
asylum-seekers 10-11, 21, 31, 33,
    172, 227-47, 245-6, 252-3
Australia, immigration to 24-5, 32,
    127
Austria, immigration to 259-60

balance of power 98
Bangladesh, emigration from 28, 38,
    40, 208, 213, 221-2
Bangkok Declaration on Irregular
    Migration 222
Bank of Central America 174
Banque protestante 54-6
Bawean pattern 214
Belize, emigration from 163
Betancourt, Rómulo 173
biologism 90-91, 264
boat people 109
Bodin, Jean 100
borders 1, 4-5, 63, 71-2, 74-5, 93,
    104, 249, 255-8, 261-2
Bosnia, emigration from 248
Brunei, immigration to 207
Buber, Martin 266
Bulgaria, emigration from 248
Business Process Outsourcing 30

Calvinists 50-5, 80
Cambodia, emigration from 205,
    208, 219
Canada, immigration to 32, 127,
    129, 160
capitalism 52-3
Cárdenas [Nicaragua] 166
Carolinians 144
Carpatia [Euroregion] 252, 257
Central American Common Market,
    migration policy of 3, 153-79
Central American Commission for
    Environment and
    Development 175
Central American Customs Union
    177-8
Central American Institute for
    Research and Industrial
    Technology 175
Central American Integration
    System 174-5
Central American University

Council 173
Central American University Federation 175
Centre for Information, Discussion and Exchange on the Crossing of Frontiers and Immigration [EU] 232-3
Centre for Information, Reflection and Exchange on Asylum [EU] 232-3
Centro Agrónomo Tropical de Investigación y Enseñanza 174
Chain migration 129, 148-9
Chamorro, Violeta 173
Chamorros 147
Charter of the Organisation of Central American States 175
China, emigration from 58, 111-2, 115, 126-7, 207-09, 211, 268
Chuuk, emigration from 139-51
Chuukese Church Association 147-8
citizenship 32, 63-8, 255
civil security 268-9
civil society 1, 9-10, 67-8, 94, 264-6, 271
Clausewitz, Carl von 5, 85
climate theory 8
colonialism 88-9, 136
Commission of Central American Directors of Migration 175
Commission on Human Security 4, 10-11, 77
Committee of Permanent Representatives [EU] 235-6
Compact of Free Association 143
confessional migration 52-3
constructivism 108
Consultative Council of Regional and Local Authorities [EU] 256
contractualism 6, 51, 74, 83, 93
Convention on the Protection of the Rights of All Migrants and Members of Their Families 38-9, 65, 73, 78, 211
Cook Island, emigration from 140, 149-50
COREPER 232
Corte Centroamericana de Justicia 175
Costa Rica, emigration from 170-171
Costa Rica, immigration to 159, 160, 162-72
Council for Security Cooperation in Asia-Pacific 117-8
Council of Europe 200
Council of the European Union 196-7
Cromwell, Oliver 55
cross-border cooperation 245-58
Credi Amigo 40
cultural innovation 150
Czech Republic, emigration from 248
Czech Republic, immigration to 246, 248-9

Dahomey 89
Dante Alighieri 100
De la Torre, Haya 173
democracy, theory of 262-5
demography, theory of 81
Denmark, German occupation of 259-60
Denmark, immigration to 34, 266
Development and Migration Nexus 34-5
development assistance 116, 142, 146, 217-18
distance 123-38
drug trafficking 113-4
Dublin Agreement 227-8, 237
Dutchwork 54

East African Community 62, 92
Edict of Nantes, revocation of 52-3,

81
Edict of Potsdam 54
education migration 144, 171
El Salvador, emigration from 153-4, 162, 167, 170, 173
elite migration 167, 174
emigration prohibitions 57-8
Engelbert of Admont 6, 99
Enschede 250
epistemological solipsism 265-7
ERASMUS 256
ethnic mobilization 181-202
Euregio 254
European Commission 195-6, 198-9, 231, 234-5, 237, 239-40
European Convention on Human Rights 237
European Court of Human Rights 199-202
European Federation of National Kurdish Federations 199
European Parliament 194-5
European Union, accession of Turkey 191-202
European Union, migration policy of 1-2, 22, 33, 66, 178-9, 225-44, 245-58
Europeanization 183-202, 225-44
Euroregions 250, 256-62

family reunification 241-4
Federal States of Micronesia, emigration from 138-51
federal theology 51
Federation of Indonesian Migrant Workers' Organizations 220
Federation of Kurdish Workers' Association 188
Federation of National Kurdish Federations 199
feminization of labour migration 207-08, 220-1
Festival of Pacific Art 149-50
financial market 54-6, 58-9

Fishing Project Fund [Chuuk] 142
Fondaco dei Tedeschi 47, 49
Fondaco dei Turchi 47
Fonseca, Carlos 173
forced migration 136
France, emigration from 52-3
Frontier Workers 256-7
functionalism 90-92, 156-7

General Agreement on Trade and Services 23, 176
General Agreement on Tariffs and Trade 127
Geneva, immigration to 54
geno group 7-8
Germany, immigration to 52, 86, 183, 187-8, 241, 245-6, 266
ghetto 47, 50
Ghura Low Income Public Housing Scheme 146
glass industry 58
global cities 155-6, 163
Grameen Bank 40
Greece, emigration from 50
Greece, immigration to 56-7
Gronau 250
Guam, immigration to 141-9
Guatemala, emigration from 162, 167, 173
Guatemala, immigration to 162
Guayana, emigration from 36-7
Gusii 261

Hague Peace Conference (1899) 96-7
Haiti, emigration from 27
HELP Asian Women's Shelter 221
Helsinki Final Act 75-6, 97, 101
Hesse-Kassel, immigration to 81
Hobbes, Thomas 6, 96, 263
Honduras, emigration from 170
Honduras, immigration to 160, 162
Hong Kong, immigration to 39, 129, 133, 207, 210, 220

horizontal migration 157-8, 179
Huguenots 50-5, 81
human security 70, 75-7, 94-100,
    103-19, 205-224
Hume, David 8. 97-8
Hungary, emigration from 248
Hungary, immigration to 246

Ibaraki Christian Center 134
Immigration Crisis 22
India, emigration from 37-8, 41,
    135-7, 248
Indonesia, emigration from 205, 207,
    211, 213-6, 220-2
Indonesia, immigration to 268
IndUS Entrepreneur 37-8
Innocenti Research Centre 42
Instituto Interamericano de
    Cooperación para la
    Agricultura 173
intellectuals 156, 174
Intergovernmental Europeanization
    225-44
International Aristocracy of Money
    58
International Labour Organization 1,
    34, 38-40, 65
International Organization for
    Migration 1, 4, 34, 37, 222
INTERREG 251-5, 262
inter-regional migration 255-6
Israel, immigration to 207
Italy, immigration to 39, 47

Jakarta 260
Jamaica, emigration from 36-7
Japan, immigration to 111-3, 115,
    127, 129, 133-5, 207, 210,
    216-18
Japan Institute for Labor Policy and
    Training 223
Japan International Training
    Cooperation Organization
    217-18

Jews 50-2, 56-8, 259-60
Justi. Johann Heinrich Gottlob 81-2,
    98
Justice and Home Affairs pillar
    [EU] 228, 230, 232

Kadek 191, 197
Kalenjin 261
Kenya 261
Komkar 188-9
Kon-kurd 199
Korea, Republic of, emigration from
    207
Korea, Republic of, immigration to
    110-1, 129, 210-1
Kosovo, emigration from 248,
    257-8
Kurdish National Congress 197, 199
Kurdistan Human Rights Project
    197
Kurds 181-202

La Cruz [Costa Rica] 166
labour migration 24, 38-9, 45-59, 61,
    65, 125-6, 128-32, 139-51,
    164-7, 188-9, 205-24, 256,
    260-261, 266-8
Laos, emigration from 208, 219
*Laws of Migration* 124-5
LEONARD [EU] 256
life cycle migration 260, 266
Lipsius, Justus 6, 100
livelihood strategy 24-7, 154-5
Locke, John 6
Lombok pattern 214
London 54-5
long-distance nationalists 27, 41,
    151
López, José Roberto 173

Maastricht, Treaty of (1992) 228,
    230-231
Macedonia, immigration to 257-8
Malawi, emigration from 26-7

Malaysia, immigration to 109-10, 136, 205-7, 210, 212-6, 221-2
Malaysian Employees Provident Fund 214
Marsilius of Padua 100
Maritime Safety Agency [Japan] 112-3
Mauritius, immigration to 136
Menjivar, Rafael 173
Mennonites 52, 168
*merantau* 260, 267
mercantilism 47-8, 58
Mexico, emigration from 32, 41-2
Mexico, immigration to 160, 162, 167
Microfinance Institutions 35, 40
Micronesia, emigration from 139-51
Middle East Indonesian Manpower Supply Association 220
migration, perception of 78-9, 86
migration industry 66, 117-8
migration motivation 7, 9, 68, 80
migration networks 37-8, 208-9
migration statistics 11-2, 124-5
Minangkabau 260, 266-7
Mission for Filipino Migrant Workers 220
Mitrany, David 96-7
mobilization 190, 193-7
Mongolia, emigration from 211
Montesquieu, Charles de Secondat, Baron de la Brède et de 9, 263
Moriscos 50, 58
Mortlocker Island 148
Mouraviev Memorandum 96-7
Mughal Empire 88
Murano 58
Myanmar, emigration from 109-10, 205, 208, 219
Myanmar, immigration to 136

Nandi 261

National Network in Solidarity with Migrant Workers [Japan] 221
nationalism 6-7, 75, 83, 85, 89-91, 114-5, 263-4
nationality legislation 6-8, 32-3, 97, 114-5
Neiße/Nisa/Nysa [Euroregion] 250-251
neo-functionalism 8, 73-4, 92-3, 156-7
Netherlands (Spanish), emigration from 52-3
Netherlands (Kingdom of), immigration to 130
New Migration 8-12, 68-77
New Regionalism 8-12, 69-77
New Security 8-12, 69-77
New York 155-6
New Zealand, immigration to 24-5, 149-50
Nicaragua, emigration from 163-6, 172, 173
Nippon Keidanren 218
Non-Resident Indians 41
non-traditional security concerns 109-114
North Korea, emigration from 110-1
Nueva Granada 173

ODA 116, 142, 146, 217-8
Odyseeus Programme [EU] 233-4
Öcalan, Abdulah 182, 189-91, 196, 199-200
OECD 22-3, 26, 31, 35
Ogata, Sadako 116
Organization of Central American States 174

Pakistan, emigration from 213
Palau, emigration from 140
Parem 141-2
Parlamento Centroamericano 175
periphery-centre migration 154
personhood 95, 97

PHARE 252-5
Philippine Overseas Employment
    Agency 38
Philippines, emigration from 25-6,
    38-9, 125-6, 128-35, 146,
    205-7, 211, 213, 220-2, 267
Philippines, immigration to 135-7
PKK 182, 189-91, 194, 196-7, 199,
    201
Poland, emigration from 248, 266
Poland, immigration to 52, 246, 252
political opportunity structure 194-8
Polynesians 140, 149
population policy 6, 71, 81-3
Proceso Puebla 174
Protest Event Data 184-5
Prussia, immigration to 81
Puritans 50-2
push-and-pull factors 7, 68, 126,
    157-9, 208-210, 247

Quakers 50, 168
Qualified Majority Voting 228-9,
    231, 236, 240, 242-4
quasi-migration 246

Ramírez, Sergio 173
Ravenstein, Ernest George 7, 124-5
realism 87, 93, 104-5, 108
refugees 10, 21, 31, 108-11, 115,
    160, 162, 165, 173, 188-9,
    225-44, 245-6, 252-3
Regional Committee of the EU
    252-3
Regional Conference on Migration
    [Puebla] 174
Regional Ministerial Conference on
    People Smuggling [ASEAN]
    118
regularization 32
remittances 35, 39-42, 140, 143,
    150-151, 154-5, 162-3, 209
residentialism 3, 7
Return of Qualified Afghans

    Programme 37
Royal Statistical Society 124
Rumania, emigration from 248
rural-urban migration 46-7, 154,
    164

Saipan, immigration to 133, 141-9
Salzburg, emigration from 52
Samoa 149-50
San José (Costa Rica) 163
San Vito (Costa Rica) 168
Saudi Arabia, immigration to 129,
    207
Schengen Agreements 226-8, 230,
    234, 247, 249, 258
Schengen Information System 234
seasonal migration 256
securitization 107
security, concept of 96-7, 103-7
security policy 77-101, 117
separatism 189
Sephardites 56-7
Singapore, immigration to 129, 136,
    205, 207, 210
Single European Act (1986) 226-7
Silicon Valley 28-9, 37-8
Sistema de Integración
    Centroamericana 173
Skopje-Pristina Corridor 257
Slovakia, immigration to 246
social welfare policy 75-6, 84
South Africa, emigration from 38
South African Network of Skills
    Abroad 38
sovereignty 72-3
sports migration 261
space 123-38
Sri Lanka, emigration from 211, 248
step migration 142
Strategic Committee on
    Immigration, Frontiers and
    Asylum [EU] 235-6
sub-migration 247-8, 250-251,
    256-7

Süßmilch, Johann Peter 81-2
Sumatra 2630 271
Sweden, immigration to 33-4, 52

Tahiti 149
Taiwan, emigration from 28
Taiwan, immigration to 112, 207, 210
Technical Intern Traineeship Program [Japan] 217-8
technology transfer 45-59
textile production 53-4
Thailand, emigration from 207, 211, 213, 221-2
Thailand, immigration to 109-10, 208, 210-1
Torres Rivas, Edelberto 173
Tokyo 155-6
Toll Island 148
Transnational Communities Programme [EU] 35-6
transnational entrepreneurs 29, 30, 37-8, 154, 168-9
transnational social spaces 1, 27-42, 64-5, 67-8, 153-9, 245-58, 271-2
Turkey, accession to the EU 191-202
Turkey, emigration from 183, 187-8
Typhoon Aid Project [Chuuk] 142

Ukraine, emigration from 248
ul-Haq, Mahbub 95, 97
undocumented migration 32, 78, 109-110, 207, 220, 256
United Arab Emirates, immigration to 129, 207
United Nations, Convention on the Protection of the Rights of All Migrant Workers and Members of Their Families 38-9, 61, 65, 73, 78, 211
United Nations Development Program 10, 97, 104

United Nations Economic Commission for Latin America 160
United High Commissioner on Refugees 1, 116, 162
United Nations, High Level Dialogue on International Migration and Development 34-5
UNMIK 257-8
United Kingdom, emigration from 24-5
United Kingdom, immigration to 28, 34, 36
United States of America, immigration to 27-32, 37, 41-2, 129, 135, 139, 141, 151, 160, 162-3, 167, 170, 178
universalism 101
urban in-migration 46-7, 154, 163

Vattel, Emerich de 98-9
Venice 47, 49-50, 57-8
Vietnam, emigration from 109, 205

Waldensians 50, 52, 58
war, theory of 85-8, 90, 99
Weno 141-2, 145, 148
wool industry 53-4
Working Group on Freedom, Security and Justice [EU] 241
World Trade Organization 23, 38-9, 127, 203
world economy (notion of) 59

Yanban 110
YOUTH [EU] 256
Yugoslavia, emigration from 248

Zulu 89